FAMILY MEDIA
THEORY AND PRA

FAMILY MEDIATION: THEORY AND PRACTICE

Jane C. Murphy
Professor of Law
Associate Dean for Academic Affairs
University of Baltimore School of Law

Robert Rubinson
Professor of Law
Director of Clinical Education
University of Baltimore School of Law

2009

ISBN: 978-1-4224-1847-5

Library of Congress Cataloging-in-Publication Data

Murphy, Jane C.
Family mediation : theory and practice / Jane C. Murphy, Robert Rubinson.
p. cm.
Includes index.
ISBN 978-1-4224-1847-5 (perfect bound) 1. Family mediation--United States. 2. Domestic relations courts--United States.
3. Dispute resolution (Law)--United States. 4. Domestic relations--United States. I. Rubinson, Robert. II. Title.
KF505.5.M87 2009
346.7301'5--dc22

Editorial Offices
121 Chanlon Rd., New Providence, NJ 07974 (908) 464-6800
201 Mission St., San Francisco, CA 94105-1831 (415) 908-3200
www.lexisnexis.com

MATTHEW◆BENDER

(2009–Pub.3251)

DEDICATIONS

To Chris, Brendan, Margaret, Cat and Gracie, with thanks for your love and patience
—JCM

To my wife Randi Schwartz and to my children Stella and Leo, with love and gratitude
— RR

PREFACE

This text is the result of the convergence of two trends in the resolution of disputes within families.

The first trend is a broad consensus that the unique characteristics of family disputes frequently do not lend themselves well to traditional adversarial litigation. Adversarial litigation almost always intensifies emotions — hardly a welcome development in family disputes, where passions, resentments, and recriminations often flow freely even without the spur of advocacy. Moreover, this very intensification often works to the detriment of individuals who may not formally be "parties" to a family law dispute but surely are, in many respects, the most vulnerable and the most profoundly affected by its consequences, namely, children. Family disputes are also bound up with social ills that extend well beyond the adjudication of legal rights and duties: domestic violence, child abuse, substance abuse, poverty, and much else. Such ills often implicate skills — particularly medical and therapeutic — that lawyers and judges may well not possess by temperament or training. Furthermore, there is the sheer volume of these cases: no single category of civil cases remotely approaches family law in the number of matters presented to courts for adjudication. And, given that there is currently no right to counsel in most family cases, the massive need for legal representation in family law cases for those of low or modest means cannot even begin to be met by underfunded legal services organizations.

These factors have led in recent years to substantial changes in how family law disputes are resolved. Some of these changes are doctrinal: the shift in focus from adults to children as reflected in the rise of no-fault divorce and the increasing use of parenting plans, and changes in the legal construction of parenthood and the financial consequences of divorce. Some are judicial, such as the rise of "unified family courts" and shifting conceptions of a family law judge's appropriate role in such matters. Some advocates for family court reform argue that the nature of family disputes renders the traditional judge as finder of fact and applier of law inadequate to the task of confronting the multi-dimensional complexities of these sorts of cases. Other reforms focus on the lawyer's role. Some lawyers, for example, claim that conventions of "zealous advocacy" so embedded in American legal tradition are counterproductive in such cases, and have become practitioners of "collaborative law," which focuses on problem-solving rather than advocacy.

The second trend is the extraordinary rise in the last few decades of mediation as an alternative for the resolution of disputes. The importance and consequences of this sea-change cannot be exaggerated. As we elaborate throughout this text, the danger in approaching mediation is in underestimating its strangeness in a culture suffused with the norms of traditional advocacy. There is no fact-finder, there is no decision-maker apart from the parties in mediation. Rather, a mediator *facilitates* the parties in resolving their own disputes. In appropriate cases, such a process can empower parties, enhance the ability of parties to work together in the future, and promote flexible and creative problem-solving.

While mediation has spread as a means to resolve virtually all types of disputes, in no area has this been more apparent — or more controversial — than in family law. Increasing numbers of individuals are voluntarily turning to mediation as a means to resolve family disputes. Legislatures and courts in numerous jurisdictions have adopted rules and statutes that refer and sometimes mandate that family law cases be mediated and set forth procedures under which such mediations are to take place. These mediations

PREFACE

happen in the tens of thousands every day. Indeed, it is no exaggeration to state that at the beginning of the twenty first-century, mediation and family law are increasingly intertwined in an intricate web of procedures and practices that has generated a new, distinct subject: "family mediation." Knowledge of mediation or knowledge of family law no longer suffices as a means to understand this new terrain. Family mediation's melding of the unique characteristics and challenges of family law with the unique practices and goals of mediation, and the many issues of practice and policy this implicates, is the subject of this book — the first of its kind directed to law students.

A number of principles guide us throughout this text. First, we believe that mediation can be an effective means to resolve family disputes both from an individual and a societal perspective. That said, family mediation — like any other activity — can be done well or poorly, can be appropriate or inappropriate, can be effective or ineffective. We have sought to explore the complexities of the subject, and, as a result, allow future mediators and lawyers to assess issues of quality, appropriateness, and effectiveness in family mediation both at a systemic, legislative, and individual case level.

Second, law students who may soon enter the practice of law might find themselves mediating family conflicts or representing clients in family mediations. These are different activities that raise distinct issues, just as judging is different than lawyering. As the subject of family mediation continues to mature, there will likely be separate courses addressing these different activities. We are not there yet, however, and we have thus included materials regarding both here.

Third, we strongly believe that family mediation should be viewed in a specific social and procedural context. We will not assume a perfect world, with parties with sufficient resources to afford attorneys and a mediator with abundant time to facilitate a resolution. We will also not assume that there is a consistent conception of what effective family mediation is or should be. All of these matters are contested, and we have sought not to mislead readers into thinking that "real world" mediation approaches any single "ideal" of family mediation. We also recognize that participation in mediation can, in some contexts, pose a serious risk that parties may waive important legal rights or enter into agreements that exacerbate conflict. To this end, we have included readings and simulations that explore the feasibility and effectiveness of mediation when time and resources are limited.

Finally, family mediation, even more than family law, must be approached in an interdisciplinary fashion. We all have views about right and wrong, good parenting and bad parenting, and so forth, but family dynamics and child development have been the subject of intense study by social scientists. What they have found has crucial implications for our subject, and we include a sampling of their conclusions in the text.

We welcome readers to an exciting and challenging subject that is at the forefront of how we, as lawyers and as a society, approach resolving the most intimate and, in many respects, consequential of disputes.

ACKNOWLEDGEMENTS

This book is a collaboration in the full sense of the word. We have benefited enormously from the help of others. Wendy Seiden drafted Chapter 4's section on Parents v. State Child Access Disputes and prepared simulations included in the Teacher's Manual. Andrew Schepard was a supporter of this project from its earliest stages and his critique of an earlier draft was of incalculable importance. We have drawn upon Carl Schneider's deep insights about family mediation and we and readers of this book benefit from the material he has generously permitted us to reproduce. We are also grateful to the many other family mediators who have contributed to our classes and our understanding of mediation, including Louise Phipps Senft, Theresa Furnari, Mark Scurti, and Amaza Scott Reid. We have also received wonderful research assistance from University of Baltimore law students and graduates Sarah Hale, Megan Beechener, and April Nelson. We also thank Library Director Will Tress and his talented colleagues in the law library for all their help in the preparation of this book.

There are many others, too numerous to name, who have been de facto co-authors. Our work has been enriched by the many mediators we have spoken to, mediated before, and observed. Our students in our Family Mediation Seminar and Clinic have taught us a great deal about teaching, learning, and mediation and have provided helpful feedback on earlier versions of the text.

We also thank the University of Baltimore Foundation for its financial support and the many faculty and administrators at the School of Law who have provided encouragement and various kinds of expertise while we were writing the book.

Finally, our deepest thanks to the many participants in mediation we have represented and with whom we have mediated. They have been the greatest teachers of all.

TABLE OF CONTENTS

TABLE OF CONTENTS

TABLE OF CONTENTS

TABLE OF CONTENTS

Chapter 1

AN OVERVIEW OF FAMILY MEDIATION

A. INTRODUCTION

Family mediation melds distinct disciplines into one subject: family law, mediation (itself a multidisciplinary undertaking), and the psychology of family relations. Each of these disciplines has a distinct history and a distinct role to play in understanding and, ultimately, mastering the intricacies of family mediation. Although we will assume a working knowledge of family law, we make no such assumption about knowledge of mediation generally or family mediation in particular.

This Chapter will begin the process of understanding and, even more importantly, internalizing ways of thinking that are alien in a culture — both legal and non-legal — that is dominated by the norms of adjudication. The following will do so with a historical approach. The history that follows is both intellectual history and the history of growth of family mediation.

B. AN INTELLECTUAL HISTORY OF MEDIATION

Mediation did not arise in the context of family disputes, yet family disputes are now where mediation is most pervasive. The history of family mediation is thus necessarily bound up with the history of mediation more generally.

Mediation has a much longer intellectual history than is often recognized. The following excerpt introduces intellectual forebears of mediation. Some, but not all, of this excerpt addresses family mediation. In reviewing this material, it is important to filter these ideas through the lens of family disputes. Is it relevant? To what extent can these early critiques apply to our current approaches to family mediation?

The themes introduced in the following excerpt presage current debates about the intellectual and institutional foundation of family mediation — debates to which we will return in succeeding Chapters.

MOTHERS AND FATHERS OF INVENTION: THE INTELLECTUAL FOUNDERS OF ADR[1]

16 Ohio St. J. on Disp. Resol. 1, 1-37 (2000)

By Carrie Menkel-Meadow

[The ADR Movement] has been an eclectic field intellectually, and we have used, borrowed, and elaborated on ideas that have come to us from many different fields, not only from law and legal theory, but from anthropology, sociology, international relations, social and cognitive psychology, game theory and economics, and most recently, political theory . . .

[In the 1920's] Mary Parker Follett, one of the leading "mothers" of invention in ADR, talked about "constructive conflict" in the context of organizational and labor disputes . . . For Follett, there were three ways conflict was dealt with: domination, compromise, or integration. She urged integration as a process where new solutions would emerge from parties trying to meet their desires without the compromise of having to give up something. It is her story we often tell when we describe integrative solutions, when she was one of two readers in a library, arguing about an open window. She wanted the window closed because of a draft; the other patron wanted fresh air; the solution was to open a window in another room for indirect air to circulate. In her view, the likelihood of integrative solutions, in which parties do not necessarily have to give anything up, are increased by bringing differences out into the open, facing the conflicts and underlying desires, evaluating and re-valuing desires and preferences when the other parties' desires are made known, and looking for solutions in which the "interests may fit into each other." . . .

[The anthropologist Laura] Nader reminds us that disputing processes are intimately tied to the culture in which they are situated . . . Nader reminds us that methods of dispute resolution, in all of its forms, are not neutral — they are designed and implemented by parties, court administrators or governments with substantive agendas. Thus, we must always interrogate the purposes for which a process of dispute resolution is being invoked. How did this particular institution come to be? What values does it serve? Who is achieving what with the particular structure of the system in place? . . .

Nader's attention to the social and cultural situatedness of dispute resolution has resonated with a number of critics of ADR, both about mediation and arbitration, usually in their compulsory or mandatory forms. Thus, where mediation is thought to be designed to provide flexible, future-oriented solutions, critics point out that in cases of divorce, wronged and financially less secure women may be manipulated to compromise and give up too much. Similarly, others have argued that without the protection of the "rule of law" and the formality of the courtroom, racial and ethnic minorities as well as the economically disadvantaged will be taken advantage of by the more contextually powerful within the informal settings of ADR. Though she is not the only one, Nader's political and anthropological critique has provided an important standard against which to measure whether justice is being compromised in the quest for other values, like peace, harmony, or simple caseload reduction. . . .

---

[1] This article was first published in the Ohio State Journal on Dispute Resolution. Copyright ©2000. Reprinted with permission.

In his efforts to elaborate the different structures, functions, and moralities of different legal processes, [Lon] Fuller wrote the first description of, and most sustained argument for, mediation. He said that this conciliatory process, which did not require a decision of state-made law, would "reorient the parties to each other" and "brin[g] about a more harmonious relationship between the parties, whether this be achieved through explicit agreement, through a reciprocal acceptance of 'social norms' relevant to their relationship or simply because the parties have been helped to a new and more perceptive understanding of one another's problems." For Fuller, as for other theorists of mediation, its principal functional strength lay in its release of the parties "from the encumbrances of rules and of accepting, instead, a relationship of mutual respect, trust and understanding that will enable them to meet shared contingencies without the aid of formal prescriptions laid down in advance" . . . Fuller's functionalist definition of mediation, as being confined to either the improvement or termination of relationships (he focused on collective bargaining, divorce, and other familial relations and long-term business contracts), remains an important strand in the current justification of mediation . . .

Soia Mentschikoff, one of the first women to leave a deep imprint on legal institutions, also argued for the particular strengths of non-adjudicative forms of dispute resolution . . . Like a wise and modern student of ADR, Mentschikoff refused to pronounce on which processes were "better" than others . . . [I]t could not be said that any one process was perfect or appropriate for all kinds of matters . . .

Though few have made the argument explicit, much of the current penchant for "menus," "multi-door courthouses," and "fitting the forum to the fuss" can find its historical roots in the work of the Legal Process scholars, Henry Hart and Albert Sacks . . . Hart and Sacks make among the first references to the lawyer's role as negotiator and dispute resolver by suggesting that the lawyer's function as a "representative in the private settlement of disputes without litigation" was every bit as important as the more well-known role of the lawyer in court . . .

Much of the underlying and often implicit assumptions of negotiation and bargaining processes in modern ADR theory draw from the work of George Caspar Homans [who noted that what] might be good for trial (narrowing issues) is actually dysfunctional for settlement — the more issues, the merrier, for more possible trades . . .

Some legal scholars of dispute processing and conflict resolution have also drawn on the work of fathers in cognitive science to help us understand why resolving conflict is sometimes so difficult. In Kenneth Arrow's edited volume on Barriers to Conflict Resolution, psychologists describe the various reasoning errors and biased heuristics we use when reasoning alone or with others in the negotiation process . . .

[D]ispute resolution lies at the center of an intersection of many disciplines and is a discipline and practice for which the term "applied science" might have been invented . . .

NOTES AND QUESTIONS

1. Many of Menkel-Meadow's "mothers and fathers" focused on dispute resolution in ways other than traditional adjudication. When and under what circumstances is traditional adjudication most appropriate? When and under what circumstances is it least appropriate?

2. Are the ideas described particularly appropriate given the nature of family conflicts? Which ideas might be particularly inappropriate?

3. One of the themes that Menkel-Meadow develops is the influence of a range of disciplines on the development of mediation. What training do most lawyers bring to mediation that would be useful or not useful? In terms of family disputes, what other disciplines would be particularly pertinent?

4. Gender as a distinct issue in family mediation has been a contested issue and one to which we will turn particularly in Chapter 8. A substantial number of Menkel-Meadow's intellectual founders are women. Does a women's perspective (if there is a distinct "women's perspective") relate to the development and practice of mediation generally and to family mediation in particular?

C. A HISTORY OF FAMILY MEDIATION

The excerpts below explore the development of what has become a recognized ADR specialty — family mediation. As the readings note, most of the early recognized work in family mediation involved divorcing couples — first in mediation designed to facilitate reconciliation between husbands and wives and, later, to resolve post-divorce issues. Court-sponsored programs evolved to address primarily custody and visitation issues of both married and unmarried parents. Child access remains the focus of most family court programs but private family mediation has expanded to address a wide range of issues among traditional and nontraditional families.

As you read these excerpts consider some of the broader issues facing family mediation today:

- What are or should be the goals of family mediation?
- Do the goals change when you move from a private to a public setting?
- Would you recommend mediation to a client seeking a divorce or other family law remedy? Why or why not?
- Are there any circumstances when litigation would be a preferred dispute resolution method?
- Who is the ideal mediator in family cases? What training is needed?

THE EVOLUTION OF DIVORCE AND FAMILY MEDIATION[2]

From DIVORCE AND FAMILY MEDIATION 4-7 (Jay Folberg, Ann L. Milne & Peter Salem, Eds.) (2004)

A Brief History

The increase in, and growing acceptance of, divorce in our society has led to sweeping changes in the substantive law of divorce, the most significant being the adoption of no-fault grounds for divorce. All states now provide some form of no-fault divorce, which shifts the responsibility for determining whether or not a divorce is warranted from the court to the parties involved. Other substantive legal changes included legislative provisions for shared parenting and joint custody, as well as the requirement in some states that parents submit parenting plans for how responsibility for children will be allocated. Alimony based on fault and entitlement has given way to financial arrangements based on need and ability to pay. Rigid rules of property division have been replaced in many states by consideration of equity and fairness based on the unique circumstances of the parties.

In addition to these substantive legal reforms are changes in the procedural aspects of divorce. Traditional divorce embodied adversarial norms intended to minimize direct communication and maximize third-party decision-making. Divorce actions were initiated by a lawsuit naming a plaintiff and a defendant, and settlement negotiations were conducted under the threat of a trial that only reinforced the competitive underpinnings of the "winner-takes-all" mentality. In the early 1970's a handful of attorneys took to heart the emerging no-fault divorce philosophy and began offering "nonadversarial legal services." These attorneys risked bar association sanctions by meeting with both spouses to help settle financial, property, and child custody issues. The concept of a neutral attorney set the stage for other members of the legal profession to promote the principles of mediation in divorce-related matters.

About the same time, mental health professionals began offering new options for divorcing family members. Historically, divorce was viewed by the mental health professionals as lying outside the domain of psychotherapy. The psychodynamic model, with its focus on an individual's unconscious conflicts and intrapsychic pathology, did not allow couples in conflict to be treated together in a clinical setting. The more traditional schools of therapy did not direct themselves to psychological and emotional issues of the divorcing family. These practitioners saw divorce solely as a legal process that begins at the point of separation.

As more therapists began to identify themselves as divorce counselors specializing in services directed toward the mental health concerns of the divorcing family, they created therapeutic interventions that combined an insight approach with the action-oriented focus of the behaviorists. Divorcing spouses enlisted the help of clinicians in an attempt to resolve conflicts to effect a satisfactory post divorce adjustment. Out of these efforts emerged a body of theory that addressed emotional-psychological aspects of divorce. This divorce theory moved professionals from the one-dimensional view of divorce as a legal process to a more integrated view of divorce as a multidimensional process involving both legal and

---

[2] Copyright ©2004. Reprinted with permission.

psychological matters. Some mental health professionals began offering mediation as a means of helping the divorcing family with both the psychological dissolution of the marriage and with working out a contractual agreement on parenting responsibilities, property division, and finances.

California first established court-connected conciliation services in 1939. The initial focus of these services was to provide marriage counseling aimed at reconciliation. Conciliation court personnel were probably the first to offer mediation services, as the focus of conciliation shifted from reconciliation to divorce counseling and custody mediation. In 1980 California became the first state to mandate all parents with custody or visitation disputes to participate in family mediation prior to a court hearing. Disputants could choose to use either court-based or private mediators. Most states today have statutes and court policies governing family mediation and selected jurisdictions in at least 38 states mandate mediation when there are disputes over custody or visitation.

The first private-sector family mediation center was established in 1974 in Atlanta, Georgia, by O.J. Coogler, an attorney and marriage and family counselor. Spurred by his emotionally and financially costly divorce, Coogler helped popularize the idea of divorce mediation through the publication of his book *Structured Mediation in Divorce Settlement*. To assist couples in contractually resolving issues of finances, property division support and child custody, Coogler proposed a structured framework for third party mediators, using communication and intervention techniques borrowed from labor mediation and the social sciences. In 1975 Coogler established the Family Mediation Association (FMA), an interdisciplinary organization of individuals interested in the development and advancement of divorce mediation. Like many pioneers, Coogler and his "structured mediation model" were harshly criticized. Bar associations declared mediation by nonlawyers to be the unauthorized practice of law and attempted to discourage lawyers from mediating through the threat of ethical sanctions.

Nonetheless, the practice of divorce mediation continued, encouraged by judges who welcomed both the reduction of cases on their dockets and relief from making difficult decision about the best interests of children. Court administrators supported legislation that compelled family mediation, as evidence mounted that mediation was less expensive than court hearing and resulted in less post divorce litigation and enforcement problems. The divorcing population, through a number of grassroots organizations, began demanding reform. Legislative changes supporting co-parenting, joint custody, and shared parenting set the stage for the institutionalization of divorce mediation.

Following a dispute within the leadership of FMA over organizational direction, John Haynes, Stephen Erickson, and Samuel Marguiles founded the Academy of Family Mediators (AFM), in 1982. AFM became the professional association for family and divorce mediators. The organization sponsored mediation-training programs, addressed public policy issues (including diversity, standards of practice, and supervision qualifications), and published a newsletter and journal for its members. In 2001 AFM merged with the Society of Professionals in Dispute Resolution (SPIDR) and the Conflict Resolution Education Network (CREnet) to form the Association for Conflict Resolution (ACR)-a membership organization dedicated to "enhancing the practice and public understanding of conflict resolution."

Other national organizations, including the Association of Family and Conciliation Courts, the American Arbitration Association, and the American Bar Association, began to encourage divorce and child custody mediation and added mediation topics and programs to their conferences, newsletters, and journals.

Today, the largest dispute resolution membership organization, with more than 9,000 members, is the American Bar Association Section of Dispute Resolution. In April 1999, the Section Council called for the inclusion of people from all backgrounds as neutral participants, regardless of whether they are lawyers, and in 2002 passed a resolution stating that mediation is not the practice of law.

The early years of the divorce mediation field focused on attempting to establish a foothold of credibility. Research, limited as it was, established the benefits of mediation over lawyer-assisted negotiation, custody evaluation, and litigation. Funding for court mediation programs-through the use of filling fees dedicated to support these programs-was established in some jurisdictions.

Since its inception in the early 1970's, the landscape of the mediation field has evolved as more programs and services had been established. Mediation is now used in thousands of divorce-related disputes annually. The field has matured, as evidenced by current professional issues and controversies. Topics such as the use mediation in cases involving allegations of domestic abuse, same sex partners, and members from blended families as well as unmarried parents have moved our professional discourse beyond the benefits of mediation.

Model Standards of Practice for Family and Divorce Mediation were developed through a cooperative effort of the Association of Family and Conciliation Courts, the Family Law Section of the American Bar Association, the Dispute Resolution Section of the American Bar Association, the Academy of Family Mediators, the Conflict Resolution Education Network, the National Association of Community Mediation, the National Conference on Peacemaking and Conflict Resolution, and the Society of Professionals in Dispute Resolution.

The training and education of mediators have expanded from 1-5 day programs with no entrance or exit requirements to academic programs that confer a degree in conflict resolution upon completion of course work and a field practicum (e.g. Marquette University, Antioch University, University of Missouri Law School, George Mason University, Pepperdine University).

New models of mediation that extend beyond the traditional problem solving facilitative approach are being touted together with accompanying training curricula. Some blanch at these new approaches and decline to call them *mediation*, whereas others welcome them and point to the benefits of having a diversity of tools in the mediator's tool kit.

*   *   *

As family mediation becomes more established as an alternative to litigation, more and more court systems established mediation programs. Many of these programs mandate the use of mediation, particularly for child access disputes. The following excerpt raises a variety of issues about the structure of such programs, and the implications for providing access to these new types of "justice" for low income families.

BURDENING ACCESS TO JUSTICE: THE COST OF DIVORCE MEDIATION ON THE CHEAP[3]

73 St. John's L. Rev. 375, 390–93, 397, 473–74 (1999)

By Carol J. King

Early in this century, a number of states passed family law conciliation statutes or formed specialized family conciliation courts in an attempt to encourage reconciliation between divorcing spouses. If private reconciliation efforts did not succeed, the laws or courts encouraged the parties to reach agreement by arranging for custody and visitation with the minor children. The conciliation movement was spurred by the desire to find a way to reduce the bitterness created by contested divorce trials, a goal that continues to drive the modern mediation movement. Due to low voluntary use, the statutes fell out of favor and subsequently failed to serve their intended purpose.

Over twenty years ago, several well-known scholars and practitioners who found themselves frustrated by certain aspects of the adversarial divorce system proposed divorce mediation as an alternative to litigation. In the early 1970s, O.J. Coogler began to experiment with a model of divorce mediation. Coogler proposed using a neutral mediator to structure settlement discussions between the parties. At the 1976 Pound Conference on the administration of justice, Professor Frank Sander discussed the potential benefits of mediation of family matters. He further proposed the idea of the "multi-door courthouse," in which disputants could be directed to a variety of dispute processing avenues, including mediation and trial. Therapists and others outside the legal system also became interested in divorce mediation as a way to resolve family conflicts more productively. As did Coogler and Sander, therapists often observed the destructive fallout of adversarial divorce and sought a better way to minimize the pain and trauma experienced by many divorcing couples. The interests of children were often noted as a reason to avoid litigation.

Originally, most divorce mediation practitioners were privately retained and paid by the parties, while a few community mediation centers provided free services. This was in line with one of the primary rationales for advancing the mediation movement — avoiding the court system. Mediation was intended to provide a dispute resolution process that differed greatly from the adjudicatory model, by emphasizing consensual, voluntary participation in both the process and outcome of mediation. People were not ordered to attend mediation. Instead, they were given the opportunity to negotiate freely. Mediators were philosophically opposed to forcing a settlement on an unwilling party. One of the goals of mediation was to address the root causes of the conflict by generating understanding and consensus. Rather than focusing on fault-finding or seeking to impose a decision on the parties in conflict, mediation sought to promote lasting resolutions.

Recently, mediation has begun to diverge greatly from many of the precepts originally guiding the movement and mandatory mediation is no longer viewed as being antithetical to the goals of mediation. Early experience in community mediation pilot programs showed that voluntary usage rates were low. In many cases, one party was interested in trying mediation, but one or more of the other

---

parties would decline to participate. Policy makers grew more interested in mandating participation, particularly in light of studies indicating that satisfaction rates were high even under mandated conditions. Interest in expanded use of mediation through mandatory participation was not limited to the types of cases typically seen in neighborhood or community mediation centers. Family courts began to explore mediation when possible systemic benefits, such as docket reduction and cost savings, became known. In the past few years, there has been a significant increase in the number of states authorizing mandatory divorce mediation — there was a vast leap in a single year, from reports of four to six states in 1993, to thirty-three states in 1994. Courts have taken several different approaches to funding mandatory divorce mediation programs. On one end of the continuum, courts fully fund mediators for the disputants. On the other end, judges are permitted to refer cases to private providers at party cost, manifesting little official concern for the financial constraints on the parties.

Systems of funding are crucial to the implementation of mediation. Unfortunately, private mediation can be costly. In St. Croix, mediators charge $150 per hour. In St. Thomas, the hourly rate increases to $200 . . .

Parties are generally required to pay the mediator's fees. Sometimes, free services are made available at least to some of the very poor. Unfortunately, many low-income divorcing parties, who are unable to pay mediation fees on their own, do not qualify for free services. A few programs attempt to mitigate the financial strain on lower-income mediation participants through sliding fee scales. The actual affordability of mediation services offered under sliding fee scales remains unexamined. Statutory provisions allowing parties to request fee waivers may be ineffective because the parties are often unaware of them. Some courts do not address the affordability problem at all, and leave the allocation of fees to the court's discretion if the parties cannot agree. If the fees are substantial, which is often the case, the allocation of such fees is a deciding factor when parties are determining whether to pursue mediation . . .

The American legal system has historically valued the ideal of access to justice for all members of society. Until recently, court adjudication was recognized as the primary model for dispensing justice. Within approximately the last twenty years, the use of mediation has been advanced as a different alternative for fair, satisfactory resolution of disputes through a participatory process leading to a consensual outcome.

Courts have encouraged greater use of mediation with hopes of controlling dockets and reducing the delays and costs of modern litigation. Domestic relations courts also aspired to reduce the negative impact of bitterly fought divorce and custody disputes on children by diverting cases to a forum seen as more capable of resolving the underlying conflicts between parents than traditional adjudication or attorney negotiation.

Totally voluntary mediation programs did not handle a sufficient volume of cases to have any significant impact on the court system's goals. Mandatory mediation became more appealing, especially as research showed continued participant satisfaction even when mediation was involuntary.

Unfortunately, as courts have demonstrated increased interest in adding mediation to the range of available dispute resolution services, money for funding new programs has become less readily available. Funding problems have led to the passage of statutes and rules allowing courts to require parties to use and pay for mediation as a prerequisite to having their cases heard in court. An increasing number of litigants, both in general civil and family law cases, have been compelled to pay for mediation in addition to the other costs of litigation.

In the civil case context, this practice may be more expedient than wise. In the domestic relations case context, it raises serious concerns about functional denial of the due process guarantee of access to the courts where parties cannot afford both mediation and litigation. In addition, the practical reality of the significant financial constraints facing most divorcing parties makes a party payment approach punitive. It clearly places the interests of the court in case diversion ahead of the litigants' needs and interest in free choice of dispute resolution options. The weight of argument and preliminary research favor publicly funded divorce mediation as the best way to guarantee equal access to both alternative dispute resolution and the courts . . .

NOTES AND QUESTIONS

1.   What are the range of goals of family mediation identified in the readings? Should any of these goals be given priority when developing a family mediation program?

2.   Do the goals of family mediation change if the mediation program is court sponsored? Some statutes require parties seeking divorce or child access remedies to try mediation before they are permitted access to the courts. See e.g., MD Rule 9-205; ME. REV. STAT. ANN. Tit.19-A § 251; W. VA. CODE § 48-9-202. What issues do these statutes raise? Does the method for payment of mediators affect these issues?

Chapter 2

MODELS OF FAMILY MEDIATION

A. INTRODUCTION

Family mediation, like all types of mediation, encompasses an extraordinarily broad range of activities.

This is often the result of a range of factors — for example, whether the matter is "court-referred" or not and the resources available to the parties. At this introductory stage, however, we will explore this issue more broadly.

In recent years, there has been an intense debate among mediators and mediation scholars about what "model" of mediation is most effective, or even if certain "models" constitute "real" mediation at all. We will begin by offering a brief overview of three primary "models" that are usually the basis of this debate: "facilitative mediation," "evaluative mediation," and "transformative mediation."[1]

B. THREE MODELS OF FAMILY MEDIATION

CHILDREN, COURTS AND CUSTODY: INTERDISCIPLINARY MODELS FOR DIVORCING FAMILIES 52–53 (2006)[2]
By Andrew Schepard

The mediator's goal is to generate an agreement that satisfies the parties' diverse needs and interests, defined in largely psychological and economic terms. Mediators, however, do not universally agree on the theory and practice of their

---

[1] The initial articulation of the distinction between "facilitative" and "evaluative" was originally put forward by Leonard Riskin. Leonard Riskin, *Understanding Mediator Orientations, Strategies and Techniques*, 12 Alternatives to High Cost Lit. 111 (1994); Leon Riskin, *Understanding Mediators' Orientations, Strategies, and Techniques: A Grid for the Perplexed*, 1 Harv. Negot. L. Rev. 7 (1996). The distinction pervades both the theory and scholarship of mediation, although Professor Riskin himself has expressed subsequent reservations about how the distinction has come to be used. Leonard Riskin, *Decision in Mediation: The New Old Grid and the New New Grid System*, 79 NOTRE DAME L. REV. 1 (2003).

[2] Copyright ©2006. Reprinted with the permission of Cambridge University Press.

craft. Differences between them can be usefully categorized on a continuum between "facilitative" and "evaluative." One end of this continuum contains strategies and techniques that facilitate the parties' negotiation; at the other end lies strategies and techniques intended to evaluate matters that are important to the mediation.

A primarily facilitative mediator uses techniques to help parents better communicate. He or she asks probing questions to encourage parents to articulate why they want custody and what role they see for the other parent in the child's life. The facilitative mediator asks parents to complete parenting plans to exchange concrete proposals for what days each wants a child to live with that parent and how differences can be resolved.

A primarily evaluative mediator seeks to get the parents to understand the strengths and weaknesses of their positions and interests. An evaluative mediator might predict what will happen in court if the parents do not settle, will evaluate proposed solutions, and will offer his or her own suggestions for settlement and solutions to impasses. The differences between evaluative and facilitative are often a matter of degree, rather than of kind; many mediators combine facilitative and evaluative techniques, as they deem appropriate.

Another school, transformative mediation, views conflict as a crises in human interaction that results in hostile and aggressive communication patterns between parties that in turn causes further deterioration in each party's perception of self and the other party. The goal of the transformative mediator is to change the quality of the parties' interaction, not to solve the problems that divide them. Success in mediation is not measured by agreements reached, but rather by party shifts toward greater self-confidence, responsiveness to the other party, and constructive interaction . . .

C. "FACILITATIVE" MEDIATION

The debate between proponents of "facilitative" mediation and proponents of "evaluative" mediation has been intense. As with much else, the debate takes on particular meaning in the specialized context of family mediation.

Many family mediators, particularly in private practice, advocate facilitative approaches. Indeed, the facilitative dimension of mediation is "sold" to potential participants as a particular advantage of mediation over litigation, with facilitation generating more self-determination and empowerment for parties. Indeed, there are few published defenses of an explicitly evaluative approach.

The following excerpt describes basic premises of facilitative mediation.

CLIENT COUNSELING, MEDIATION, AND ALTERNATIVE NARRATIVES OF DISPUTE RESOLUTION[3]
10 Clin. L. Rev. 833, 846–54 (2004)
By Robert Rubinson

The story of litigation has been so thoroughly internalized by litigants, judges, and lawyers alike that it operates below the level of consciousness. [E]verybody — lawyers and non-lawyers alike — knows what it is. In contrast, for a culture steeped in litigation, the risk in approaching mediation is in underestimating its strangeness. In its more sophisticated forms, mediation is bizarre indeed: it proceeds from fundamentally different premises as to what resolving disputes is about and, even more fundamentally, as to what a dispute is.

*   *   *

1. Actors and Owners

Once litigation is commenced, parties are actors compelled by force of law to act within a system: this is most obvious in criminal cases, where criminal defendants cannot unilaterally "opt out" of a case, but it is also true in civil litigation, where one party can compel the participation of another party or risk entry of a default judgment. Moreover, all litigation operates in the shadow of a simple fact: a court can impose its judgments by force on parties . . .

In contrast, mediation is a voluntary process. While this picture has been clouded by the rise of "court-referred" and "court-ordered" mediation and enforceable "agreements to mediate," a preeminent — if not the greatest — value in mediation is "the principle of self-determination" through which parties "own" the process. The ultimate way to "own" a process is to have power to decide whether to engage in it or not. Put another way, mediation must sell itself to parties because the parties can walk away without buying.

2. Perspectives

[L]itigation is consumed with determining "what happened" in order to determine liability. Judges and juries decide "what happened" and sort liability (or penalties) accordingly.

In contrast, mediation rejects the idea that "what happened" is a unitary or stable "truth" to be found "out there." Instead, a primary — if not the primary — thrust of mediation is that conflict resolution entails some recognition on the part of disputants that "what happened" is informed by perspective. Literature on mediation is rife with this idea: a critical component of mediation is that parties "begin to acknowledge another view of the situation," or "[t]he challenge for mediation is to somehow lead people to a situation where they can, at the very least, allow two contending perceptions to coexist," or to "enable each person to see the other as the victim, and in the process, build a new moral framework" . . .

---

[3] Copyright ©2004. Reprinted with permission.

3. Rights and Wrongs in Mediation

Given the importance of "perspective" in mediation, the very notion of "judgment" is alien to mediation, as are notions of "fault" and even "responsibility." Issuing "judgments" (both in its legal and non-legal sense) and finding "fault" or "responsibility" impede mediation because mediators want parties to be the authors of their own mediation. A morality tale which identifies one party as "moral" necessarily brands the other party as not, and the "immoral" party is not likely to "own" a process that produces such a result.

4. "Time" in Mediation

Litigation looks backward in time: it seeks to resolve disputes through historical reconstruction of past events. In contrast, mediation focuses on what needs to be done to resolve disputes in light of present and future interests. This is not to say that history — or at least perspectives on history — does not have its place in mediation: indeed, history in mediation might offer clues about how to resolve controversy in the here and now, or parties might require validation of their perspective on history — and the catharsis that describing that history might bring — as necessary before meaningful progress can be made towards resolving a controversy. Nevertheless, the past in mediation is typically not the foundation for resolving conflict . . .

5. Narrowing and Expanding

Litigation seeks to "narrow issues" — and thereby the contested narrative — through a panoply of procedural and substantive mechanisms: responsive pleadings, motions to dismiss, pretrial orders, the requirement of relevance. . . . In contrast, rather than narrowing issues, the mediation process tends to embrace openness in dialogue. Such openness encourages parties to discuss and disclose anything that would facilitate the resolution of controversy. The idea is that the more circumstances and possibilities are shared by the parties to mediation, the greater the chances that the parties, with the assistance of the mediator, can find creative ways to resolve disputes . . .

D.   THE "FACILITATIVE" VERSUS "EVALUATIVE" DEBATE

As generally conceived and as its name suggests, "evaluative mediators" assess the strength of a case in mediation, much as a judge might in a settlement conference. In this sense, an evaluative mediator engages in a process that is not particularly different from the normal mode through which judges render decisions, albeit without the power to issue binding decisions. As a result, evaluative mediation does not proceed from the "fundamentally different premises" alluded to in the prior article.

Many family mediators reject evaluative mediation at least in its pure form, although there remains strong disagreement on this issue. The following excerpt articulates the "facilitative" side of the debate.

THE TOP TEN REASONS WHY MEDIATORS SHOULD NOT EVALUATE[4]

24 Fla. St. U. L. Rev. 937, 937–38 (1997)

By Lela P. Love

I. THE ROLES AND RELATED TASKS OF EVALUATORS AND FACILITATORS ARE AT ODDS

. . . [D]ifferences between evaluators and facilitators mean that each uses different skills and techniques, and each requires different competencies, training norms, and ethical guidelines to perform their respective functions. Further, the evaluative tasks of determining facts, applying law or custom, and delivering an opinion not only divert the mediator away from facilitation, but also can compromise the mediator's neutrality — both in actuality and in the eyes of the parties — because the mediator will be favoring one side in his or her judgments . . . "No one can serve two masters." Mediators cannot effectively facilitate when they are evaluating.

II. EVALUATION PROMOTES POSITIONING AND POLARIZATION, WHICH ARE ANTITHETICAL TO THE GOALS OF MEDIATION

When disputing parties are in the presence of an evaluator — a judge, an arbitrator, or a neutral expert — they act (or should act) differently than they would in the presence of a mediator. With an evaluator, disputants make themselves look as good as possible and their opponent as bad as possible. They do not make offers of compromise or reveal their hand for fear that it weakens the evaluator's perception of the strength of their case. They are in a competitive mind-set seeking to capture the evaluator's favor and win the case.

While adversarial confrontations between parties are helpful to a neutral who must judge credibility and clarify the choices he or she must make, such confrontations are not helpful to collaboration. Adversarial behaviors run counter to the mediator's efforts to move parties towards a different perception of their own situation and of each other. While parties typically enter the mediation process in a hostile and adversarial stance, the mediator seeks to shift them towards a collaborative posture in which they jointly construct a win-win solution. An atmosphere of respectful collaboration is a necessary foundation for creative problem-solving.

III. ETHICAL CODES CAUTION MEDIATORS — AND OTHER NEUTRALS — AGAINST ASSUMING ADDITIONAL ROLES

The ethical codes explicitly include a preference to keep processes "pure." Consequently, a mediator undertaking to give an opinion on the likely court outcome of a particular claim or a fair resolution of a particular matter should give an accurate label of the new role he or she is assuming and obtain the disputants' informed consent for undertaking the new role. Also, the mediator should be sure that the disputants understand that taking on an additional role might adversely impact the ability to facilitate discussions. When processes become "mixed," such

---

[4] Copyright ©1997. Reprinted with permission.

as when an arbitrator mediates or a mediator evaluates, it should be at the request and with the informed consent of the parties.

IV. IF MEDIATORS EVALUATE LEGAL CLAIMS AND DEFENSES, THEY MUST BE LAWYERS; ELIMINATING NONLAWYERS WILL WEAKEN THE FIELD

If it is acceptable or customary for mediators to give opinions on likely court outcomes or the merits of particular legal claims or defenses, then only lawyers and substantive experts will be competent to mediate . . . While this result may be good news for lawyers, the mediator pool would be substantially weakened by the loss of the talents and perspectives of nonlawyers. Furthermore, if the field is theirs, lawyer-mediators will likely pull mediation into an adversarial paradigm. One noted authority in the mediation field, reacting to a Florida rule requiring mediators of certain cases to be either experienced lawyers or retired judges, proclaimed this requirement to be "the end of good mediation."

V. THERE ARE INSUFFICIENT PROTECTIONS AGAINST INCORRECT MEDIATOR EVALUATIONS

Even assuming that mediators could be governed by and held to appropriate standards when they evaluate, growing concerns about the quality of justice that disputants receive when they are diverted from courts into private alternative dispute resolution (ADR) processes argue for leaving evaluation to adversarial processes where due process protections are in place. In the courts, disputants can appeal decisions they feel are wrong. In arbitration, disputants pick arbitrators based on the arbitrator's substantive expertise or wisdom and consciously waive the right to appeal.

In mediation, little protection exists from a mediator's inadequately informed opinion. Confidentiality statutes, rules, and agreements keep sessions private. Quasi-judicial immunity in some cases can shield mediators from liability for careless opinions. . . . Service as a mediator does not qualify a mediator to be a judge any more than service as a judge qualifies a judge to mediate.

VI. EVALUATION ABOUNDS: THE DISPUTING WORLD NEEDS ALTERNATIVE PARADIGMS

Mediation has the potential of being shifted towards an adversarial framework in which mediators "trash and bash" to get parties to settle. They "trash" the parties' cases, predicting loss and risk if litigation is pursued. They "bash" settlement proposals that the other side will not accept. We lose a great deal if mediation becomes a mere adjunct of the adversarial norm. Having mediators use evaluation as a technique to get movement takes us in that direction.

VII. MEDIATOR EVALUATION DETRACTS FROM THE FOCUS ON PARTY RESPONSIBILITY FOR CRITICAL EVALUATION, RE-EVALUATION AND CREATIVE PROBLEM-SOLVING

. . . The mediator's task of elevating the dialogue from recriminations and blame to the generation of possibilities and breakthrough ideas is a task we are just beginning to understand. If we allow mediation and mediators to slip into the comfortable (because it is the norm) adversarial mind-set of evaluation, we kill the turbo-thrust of the jet engine of idea generation. So-called "evaluative mediation" pulls mediation away from creativity and into the adversarial frame. If we are to continue to survive and evolve as a species, we need to nurture the processes that tap our affinity to create and imagine.

VIII. EVALUATION CAN STOP NEGOTIATION

When mediators provide opinions, the opinions have consequences. An unfavorable opinion can seriously disadvantage one of the parties. When a party disagrees with the unfavorable opinion, the party is likely to withdraw from the mediation, believing that the mediator has "sided" with the other party. On the other hand, a party advantaged by a favorable opinion may get locked into an unacceptable claim or position and negotiations may stop altogether. Because mediators are charged with furthering negotiation, this result is undesirable.

IX. A UNIFORM UNDERSTANDING OF MEDIATION IS CRITICAL TO THE DEVELOPMENT OF THE FIELD

When attorneys advise clients about the advantages and disadvantages of mediation, when courts and institutions create mediation programs and panels of mediators, when consumers go to the Yellow Pages to find a mediator, they should know what they are getting. They should have a clear understanding of the goals of the process and the tasks the neutral will perform.

In an article criticizing ADR, Noreen Connell, former president of the New York State chapter of the National Organization for Women, describes a case in which a married couple elects to mediate their divorce to avoid dissipating marital assets in litigation:

> At the sessions, the mediator, who is a woman, echoes the husband's complaints that the wife is "too angry and too suspicious" when he claims that he no longer has a pension and that he has lost the credit card records. The wife is told her complaintss [sic] about not getting enough money to pay the mortgage since her husband moved out of the house are emotionally damaging to their son and that responsible parents choose joint custody.

Ms. Connell's conclusion about mediation is contained in the article's title, "Beware of Alternative Dispute Resolution." Another conclusion based on the same story is that the mediator was so busy evaluating who was right and wrong and what the outcome should be that the mediator did not mediate at all. The mediation community must make the meaning of mediation so clear that, in her next article, Ms. Connell will criticize the mediator involved in this case, not the mediation process itself.

X. MIXED PROCESSES CAN BE USEFUL, BUT CALL THEM WHAT THEY ARE!

Parties sometimes request that neutrals assume a variety of roles. "Mixed processes" abound: med-arb, arb-med, mini-trials, summary jury trials, and mediation and neutral evaluation. These mixed processes can address particular needs of a situation and can be very helpful.

Mediators are not foreclosed from engaging in some other process or helping parties design a mixed process. Whatever the service being provided, however, it should be requested by the parties and accurately labeled. When a process is "mixed" and the neutral has multiple roles, he or she is bound by more than one code of ethics and is charged with separate goals and tasks. A properly labeled process — or, conversely, a label that has a clear meaning — promotes integrity, disputant satisfaction, and uniform practice.

Mediators who regularly give case assessments and expert opinions should continue those practices only if they are requested by the parties, properly advertised, and accurately labeled.

NOTES AND QUESTIONS

1. Are you convinced by Love's reasons why "mediators should not evaluate"? Why or why not?

2. While sometimes writers charge "evaluation" is never appropriate in mediation, such as in the excerpt above, others claim that the debate presupposes a kind of stylistic "purity" that is not to be found in practice. In other words, many — if not most — family mediators will sometimes be "facilitative" and sometimes "evaluative" along a continuum, with the more sophisticated mediators deploying a particular "style" when the situation so demands. *See, e.g.*, Jacqueline M. Nolan-Haley, *Lawyers, Non-Lawyers and Mediation: Rethinking the Professional Monopoly from a Problem-Solving Perspective*, 7 Harv. Neg. L. Rev. 235, 276–280 (2002) (arguing that all mediations contain explicit or implicit "evaluation" by mediators). If this is true, do you think issues relating either to child access or marital property lend themselves to a more "evaluative" or a more "facilitative" approach? Why or why not?

3. Love is careful to limit her use of the term "mediation" to facilitative mediation. Indeed, she argues that the role of an evaluator is inconsistent and subverts what mediation seeks to accomplish. Do you agree that evaluative mediation is not mediation at all?

4. Are some forms of evaluation more legitimate than others in family mediation? For example, should mediators "evaluate" — or at least share views — on what is best for children of divorcing couples? Is your view influenced by how children are not formal "participants" in mediation?

5. As with much else in debates about family mediation, the issue of the involvement of lawyers percolates at or just beneath the surface. It has often been noted that lawyers in mediation and mediators who are lawyers are more likely to tend towards and be comfortable with an "evaluative" style because that is the norm of adversarial adjudication. *See* Robert Rubinson, *Client Counseling, Mediation and Alternative Narratives of Dispute Resolution*, 10 Clin. L. Rev. 833, 858–59 (2004). Indeed, as Love notes, some — particularly non-lawyers — argue that the involvement of lawyers in mediation, and the evaluative orientation that they may often bring, signal "the end of good mediation." Do you agree?

6. Facilitative mediation can often be time-consuming. In situations where mediation is "court-referred" or "mandated" — as we shall see, an increasingly

common circumstance in family mediation — it is often more likely that mediators will be "evaluative" simply because there is not enough time for facilitation to work. This is one issue among many that call into question the efficacy of court-annexed programs.

E.   "TRANSFORMATIVE MEDIATION" IN FAMILY DISPUTES

In the 1990s, Robert A. Baruch Bush and Joseph P. Folger elucidated "transformative mediation" — a form of mediation that has since been the subject of extensive debate and commentary. Robert A. Baruch Bush & Joseph P. Folger, THE PROMISE OF MEDIATION: RESPONDING TO CONFLICT THROUGH EMPOWERMENT AND RECOGNITION (1994).

In the following excerpt, one of the developers of this approach describes the goals of transformative mediation and how it differs from other conceptions of mediation.

TRANSFORMATIVE MEDIATION: CHANGING THE QUALITY OF FAMILY CONFLICT INTERACTION[5]
From DIVORCE AND FAMILY MEDIATION 54, 56, (Jay Folberg, Ann L. Milne & Peter Salem, Eds.), (2004)
By Robert A. Baruch Bush & Sally Ganong Pope

. . . T]here are problems to be solved at the end of a marriage — the assets to be divided, the parenting plan to be created — and parties do want to solve those problems. The reality is, however, that they want to do so in a way that enhances their sense of their own competence and autonomy without taking advantage of the other. They want to feel proud of themselves for how they handled this life crisis, and this means making changes in the difficult conflict interaction that is going on between them, rather than simply coming up with the "right" answers to the specific problems. The corollary, explored below, is that in order to be useful to parties, conflict intervention must directly address the interactional crisis itself; it cannot be limited to problem solving and satisfaction of interests . . . Therefore, what they most want from an intervener-even more than help in resolving specific issues-is help in reversing the downward spiral and restoring a more humane quality to their interaction . . .

In the transformative model, reversing the downward spiral is the primary value that mediation offers to parties in family conflict. That value goes beyond the dimension of helping parties reach agreement on disputed issues. With or without the achievement of agreement, the help many parties want most in family conflict (and probably in all conflict) involves helping them end the vicious circle of disempowerment, disrespect, and demonization — alienation from both self and other. Because without ending or changing that cycle, the parties cannot move beyond the negative interaction that has entrapped them and cannot escape its crippling effects . . .

In effect, without a change in the conflict interaction between them, parties are left disabled, even if an agreement on concrete issues has been reached. Their

---

confidence in their own competence to handle life's challenges remains weakened, and their ability to trust others in relationships remains compromised. The result can be lasting damage to the parties' ability to function, not only in family relationships but in general. "Moving on," therefore, necessarily means moving out of their negative conflict interaction itself, and parties intuitively know this and want help in doing it. . . .

Conflict is not static. It is an emergent, dynamic phenomenon in which parties can and do move and shift in remarkable ways. They move from weakness to strength, becoming (in more specific terms) calmer, clearer, more confident, more articulate, and more decisive. They shift from self-absorption to responsiveness, becoming more attentive, open, trusting, responsive toward the other party. [T]hese shifts that parties make — from weakness to strength, and from self-absorption to responsiveness to one another- . . . are called "empowerment" and "recognition" . . . [T]here is a reinforcing feedback effect . . . The stronger I become, the more open I am to you. The more open I am to you, the stronger you feel, the more open you become to me, and the stronger I feel . . .

Defining Transformative Mediation

What many divorcing parties want most from mediators, and what mediators can, in fact, provide-with the proper focus and skills, as discussed below-is help and support in making these critical shifts from weakness to strength and from self absorption to responsiveness. . . .

- *Mediation* is defined as a process in which a third party works with the parties to help them change the quality of their conflict interaction from negative and destructive to positive and constructive, as they explore and discuss issues and possibilities for resolution.
- The *mediator's role* is to help the parties make positive interactional shifts (i.e., empowerment and recognition shifts) by supporting the exercise of their capacities for strength and responsiveness through deliberation, perspective taking, communication, and decision making.
- The *mediator's primary goals* are (1) to foster empowerment shifts by supporting, but never supplanting, each party's deliberation and decision making, at every point in the session where choices arise (regarding either process or outcome); and (2) to foster recognition shifts by encouraging and supporting, but never forcing, each party's freely chosen efforts to achieve new understandings of the other's perspective . . .

The transformative model does not ignore the significance of resolving specific issues, but it assumes that, if mediators do the job just described, the parties themselves will very likely make positive changes in their interaction and, as a result, find acceptable terms of resolution for themselves if such terms genuinely exist. More important, they will have reversed the negative conflict spiral and begun to reestablish a positive and connecting mode of interaction that allows them to move forward on a different footing, both while and after specific issues are resolved-and, indeed, even if they cannot be resolved.

The transformative model posits that this is the greatest value that many families in conflict will find in mediation: It can help them conduct conflict itself in a different way. It can help them find and take the small but meaningful opportunities for empowerment and recognition shifts as they arise. It can support the virtuous cycle of personal empowerment and interpersonal recognition that de-escalates and de-embitters conflict (so that, with the bitterness drained out, even if there may still be conflict, it's no longer dehumanizing and demonizing). It can turn conflict interaction away from alienation, from both self and other, toward a restored connection to both-strength of self and appreciation of other-even while conflict continues. Mediation can thus help divorcing parties to "move on with their lives," with the capacities for living those lives restored-including both the sense of their own competence, and the confidence in their ability to connect with others . . . Transformative mediators allow and trust the parties to find their own way through the conflict, and even more important, find themselves and each other, discovering and revealing the strength and compassion within themselves . . .

Following the parties in their discussion highlights all of the issues they choose to put out on the table. Pushing them, probing and asking questions to get them to do more, is experienced as just that. The parties feel they are being pushed, and opportunities for empowerment and recognition are almost certainly lost. "Hypothesizing" by the mediator about what is important to one of the parties, or what would be an acceptable settlement, detracts from the intense focus needed to pay attention to what is actually going on right in front of the mediator. Hypothesizing requires the mediator to develop a line of questioning to follow up on and test the accuracy of the hypothesis; the result is the pursuit of the mediator's agenda, not the parties', and the loss of focus on transforming the conflict interaction . . .

NOTES AND QUESTIONS

1.   In another article, the authors claim that transformative mediation "differs markedly from the normal definitions found in training materials and literature on mediation." Robert A. Baruch Bush & Sally Ganong Pope, *Changing the Quality of Conflict Interaction: The Principles and Practice of Transformative Mediation*, 3 PEPP. DISP. RESOL. L.J. 67 (2002). Based upon your current understanding — an understanding that will deepen as we explore family mediation — do you agree? The authors note "transformative mediation" seeks to encourage "positive interactional shift" with the parties rather than resolve specific controversies. Does facilitative mediation — at least in terms of its promise — seek to do the same thing, albeit as a means to resolve a specific conflict? Is the difference then one of emphasis rather than of kind?

2.   In line with the prior question, formulate, building upon the earlier article by Lela P. Love, ten reasons why a "mediator should not transform" and ten reasons why a "mediator should transform."

3.   On their face, the goals of transformative mediation are ambitious. Do you believe that these goals have particular resonance for family mediation? Are there particular obstacles in meeting these goals in family disputes? Are there particular opportunities for meeting these goals in family disputes?

4.   As noted above, facilitative mediation requires time, which is not always available in court-referred or mandated contexts. Anecdotally, some mediators involved in court-annexed programs find transformative mediation compelling in theory but unworkable in practice due to time and resource constraints. Is transformative mediation only plausible for parties with the available and time and resources to be transformed? Do you believe that, nevertheless, the perspective and

insights set forth by theorists and practitioners of transformative mediation can inform mediations where time and resources are limited?

5.   Apart from the typical time limitations in court annexed mediation, do you believe courts would be inclined to support a more transformative orientation? In thinking this through, consider not only potential time demands of transformative mediation, but also its promise of permanently altering how parties interact with each other and, indeed, with others and within themselves. Could this be viewed as minimizing the possibility of future litigation?

6.   Whatever one's views of transformative mediation, Bush and Pope's model builds upon an important idea: "conflict is not static" and "is an emergent, dynamic phenomenon." This, again, differs from the norms of litigation. Are there special ways that you anticipate conflicts about child access mediation might be "dynamic"? Would this be about the past history between the parties, the nature of their future relationship, or some other sense? Does or should mediation draw upon this "dynamic" element of conflict? Are financial issues in family mediation more or less dynamic than child access issues?

Chapter 3

AN OVERVIEW OF THE FAMILY MEDIATION PROCESS

A. INTRODUCTION

Most family mediation involves child access and/or financial issues. This standard distinction, however, can be a simplification. They can overlap, that is, financial considerations might have an impact on child access and vice versa. Moreover, as we will see in Chapter 7, a range of disputes fit under the category of "family mediation" and while these have much in common with the mediation of more commonly recognized family conflicts, they also have distinct issues to be resolved.

Nevertheless, it is often helpful for family mediation — like other forms of mediation — to be conceptualized as proceeding through a number of "stages." Before reading the following material, it should be noted that it assumes a general facilitative orientation as set forth in Chapter 2. As you review this material, consider how an evaluative and, especially, a transformative style might imply different stages and/or techniques. We will have an opportunity to compare and contrast at the conclusion of this Chapter.

B. THE "STAGES" OF FAMILY MEDIATION

Many mediation practitioners and scholars suggest that there are "stages" or "segments" of mediation. There is no consensus on precisely what these "stages" are or should be and what they should be called. Whatever "stages" one identifies, these should never be viewed in a linear, overly rigid fashion. Flexibility in form and process is often the hallmark of effective mediation. Nevertheless, a roadmap of stages often helps keep the mediator and parties oriented. In this sense, the idea of "stages" is as much an aid to mediators as it is descriptive of how mediation actually proceeds.

One plausible approach contains six stages:

- Setting the stage
- Gathering information
- Identifying Issues and Interests
- Generating options
- Negotiation
- Formalizing decisions

We will briefly consider each of these in turn. In so doing, we will consider the context in which the mediation takes place, particularly whether the mediation is court-referred (or ordered) or private.

1. Setting The Stage

a. Preliminaries

It is crucial that certain preliminaries be attended to in family mediation, whether they be formal paperwork, background about what mediation is, and, if appropriate, agreements about fees.

There is a vast range of how mediators approach these and other matters. Approaches are a function of personal style, experience, and sometimes the time frame in which the mediation must take place. The mechanism through which the content is communicated varies considerably. Some private mediators send prospective mediation participants packages containing "setting the stage" information and then conduct a separately designated "orientation session" for parties to learn about mediation, ask the mediator questions about the process, and fill out paperwork relating to, for example, confidentiality, payment of fees, and detailed statements about financial matters. Depending on the mediator, this orientation may include an "Opening Introduction" (detailed below) by the mediator, or the mediator may defer the Introduction to the first actual mediation session.

Court-annexed programs rarely, if ever, have the luxury of separate orientation sessions with mediators, so the "setting the stage" activities must take place as part of the initial session. One option that, on occasion, courts employ is to show participants a brief video introducing mediation. These videos typically emphasize how mediation can benefit participants and children. That said, given the generally compressed time frame of court-annexed mediations, most, if not all, of this information is communicated through an initial "Opening Introduction" by the mediator.

Another factor to consider is how family mediation can take place prior to or after the commencement of formal proceedings. Some participants still might hope to reconcile. Given that most family mediators do not conceive of their role as couples' therapists or of mediation as a mechanism through which to preserve a relationship, some mediators ask parties early in the mediation process whether they have decided to divorce, thus clarifying the mediator's role and what mediation is and is not. Of course, on occasion parties might decide to reconcile. This might or might not be the result of how mediation offers a rare or unique opportunity for parties to share perspectives. If this is the case, it is not unheard of for parties to agree to come to mediation should future conflicts arise or if reconciliation does not succeed.

b.   Seating Arrangements and Space

An important aspect of how challenging mediation can be is the importance of thinking through where the mediator and participants sit. This is, of course, a non-issue in courts, with bench, witness stand, and jury box not subject to discussion. In mediation, however, these are decisions to be made and these decisions can have meaningful consequences. Should participants sit across from each other or next to each other? Should one participant have to physically turn to address another participant as would be the case if they were side by side? Where should the mediator be? What sort of table, if any, should be included in the arrangement?

Needless to say, sometimes options are limited as is usually the case when mediations take place in a designated space such as "mediation rooms" in courts. Even so, there are usually options to consider. As always, skilled mediators often revisit decisions based upon particular mediations. Is this a "high conflict" divorce? Are there "third parties" such as relatives or friends who will be attending?

There are also other basic issues to be attended to. It is often crucial to have a whiteboard or some means to write in a way that is visible to all parties. This is especially crucial in family mediation. Having a calendar with which to craft child custody schedules or written means to work through financial arrangements is immensely helpful.

In addition, mediators should think through how they plan to conduct a private caucus. This would usually entail having some means for the participant who is not in caucus to wait in a comfortable setting in which what is being said in private caucus is not audible.

c.   The "Opening Introduction"

It is close to a universal that mediators deliver some sort of Opening Introduction when both parties are first present at the mediation. What mediators actually say varies based on numerous variables: mediator style, mediator personality, time available, whether attorneys are present or not. It is also important to reflect on what tone to employ and atmosphere to cultivate at this initial stage of the mediation. The Opening Introduction still tends to be far more stable than other aspects of family mediation, largely because it is often the only time when the focus is primarily on the mediator.

As with much else in mediation, your initial challenge is to consider goals. What are the goals of an Opening Introduction? Many mediators would view one goal as educating participants about relatively specific matters. It is often, for example, an opportunity to educate participants about what mediation is, share substantive information about confidentiality, and, if appropriate, talk about legal procedures that will ensue should an agreement is reached.

To view an Opening Introduction solely in these terms, however, misses equally important opportunities that are less information-driven. Mediators might wish to "model" in intonation and body language a calmness and spirit of collaboration that participants might emulate or absorb. Many mediators start on a note of optimism, perhaps congratulating parties on their willingness to enter into mediation. Another possibility is to offer parties an opportunity to make decisions about the mediation process such as, for example, eliciting a verbal agreement to mediate and suggesting to participants that they might call for breaks as they wish. This communicates that mediation is the participants' process and, equally important, that a mediator is not an authority figure like a judge. It is worth noting how these sometimes indirect actions are far more valuable than simply saying "this is your process" or that "I am not a judge." Participants are *experiencing* these principles rather that merely hearing about them.

The following list incorporates these and other ideas into a menu of options to consider as you develop your own Opening Introduction:

- Communicate optimism about the potential for a productive and successful mediation.
- Support, compliment and confirm participants' decision to proceed with mediation.
- Make participants comfortable by discussing the location of rest rooms, the possibility of taking a break if needed, the availability of refreshments, and so forth.
- Inquire of participants about how they wish to be addressed.
- Present and complete forms, such as agreements to mediate and agreements regarding confidentiality. If the mediation is court-annexed, certain forms are likely required by the court.
- Introduction of the mediator, including the mediator's relevant experience.
- General description of the goals and process of mediation, including how mediation differs from litigation, the differences between the role of mediator and judge, and the voluntary nature of whether to reach a mediated agreement.
- A discussion of private caucuses, including how the mediator might consider it useful to meet with each participant separately and how confidentiality will be handled. This process should be "normalized," that is, it is a natural part of mediation and not some sign that the mediation is "going badly."
- A discussion of confidentiality — a particularly delicate matter that we will explore in greater detail in Chapter 10.

- "Ground rules," such as, for example, no interruptions or shouting.
- Discuss whether you plan on taking notes and, if appropriate, assuring participants that notes will be destroyed after the mediation.

NOTES AND QUESTIONS

1. Decisions about *what* to raise do not address the equal, perhaps greater challenge of *how* and *when* to raise them. Consider the following non-exclusive range of decisions to be made:

1. In terms of experience, what should you say if, as is always the case at the start of a mediator's career, you have limited experience?
2. How about paperwork? Assuming that you do not have the luxury (as is true in most court-annexed programs) of sending participants paperwork ahead of time, how do you present the paperwork? Do you present the paperwork prior to any other aspect of the Introduction to "get it out of the way" or do you wait to the end of the Introduction or somewhere in between? To what extent do you describe what the paperwork is?
3. When do you inquire about children assuming this is child access mediation? Is this something to do immediately to emphasize the "real" concern of the mediation or should you wait until parties are more comfortable with you and the process?

It is worth noting that, as with much in mediation, these answers often have no definitive "yes" or "no" answers. Rather the most important lesson to be learned at this point is that these questions are worth asking and resolving through a systematic decision-making process. Though they may seem minor, such decisions can be of great consequence. The charged nature of many family mediations means that seemingly small details can have an important impact on the dynamic of mediation communcations. As always, decisions can be changed as you gain experience or as a particular mediation unfolds.

2. Consider the issue of how and if to raise specifics about children who will be part of the mediation conversation. Some mediators ask for pictures and then place them in the middle of the mediation table. Some may do so verbally, emphasizing to the parties that the wellbeing of children is the core issue in the mediation. Some do nothing and wait for the parties to express thoughts about children as the mediation unfolds. Without knowing any details about a particular mediation, do you see pros and cons to these choices? What are they?

2. Gathering Information

a. Beginnings

Unless a mediator has a specific reason to do otherwise, the "gathering information" stage virtually always begins with a joint session that, as its name implies, includes the presence of all participants. One exception might be a "high conflict" mediation or a mediation involving allegations of domestic violence — the latter being a particularly important and controversial issue that we will cover in Chapter 9. Such situations, however, are not the norm. Rather, most family mediators typically begin information gathering with a request that each participant present without interruption his or her perspective on issues without predefining what those issues might be.

b.   What Is "Information"?

The term "gathering information" is perhaps misleading. "Information" in litigation is usually associated with "facts" yet it is important at this early stage for mediators to avoid replicating patterns of litigation. It is all too easy for a mediator — as participants often do — to view this exchange as akin to an "Opening Statement" at trial. To counter this tendency, mediators may, for example, ask for parties' "perspective" or "description of the situation." In light of research that shows that parties who speak second often "respond" to the first participant point by point and thereby cede power to the first speaker for setting at least the initial agenda for the mediation,[1] some mediators will explicitly tell both participants that they need not engage in such a "response" and explicitly note that this exchange is about sharing information and perspectives. The litigation norm looms large at all points in mediation — indeed, sometimes it never disappears — so mediators should be alert at all points about opportunities to educate the parties explicitly or implicitly about the distinctive norms of mediation.

In any event, unlike litigation, mediators often facilitate parties sharing as much background as possible in order to more effectively build the foundation for identifying issues and generating options. Information in this sense might include emotions — things that might be not "relevant" in a legal sense.

c.   Who Goes First?

An initial question that often arises prior to this initial exchange is the decision as to who should go first. There are different schools of thought on this point. If there is some neutral basis upon which to make this decision — for example, the party who filed for divorce if there is pending litigation or the party who requested mediation — the mediator may ask this party to speak first, explaining the neutral reason why. Other mediators employ by design entirely arbitrary criteria — "I start with folks on my right" — which has the virtue of enhancing the message of neutrality. Some mediators may ask the parties who should speak first, which signals to the parties that this is *their* process and might establish a pattern of collaboration at this early stage of mediation. However handled, there tends to rarely be disputes on this issue.

After this initial exchange, mediators often prompt parties to share more information with open questions. Given that the hallmark of effective mediation is often flexibility and openness as to what is useful "information," it is crucial, as much as possible, to allow the parties to share what information *they* see as significant, even if, to the mediator, it may appear irrelevant or even counterproductive. Put another way, there is a pervasive risk for mediators — especially those trained as lawyers — to jump over the "information gathering" stage and start "issue spotting" and "problem solving" immediately and to ask questions in light of these ideas. This is not to say that mediators should not engage in at least considering these later stages; rather, mediators should allow the participants "space" to themselves shape the contours of how to conceptualize

---

[1] Sara Cobb & Janet Rifkin, *Practice & Paradox: Deconstructing Neutrality in Mediation*, 1991 LAW & SOC. INQUIRY 35, 54–59.

their conflict before mediators, if necessary, help parties narrow the focus to specific issues.

In addition, mediators need not always intervene at this or other stages of mediation. Indeed, it is sometimes counterproductive to do so. The stereotype of high conflict divorce is common, but "amicable divorces" are common as well. Effective family mediators should cultivate no particular expectations as to which category (or middle category) a particular mediation might fall into. If parties are collaborating in sharing information productively, the mediator should hold back except to listen and concentrate on what is being said, with an eye to facilitating, if necessary, the later stages of mediation. The mediator *facilitates*, but "facilitation" might simply be bringing participants together in a collaborative atmosphere with the mediator saying virtually nothing. Sitting and saying nothing is a legitimate and sometimes advisable mediation technique.

Most family mediation, however, usually entails gathering basic information for the benefit of the mediator and sometimes the parties themselves. The mediator typically should know and, if necessary, seek to elicit information about the following:[2]

- Children. Of course, in custody mediation, it is understood that children are involved, but it is important to know about any children even in mediations where custody is not contested. Apart from the obvious questions regarding names and ages, the mediator might wish to explore where each party believes the children should live, go to school, and the nature of the relationship each hopes to maintain with the children. This does not mean that there is necessarily conflict about any or all of these issues, but knowing how parties perceive such issues is often crucial for a mediator to understand the parties' situation and thereby facilitate solutions. Of course children are not involved in all family mediations.
- Finances. Even if the issue to be mediated is solely custody, it is rare that issues about finances are not at least significant background information. The degree to which it is necessary to delve into details, of course, is contingent on the nature of the mediation and the resources of the parties, but when resources are at issue detailed information about assets, liabilities, and cash flow are virtually always necessary. Even when parties have no or minimal resources, issues about child support may arise. These calculations are contingent upon the law of a particular jurisdiction and may even not be within a parties' discretion, although even then mediators may be involved in issues about or surrounding the award.
- The parties' future plans. How do the parties see themselves in the future? This may entail information about professional or personal goals or redressing personal problems that might have inhibited their ability to act as a parent or to work, such as alcoholism or substance abuse.

In regard to all of these subject matter areas, it is important to note that some parties might have access to more information and, indeed, to more "power" based upon, among other things, personality and the history of a relationship. We examine these issues in Chapter 8.

---

[2] Each of the following categories of information is addressed in more detail in Chapter 4 ("Mediating Child Access Cases") and Chapter 5 ("Mediating Financial Issues").

3.   Identifying Issues and Interests

At some point, "gathering information" will usually transition into identifying specific issues to be addressed and the parties' interests underlying those issues. Again, this process is not linear; indeed, in some sense, "gathering information" never stops as the parties and mediator explore issues, interests, and options for agreement.

a.   What Is an Issue in Family Mediation?

A GUIDE TO DIVORCE MEDIATION 39–42 (1993)[3]
By Gary Friedman

. . . With the information gathered, we are now ready to address the conflict. But what is the conflict? It's critical at this point to determine precisely what the parties disagree about. It is my practice to work with the spouses to identify areas of agreement and disagreement. This may sound simple, and sometimes it is, but more often this step is complex and full of surprises.

Consider Art and Mary, who both assumed at the outset that their case would be easy to resolve. "Well, maybe we should start with the house," began Art, "and who will live-" That was as far as he got. "The house is easy," Mary interjected. "There can be no disagreement there. I need it. The kids are going to be with me and they need it. A court would award it to me. Art surely agrees. We can go on to the next issue." At this point I came in: "It takes two to agree. It only takes one to disagree. Unless both of you feel we have an agreement, I assume that for now that this is an area of disagreement." "You're damn right," Art told me, to Mary's obvious surprise, and now the abstractions about two-party agreements started to take on a starker reality.

While facilitative family mediation seeks to empower parties to determine issues to be addressed, family mediators still routinely raise issues parties might not have considered. To continue with the custody example, while Christopher's location during holidays might be an issue, so may the parenting arrangement during summers and other school holidays — issues that might not have occurred to parties. If Christopher's parents do not raise this issue, a mediator should ordinarily do so. This minimizes the possibility that the parties will reach an agreement in mediation that unravels once summer arrives.

In characterizing issues, mediators often seek to adopt more "neutral" language that retains the substance of the issue without alienating the other party. For example, one party might note angrily that "that SOB will never get Christopher for Christmas" might be reframed as "determining where Christopher will spend holidays."

b.   Organizing Issues

As noted above, in family mediation, there are often obvious issues:

- Children
- Finances

---

[3] Copyright © 1993. Reprinted with permission.

In some sense, these are "issues" and might be useful as a way to divide the substance of the mediation. Under each broad category, however, it is almost certain that there are subissues to be addressed. Consider children:

- Children
    - Choices of school.
    - Transportation to father and mother's house.
    - Where to spend the holidays

Perhaps all or some of these are issues to be resolved. To dig down deeper, perhaps issues might break down as follows:

- Children
    - Where to spend the holidays
        - Birthdays
        - Major family holidays (Christmas and Thanksgiving)

These can be, plausibly, subdivided. It is often the mediator who can be helpful in identifying and conceptualizing issues. It is usually crucial, however, for the mediator to "check in" with participants to ensure that the structure and characterization of an issue is acceptable to both parties.

c.   Framing Issues

As we have noted throughout this Chapter, word choice is key at many levels of mediation. We will shortly address questions surrounding categorizing and characterizing options. At the framing issue stage, consider the following strategies for how mediators should frame issues:

GUIDELINES FOR FRAMING ISSUES IN MEDIATION[4]
Mediation Matters Manual (2005)
By Carl Schneider

1.   **Get a Buy-In**
2.   **No Blaming**
3.   **Neutrally**
4.   **Not the Past**
5.   **Mediation is not about Finding "the Truth"**
6.   **Towards the Future**
7.   **Normalize**
8.   **Involve the Needs and Interests of Both Parties**
9.   **Capable of Being Resolved in Mediation**
10.   **Not Character**
11.   **Behavior [Moving Forward]**
12.   **No Advice/Solutions**
13.   **Don't be Invested in Outcomes**
14.   **Go to Options**

---

[4] Copyright ©2005. Reprinted with permission.

QUESTION

Consider the situation of Art and Mary excerpted above. How could a mediator formulate questions employing each of these guidelines? Do you think any would be particularly appropriate or less appropriate? Why?

d.   Interests versus Positions

One of the foundational tenets of mediation is that mediators help parties identify "interests" rather than "positions."[5] A classic description of the difference between "positions" and "interests" is a couple who is planning a vacation. The husband wants to go to a beach; this is his "position." The wife wants to go to the mountains; this is her "position." If one considers, however, *why* the husband wants to go to a beach, it is because he enjoys swimming and sunbathing. These are his "interests." If one considers *why* the wife wants to go to the mountains, it is because she enjoys hiking. This is her interest. While "beach" and "mountains" seem incompatible "positions" with no room for compromise, understanding what motivates these "positions" — the parties' interests — helps to generate possible compromises, such as a trip to a mountain lake.

Parties to family mediation, drawing from litigation norms, often take "positions" akin to the beach/mountains. Here a few examples:

- "I want sole custody."
- "I need to get the house."
- "We have to sell the house."
- "There's no way your mother will have anything to do with Jane."

How may a mediator seek to facilitate parties' recognition and articulation of interests in the often emotionally charged environment of family conflict? One technique is to ask "why" or "what for" questions, which tend to elicit interests. Another technique is more subtle. Sometimes parties do not express a pure "position," but a "position" embedded with some expression of an underlying interest. A parent might, for example, state that he wants "joint custody," which is a "position" that might be incompatible with the other parent's position that she have "sole custody." Nevertheless, a position that a parent wants joint custody may embody a desire to maintain a close and continuing relationship with a child. In such cases, a mediator listening to a party closely can glean underlying interests, state them, and thereby enable each party to better understand what the other party wants. It is usually advisable in such instances for the mediator to confirm with a party that a mediator's statements about interests are accurate — the "check-in" alluded to earlier.

4.   Generating Options

a.   The Option Generating Process

Once some progress has been made in identifying issues and underlying interests, the parties and mediator can collaborate in generating options.

---

[5] The most famous articulation of this distinction is in ROGER FISHER, BRUCE M. PATTON & HAROLD L. URY, GETTING TO YES: NEGOTIATING AGREEMENT WITHOUT GIVING IN (1992).

A basic premise of literature on problem solving is that it is most productive to generate as many potential solutions to problems as possible before eliminating them as not feasible or inappropriate. While this is easy to state, it is exceptionally and understandably difficult in practice, especially in family mediation which so often embodies intensely felt views of what is "right" or "wrong." Thus, it is the norm and not the exception for parties to immediately reject many potential options suggested by another participant. On occasion, however, a new idea might arise that the other party — or even the party stating the new idea — might not have thought of before.

It is usually advisable for the mediator to defer supplying options prior to insuring that the parties suggest their ideas. This can take a prodigious amount of self-control on the part of the mediator: the mediator will defer expressing what seems to be a transparently obvious solution. Nevertheless, what is transparent to the mediator might be opaque or wrong to the parties, and, conversely, the parties themselves are experts on their own situations and are likely to offer potentially creative, constructive, ideas that would never occur to the mediator. Moreover, the notion of parties as controlling the subject of mediation and the mediator as facilitator suggests that premature option generation by the mediator herself might be counterproductive.

Of course, if the problem-solving phase is not productive or no other options are forthcoming from the parties, it might be advisable for the mediator to suggest a possibility to the parties — a "trial balloon." This might be accepted with enthusiasm or rejected immediately or met with a reaction that is something in between. As always, it should be the parties who are the ultimate decision-makers in how they choose to accept or reject or reformulate options.

b.   Framing Options

Effective mediation entails sensitivity to words. In family mediation, options can be framed in multiple ways suggested by the parties or by the mediator. Note that in facilitative mediation, mediators may choose, when appropriate, to subtly shift how an option is articulated either in joint session or private caucus, again with the ever-present check-in advisable.

Consider the following example. The distribution of an art collection is at issue. While the following excerpt addresses negotiation, not mediation, it starkly demonstrates the fluidity of potential options and how these options may be framed. As you read this discussion, consider how a mediator may facilitate the different potential dispositions of the collection and determining whether different dispositions might accord with the parties "interests" relating to the collection.

AN INTRODUCTION TO THE PLANNING AND CONDUCT OF NEGOTIATIONS (1989)[6]
By Anthony G. Amsterdam

. . . If personal property is being divided upon the divorce of a wife (a lawyer) and a husband (an architect), the art collection can be handled by giving a portion of it to each party, or by giving the entire collection to one party and "balancing" it by giving some property of equal value to the other. The party urging the latter

---

[6] Copyright © 1989. Reprinted with permission.

disposition can argue that it is appropriate (or "natural") to "keep the collection together" for aesthetic reasons, or for economic reasons. Notice that the very description of the subject matter as an "art collection," rather than as "the pieces of artwork in the house" works subtly in favor of keeping it together. If the collection is divided, it may nevertheless be "natural" to keep some subparts of it together. Again, differing divisions can be urged. It can be said to be "natural" to keep the Daumier prints together (for the same aesthetic or economic reasons, or others), or "natural" to keep all of the prints from the living room (which include some but not all of the Daumiers) together. The latter disposition will be more "natural" if the furniture has been divided earlier in the negotiation, on a room-by room basis. If the Daumiers are kept together, it may be "natural" to give them to the wife because they deal with legal subjects, or "natural" to give them to the husband because he was the one who originally selected them. Or it may be "natural" to sell the art collection and split the proceeds equally. The party who urges this course will point out that the art collection was "held for investment" — indeed, that the couple has previously claimed tax deductions for framing which were allowable only because the art collection was "held for investment."

NOTES AND QUESTIONS

1.   Consider the impact of the different formulations described by Professor Amsterdam. To what extent are they merely descriptive? To what extent do they characterize what the art collection *is*?

2.   Art collections, of course, are not the only options that might be subject to the verbal reformulations detailed in the above excerpt. Consider how to recharacterize the following:

- A house purchased by a divorcing couple with children in which the mother currently resides with the couple's children.
- A girlfriend who now resides with the husband of a divorcing couple.
- A 10-year-old child from the prior marriage of the wife of a divorcing couple who has resided with that couple.

5.   Negotiation

This stage in mediation involves how to choose options generated as a result of working through the prior stages.

One question is the order in which to tackle issues. Some mediators may suggest beginning with something "easy" or likely to generate agreement as a means to establish positive momentum. Alternatively, some mediators may tackle a difficult problem first, in the hopes that a successful resolution will generate momentum that will carry everything else along to a positive conclusion.

Another concern is, as with everything else in mediation, that mediators should be mindful of not appearing partial to one party or another. One issue may be of greater importance to one party, or may involve the giving up of something that a party currently has. In such situations, mediators should try to "alternate" issues to ensure that parties feel that the mediation is proceeding fairly.

As always, mediators should seek to elicit parties' "buy-in" as to the order or consideration of a particular issue. Mediators should also always keep in mind the option of a private caucus. It is often at this negotiation stage that individual meetings with parties can generate positive movement towards agreement.

6.   Formalizing Agreements

How agreements reached in family mediation are formalized depends on the posture of the matter and the jurisdiction in which the mediation takes place. In mediation generally, it is often typical for a mediator to draft a "Memorandum of Understanding" to memorialize the parties' agreement and to guide the parties' future conduct. This "Memorandum" may then serve as a contract, the breach of which may entitle the aggrieved party to seek damages in a lawsuit. While such a document may be the result in some forms of family mediation, more typically the ultimate goal of the mediation — the granting or modification of a divorce decree, for example — may only be ordered by a court, even if the mediation is "private" and not court-annexed. A court also may be required by law to undertake an independent review of custody arrangements agreed to in mediation or ensure that an agreement does not violate some other law relating to, for example, child support. It is thus often the case that an agreement reached in family mediation must be put into a form appropriate for judicial review.

While a mediator who is an attorney may draft such a document, it is crucial, as always, to keep in mind that the mediator is not acting as a lawyer even if the mediator is a lawyer. The mediator should view her role more as scrivener, albeit one whose expertise in law might help ensure that the parties' agreement conforms to the format courts look for or expect. We will defer for now the difficult ethical issues that may arise when a mediator who is a lawyer recognizes that an agreement will differ from the result likely be obtained in court.

A final point about the Formalizing Agreements stage is to recall the important idea that the whole conception of "stages" imposes a false linearity on the mediation process. Conflicts can arise at any point and one stage might go "backwards" or meld into one another. It is rare indeed for a mediation to proceed logically in line with discrete stages. To the dismay of many a new mediator, this can happen even after participants seem to have reached an agreement as to all matters and the mediation has reached the point of writing down the agreement. It is important to realize that it would be optimistic in the extreme to assume that mediation, while a powerful tool, can permanently shift longstanding personal dynamics that might have emerged over many years. If conflict should flare at the formalizing agreement stage, this is not necessarily a "failure" or "setback." Rather, it might suggest more work needs to be done by the participants and mediator, and this work might well enhance the chances of a durable and comprehensive arrangement and understanding. Viewed in this way, it can demonstrate the power and effectiveness of mediation.

C.   JOINT SESSIONS AND PRIVATE CAUCUSES

There are two primary procedural mechanisms family mediators use in mediation: the "joint session" and the "private caucus."

1.   The Joint Session

Given the collaborative spirit of mediation, it is no surprise that most mediators prefer "joint sessions" at which both parties are present, as well as attorneys if the parties have them and the attorneys have chosen to attend. Given that all participants are present, it is crucial that the mediator recognize that what is said or done has multiple audiences. To take a simple example, if a mediator asks one spouse a question, the other spouse hears both the question and the response. Mediators should be aware of reactions on the part of non-speaking party. These reactions can be non-verbal, such as through facial expressions or body language.

2.   The Private Caucus

As its name implies, a "private caucus" involves a mediator meeting separately with a party and the party's attorney if there is one. As with much else regarding mediation, mediators vary widely in how often or even whether they use private caucuses. Among the situations where a private caucus might be warranted are:

- When parties are too emotional or volatile to be productive in a joint session. Sometimes this situation is referred to in shorthand as "high conflict mediations," although, of course, it is difficult to make that determination without details of a given matter.
- When the mediator believes that a party may share information confidentially with the mediator that is too intimate or sensitive to share with the other party.
- To help one party consider or make a proposal or suggest ways of framing issues or proposals in light of the other party's perspective.
- When impasse looms or the mediation seems "stuck."

There are some basic rules to follow in conducting private caucuses:

- Never conduct a private caucus with only one party without then conducting a private caucus with the other party.
- If you are co-mediating, both co-mediators should meet with each party at the same time.
- Ensure that all parties understand confidentiality "ground rules" prior to the private caucus and that you, as mediator, strictly adhere to these ground rules. Thus, some mediators choose to go into a private caucus with the understanding that unless a party requests otherwise, all information shared in the private caucus may be shared with the other party either in the private caucus or in a joint session. Alternatively, some mediators choose to go into private caucus with the understanding that everything said in the private caucus will be kept confidential unless a party explicitly authorizes the mediator to make a disclosure.
- Ensure that the parties understand that they can request a private caucus if they wish.

D. PROCESS AND STYLES IN EVALUATIVE AND TRANSFORMATIVE FAMILY MEDIATION

As noted at the beginning of this Chapter, this discussion has assumed a mediator "style" that is generally facilitative. As noted in Chapter 2, however, "evaluative" and "transformative" mediators might well take issue with some of the approaches this Chapter has presented. As always, it is important to note that many, if not most, practicing mediators would state or admit that they employ a range of styles as appropriate in a given mediation. Stylistic "purity" is perhaps not nearly as pervasive as the literature might suggest.

Consider the following set of elements that a transformative mediator might employ.

TRANSFORMATIVE MEDIATION: CHANGING THE QUALITY OF FAMILY CONFLICT INTERACTION[7]
From DIVORCE AND FAMILY MEDIATION 54, 56 (Jay Folberg, Ann L. Milne & Peter Salem, Eds.) (2004)
By Robert A. Baruch Bush & Sally Ganong Pope

. . . Learning the Vocabulary of Empowerment and Recognition

In order to notice the opportunities for supporting empowerment and recognition, the mediator pays close attention to the parties' conversational cues in the immediate interactions between them-what they say and do. . . . [T]he mediator must know what he is listening and looking for. In effect, the mediator is learning to listen to the exchanges between the parties in a whole new way, on a new level, and in a new language-the language of conflict transformation . . . For example, asking "What should I do?" shows that the party sees the mediator as the decision maker and feels dependent on his guidance. "I'm really confused" expresses lack of clarity and probably uncertainty. "I've had enough of this!" expresses strong emotions and feelings and shows a sense of helplessness or frustration. "What do you expect from someone like that?" indicates a negative view of the other party and, hence, self absorption. "It's not like me" and "You don't understand what it's been like for me" are requests for understanding that suggest the experience of nonrecognition.

A mediator listening with a transformative ear does not ignore or dismiss statements of this nature as "resisting" or merely "venting." Such statements are viewed as important markers of opportunities for shifts in the conflict interaction . . .

SUPPORTIVE RESPONSES

. . . *Reflection* is another primary supportive response. In reflecting a party's statement, the mediator simply says what she hears the party saying, using words close to the party's own language, even (or especially) when the language is strong, loud, negative, or strongly expressive. The mediator does not soften the party's language or remove its "sting." . . .

---

[7] Copyright ©2004. Reprinted with permission.

Here is a one example of reflection in practice, in a portion of a divorce mediation that concerned division of assets:

> The husband, John, says,"Our house in the country is mine. I bought it before we got married. After we got married and spent more time there. I completely renovated it myself. I gutted the inside to open it up, put in windows, and added a new room. Oh, and a new roof and cedar shingles on the outside walls. It's worth a lot more now, and there is no way she is going to share in the value!"

> The mediator's reflection could be: "So, you feel strongly that the country house is entirely yours and that Lois should not share in its value at all. You bought the house before you married, and after your marriage you spent more time there, and you did extensive renovations. You gutted the inside, put in new windows, added a new room, a new roof, and shingles. You are saying that it's worth a lot more now, and you put a lot of personal labor into making the value increase, and you see the house as yours." . . .

AVOIDING DIRECTIVE RESPONSES

Using the essential skills of reflection, summary, and checking in, the mediator "follows" or "accompanies" the parties; he does not have a set agenda of steps to accomplish in a divorce mediation. The parties begin where they choose to begin, and in the course of the discussion, they talk about anything of importance to them. The mediator does not rule out any subject as inappropriate or unhelpful, nor does the mediator tell the parties how to have their conversation or when to continue or end it . . .

While intensely engaged in listening, observing, and enacting supportive responses, the mediator constantly maintains an awareness of-and represses-his directive impulses. One of the parties may say, "I just don't know what to do. I'm afraid to be on my own." An almost automatic response would be to explain that most people feel that way when going through a divorce and then to move on with the "real business" of the mediation. To do so, however, minimizes the feeling of the confused party by making the confusion normal, usual, and therefore ripe for ignoring-perhaps with a referral to a popular book on divorce. It is also a directive response in that the mediator is attempting to control the content of the discussion by characterizing the feeling and then changing the topic. In contrast, a supportive response that utilizes the opportunity for empowerment being presented would be to simply reflect the statement and then allow time for the party to respond as he or she chooses. A party might choose to move on to other business, or comment that "It's just normal, I guess," or request more time to deal with the shock, or elaborate on how he feels, how the other party is behaving, or what he wants to do about it. Any of these possible responses would be empowering for the party who is feeling weak and confused at the moment.

Another example: Even if many women going through divorce fear they will end up as "bag ladies on the street," it does not help a particular woman dealing with these circumstances to be told that "Everyone feels that way." Rather than offering empathy and assurance, it is dismissive of a very real fear. Instead, the transformative mediator simply reflects the fear, using words close to those used by the party. The mediator might say, "So you are scared and worried about becoming destitute and, to use your words, 'winding up on the street.' " That kind of reflective statement allows the woman to know the subject is, in essence, now on the table for discussion if she chooses to pursue it and that the others in the room are now aware of how she feels and the depth of that feeling. She can then choose where to take the discussion at that moment . . .

NOTES AND QUESTIONS

1.   The above excerpt is only a sampling of a much more comprehensive set of strategies transformative mediators would employ. Consider which are consistent with techniques in facilitative mediation.

2.   Evaluative mediation is often considered the most "directive" style of mediation, with facilitative and transformative moving, respectively, towards the less directive. Do you agree?

3.   Some transformative mediators argue that there is no such thing as deploying a select group of transformative strategies and that, indeed, characterizing individual strategies as "transformative" is wrong since only a full deployment of the norms of transformative mediation is transformative mediation. Do you agree?

Chapter 4

CHILD ACCESS MEDIATION

A. INTRODUCTION

Child custody and visitation have traditionally been viewed as especially appropriate for mediation. As discussed in Chapter 1, almost all states have enacted statutes or court rules that encourage or mandate participation in court-sponsored mediation for child access disputes between parents or between a parent and a third party. Increasingly, courts are also experimenting with some form of alternative dispute resolution in child access cases in which the state is a party.

The potential virtues of mediation and the problems with the adversary system seem to make mediation particularly appropriate in the child access context. The adversary system, with its emphasis on the past and parental fitness, may encourage parents to focus on weaknesses of the other parent and thus escalate conflict and destroy relationships between individuals who will have to co-parent after the dispute is resolved. Crowded court dockets mean delayed decisions which are particularly problematic for children who need certainty and predictability to reduce the harm from parental break-up. Applying the legal standard governing most child access disputes, the "best interests of the child," calls for an understanding of the particular child(ren) involved in the dispute and expertise about child development that are not ordinarily part of judges' range of talents or knowledge. Finally, the decision in a standard custody case relies on terms and concepts "custody" and "visitation" that do not permit nuanced and detailed plans for children, often resulting in post-judgment proceedings in court.

Mediation, on the other hand, is said to look to the future rather than the past and encourage parents to rethink their roles as parents for the common goal of helping their children. Mediation generally leads to quicker resolution of child access disputes in a setting that permits more privacy than litigation to discuss intimate details of family life. Mediation's flexibility also permits the involvement of more interested parties and informal consultation with experts. Mediation permits detailed planning for children resulting in agreements that often contemplate greater involvement of both parents than existed while they were together. To the extent the agreements reflect genuine agreement and realistic expectations, mediated agreements may require less judicial intervention for clarification or enforcement than court-imposed solutions. Finally, mediation may be a particularly helpful option in cases where existing legal standards do not adequately address the interests of particular family members. These include non-biological "de facto" parents in families with same sex parents or cases where multiple potential parents exist as a result of artificial reproductive technology.

The readings will explore these and other assumptions about child access conflict resolution. They examine the use of parenting plans in mediation, the benefits and problems with joint custody and the use of mediation related approaches in child welfare cases where the state is a party.

B.   PARENT VS. PARENT IN CHILD ACCESS DISPUTES

1.   Parenting Plans

The following excerpt discusses the benefits of parenting plans and provides practical suggestions for working with parents to achieve such agreements in child access mediation. Examples of parenting plans, from form plans used in court ordered mediation to more extended plans developed in multiple session private mediations, can be found in Appendix B.

THE PLAN TO SEPARATELY PARENT CHILDREN AFTER DIVORCE[1]

From DIVORCE AND FAMILY MEDIATION, 129–133 (Jay Folberg, Ann L. Milne & Peter Salem, Eds.) (2004)

By Marilyn S. McKnight & Stephen K. Erickson

As 9-year-old David leaves Mom's car at a neutral exchange site to enter Dad's waiting vehicle, he kisses his mother goodbye and says, "Mommy, if I were dead, maybe then you and Daddy wouldn't fight over me so much." David's parents are now on their second round of appeals to the Minnesota Supreme Court over the issue of custody. Beginning with the report of the custody investigator, the guardian ad litem's report, the testimony of the expert psychologists hired by both sides, and continuing with the countless motions, hearings, and endless rounds of appeals, it never seems to end for David. David's parents have each spent in excess of $150,000 on legal fees fighting over custody of him. They may soon realize that they have nothing left to fight over. They will certainly be awarded damaged goods once the hearings are over. David's parents are wealthy and have the means to carry on the custody battle as long as they can find attorneys who are willing to take their money. Even though many jurisdictions have passed legislation attempting to limit this type of continual litigation, all jurisdictions permit recourse

---

[1] Copyright ©2004. Reprinted with permission.

to the court upon a showing of child endangerment. This change usually allows an opening for yet more litigation, as each parent can allege that the other parent's conduct is endangering the child. As we know from the research and our own observations, each parent's conduct *is* definitely endangering the child. But now, David on his own may have figured out a way to truly end the battle that is so deeply affecting him.

THE CUSTODY CONTEST

There are many more Davids in this country than we, as a society, are willing to acknowledge and they all have something in common. Children such as David have parents who have sufficient funds to engage in legal battles, and they have a legal system willing to give parents the weapons with which to wage the battle. Most observers want to blame the parents, but in reality the genesis of David's problem is a system of adversarial conflict resolution that provides fuel for more conflict by forcing parents to compete with each other instead of encouraging parents to cooperate. The adversarial assumptions are deeply ingrained. They are subtle but powerfully damaging to families and children, because these assumptions create a contest mentality.

One of the more destructive impacts of this contest mentality is the relentless need to evaluate. This demand for evaluation is created by a faulty premise that says, in essence, "Well, if they can't live together as husband and wife, then we certainly can't expect them to raise their children together, and we'd best put one of them in charge." In order to determine who should be in charge, it becomes necessary to evaluate each parent's past behavior in light of a set of standards, called the "best interest tests" and then apply these standards to the past conduct of the parents. This focus has three major flaws that create unfairness and suffering:

1. It assumes that people cannot and will not change.
2. It assumes that circumstances are static and will never change, in that past conduct is evaluated in light of the past circumstances — which are always certain to change, once two homes have been established and the children begin to move between those homes.
3. It ignores the high cost of the contest. The transaction cost of evaluating past conduct and assigning it a score is always exponentially greater than the process of building a Parenting Plan in mediation.

Moreover, a custody evaluation approach diminishes the likelihood of future parental cooperation by virtue of the destructive impact of the contest itself . . .

Beginning with Kelly and Wallerstein's (1980) earliest research about the harmful effects of custody battles, all subsequent research has reached the same conclusion: that children's negative adjustment to their parents' divorce is directly related to the level of the parents' conflict. If we were really willing to accept the truth of this research, we would dismantle the custody trial apparatus that exists in this country and start teaching people how to cooperate. However, the courts cannot do this, and as a result, the adversarial process continues to encourage parents to fight by holding on to the notion that it is necessary to put one parent in charge and call the other less qualified.

CHANGING THE GAME

If we can remove divorcing parents' fear of losing their children, we will end the need to have custody battles. The most constructive way to accomplish this goal is by changing the game from a *contest* to a *process of future planning*. Parents fear losing when each parent is advised that it is necessary to compete with the other parent to win custody of the children. Parents do not fear losing their children when they are assured that no one is trying to minimize their importance by attempting to turn them into a second-class visitor. Removing the fear can be accomplished in the mediation room [.] The impetus for such an approach comes from research and simple observation of children's suffering in the course of custody battles.

Ricci (1997) has pointed out that children can easily adapt to moving between two loving homes; the struggle begins with the need to fight over which home is better. Her book, *Mom's House, Dad's House* (Ricci, 1997), has been read by millions. She observed an 8-year-old simply say, "I'm going to be at my dad's house this weekend," or "I'm going to be at my mom's house this weekend." He does not say to his friend on Friday afternoon that he is going to spend the weekend with his noncustodial, nonprimary, non psychological, nonresidential, secondary, nonmanaging, Disneyland, deadbeat, visitation parent.

Mediators who practice a facilitative rather than an evaluative method of intervention have seen the pain children experience at the hand of their parents' conflict. After 25 years of observing couples in our own daily mediation practice, we have come to the only conclusion possible: that most of the battle created in the minds of parents and their advocates is more a result of the statutory adversarial process we impose on divorcing couples and less a result of their own misfortunes and tribulations. As mediators, we have also learned that the battle is fueled by two other forces in addition to the evaluative force: (1) a focus on the past, and (2) the impact of words. Think of the associative differences between the word *custody* and the word *parenting*:

Impact of, and assumptions associated with, the word *Custody*	Impact of, and assumptions associated with, the word *parenting*
Ownership	Sharing
Control, power over other parent	Empowering each parent
Possession	Cooperation
Static situation; signifies a position won at trial and assumes the ruling solves all problems; does not address future interaction.	Evolving and changing relationship in light of future tasks; *to parent* is a verb and assumes an ongoing relationship and ongoing interaction between the parents
Requires evaluation of past conduct to determine who wins custody	Requires discussion about future changes needed and parenting ground rules, to be observed jointly
Used by proponents of an adversarial approach	Used by mediators in an attempt to create a cooperative approach
Serves the judicial system's need for simple outcomes dictated by evaluating the weight of the evidence as applied to the case.	Serves parents' needs to remain parents; does require more complex discussion and planning than simply determining who is better or worse

Impact of, and assumptions associated with, the word *Custody*	Impact of, and assumptions associated with, the word *parenting*
Creates losers who are branded non-custodial visitation parents.	Creates new status for parents, who are then viewed equally in the eyes of their children
Establishes a number of "prizes" or benefits that accompany the parent who is anointed as the custodial winner.	Disconnects the award of child support, possession of the house, and other normal spoils of custody, and requires fairness on all issues
Emphasizes rights of parents	Emphasizes obligations of parents
Past focused and evaluative	

2. The Evolution of Parenting Plans

The approach outlined in [the parenting plan used by the authors] follows the understandings first discovered by a small group of mediators in the early 1980s who noticed that it was much easier to reach resolution of the custody issues when the entire content of the parenting arrangements were first agreed upon prior to engaging in discussions about custody labels. This approach attempted to neutralize the framework of the adversarial system of divorce by eliminating the connection between winning custody as the key to so many other "prizes" that are attached to the custody label. Although at the time we did not think of it in terms of building a Parenting Plan, the approach essentially called for the mediator to refuse to mediate *custody* and to instead mediate schedules, housing, even how the clothes would be exchanged or handled.

When following such an approach, the mediator's responsibility is to provide a cooperative environment wherein the couple can begin to experience positive progress and improvement. The mediator moves beyond each parent's claim that he or she is entitled to be the primary custodial parent by asking each to flesh out the details of proposed schedules for exchanges and other important conditions and ground rules for future parenting. This approach moves parents, almost exclusively, into future planning arrangements, even though the parents may still be caught in the pain of the past and prone to ruminate about the other's past misconduct.

[M]any mediators do not practice the Parenting Plan approach but use a law-centered approach and make evaluative determinations about who should have custody-which, of course, then imposes the role of *visitor* upon the parent deemed less likely to prevail in a custody trial. The public may think this is mediation, but it mediates the wrong issue. It mediates the winning or losing of custody. Our focus is on mediating a Parenting Plan, not a custody dispute, and it calls for asking an entirely different question of the parents. Instead of asking who is a better or worse parent, the parents are asked if they wish to build a plan detailing the future parenting of the children that views the parents as significantly involved in their children's lives after divorce.

Sample language used in our practice may be helpful in understanding how a Parenting Plan is mediated. The plan itself is essentially a series of detailed agreements about each parent's conduct in the future. Most Parenting Plans include some statement about the processes and philosophies by which parenting decisions will be made, a schedule of time that each parent spends with the children, a mechanism for sharing the costs of raising the children, rules that address concerns specific to the particular couple, and a method of dispute resolution for use if the parents are unable to resolve future parenting conflicts on their own. In those jurisdictions that do not follow a Parenting Plan approach, the person awarded custody is generally presumed to be in charge of determining the scope and content of these ground rules, often without any input from the other parent, other than perhaps active or passive resistance to the wishes of the custodial parent . . .

NOTES AND QUESTIONS

1. Appendix B includes the Parenting Plan discussed in the McKnight and Erickson excerpt. The Appendix also includes a Parenting Plan used in a court sponsored mediation program in Baltimore, Maryland. What are the primary differences between the plans? Evaluate the pros and cons of each plan and consider which you would prefer to use in your mediation practice and why.

2. McKnight and Erickson encourage the use of parenting plans in mediation. Do such plans encourage any particular type of child access (custody) arrangement? One of the stated benefits of such plans is that their detail provides for a wide range of post-separation situations not contemplated in the usual separation agreement or courts imposed custody and visitation order and therefore result in fewer trips back to the court. Others claim that these plans actually encourage greater involvement by the courts. Which view do you find more persuasive?

3. As discussed in Chapter 2, the dominant model of mediation in this country is the neutral mediator. They facilitate communication and, in some cases, agreements but do not encourage or impose any particular child access arrangement. Is that view consistent with McKnight and Erickson's approach?

2. Joint Custody and Mediation

Enthusiasm for joint or shared parenting is a consistent theme in mediation literature. *See, e.g.,* Carol Bohmer & Marilyn Ray, *Effects of Different Dispute Resolution Methods on Women and Children After Divorce,* 28 Fam. L. Q. 223, 227, 233–234 (1994). Some commentators believe such a preference in child access arrangements may pose risks in certain families. The following excerpt critiquing one jurisdiction's adoption of a joint custody presumption illustrates some of the concerns about joint parenting agreements, and related concerns about mediator preference for these agreements.

THE DISTRICT OF COLUMBIA'S JOINT CUSTODY PRESUMPTION: MISPLACED BLAME AND SIMPLISTIC SOLUTIONS[2]
46 Cath. U. L. Rev. 767, 767–75, 780–801, 806–807, 814–824 (1997)
By Margaret Martin Barry

Joint custody made its statutory debut in 1979 with the passage of California's Family Law Act. Today, most states acknowledge joint custody as an option. Several jurisdictions, however, have significantly limited the applicability of joint custody, while only eight have made it presumptive. In 1996, the District of

---

[2] Copyright ©1997. Reprinted with permission.

Columbia joined the small minority when it enacted a presumption in favor of joint custody. In so doing, the District entered into a realm of domestic relations law that has been described as frightfully lacking in linguistic uniformity and consistency in outcome.

This Article discusses the District of Columbia's version of joint custody. . . . This Article concludes by observing that the District's new law is of particular concern given the demographics of the jurisdiction. As with welfare reform, rhetoric supporting this law places considerable blame for societal woes on the parent who is raising children single-handedly, and in poverty. The law must not be used as a wedge to further isolate welfare mothers, causing more division where unity of spirit and purpose need to be fostered. Yet, it has the potential to do this if parents are placed in artificial and unfamiliar unions that can undermine the efforts being made by single parents.

The serendipitous approach to custody reflected in the District's presumption does not account for the real harm done to relationships when marriages or other familial unions dissolve, or when they never formed. Because courts must meet their obligation to protect children, the new law cannot be interpreted as a license to abandon analysis of the many factors — impact of anger, lack of trust, fear, and/ or irrelevance due to lack of involvement — that indicate what may be in the child's best interest. The new law cannot be viewed as a shortcut to custody decision-making since it raises far more questions than it answers. . . .

I. Custody By What Rule?

From the beginning, courts have viewed their role with regard to child custody determinations as one of parens patriae — a duty to protect vulnerable citizens. Consistent with that role, the best interest of the child has been the driving standard, and, as such, statutory presumptions have generally been stated in those terms. This judicial function consistently has been muddled with parental interest in the companionship, care, custody, and/or management of their children. Thus, the law reflects an often unresolved conflict between the child's needs and those of the parents.

The roots of the authority in Anglo-American law to act on behalf of the safety and welfare of children dates back to the seventeenth century and the equitable jurisdiction of the English courts. Determining custody was simple: the father received sole custody except in cases where the father was found to have gone beyond accepted norms. The paternal preference was based on the English common law rule recognizing the father's right to his children's services (the "fruits of their labor") in return for his obligation to provide for their welfare. . . .

[T]he paternal preference was not firmly replaced by the "tender years" doctrine until the early twentieth century. This doctrine acknowledged that both parents had equal custodial rights, but presumed that mothers were the best custodians of children of "tender years." . . . The "tender years" doctrine has been largely discredited for its inconsistency with the concepts of gender equality and the role of the father in child rearing.

Another alternative that has been suggested is the primary caretaker presumption. This presumption is not inherently gender driven and, instead, focuses upon which parent has been most involved in the child rearing responsibilities. This approach is more consistent with the "best interest" paradigm since it is tied directly to parental involvement with the child, as opposed to generic assumptions about gender roles. . . .

Somewhat recently, yet another presumption with a shift in focus, mid-way between the father-mother poles, has invaded the child custody landscape. Over the past two decades, joint custody has been the solution a la mode. Joint custody ostensibly strives for gender equity in its allocation of parental rights and obligations. Unfortunately, in its preoccupation with parents this approach tends to invert the wisdom of Solomon by instructing the courts to divide the child in the name of settling the parents' conflicting claims. . . .

II. What Does A Rebuttable Presumption in Favor of Joint Custody Mean?

A. What Does Joint Custody Mean?

Joint custody can refer to joint legal custody, in which both parents share in the decision-making. How that decision-making is shared can vary: one parent may play a consultative role only, or one parent may make all of the major decisions while the physical custodian handles the day to day supervision, and so on. Joint custody can also refer to joint physical custody, in which the child spends time with each parent, either on a roughly even basis or in blocks of time that are, in effect, no greater than visitation under a sole custody arrangement. The D.C. Court of Appeals recently made the distinction that joint legal custody refers to long-range decisions, and physical custody refers to control over the child and decisions related to immediate control. Joint legal custody generally accompanies joint physical custody, but the converse is not always the case. In fact, most joint custody awards grant physical custody to one parent, but limit that parent's decision-making power by requiring collaboration with the other parent.

Many state statutes suggest that joint custody is monolithic; however, this ignores the subtle and not so subtle distinctions it encompasses. The silence in many statutes on the issues of the child's physical location and which parent has responsibility for the child reflects a desire to allow for greater flexibility in fashioning joint custody orders consistent with the best interests of the child. Yet, this very concern inculpates a joint custody presumption: if flexibility to the point of being completely amorphous is necessary to make the presumption palatable, why state the concept as firmly as the District of Columbia has done? . . .

. . . .

The new law provides, in both sections of the statute, a list of factors for the court to consider in making a joint or sole custody determination. These new factors generally offer useful guidelines for judicial assessment of custody petitions; however, they neither simplify the custody process nor suggest that joint custody is ideal. A discussion of the new factors as they relate to joint custody follows.

a. Shared Decision Making

The capacity to communicate and reach shared decisions is central to the success of any joint custody arrangement. Studies have shown that, without cooperation between the parents, joint custody arrangements are doomed to fail.

Even where there is a commitment to communicate and cooperate, a joint custody order can be risky. Changing demands on one or both parents due to employment, marriage or remarriage, or relocation can cause tensions that undermine and ultimately destroy the arrangement. While such eventualities would not necessarily preclude a joint custody award, they do underscore the difficulty of imposing interaction implicit in the marital relationship upon parties who are not in that relationship. It is even more difficult to contemplate such interaction for parents who have no previous familial relationship. Furthermore, to make a child the focus of the imposed interaction can be harmful to a child who feels responsible for any resulting discord or who has conflicting or insufficient guidance.

b. Willingness to Share Custody

The "willingness to share custody" factor could be interpreted to mean that where parents are unwilling to share custody, joint custody should not be granted. The phrase has more commonly been viewed as calling upon the courts to penalize the "unfriendly" parent. Parents who might otherwise raise good faith objections to the wisdom of a joint custody arrangement may remain silent if raising such objections could potentially result in loss of custody entirely. A "willingness to share custody" provision can be particularly treacherous for women, since women generally are held to higher parenting standards than men and tend to be blamed for breakdowns in custody and visitation arrangements. Furthermore, women usually are believed less than men and/or their concerns are more often trivialized. This is particularly true for poor, black women who are often considered suspect by nature and treated with disdain.

Generalizations that discount objections to shared custody are unwise. A custody award cannot be driven by a desire to punish the parent who believes that co-parenting is not a reasonable solution. That parent may have sound reasons for the objection, and, may prove to be the most involved, the most nurturing, and, therefore, the best candidate for custody . . .

d. Prior Involvement in the Lives of the Children

Assessing prior involvement in the lives of the children is consistent with the concept that the primary caretaker is usually the preferred custodian. With joint custody, the court must still be concerned with the non-primary caretaker parent's involvement in the child's life. If that involvement is minimal, the interest in joint custody is suspect. When one parent's involvement in child rearing has been minimal, the court needs to assess carefully the motivation and commitment to raising the child. Furthermore, if the court orders shared physical custody or visitation for a previously uninvolved or minimally involved parent, a course of adjustment for the child and the parent may need to be specified.

A corollary of the lack of involvement in child rearing is the situation in which one parent is not really committed to the arrangement. Often, this parent pursues joint custody and gets it, but then fails to assume responsibility. The parent raising the child does not have clear authority and can be subjected to the whim of the uncooperative parent. Currently, there is no precedent for sanctioning a failure to exercise visitation rights, nor is there precedent for enforcing a parent's failure to meet the custodial responsibilities under a joint custody arrangement. Consequently, the opportunity to abuse joint custody by using it as a means to avoid child support or to maintain control over a partner without acquiring any greater childrearing responsibilities is considerable.

e. Age of the Children

Many experts, as well as the D.C. Court of Appeals, have raised concern over the age of the children in the context of issuing joint custody orders. The concern focuses on the particular need for stability for very young children in meeting their developmental and emotional needs and the disruption that shared physical custody can cause. Some have argued, however, that younger children can adjust better to such disruptions in the long term than older children. Still, others have raised sufficient concern with regard to the impact of shared custody on children of all ages to give courts pause in fashioning arrangements that will require awkward or disruptive schedules.

f. Stability

Interaction with siblings and significant others, disruption of social and school life, and the geographic proximity of parents all speak directly to a child's stability. Joint physical custody is inherently problematic in this regard, and is second only to parental collaboration in the hierarchy of concerns that must be addressed. Studies have shown that a significant number of children suffer when they constantly are shuttled from one household to another, particularly when this involves leaving their neighborhood. No studies appear to analyze the impact such movement has on children in poor, inner-city neighborhoods. There is no basis, however, for expecting that the impact of such disruption would be any less difficult for these children.

Parents committed to joint physical custody can compensate for the disruptions it causes by working to coordinate safety, as well as access to friends, family, school activities and social events. This scenario is not realistic, however, when resources are extremely limited, when the parents live more than a few miles apart, when the parents have no premise for such collaboration, or when the children find the organizational pressures of living in two households so intrusive that they outweigh the benefit of the other parent's involvement.

g. Financial Consequences

The very premise of the Child Support Guidelines indicates that financial comparisons were not intended to result in custody being awarded to the more affluent parent, or to the parent whose earning potential may seem greater. It is more likely, particularly given the statutory context, that the "parent's ability to financially support a custody arrangement" refers to the financial hardship, if not impossibility, for most parents to provide adequately for children in two households. The number of children factor compounds this consideration since dual households reduce resources available to meet the child's needs. Diffusing the resources available for children is particularly troublesome in a jurisdiction like the District of Columbia where many households fall close to, or below, the poverty line. As discussed below, listing the impact on Aid to Families with Dependent Children and Medicaid as yet another factor for the court to consider is not helpful since it is unclear what the impact might be. It has been argued that orders making both parents equally responsible for childrearing would reduce the disparity between the mother's and the father's standard of living. Such an argument does not take into account the increased costs of providing for dual residences for the children or the impact of disabling choices implicit in shared parenting. Significantly, it does not take into account another side effect of joint custody: the hardship faced by the parent who shoulders the bulk of the financial responsibility by virtue of de facto sole physical custody, with little contribution from the parent who fails to meet the obligations ordered by the court. Although such a situation may be remedied by returning to court, anticipation of court costs, fees, time, child care, lost wages, the unavailability of legal help, the proof required and the hostilities such action would reignite may lead to the unintended consequence of one parent shouldering the burden with little or no contribution on any level from the other parent.

h. The Demands of Parental Employment

Complimentary time frames may drive how physical custody is divided and result in a schedule in which children have regular access to each parent. This might occur, for example, where one parent works days, and the other works nights. This exceptional scenario often is alluded to by proponents of joint custody who argue that the presumption of joint custody can be financially neutral or even beneficial since procuring childcare is obviated. In contrast, if one parent has a very demanding job which involves long hours or travel, sole physical custody should be granted to the more available parent, with flexible visitation for the more encumbered one. This arrangement may be viewed as shared physical custody, with no more than the amount of visitation provided in a sole custody order. The goal is to ensure supervision, caring, and attention to the children; one parent may, by virtue of professional demands, be less able than the other to do so.

i. Benefit to Parents

As the Maryland Court of Appeals pointed out in Taylor v. Taylor, the benefit to the parents is relevant not only because their feelings and interests are worth considering, but because the parents' improved self-image is likely to benefit the child. However, the very nature of a custody battle voices parents' interests. The consideration of this factor underscores the danger that a joint custody presumption poses when the focus shifts from the child's needs to those of the parents. An earlier version of the Act read "the benefit to the parents, not to be outweighed by the best interest of the child." Fortunately, since it would seem to have supported a definite conflict with the statute's emphasis on the primacy of the child's interests, the latter phrase was dropped.

Implicit in custody law is this tension between the fundamental liberty interest of natural parents in the raising of their children and the obligation of courts to limit that interest when the parents are not prepared to exercise it in unison, or where they endanger the children. This strong sense of right finds expression in joint custody presumptions that subject the assessment of the children's needs to a reflexive conclusion that two parents are ideal under just about any circumstance. In essence, children are reduced to chattel in that they are subordinated to the proprietary interest of their parents. That is why, when the courts do intervene as the family structure is dissolving, it is primarily the parents who are heard. Custody is about the raising of children. Children's voices are silenced if their interests are not made the court's central concern.

3. Parenting Plans

. . . Much has been said in the joint custody debate about the importance of parenting plans, and several state statutes specifically refer to them. Parenting plans have the benefit of compelling parties to hash out the specifics of the arrangement they are undertaking. The use of a standard parenting plan form provided by the court may be useful to parents and judges when joint custody is to be awarded. The danger is that the court may rely too heavily on the forms, using them as checklists, instead of making less mechanical custody determinations. Furthermore, simply providing parenting plan forms will not give pro se litigants insight into the level of detail needed to make the forms useful. The forms also will not alleviate the difficulty and stress involved in providing the necessary information. Trained personnel will be needed to render assistance to these parties. Given the number of pro se litigants in the District of Columbia, this will require resources that were not anticipated by the court or the legislature when the new Act was passed. . . .

Judges should choose whether to use parenting plans with caution since they can open a Pandora's Box of infractions for the court to address. Even with the counseling or mediation suggested in statutes, once parenting plans are adopted, the court is the ultimate arbiter if these negotiations break down, and it has virtually no options for reasonably resolving much of the conflict.

4. Providing For Which Parent Makes Decisions Requiring Immediate Attention

. . . [The new statute] requires the court to designate a parent to make decisions that need "immediate attention" regarding the health, safety, and welfare of the child. Giving one parent clear authority in emergency situations avoids the horror stories told of parental impasses as a child lays on the operating table. The phrase "immediate attention," however, encompasses more than pure emergencies. The parent with such authority can make decisions regarding non-routine medical care, schooling, counseling, travel, and so on.

Arguably, this decision-making authority subsumes the concept of joint legal custody. However, if joint legal custody refers only to long-range decisions, as indicated by the D.C. Court of Appeals in Ysla v. Lopez, then the bulk of the issues requiring immediate decisions will fall to the physical custodian. In any event, children cannot be protected effectively if important decisions are hamstrung by the inaccessibility of one parent or by an impasse. Such situations will come up over the course of the child's minority, and without a mechanism to resolve them short of judicial intervention, children will suffer and the court will be overwhelmed.

As suggested by the Ysla court, the parent having such authority to make immediate decisions should be the parent with the most significant contact with the child. It would be inappropriate to give less weight to the decision-making authority of the more involved parent. A reasonable award of joint legal custody would anticipate and foreclose manipulation of long range decisions by the authorized parent who may otherwise be tempted to delay action until situations require an immediate response. Thus, while choice of the child's school would not normally fall under this provision, a parent should not be able to put off the issue to the point at which collaboration is no longer an option. Although parenting plans set out parental responsibilities, it is difficult to expect that the court will be equipped to handle the occasions on which breach may occur. . . .

6. Child Support

The application of the Child Support Guideline does not extend to shared physical custody arrangements in which the child spends forty or more percent of the time with each parent. Unfortunately, it is not clear how child support will work in cases where shared physical custody is approximated, or how the resulting lack of child support will benefit the child when resources must be stretched between separate households. While there are formulas within the statute for determining support in these cases, the only requirement that stands when joint physical custody is roughly equal is that the standard of living of the child should not be less than that of the noncustodial parent. The meaning of this requirement is left to judicial discretion. The very existence of child support guidelines throughout the country demonstrates that the exercise of such discretion has not resulted in adequate support for children . . .

7. Domestic Abuse

. . . Abuse of one parent by another raises specific issues with regard to children that only recently have gained the recognition they warrant in custody determinations. While many children suffer physical injury as a result of being in the line of fire, children who witness violence by one parent against another often are harmed psychologically. It does neither the child nor the abused parent any good to require that the harmful contact continue, especially the level of interaction expected under joint custody. However, raising abuse for the first time in the context of a custody case is often viewed as inherently suspect. The parent whose strategy for escaping abuse does not include pressing criminal charges or seeking a protective order may risk losing custody to the abusive parent if the court disregards the undocumented evidence as opportunistic and applies an unfriendly parent penalty. . . .

The District of Columbia Code's definition of the term "intrafamily offense" does not include emotional abuse. It has long been acknowledged that emotional abuse can also be devastating as well. A degrading statement or threatening look elicits conditioned responses associated with previous psychological abuse. That abuse can take the form of isolation, induced debility, monopolization of perception, degradation, and random reinforcers or indulgences that keep alive the hope that the abuse will cease. Children who witness the anxiety, depression, and emotional withdrawal of a parent experiencing emotional abuse will present emotional or physical problems similar to those seen in children traumatized by witnessing physical abuse. Clearly, forcing contact in a jurisdiction where there is a presumption of joint custody with no specific exemption in the case of emotional abuse runs contrary to the interests of the child.

Thus, despite its strong language, the Act risks giving abusive parents a greater opportunity to use custody as a means of continuing destructive contact. This is particularly true since the presumption in favor of joint custody may preclude sufficient analysis of the impact of psychological abuse, or may preclude sufficient analysis of physical abuse if the abused parent is hesitant to raise the history of abuse or is effectively silenced in the attempt to do so . . .

11. Not Just Divorce and Separation

Finally, the Act obliquely addresses the possibility that application of the joint custody presumption may be limited to divorce cases. It is significant that the legislature included in both sections of the law a phrase that is often used in connection with joint custody, "frequent and continuing contact," and connected it to language stating that the provision applies to all relationships, "regardless of marital status." This is the first time that the legislature explicitly has applied the custody standard to unwed parents. While the best interest standard had been routinely applied to unwed parents, joint custody raises different issues because it is a policy that is tied conceptually to divorce and is intended to continue much of the unity attributed to marriage, vis-a-vis the children. The joint custody dialogue does not contemplate unwed parents, and as such, it does not reflect the reality that many couples live and raise children together without marrying. There is no legitimate basis for distinguishing between unmarried parents who are separating and parents whose marriage is dissolving, and, in this instance, the statute appropriately applies the custody options to this group of unwed parents.

There is also a large category of parents who never married, never lived together, and never coordinated their lives, however, including the responsibilities that come with having children. In these situations, undistinguished by the statute, the court should be concerned about requiring the parents to enter a relationship that is completely foreign. The statute gives the court reason to be cautious in entering a joint custody order in these situations by requiring the judge to consider prior parenting history, but it is unclear whether prior history, listed as a factor to be considered in rebutting the presumption, will gain the distinction warranted in these situations . . .

V. Joint Custody Should Not Be Presumed or Imposed

A joint custody presumption is attractive because it seeks to reconstruct, or construct, the Ozzie and Harriet ideal of the nuclear family out of a relationship that has failed, or in many cases never existed. Neither reason nor social science support such high regard.

All too often in this area of law, legislatures swing from one preference to another without requiring solid evidence in support of the approach considered. The maternal preference, for example, reinforces the notion that mothers are responsible for children while fathers are not. Joint legal or physical custody, on the other hand, forces mothers who in fact have been responsible for the children to make concessions in order to continue to raise them. Joint legal custody reinforces the notion that fathers have a decision-making, as opposed to a caretaking, role in the family. Although most statutes do not indicate a preference for the form of joint custody awarded, currently most orders award joint legal custody. Seven jurisdictions have statutes that specifically favor joint legal custody. In these jurisdictions one parent has the bulk of the responsibility for providing the day to day nurturing of the children and must negotiate with the absent parent with regard to decision-making. In essence, the absent parent has the benefit of wielding authority without undertaking the responsibility for its execution. This imbalance not only is unfair to the physical custodian, but can undermine that parent's role in child rearing since decisions are subject to negotiation with a parent who is not otherwise functioning in the daily life of the family . . .

Joint custody should certainly be available to parents who freely commit to co-parenting. Such commitment has the potential to overcome economic and social barriers that may otherwise defeat it. Too much is at stake, however, to embark on this particular variety of social engineering without both parents being vested in its success . . .

9. Conclusion

Most families . . . , from all economic and social classes, resolve custody issues by agreement. That agreement generally represents the best hope for addressing the needs of children since the court is not likely to force two unwilling parents into an alternative arrangement. Furthermore, such agreements reflect an exercise of parental responsibility that courts are, and should be, loath to second guess. The role of the court in consent situations should be to determine that the agreement was entered freely and that the children involved enjoy a level of shelter and financial support consistent with their parents' financial status. These, however, are not the situations addressed by a presumption in favor of joint custody. The presumption comes into play in the face of conflict between the parents as to what custody arrangement is best. Parental rights aside, this suggests dysfunction, and society has an interest, represented by the concept of parens patriae, in ensuring that the children do not suffer in the exchange. A joint custody presumption is a seemingly tidy response to the discomfort of choosing between the perceived wishes and needs of two parents battling for the right to raise their child. It says, "Both of you should do this together, and since we know that this solution is far from tidy in the details, you propose a plan indicating what it should mean."

Financial, organizational, and emotional stresses directly related to orchestrating joint custody anticipate commitment and resources. It is shortsighted to presume that poor families have the resources and that broken families possess the commitment. In fact, requiring collaboration can perpetuate abusive relationships, even under a statute such as the District's that specifically exempts cases in which there is a history of domestic violence, child abuse and neglect, or parental kidnapping. The language does not reach emotionally abusive relationships, and may not reach poorly documented abusive situations that do not fit within the statute. In such situations, joint custody can defeat the salvation sought by parent and child through a separation . . .

Thus, the search for an alternative to the best interest of the child standard is understandable. The premise of the standard is irrefutable, but its application is vague and inherently biased. It has been criticized as being unfair to fathers and to mothers alike. An emphasis on the primary caretaker can mitigate these failings in that it focuses on care of the child. It forces an analysis of child care, and, as such, may force the court and the litigants to bring children out of the shadows. If it is not interpreted as a mechanical checklist of daily child maintenance, it has the benefit of rewarding nurture in its most affirmative sense. This does not mean that the court should be relieved of analysis of what is in fact best for the child, or that the goal of encouraging the involvement of both parents should be abandoned. Participation in the raising of children can be a matter of ego, tied directly to the need to love, to be loved, to role identification, and to deeply held beliefs regarding fundamental rights. These are highly emotional and deeply essential feelings that are implicated when parents struggle to capture their relationship with their children. However, these feelings can be accommodated without creating contorted and tenuous arrangements that may simultaneously reward the uncommitted parent and undermine the one who is committed. As important as parents' interests and feelings may be, it is a mistake to allow them to trump the best solution for the child. The court must balance the competing interests of the parents with those of their children, and given the relative vulnerability of the latter class, the court must protect them. The court's role is to think carefully, guided primarily by the protection of the child's, not the parents' interests or ill-conceived notions of social engineering about the implications of decisions as to where, with whom, and under whose tutorship children in each case before the court will spend their lives. Joint custody may be an appropriate result, but there are far too many negative implications attached to the District of Columbia's current presumption that it is the appropriate result.

NOTES AND QUESTIONS

1. Professor Barry cautions against a statutory presumption in favor of joint custody, particularly for parties who have no history of co-parenting and have limited resources. Do you agree with this critique? Do any of her arguments also apply to divorcing couples or parties with resources? What implication does her critique have for child access mediation?

2. Many of the benefits attributed to child access mediation result from the power given to the parties, rather than the court, to make agreements about the care of their children. Indeed, in many jurisdictions trial courts are either not permitted to award joint custody over the objection of a parent or are required to make a series of factual findings before ordering it over the objection of either party. *See, e.g., Taylor v. Taylor*, 508 A.2d 964 (Md. 1986) (finding an award of joint custody reversible error unless evidence in the record that parents have a "capacity to communicate and to reach shared decisions affecting the child's welfare").

Putting aside joint custody, what is the court's role in reviewing other aspects of child access agreements? Is it ever appropriate for a court to overrule a mediated agreement when neither party is alleging unfairness or, for other reasons, seeks to set aside the agreement? *See, e.g.,* In re *Marriage of Sutton*, 233 S.W.3d 786 (Mo. App. E.D., 2007) (trial judge did not abuse his discretion when changing the parenting plan to eliminate each parent's access to the children by telephone while the children were in the custody of the other parents because it was in the best interest of the children); *Sleater v. Sleater*, 42 S.W.3d 821 (Mo. App. E.D. 2001) (trial court judge was permitted to reject the parenting plan on custody and visitation but was required to make written findings detailing the specific relevant factors (1) making its plan in the best interest of the children and (2) resulting in the rejections of the parties' proposed agreement); *Fisher v. Hasenjager*, 116 Ohio St.3d 53, 876 N.E.2d 546 (2007) (trial court may modify designation of residential parent and legal custodian of child if there is a determination that a change in circumstances has occurred, as well as a finding that the modification is in the best interest of the child). These issues will be explored in greater depth in Chapter 6 which explores the legal regulation of mediation.

C. PARENTS VS. STATE CHILD ACCESS DISPUTES

1.   What Is Meant by Child Welfare?

The child welfare system involves government agencies, usually called Departments of Social Services or Children's Services, and a combination of federal, state and local laws to protect children from physical abuse, emotional abuse, or neglect by the child's parent or parents. Child welfare cases usually come under the jurisdiction of a Juvenile Court, Family Court, or Unified Family Court. States may refer to the structure that governs child welfare cases as dependency, CINA, CHINS, or PINS. While the nomenclature of the public entities may vary by state, the structure of the child welfare system is governed by federal mandate, and these cases differ vastly from private child custody disputes in purpose, process, and law.

Child welfare cases generally begin with a call or written report by a family member, school teacher, or other citizen to the county's Child Protection Services child abuse hotline. The hotline worker, usually a Department of Social Services child welfare worker, determines whether the report merits an investigation. If the case is investigated, another initial determination is made by the worker, often an intake worker, about whether the child or children should be removed from the home pending an initial court hearing. If the child is removed, the states generally have between 24 and 72 hours before they must present the case to the judge or hearing officer. Whether the child is removed or remains in the home of the accused parent, the court may hold a jurisdiction hearing to determine if the court will exercise control over the care of the child. If the court determines that the child is at risk, and therefore takes jurisdiction, the court will also hold a disposition hearing, during which it determines the appropriate placement type for the child. Another hearing is held by the court or an administrative agency every six months, until the child is returned to the home or the reunification period, usually consisting of six to 18 months of social services to the parent and child, has ended. If a child remains in the foster care system past the point of termination of services to the parent, another review hearing is held at least every 12 months.

Mediations take place throughout this process but most often, prior to jurisdiction, at disposition, after review hearings, and at times when the child's placement is in question. In almost every state, parents and children are routinely appointed attorneys or sometimes in the case of children, guardians *ad litem*, to represent their interests. The parents and children, their representatives, the assigned child welfare worker, county counsel, foster parents, community support people, and psychosocial experts may participate in mediations. Ultimately, if the child is out of the home for 15 of 22 consecutive months, the case must move toward termination of services for the parents and may move toward termination of parental rights and later, adoption. Post-adoption contracts between biological and adoptive parents are often mediated toward the end of the child welfare process.

2.   How Should Child Welfare Cases Differ from Private Dispute Resolution?

Child welfare cases pose unique challenges to the family mediator, and some jurisdictions have or are contemplating special qualification requirements for individuals mediating child welfare cases. In contrast to child custody cases between private parties, which presume parents to be 'fit' to make decisions for their children, the child welfare system only comes into play when the fitness of the parent is in question by the state or the well-being of the child is at risk. For this reason, mediations that take place in child welfare cases begin with an imbalance of power, in that parents alleged to have brought harm to their children mediate with child welfare workers, the state agents assigned to protect and at times, remove, children from their homes. In addition, children often participate in these mediations, necessitating that the mediator have some grounding in child development or at least have the capacity to use age-appropriate language and child-friendly processes. Child welfare statutes, in contrast with child custody statutes, are rooted in federal law and tend to be more complex and involve more case law than custody matters. Child welfare cases often involve disparate but interrelated issues within a case, such as the need to apply for immigration status, the concurrent filing of criminal charges, delinquency court involvement, special education appeals, school discipline proceedings, public benefits barriers, adoption processes, substance abuse, poverty, domestic violence, and mental health issues.

Due to the complexity of interwoven law and the depth of emotions that often come to the surface during child welfare mediations, jurisdictions have experimented with having child welfare mediation facilitated by co-mediators with divergent expertise and experience. One formula would involve a mediator with a legal background co-mediating with a mediator schooled in social work or psychology. Similarly, at least one jurisdiction employs a co-mediator who herself traversed the child welfare system as a parent. The cross-pollination of insight from the complementary fields and first-hand experience assists the co-mediators in their effort to accurately reflect the feelings and values of the participants as well as to bring attention to the specific needs of the individual families.

The following excerpt discusses the results of a pilot child welfare mediation program in five California counties in the 1990s. The article speaks to the fears experienced by professionals — attorneys and child welfare workers — not accustomed to using mediation. She then discusses their experience, and that of the participating clients, once the pilot project was underway.

AN EVALUATION OF CHILD PROTECTION MEDIATION IN FIVE CALIFORNIA COURTS[3]

From 35 FAMILY AND CONCILIATION COURT REVIEW 184, 184–85 (1997)

By Nancy Thoennes

This article presents the results of an evaluation of five California counties utilizing court-based mediation services to process child maltreatment cases filed with the court. The programs employed a variety of different service delivery approaches and targeted cases at a variety of different stages of case processing. The results indicate that mediation is an effective method of resolving cases and may offer a number of benefits over adjudication, including more detailed treatment plans and fewer contested court hearings.

At the Center for Policy Research we have been fortunate to have the opportunity to conduct research in a number of courts providing dependency mediation. Some of our earliest research gave us the chance to consider the programs operating in Los Angeles and Orange counties in California and throughout Connecticut. That research reached the following very general conclusions:

Settlement rates ranged from 60% to 80% of the cases seen by mediators;

Mediated treatment plans were produced, on average, a month sooner than nonmediated plans;

In some, but not all, sites there were significant differences between the degree of compliance with mediated and adjudicated plans. Where there were differences, compliance was better in mediated cases;

Children were more likely to be mentioned as the recipients of services in mediated versus adjudicated plans;

Professional participants reported that mediation makes the court experience a little faster, and less foreign and more understandable to parents.

The results of this study have been documented elsewhere (Thoennes, 1991, 1994). In the present article, I offer the results of a similar study conducted in five California counties. The California evaluations provide an opportunity to see whether similar results are found in dependency mediation programs initiated years later, and employing a variety of different formats . . .

REFERRAL PROCESS

At most of the California pilot sites, judges had discretion about which cases would be referred to mediation. However, efforts were generally made to refer contested jurisdiction and disposition cases to mediation. Programs generally also encouraged the parties to request mediation at any time they felt it might help, and judges were inclined to order mediation when it was requested. The professionals interviewed in this study were able to cite examples of situations in which they did request mediation, For example, attorneys who represent children and parents reported that they sometimes requested mediation because discussions were at an impasse, because an issue needed immediate results, or because they needed to get

---

direction in a case. One attorney who represents parents explained why he requests mediation:

> I'd ask for it if the social worker was being evasive and didn't talk to the parents. Or maybe there's a specific problem, like I had a caseworker who did a home visit to a client who doesn't speak English and there was no interpreter there. I request it if I have a parent who just needs to vent. And some attorneys use it . . . to find out what's really going on.

Attorneys who represent parents sometimes requested mediation because they felt they had nothing to lose and might get a better deal. Others wanted their client to get another "reality check," that is, to hear from people other than their attorneys that their demands or expectations were unreasonable. Finally, in fast-moving cases, mediation was an opportunity to get fresh information about events that had happened between the time the caseworker's report was written and a court hearing was scheduled.

Attorneys who represented the child protection services agency reported that they tended to request mediation when there was a visitation issue, intrafamily conflicts, or when they felt their client, the social worker, needed to reevaluate her position.

PARTICIPANT REACTIONS

It was difficult to obtain candid reactions from parents about their mediation experiences. In addition, we felt that anonymous surveys would be better than personal interviews. Despite reassurances to the contrary, we thought parents would suspect that their comments might filter back to the court and or the caseworker, leading to less than candid responses. We chose to rely on very simple user surveys, available in both English and Spanish, which were anonymously completed immediately following mediation, rather than phone surveys.

The surveys indicated that parents felt "heard" in mediation. More than 90% of the parents at each site reported they had a chance to talk about the issues important to them, felt others listened to and understood what they had to say, and felt mediation clarified what they needed to do in order to have the child protection services agency close their case. Somewhat fewer parents indicated that mediation helped to clarify what the caseworker would do to meet the goals of the treatment plan, which suggests an area in which mediation can improve.

Parents were also asked to compare their experience in mediation with prior experiences they may have had in court. Although a few of the parents said they were simply unsure of how mediation and court compare, parents who were able to provide an assessment clearly felt that mediation was "better than a court hearing before a judge."

Although the parents were usually receptive to mediation, initial resistance to the idea of mediation was common among caseworkers, attorneys, and even some judges and hearing officers. When they first heard about the pilot project, social workers at most sites admitted to having fundamental doubts about its utility. Speaking candidly, workers at most sites said they initially suspected that mediation would prove to be a waste of time. Workers tended to feel that they could reach settlements with reasonably cooperative and motivated parents on their own, and believed that it was impossible to achieve mediated settlements with less cooperative families. These caseworkers were concerned that mediation would be used by parents and their attorneys to challenge the workers' professionalism and honesty. There was concern that "mediators would be deciding things and the caseworker would be undermined."

Legal counsel for the caseworkers worried at the outset that public defenders would simply use the session "to get some free discovery" with no intention of settling in mediation. These attorneys said they did not want to participate in the process if that meant "negotiating about what the law said or coming up with agreements that were contrary to the law."

The prospect of mediating dependency cases also met with some initial resistance by the attorneys who represent parents in dependency court proceedings. Some public defenders doubted that the process would remain truly confidential, although experience has since convinced them that confidentiality is respected. With the exception of a new disclosure that puts someone at risk, nothing goes out of the mediation session. Participants at each site now agree that "judges never ask about mediation," and that the confidential nature of the process has been honored. Some public defenders also maintained that mediation would be like every other settlement effort: "just another way to get parents to submit." Thus they worried that the compromise in mediation would be done by parents, never by the department.

Resistance to mediation on the part of the professionals was typically short lived. Education about the process and exposure to it, along with the careful selection of a mediator, served to overcome initial resistance. Once they tried mediation, most case-workers and attorneys supported the process. Some caseworkers even credit mediation with opening up communication channels between the parents and the caseworker and helping them work together. One worker said:

> I had a client who wouldn't talk to me before mediation. She saw me as sort of like the police. . . . You don't talk to them unless they ask you a direct question. Once we got into mediation, she understood the role of the caseworker and was willing to work with me.

Caseworkers noted that in court the agency becomes the "enemy." Parents "hear all this incredibly negative stuff about themselves and feel awful." The presiding dependency court judge in one site recognized that mediation might help caseworkers bridge the conflicting demands of the social services and legal systems:

> Juvenile court has two contradictory missions going on at the same time. We are supposed to be obtaining proof of bad acts and simultaneously putting the family back together. Some social workers are busy putting together the legal case and don't really do a very good job of delivering services. Others focus on services without making the legal case.

Caseworkers now agree that mediation can help reconcile the helper and investigator roles. As a result, a strong sentiment among caseworkers is that there is "nothing to lose by mediating," and that unlike trial, "mediation has never made things worse."

Parents' attorneys came to value mediation after discovering that it could be the place where all the parties are held accountable, and all the parties "test their reality." For parents who were insisting on unreasonable, hard-line positions against the advice of their attorneys, the input of the mediators was most helpful. One defense attorney noted:

> There's really no other place where someone can tell the caseworker "you need to talk to the parents" or tell the parents "you need to shape up." The mediators have a clear grasp of the dynamics among the parties and they are equally demanding on all sides.

Another attorney for parents noted that mediation was far more candid and revealing than other settlement efforts. In a system where attorneys admit they often appear in court before they know who their clients are, mediation also ensured that parents got some undivided attention. Parents' attorneys also acknowledged that parents got a lot of practical information in mediation, which was important because not all attorneys take the time to answer questions and ensure that clients fully understand the situation.

Finally, after trying it, the professionals generally came to view mediation as beneficial even when no agreement is reached. The process is believed to be effective in promoting communication and wrestling with the "real impasse issues." One defense attorney noted that "at a minimum, you will clarify the issues in mediation and maybe you will work out some interim arrangements on things like visitation that will hold you over to trial." Attorneys were even supportive in Contra Costa County, where they did not participate in the session. Initially, these attorneys expressed skepticism, but, as in other settings, their attitudes changed over time.

One key to the success of dependency mediation in each of the pilot sites was judicial support. The courts in the pilot sites fully recognized their leadership role. One presiding judge noted:

> If the judiciary doesn't support this, it won't work. Programs that are initiated more from the bottom up sometimes have trouble getting people to show up and participate. Others have to see value in mediation for themselves, but they won't go unless the judge is clear that it is required . . .

SUMMARY

The evaluation of the California pilot projects had several limitations, as have all dependency mediation evaluations. For example, the time line did not allow us to follow cases over a lengthy period of time to discover what ultimately transpired with respect to savings in court time, length of out-of-home placement, or compliance patterns. In addition, the programs were evolving even while the evaluation took place. However, despite these limitations, we can note the following:

*Mediation can produce settlements at all stages in case processing: contested jurisdictional, dispositional, and postdispositional cases.

*All types of cases settle in mediation. There is no evidence that certain types of maltreatment should be screened out of the process.

*The decision to mediate jurisdiction and disposition generally met with some early resistance from all professional groups. However, today there is widespread support for the continuation of the service, although time constraints continue to pose problems.

*Parents reported that they understood the mediation process and felt it provided them with a place to be "heard" and to hear what was required of them. Most parents preferred mediation to a judicial hearing.

*The agreements produced in mediation are similar in many respects to those promulgated by judges. However, mediated agreements are more likely than other agreements to include detailed visitation plans for children in out-of-home placements. They are also more likely to address communication problems between family members or between the family and child protection services agency. They are also more likely to have the parent specifically acknowledge the need for services.

*Evidence suggests that mediation produces savings in time and money for the dependency court. Cases mediated, rather than adjudicated, at jurisdiction and disposition are less likely to result in subsequent contested review hearings.

*Mediated settlements enjoy greater compliance by parents, at least in the short run.

*A variety of mediation models are effective.

NOTES AND QUESTIONS

1.   What are some of the perceived dangers of child welfare court mediation programs, as outlined by the Thoennes article? Do you think public defenders were justified in their concern that mediation would be used as "just another way to get their clients to submit"? Do these types of dangers exist in child access cases as well? What is your impression of the attorneys who wanted to use mediation to afford their clients "another 'reality check' "as to their demands and expectations? Do you think the attorneys were justified in thinking that mediation would be used for "free discovery" by some attorneys?

2.   Thoennes writes that "mediators have a clear grasp of the dynamics among the parties and they are equally demanding on all sides." Does this description suggest any particular style of mediating that may have been used in these California counties? What style do you think would work best?

3.   Thoennes argues in her summary that "there is no evidence that certain types of maltreatment should be screened out of the process." Do you think any particular types of issues, such as domestic violence or child sexual abuse, should be screened out from child welfare mediation?

3.   Critique of Child Welfare Mediation

Not all reviewers of child welfare mediation have been as positive as Nancy Thoennes. In the following article excerpt, Amy Sinden critiques mediation and other informal methods for resolving disputes in the child welfare context.

WHY WON'T MOM COOPERATE?: A CRITIQUE OF INFORMALITY IN CHILD WELFARE PROCEEDINGS[4]

11 YALE J.L. & FEMINISM 339, 339–40, 353–54, 355, 356–57, 379–81, 386–87, 391–92, 396 (1998)

By Amy Sinden

Reams of paper have been filled with the ruminations of countless judges and legal scholars on the subject of criminal procedure. It is the central concern of four of the ten constitutional amendments that make up the Bill of Rights. It is a major course offered at every law school. And it is the paradigmatic context in which we frame much of our debate about the relationship between the state and the individual in a democratic society.

But there is another system that exists in every county across the country, in which the state hauls private citizens into court against their will, accuses them of acts that trigger severe social reprobation, and threatens them with a deprivation of liberty that, for many people, strikes at the very core of their identity and threatens to remove the most profound source of purpose, fulfillment, and happiness from their lives. This is the child welfare system . . .

[T]he predominance of social work norms and discourse creates significant pressure on parents to resolve these cases through non-adversarial, informal means. Social workers are trained to be effective by building non-adversarial relationships characterized by cooperation and trust. From a social worker's point of view, she fails professionally if her relationship with her client becomes adversarial. While lawyers' training steeps them in the discourse of individual rights and prepares them to operate in formal, procedure-bound environments, social workers are steeped in the discourse of relationships and cooperation and trained to value informality over formality as a means of gaining trust and building rapport.

A key word in the prevailing social work discourse is thus "cooperation." This word often forms the focal point of the meetings and conversations that take place in the hallways of the courthouse: "If mom would just cooperate . . . " Running as an undercurrent to this refrain are powerful cultural stereotypes and expectations attached to motherhood. Mothers are supposed to be nurturing, loving, and above all protective of their children. Conflict is viewed as harmful to the child, and therefore the mother accused of child abuse who creates conflict by failing to "cooperate" harms her child a second time. This language of "cooperation" cloaks the substantial power differential that exists between the child welfare agency and the accused mother. The word "cooperation" implies a collaboration between equals in which each party contributes and makes compromises. In the child welfare context, however, "cooperation" is frequently just a code word for the parent doing whatever the social worker tells her to do. Where there is disagreement between the parties, it is the mother, not the social worker, who is labeled "uncooperative," and therefore blamed for creating conflict . . .

In addition to these implicit pressures that operate on a day-to-day level to de-formalize the existing adversarial system, there is currently a movement to explicitly de-formalize the child welfare court system by introducing alternative dispute resolution ("ADR") mechanisms, primarily mediation . . .

Proponents of mediation cite a number of benefits in addition to its ability to ease crowded dockets. Mediation is said to encourage participation by parents by giving them a sense of inclusion, validation, and empowerment. This decreases the likelihood that parents will withdraw from the process and leave their children feeling rejected. The parties' sense of inclusion and investment in the process is also said to give mediated agreements a greater chance of long-term success. But primarily, mediation is touted as an antidote to the adversarial process, which is viewed as inherently destructive to families and harmful to children. The adversarial process is said to break down communication, polarize disputants, create hostility, and "tear at the thin fabric that holds these families together." . . .

The formal adversarial process is designed to produce accurate decisions by bringing out all relevant facts and limiting bias and prejudice. Because adversaries each present their position in an attempt to persuade the judge to rule in their favor, each side is motivated to ferret out all the evidence that supports its position. Each side is also motivated to view its opponent's evidence critically and to undermine it through cross-examination and the introduction of contradictory evidence or evidence showing bias or lack of credibility. This motivation is critically important, particularly in a system in which professionals are juggling high caseloads. The parties' adoption of a conciliatory stance toward each other raises the danger that they will accept statements uncritically and fail to seek out contradictory evidence.

The formal rules that govern trial procedure also help to assure accuracy. Witnesses testify under oath under threat of penalty for perjury. The judge excludes unreliable evidence, like hearsay, as well as evidence likely to cause prejudice. The requirement that judges state the basis for their decisions helps to ensure that decisions are based on a rational view of the evidence and not on prejudice or bias. Numerous rules governing judges' conduct in adversarial proceedings encourage impartiality and the appearance of impartiality. Thus, judges sit higher than and at some distance from the parties, and usually address only the lawyers. When they do address the parties directly they do so formally and on the record. And they do not communicate with one party out of the presence of the other party.

Of course, these mechanisms are far from perfect, and it is beyond question that trials can and often do reach inaccurate results skewed by judges' prejudice and partiality. Where decision making occurs without these formal constraints, however, it is even more susceptible to being swayed by prejudices, stereotypes, and snap judgments based on innuendo and rumor. Mediators are trained to maintain impartiality and neutrality, but because their role is to facilitate communication between the parties rather than to judge, they do not maintain the same kind of physical and psychological distance from the parties that judges do. They sit closer to the parties, talk to them directly in an informal style, and may speak to one party without the presence of the other and without subsequently relating to the other what was said. This more intimate and informal setting may make mediation "an environment in which prejudices can flourish."

The danger that prejudice or incomplete or unreliable information will distort decisions is particularly acute in the emotionally-charged arena of dependency and termination cases. Where so much is at stake — the suffering of children — the players in the system are all the more likely to make snap judgments based on gut feelings and instinct and to cut corners in an attempt to manipulate decisions to conform to their own view of the right outcome. Imagine, for example, a social worker who is convinced in his gut that a mother is severely beating her child. Maybe it is because the look in her eyes is exactly the same one he saw in another mother who seriously injured her child after he failed to act quickly enough. In the face of such a feeling, imagine how tempted the social worker must be to remove the child immediately without bothering to confirm all the facts — to perhaps accept at face value the estranged father's hearsay statement that the doctor had said the broken bone could only have been the product of abuse. Because of these pressures, the evidentiary constraints and protections against bias and prejudice afforded by formality are particularly important in the child welfare context . . .

Proponents of de-formalization, however, argue that informal proceedings lead to more just outcomes because when parties are not locked in an adversarial win/lose posture and are able to step back from the rhetoric of blame and rights that dominates formal proceedings, they are able to find a third way — creative solutions that meet all parties needs. Certainly it is possible to imagine such a dynamic producing positive results in a child welfare case. A mediation process may encourage the parties to think outside the box of the adversarial paradigm that insists on winning and defines winning narrowly: for the parent, a dismissal; for the agency, placement of the child in foster care. Instead, in the non-confrontational, needs-centered atmosphere of mediation, the mother may be able to admit that she needs drug treatment while communicating to the agency the sincerity of her desire to improve and the strength of her bond with her child. The agency may be able to re-frame its position from insisting on foster care to simply needing assurance that the child will be safe. Out of this softening of positions the possibility for a third way — placement of the mother and child together in a mother-child drug treatment program — might arise.

But in the child welfare context, the vast disparity in power between the parties distorts this process. Too often informality results in the weaker party — the parent — simply capitulating to the agency rather than pushing the agency to find the creative third way. The "win-win" solution so frequently touted by the proponents of informality requires a creative tension between the parties that tends to arise only when the parties are roughly equally matched in power. Otherwise there is no leverage to dislodge the stronger party from its position. This is particularly true in the child welfare context where the agency's position can often be well entrenched. First, because the agency inevitably equates its own win with the best interests of the child, it may often approach a dispute resolution proceeding with the intransigence of those who believe they are "on the side of the angels." Secondly, in the child welfare context, the creative third way often involves the agency providing some innovative service to the family that allows the parent and child to stay together while addressing the problem that led to the agency's involvement — for example a mother-child drug treatment program, a supervised group home for teenage mothers, or financial assistance in obtaining housing. But these solutions are usually more costly than the standard package of services and require initiative on the part of the agency social worker. Unless the parent has sufficient power to exert some leverage on the agency, such solutions are frequently out of reach. Parents can sometimes exert leverage in a formal adversarial process by seeking a court order compelling the agency to provide innovative services in order to fulfill its legal mandate to make reasonable efforts to preserve the family. No such leverage is available in an informal proceeding, however.

Additionally, the "win-win" solution depends on the parties having a set of shared values so that there is some set of cultural norms in common that can form a basis for agreement. Otherwise informality will simply result either in a stand-off or in the weaker party capitulating to the cultural norms of the more powerful party.

Much of the rhetoric promoting the use of informal procedures in child welfare cases is borrowed from the domestic relations context, where mediation has been used extensively for many years in divorce and custody cases. But the domestic relations paradigm cannot simply be transplanted to the dependency context. The alignment of the parties is fundamentally different. Domestic relations cases involve disputes between private parties. There may be some disparity of power between them, and, indeed, many feminists have criticized the use of informal procedures in domestic relations cases for that reason, especially in instances where the power disparity is particularly acute, like those involving battering. Still, in domestic relations cases the vast power disparity between the individual and the state that exists in child welfare cases is absent. Moreover, in the domestic relations context, the parties have an existing intimate relationship which they entered into voluntarily and which they will often need to preserve — though in some altered form — in order to continue to share parenting responsibilities. Thus, often in a domestic relations case, determining accurately what occurred in some past event is less important than reaching a compromise that addresses both parties' needs and preserves a workable relationship for the future. Additionally the fact that there was at some point a voluntary intimate relationship between the parties indicates a set of shared values or at least a commitment to reconciling conflicting values.

The move to de-formalize child welfare cases attempts to squeeze these disputes into the domestic relations paradigm, locating them in the realm of family therapy rather than adjudication. Thus, one particular mediation program is touted as "cathartic" and as providing the parents a chance to "vent." The issue is viewed not as whether the parent committed some act of child abuse or neglect that warrants state intervention, but how to facilitate communication between the participants and how to reach a compromise that meets all of their needs. Principles of blame and rights are replaced with the rhetoric of compromise and relationship. The conflict is "styled as a personal quarrel, in which there is no right and wrong, but simply two different equally true or untrue views of the world."

By identifying communication as the problem, however, the proponents of mediation presume that the state is entitled to have a relationship with the parent. This involves two false assumptions: first, that all parents are guilty (i.e., intervention is warranted), and, second, that intervention is always helpful to a family (or at least not harmful) . . .

Conclusion

Child welfare bureaucracies and court systems make thousands of decisions each day that profoundly effect the lives of millions of people, touching an aspect of life that many hold central to their identity. Too often, however, the policies and doctrines that shape the procedures by which these decisions are made are based on superficial reactions to the latest tabloid horror story about child maltreatment. Resistance to the adoption of formal procedures in these cases has frequently been justified by vague allusions to the need to avoid the harshness of the adversarial process in cases involving women and children and by reference to the questionable assertion that the deprivation of liberty effected by the forcible separation of parent and child is less grievous than the deprivation that is held up as the defining standard in questions involving procedure: criminal imprisonment. While a feminist critique of values can reveal the arbitrariness of the male norm embedded in such value judgments, it also forces us to question the traditional liberal notion that important interests demand formal procedures. Ultimately the question of procedure must be resolved through a contextual examination of the peculiar set of power dynamics and incentives that operate in child welfare cases.

I have argued that, at least in termination of parental rights cases and at the initial adjudicatory phase of dependency cases, traditional formal adversarial process offers the best hope of protecting against the distortions of power imbalance and the dangers of prejudice and snap judgments. I do not mean to argue that formality offers the perfect solution. My analysis has proceeded largely based on what is, with little speculation about what might be. By endorsing formality as the best among existing alternatives, I do not mean to suggest that a better third way might not be imagined.

4.   Alternative Processes

At least two additional forms of self-determinative multi-party forums have been established in the child welfare arena: the Family Team Decision Making Meeting (FTDM)[5] and Family Group Conferencing.

a.   Family Team Decision-Making Meetings

In states where FTDMs have been rolled out, the meetings occur any time a change in the placement of the child is contemplated, including, in some states, at the child's initial removal from the parent or parent's home. Participants at the FTDMs may include parents, the child at issue, the attorney for the child, foster parents, therapists, community members, service providers, a Court Appointed Special Advocate for the child, and anyone else that the family believes can help them determine the most appropriate living arrangement for the child. The FTDMs follow a specific format, beginning with introductions and a recitation of child and/or family strengths, and then move into the sharing of ideas among participants. Like all child welfare mediations, the parties discuss the matter against the backdrop of knowledge that if they do not reach a consensus on the best plan for the child, the child welfare worker assigned to the case will determine the placement for the child. The participants, of course, can always challenge that placement in court.

---

[5] Family Team Decision Making was introduced by the Annie E. Casey Foundation as part of their Family to Family initiative.

b. Family Group Conferencing

Family Group Conferencing (FGC) found its way to the United States child welfare community by way of New Zealand, where the government introduced FGC to child welfare cases. The goal of Family Group Conferencing was to strive for a formula that stemmed from the way of life of the Maori Tribe and other native peoples of New Zealand which emphasizes family strengths and relies on involvement of community in family decision making. While Team Decision Making meetings are used by the child welfare system to determine placement for a child, Family Group Conferencing is perhaps best used to build a service and recovery plan for the family. As a family strength-based practice, Family Group Conferencing becomes a tool to enhance the chances that a child will be able to return *safely* to the biological family. One aspect unique to Family Group Conferencing is the family time portion of the meeting, during which all service providers depart from the conferencing room and leave the family and extended family members to discuss and iron out the issues privately.

RIGHTS MYOPIA IN CHILD WELFARE[6]
53 UCLA L. Rev. 637, 674–84, 687 (2006)
By Clare Huntington

I. Origins, the Process, and Theoretical Underpinnings

Family group conferencing is part of the broader restorative justice movement, which seeks to reform the justice system to incorporate victims and to allow the offender to "restore" the status quo. Although largely focused on criminal justice, the restorative justice movement has also addressed other systems, including child welfare. In that context, family group conferencing is the practice of convening family members, community members, and other individuals or institutions involved with a family to develop a plan to ensure the care and protection of a child who is at risk for abuse or neglect.

Simplified descriptions of two cases, one receiving traditional child welfare services and one receiving a family group conference, illustrate the marked differences between the two approaches. In a child welfare case under the current system, after the state agency receives a credible report of child abuse or neglect sufficient to warrant removal, a caseworker goes to the home and assesses the danger to the child. Assuming the caseworker finds sufficient evidence of such danger, the caseworker removes the child and places her in foster care pending a more thorough investigation. The state agency then files a petition in court seeking temporary custody of the child. The child is assigned a guardian ad litem to represent her interests. The caseworker then develops a case plan for the parents, requiring the parents to, for example, obtain drug treatment and attend parenting classes. If the parents do not comply with this case plan within the specified period, generally twelve to eighteen months, then the state agency files for a petition for the termination of parental rights. If the court agrees that parental rights should be terminated, the child is freed for adoption. The majority of decisions in this model are made by professionals: caseworkers, therapists, guardians ad litem, and judges.

In a family group conferencing case, the story and decision makers are decidedly different. In a typical family group conferencing case, after receiving a report, a social worker conducts an initial investigation to determine if there has been abuse or neglect. If the social worker concludes there is evidence of abuse or neglect, she refers the case to a coordinator, who has the authority to convene a family group conference. The coordinator contacts the parents, the child, extended family members, and significant community members who know the family. Before the conference, each potential conference participant meets separately with the coordinator to learn about the process. In these meetings, the coordinator screens for potentially complicating factors, such as a history of domestic violence, to determine whether the case is appropriate for family group conferencing and, if so, what additional supports may be needed for the participants.

There are three stages of the conference. In the first stage, the coordinator and any professionals involved with the family, such as therapists, teachers, and the investigating social worker, explain the case to the family. In the second stage, the coordinator and professionals leave the room while the family and community members engage in private deliberation. During the private deliberation, the participants acknowledge that the child was abused or neglected and develop a plan to protect the child and help the parents. After the participants reach an agreement, they present the plan to the social worker and coordinator, who likely have questions for the participants. Parents, custodians, social workers, and coordinators can veto the plan produced by the conference and refer the case to court. In practice, this rarely occurs: The participants come to a decision, and the social worker and coordinator accept the plan (perhaps with a few changes) if it meets predetermined criteria. The coordinator writes up the plan, sends it to all participants, and then sets a time for a subsequent conference to assess developments in the case.

The plan typically includes a decision about the safety of the child, including whether the child should be placed outside of the home for a certain period of time, and, if so, with whom. If the child is placed outside the home, she is almost invariably placed with a relative or other conference participant. The plan also identifies the services and supports needed by the parents. Finally, the plan determines which participants will both help the family and also check in on a regular basis to ensure the child is safe and the parents are complying with the plan.

As is apparent from this description, five principles characterize the philosophy of family group conferencing. First, children are raised best in their own families. Second, families have the primary responsibility for caring for their children, and these families should be supported, protected, and respected. Third, families are able to make reliable, safe decisions for their children, and families have strengths and are capable of changing the problems in their lives. Fourth, families are their own experts, with knowledge and insight into which solutions will work best for them. Finally, to achieve family empowerment, families must have the freedom to make their own decisions and choices.

As one of its proponents has stated, "[f]amily group conferences amount to a partnership arrangement between the state, represented by child protection officials; the family; and members of the community, such as resource and support persons; with each party expected to play an important role in planning and providing services necessary for the well-being of children." Family group conferences are not a means for child protection officials to relinquish their responsibilities, but rather are a different method for exercising those responsibilities. The intent is to strike a balance between the interests of child protection and family support. Family group conferencing represents a radical reorientation of child protection: Many child protection approaches attempt to enforce community standards (accountability) but lack any way for the community to reach out and weave the family back into the community fabric with the development of shared, voluntary commitments to community standards. Consequently, those strategies often create short-term relief, but do not change behavior in the long term. Those strategies also rely heavily on outside enforcers, the professional system, to solve the problem.

Family group conferencing originated with the Maori and other First Nations around the world, and New Zealand was the first country to incorporate the process into its laws. To avoid the removal of Maori children to non-Maori families, and to incorporate Maori traditions of involving extended family members in decision-making, legislative changes were made to New Zealand's child welfare system in the Children, Young Persons, and Their Families Act of 1989. The changes were in response to several government reports documenting discrimination against Maori families in the child welfare system. The legislative changes were not limited to Maori families. Rather, the law required that all substantiated cases of child abuse and neglect be referred for family group conferencing. The premises of family group conferences resonated with the idea, long-espoused by social workers, "that lasting solutions to problems are ones that grow out of, or can fit with, the knowledge, experiences, and desires of the people most affected."

There are four hallmarks of the family group conferencing process (and these hallmarks reflect the principles set forth above). First, the process is intended to find and build on a family's strengths, rather than to place blame. One method for achieving this is to focus on the problem, rather than the person, and to concentrate on healing. Although the current system is supposed to preserve families, in practice social workers often do not look for the strengths in a family and instead focus on the dysfunctional elements. Thus, family group conferencing facilitates a strengths-based practice because it requires the family and community to look within to find solutions. Second, the process respects and values important cultural practices of the relevant community. Third, the process involves the extended family and community. Those individuals with information to share, individuals who love the child, and individuals with a stake in the outcome are all included in the conference. Finally, the process views the community as a resource for the family.

In addition to the four hallmarks of family group conferencing, there are several key features of the process that set it apart from other alternative dispute resolution methods and are essential for its success. These key elements include sufficient preparation of the participants by the coordinator (often a total of thirty-five hours of preparation per conference, private family time without professionals present, consensus on the plan, and monitoring and follow-up by the conference participants and the state.

Although no country other than New Zealand requires the use of family group conferencing, many countries have started to experiment with it. In the United States, child welfare agencies have been experimenting with family group conferencing since the early 1990s. Although its use is by no means widespread, states and localities are using some version of it with increasing frequency. Notably, in the United States, social workers, rather than lawyers and legislators, have pushed for its adoption.

B. Early Empirical Research

Studies on programs implemented around the world and in the United States demonstrate that family group conferencing has had substantial success in improving child welfare systems. First, studies suggest, but are not uniform in concluding, that families who participate in family group conferences have lower levels of subsequent abuse and neglect than the typical child welfare case. This may be due in part to the way family group conferences enlist family members in monitoring the safety and welfare of children.

Second, research indicates that in the vast majority of cases families are able to devise a plan for the care and protection of their children. Family members, including fathers, participate in numbers far greater than in the traditional child welfare model. Caseworkers report that the plans devised by the participants often require more of the parent than the agency typically would. Conference participants play an active role in finding a solution for the troubles facing the family by providing, for example, child care, home furnishings, transportation, housing, and help with managing the household. Although participating family members have multiple problems, including substance abuse and histories of violence, these participants are able to create thoughtful and detailed plans to keep the children safe. These plans draw on familial and professional resources . . .

Third, participants report satisfaction with the process and result. For example, one mother described her experience as follows:

There comes a time when you think "I can take control now" and that's when I think the normal way of running social services departments falls down. Yes people come initially because they do need a certain amount of support and a certain amount of help. But if you go on trying [to] nursemaid and suffocate that person then their growth isn't going to take place. The social services, the way it's run at the moment actually doesn't allow the person who has to . . . take control, they're very reluctant to give that person back the control of the family. So social services becomes the head of the family, and the mother and the father, or one of them, becomes more or less like a child themselves, and they regress into no responsibility, because they're instructed all the way, what their responsibilities are. But they are not actually helped to rebuild their confidence to enable them to take up the full responsibility.

Fourth, there is evidence that family group conferencing fosters development of a strong support network within the child's extended family and community. For example, when the plan does recommend placement outside of the immediate family, children are more often placed with extended family members . . .

The process also fosters stronger ties between the family and the community. Research has demonstrated that ties to the community are particularly important to help an at-risk child overcome difficult family circumstances and that emotional support outside of the immediate family can be a crucial protective factor for children who grow up in high-risk environments.

Finally, to the extent the process prevents the placement of children in the foster care system, it could well generate significant savings for federal, state, and local governments . . .

Family group conferencing holds great potential for the child welfare system. Although it may be no panacea for the very difficult issues facing the system, the relevant question is whether family group conferencing, and a problem-solving model more generally, is a marked improvement over the current legal framework, which clearly is not serving the interests of parents or children.

NOTES AND QUESTIONS

1. What do you see as the primary distinctions between Family Group Conferencing and other forms of alternative dispute resolution? What makes Family Group Conferencing particularly well-suited to child welfare cases? Can you think of other forums in which Family Group Conferencing would aid in the resolution of disputes?

2. Would you suggest using Family Group Conferencing in child access cases? How would this practice change the nature of child access mediations? What would be the advantages and disadvantages of using such a practice? What is meant by "strength-based practice" and how could this apply to child access and other types of mediation?

3. What do you think of the practice of the participants meeting in private session, without any of the professionals? Should it be necessary that they "acknowledge that the child was abused or neglected" during this private meeting? Why does this acknowledgement happen as part of the private session? What else do you imagine might happen during the private session?

4. Why do you think Clare Huntington describes Family Group Conferencing as falling within the restorative justice movement? Who is restored? Would you describe other forms of mediation and alternative dispute resolution in this way?

5. Do you think that these alternative methods of resolving child welfare matters can change the nature of this system from one of accusation and defense to one of gathering resources from and for the community?

6. Dorothy Roberts and other legal scholars accurately point to a disproportionate percentage of children of color and poor families embroiled in the child welfare system in the United States.[7] What do you see as reasons for this disparity and how should alternative dispute resolution mechanisms be structured in light of this reality? Compare the manner in which New Zealand responded to the family system and needs of the Maori Tribe with the way in which the United States removed Native American children from their tribes and families en masse in the last two centuries. Do you think that Family Group Conferencing might be particularly well-suited in cases involving Native American children, under the Indian Child Welfare Act, in the United States?

---

[7] *See, e.g.,* Dorothy Roberts, *Under-Intervention versus Over-intervention, in* Symposium: *Advocating for Change: the Status & Future of America's Child Welfare System 30 Years After CAPTA,* 3 CARDOZO PUB. L. POL'Y & ETHICS J. 371, April, 2005.

Chapter 5

MEDIATING FINANCIAL ISSUES

A. INTRODUCTION

Family mediators are often called upon to mediate issues concerning the post-dissolution finances of a divorcing couple. Courts tend to view "finances" as a series of related but discreet issues — marital property, alimony, or child support. Mediation gives families the opportunity to take a much more holistic approach to their finances. Where children are involved, this allows parents to focus on what the children's financial needs will be post-divorce, rather than the parents' legal rights to property. It also may promote parties to work collaboratively to build budgets that are designed to permit adults to meet their increased expenses post-separation rather than maximizing financial gain for one or other of the parties under existing legal norms. On the other hand, some mediation scholars have identified the risks of this approach for the financially dependant partner. They argue that legal norms cannot be ignored by mediators when mediating financial disputes. The readings below will address this debate about the mediator's role in mediating financial conflicts. They also provide an example of a mediation involving post-dissolution distribution of marital property and a discussion of alternative approaches to mediating child support.

B. THEORETICAL MODELS FOR MEDIATING FINANCIAL ISSUES

As discussed in preceding Chapters, there is no firm consensus about the "best" approach to mediation. The transformative, facilitative, and evaluative approaches all have their proponents. While many are most comfortable with the facilitative approach in family mediation, many mediation theorists and practitioners endorse using a mixed model to enable parties to reach sound and lasting solutions to their family conflicts. Different issues may also suggest the use of different approaches. In the following excerpt, mediator and law professor Ellen Waldman offers an alternative framework for analyzing and discussing approaches to family mediation. Her discussion of "norm generating, norm educating and norm advocating" models of mediation is analogous to the discussion of different models of mediation. While recognizing that many mediators might employ a variety of approaches in a single case, Professor Waldman suggests that each of these models may be particularly appropriate to particular disputes. She focuses on "norm educating" for mediation of financial issues at divorce. Noting the importance of both social and legal norms to these disputes, she gives mediators "permission" to employ their knowledge of family law to help the parties achieve agreement on financial issues where informing parties about legal entitlements may be important in reaching informed and equitable agreements.

IDENTIFYING THE ROLE OF SOCIAL NORMS IN MEDIATION: A MULTIPLE MODEL APPROACH[1]

48 Hastings L.J. 703, 704, 707–709, 723–32, 738–45, 753, 755–64, 768–69 (1997)

By Ellen A. Waldman

Reports from the field suggest that the "quiet revolution" in dispute settlement continues. The steady growth of mediation supplies persuasive evidence. Once primarily limited to labor-management negotiations and neighborhood disputes, mediation has spread to a wide variety (of settings. Rather than suffer the delays and expense of adversary proceedings, couples pursuing divorce, environmental agencies seeking compliance with governmental regulations, communities embroiled in public policy debates, employers facing discrimination charges, law enforcement agencies handling certain misdemeanors, and other civil disputants, have turned increasingly in recent years toward a "mediated solution." But, at the risk of belaboring the seemingly obvious, what exactly is a "mediated solution?" . . .

This Article proposes a refinement of mediation theory in an effort to clarify discussion and comprehension of the field. It seeks to separate out the variety of processes grouped together as mediation and distinguish them based on their divergent treatment of social norms. It suggests that what passes as mediation today constitutes not one, but three separate models. It terms these models "norm-generating," "norm-educating," and "norm-advocating"respectively. These interventions are similar in that they all employ mediative techniques. However, they differ in their relationship to existing social and legal norms.

The model characterized as "norm-generating" corresponds to traditional notions of mediation, in which disputants are encouraged to generate the norms that will guide the resolution to their dispute. In this model, disputants negotiate without recourse to existing social norms. The models characterized as "norm-educating" and "norm-advocating" constitute more recently evolved paradigms, in which societal norms occupy a significant role in the disputants' negotiations.

This Article contends that drawing a conceptual distinction between these related but separate processes is necessary if mediation theory is to keep pace with actual practice. Although existing classifications fruitfully illuminate certain issues, answers to other increasingly pressing questions remain obscure. As the mediation field moves to assume the insignias of an established profession, it faces a number of challenges. How is mediator education and training to be organized and evaluated? Is licensure or certification necessary to protect the consumer? If so,

---

[1] Copyright ©1997. Reprinted with permission.

how are such programs to be established? What core set of ethical principles should guide mediator behavior?

The existing theoretical framework cannot do the work required to adequately confront these questions. Adherence to an all-encompassing definition of mediation creates confusion within the mediation literature, performance standards, and ethical codes. The tripartite model this Article proposes will help dispel this confusion and will allow for the creation of more useful professional guidelines . . .

The Norm-Educating Process Using Mediative Techniques

A. The Development of Norm-Educating and Norm-Advocating Mediation

As noted earlier, mediation first attained widespread use in this country in labor negotiations and community disputes. The norm-generating model which evolved in these contexts fits comfortably with the subject matter of those disputes. The collective bargaining topics most frequently and successfully handled in mediation involve salary, sick leave, working hours, and other conditions of employment. In these types of conflicts, the bargaining frequently occurs between relative equals. Furthermore, discussions of salary and vacation time, absent extreme and outrageous party demands, do not ordinarily call into play defined social norms or principles. The same can be said where two neighbors are arguing over the volume at which one plays music late at night.

However, once mediation began to play a role in the resolution of divorce, environmental, criminal, and civil rights disputes, critics began to express concern about the process' inability to assimilate and apply social norms to the problems at hand. The opportunity mediation created for parties to dictate the norms that would guide the solution to their dispute began to appear, to some, as a threat to the continued articulation and enforcement of principles that society holds dear.

Feminists, for example, argued that channeling support and custody issues into a process which often excluded lawyers and eschewed "rights-talk" deprived women of the fruits of divorce law reform. Others critiqued the application of mediation to criminal offenses, arguing that Victim-Offender Mediation (VOM) devalues the substantive and procedural norms observed in public prosecutions. The mediation of public policy and environmental disputes sparked similarly framed debates. Who, it was asked, would advance society's interest in preserving scarce resources? Who would protect the rights and entitlements of those not directly involved in the mediation? Viewing mediation as a broadside assault on the rule of law, one observer advised that lawyer-mediators evaluate the fairness of any mediated agreement according to its approximation to the likely adjudicated outcome.

The mediation field responded to these concerns. Disputes surrounding issues where societal norms are clear and compelling may still be mediated. However, what is termed mediation in these specialized areas often constitutes a norm-based process utilizing mediative techniques. . . .

B. A Description of the Norm-Educating Model Using Mediative Techniques

What follows is an example of the norm-educating model applied in a divorce dispute. While the model is now used in a variety of settings, it is perhaps most closely identified with divorce mediation practice.

Dan and Linda had been married 15 years when they decided to divorce. Dan earns $65,000 a year; Linda earns $300 a month as a part-time secretary at the local church. She is resistant to the divorce, but knows she cannot prevent it. They have two daughters, Denise, age three, and Marie, age nine. They have been separated for five months. In that time, Dan has had very little contact with Denise and Marie. To avoid acrimony and expense, Dan and Linda have decided to mediate their divorce.

At the first mediation session, the mediator, Ms. K., provided Dan and Linda detailed information about the goals and assumptions of the mediation process. She showed them a copy of her Rules and Guidelines (Rules) which discuss confidentiality, courtesy, the nonrepresentational, neutral role of the mediator, and the necessity of obtaining outside counsel to review whatever mediated settlement is reached. In addition, the Rules require the parties to refrain from selling marital property or incurring large debts without first obtaining the other's approval. She then inquired briefly about their most pressing issues. She learned that, for Linda, finances presented the most urgent problem, while, for Dan, his scant contact with his children was his greatest concern. After securing from both a commitment to the mediation process, Ms. K. then asked them to independently fill out a six-page questionnaire providing property, income, expenses, and other financial information before meeting for a second session.

Having assessed Dan's concern about not seeing his children as the most urgent, Ms. K. began the next session by suggesting that they begin talking about the children and custody issues. Ms. K. redefined the custody issue by explaining that the discussion was not about who would control the children, but rather an exploration of how both Dan and Linda could continue to be the kind of parents they wished to be. Ms. K. asked Dan and Linda to speak briefly about their hopes and fears about post-divorce parenting and to describe the parenting arrangements throughout the separation. After learning about the ad hoc arrangements that had developed, Ms. K. explained that current psychological data reveals that most couples and children benefit from having a definite exchange schedule. In this way, each family member can plan and be certain about his or her schedule. Ms. K. then drew a twenty-eight box grid on a flipchart, with each box standing for a day of the month, and began to work with Dan and Linda on developing a custody and visitation plan that would accommodate their own, and the children's schedules. The presence in Dan's apartment of Dan's new girlfriend was a sticking point for Linda. However, when Ms. K. reflected back to Linda her resentment toward the woman and probed the lack of connection between the girlfriend's presence and the children's ability to spend quality time with their father, Linda dropped the objection. By the end of the session, they had worked out a temporary schedule for the next month.

At the next session, Ms. K. complimented the couple on reaching agreement concerning the children and suggested moving to the financial issues. Both Dan and Linda listed their income and expenses and constructed a budget of what they needed to survive. Ms. K. pointed out that given their combined income and expenses, the couple as a whole were 786 dollars short each month. Ms. K. suggested that couples generally chose one of four options when facing a shortfall: 1) cutting expenses; 2) increasing income; 3) borrowing from assets; or 4) using tax-planning principles to reduce taxes, thereby yielding more income to meet their needs.

After Dan and Linda explained to each other the basis for some of the expenses listed, they agreed to divide the shortfall equally. Dan did state, however, that the finances would be easier if Linda would get a real job instead of "volunteering" her time at church. Linda expressed interest in developing a more lucrative career, and Ms. K. suggested she give some thought to a plan to increase her earning potential. Dan was asked to obtain detailed information about his pension plan.

At the next session, when Linda began to talk about her financial future, it became clear that schooling was essential. Linda's nursing studies had been interrupted by the marriage, and she now wished to continue those studies. Dan, however, did not want to pay the $4,000 per year tuition. Dan stated that Linda could pay for the tuition and books from her 1/2 share of the $18,000 money market account they planned to divide equally. Linda felt Dan should pay for tuition since she had dropped out of nurse's training in the first year of their marriage to help Dan obtain his M.B.A. degree. When Linda queried Ms. K. if she had a right to a share in Dan's M.B.A. degree, the mediator replied that several courts, particularly New York State Courts, had ruled that a wife had an ownership interest in her husband's medical degree.

As the conversation degenerated into bickering over who had worked harder at the marriage, the mediator interrupted, shifting the focus from the past to the future, from casting blame to solving problems. Ms. K. advised:

I'm quite sure that if I sat here for the next three hours and listened to both of you, I would never be able to figure out all the facts exactly the way they happened. In fact, you didn't hire me to listen to the two of you present evidence about why Linda is now dependent on the marriage for support. I'm sure that each of you would have made very different choices during the last fifteen years had you known you would be sitting in my office today.

Ms. K. then pointed out that Linda and Dan shared a mutual desire to facilitate Linda's economic independence from Dan and suggested they work at brainstorming ways to accomplish that goal. They ultimately agreed that Linda would receive $14,000 from the money market account, and Dan would receive $4,000. Ms. K then wrote up the custody and financial agreements in a memorandum, and sent a copy to Dan and Linda, with copies to their attorneys to file with the court.

Clearly, the model which Ms. K. employed is similar in many ways to the [norm generating] model. Ms. K. proceeded through the standard mediation stages, beginning with an introduction to and explanation of the process, and moving on to story telling, agenda-setting, option-generating, option-selection, and, finally, the concluding agreement writing stage.

In addition, Ms. K. availed herself of the full panoply of mediative techniques displayed in norm generating mediation. She engaged in active listening, reframed issues so as to avoid a win-lose perspective, encouraged empathic understanding of opposing views, separated needs from positions, helped the parties generate and evaluate options according to explicitly articulated criteria, and refocused the parties on the future instead of the past.

Ms. K.'s approach differed from the traditional norm generating approach in her reference to relevant social and legal norms, which she used to provide a baseline framework for discussion of disputed issues. She adverted to these norms twice: first when Dan and Linda were beginning to consider what sort of custody and visitation arrangement to adopt, and, second, when questions arose as to whether Dan should be required to pay Linda some share of her tuition. In the first instance, the mediator educated the parties about existing norms in the child psychology field. In the second, the mediator informed the parties about prevailing legal norms.

Ms. K. did not insist that the parties' agreement implement these norms. It is likely that if Dan and Linda both strongly desired to retain a visitation schedule that was ad hoc and changeable from day-to-day, the mediator would have assisted them in codifying that agreement. Similarly, if Dan and Linda both agreed that Dan's M.B.A. could fairly be excluded from all consideration, the mediator would likely have supported that conclusion, so long as she felt that the parties understood the implications of their decision.

This model, then, is a norm-educating model which utilizes mediative techniques. Contrary to the norm-generating model, where discussion of societal standards is thought to impede autonomy and distract parties from their true needs, this model's consideration of social norms is thought to enhance autonomy by enabling parties to make the most informed decisions possible.

C. Uses of the Norm-Educating Model in Multiple Settings

This model is most visible in the divorce arena. The mid-eighties divorce mediation literature reveals skirmishes between those who thought that divorce mediation should mirror the generic norm-generating model and those who believed that disputants should be educated about the norms encoded in family law. Today the battle has largely subsided. Most commentators agree that a divorce mediator should have some familiarity with family law issues. Descriptions of ongoing programs reveal that the mediator is active in ensuring that disputant negotiations are informed by relevant legal and social norms, either by educating the parties himself or by ensuring that they are educated by retained counsel . . .

D. Identifying Paradigm Case(s) for Use of the Norm-Educating Model

Like the norm-generating model, the norm-educating model is appropriately used in disputes where party autonomy and relational concerns are the preeminent values for consideration. Yet, in these conflicts, unlike in disputes that call for the norm-generating model, application of social or legal norms is possible, conclusive, and relatively compelling. These disputes invoke norms that embody certain societal conclusions about what is just and unjust and confer entitlements on those who might otherwise remain disadvantaged and marginalized in private bargaining. Elsewhere, I have called these norms "protective norms" because they serve to protect one (or both) of the parties from exploitation or abuse. Norms that require payment of permanent spousal support to a nonworking spouse after breakup of a long marriage, or prohibit the firing of an elderly worker solely because of his age could be characterized as protective norms. These standards grant rights to the displaced homemaker or terminated employee and safeguard both from impoverishment and rank injustice. Because these norms are protective in design and effect, it is important that parties be informed of their existence before making decisions which unknowingly dispense with the conferred entitlements.

The fact that a dispute implicates norms of which the parties should be informed does not, however, imply that the parties must adopt or implement them. In disputes calling for the norm-educating model, the parties' interests in reaching settlement, even a settlement that disregards social and legal norms, outweigh whatever societal interest exists in the application of those norms. Disputes in which party interests in settlement subordinate societal interests in norm-enforcement often share certain qualities.

First, the parties approach the mediation with sufficient resources such that their waiver of a legal entitlement does not appear coerced by circumstance. Although the parties may not enjoy equal power, they each possess sufficient competency that a decision to settle for less than the law might award represents a conscious, capable expression of will rather than a capitulation to oppressive conditions.

Second, the resolution of these disputes will primarily affect only the parties or entities at the table. The parties' resolution will not adversely affect third parties absent from the mediation. Equally important, while the dispute calls into play protective norms, they are not implicated so profoundly that their bypass will weaken social bonds and do violence to important public values. In certain contexts, the disregard of a protective norm, such as the antidiscrimination norms embodied in civil rights or gender equality legislation, creates a ripple effect. Far from affecting only the disputants, it places significant strains on the social fabric and casts doubt on the power and influence of the norm and its centrality in American life and institutions. A settlement in which one waitress trades her right to be free of admiring but objectifying comments at work for higher pay is less disturbing from a public policy viewpoint than a class action settlement in which thousands of women workers "agree" to continue to work in an obscene, insulting, and intimidating environment. The norm-educating model is only appropriate in conflicts in which the relevant norms may be disregarded without weakening the ideals upon which our government and legal structure are based.

To further concretize this discussion, consider the custody dispute discussed in Part One. Imagine that both parents are relatively stable, resourceful, and powerful people. Imagine too that the father is threatening to withhold child support from the mother if she does not allow him to take the children five months of the year. In this situation, it is important that both parties be alerted to the legal norms which require noncustodial parents to pay child support, even when they object to existing custody arrangements. This norm protects both the child as well as the custodial parent, usually the mother.

Now, with this information, the mother may agree to the proposed seven-five month split, even though a court might have awarded her primary custody over the children for eleven and a half months of the year, and the same amount of child support being offered by the father. If so, the mother's desire to avoid a judicial proceeding and to settle for "less" than she might have obtained in court should be respected, so long as her decision is not forced or coerced.

Another important consideration involves whether the arrangement is beneficial or harmful to the child, a third party whose interests are unrepresented at the mediation. If norms in the field of child development indicate that such an arrangement would be detrimental to the child, as it would likely be if the child were school age, then arguably the parents should not be allowed to waive the standards established by those norms.

Waiver of legal norms should also be discouraged if the resulting agreement would seriously undermine the norms of gender equality, as it would if the child support payments were so low as to represent an effective abandonment of the mother and child. Arguably, the "divorce revolution" of the last twenty years represents a societal commitment (though not entirely successful) to avoid the impoverishment of women and children following divorce. Private agreements which do injury to this commitment should be discouraged.

If, however, the parties' proposed custody and child support arrangement imperils neither the child nor the mother, and avoids seriously compromising the norms of gender equality, the parties should be permitted and encouraged to adopt and abide by it. Agreements which deviate from the legally determined outcome are permissible and encouraged, so long as the benefit to the parties outweighs any harms created.

The norm-educating model of mediation strikes a compromise between those who would bar discussions of law entirely from mediation practice and those who would outlaw mediation because it strays too far from the normative moorings of our adversary system. It stands for the proposition that the parties should be educated about their legal rights. However, if one or both of the parties decides to waive those rights, the mediator does not object. The norm-educating mediator views the parties, not society, as rightful possessor of the dispute. Consequently, the parties may, if they choose, reach a resolution that does not correspond entirely with societal norms.

This model, then, may be sensibly applied in disputes where the social or legal norms implicated are sufficiently important that the disputants should be made aware of them — but, the position of the parties and the context of the dispute does not demand their enforcement. In other words, the disputant benefited by these norms may waive them, and such waiver is unproblematic, both from the disputant's and society's vantage point.

Although parties under this model may waive their rights and entitlements, such waivers, in the face of complete knowledge, seem less likely to occur and will likely be less dramatic than in the norm-generating mediation model. Moreover, such rights-waivers, if made knowingly, may represent a party's conscious trade-off to obtain an alternate form of satisfaction. In such a situation, the legal right has served as an important bargaining chip, and, to the degree that the legal entitlement has empowered one party to advance claims that she would otherwise be poorly situated to assert, the right has served its purpose; the norm has been effectuated. Thus, if a disgruntled employee, fired after alleging discriminatory treatment by a supervisor, waives her right to sue for wrongful termination in return for reinstatement, back pay, and contrite assurances of more respectful treatment, the legal norm prohibiting retaliatory discharge has, to some degree, been respected.

In some contexts, however, the norm-educating model is insufficiently protective of party and societal interests. This is true when the power imbalance between the parties is so extreme that one party cannot provide a trustworthy waiver, when the institutions administering mediation have a mandate to enforce statutory law, and/ or when the dispute involves public resources or implicates public values in such a profound way that their enforcement outweighs the disputants' interests in achieving settlement. In these instances, a norm-advocating model better suits the task at hand.

III. The Norm-Advocating Process Using Mediative Techniques

A. A Description of the Norm-Advocating Model

The following mediation case illustrates the model I term norm-advocating. It involves an ethical conflict which has arisen in the course of patient care. [Author describes a mediation involving a patient and her physician who wants treatment withheld under circumstances that would violate the hospital's ethical standards and might violate criminal law. The mediation involves the patient and her doctor on one side and various representatives of the hospital on the other and is conducted by a"bioethics mediator."]

In this model, the mediator proceeded through the familiar stages common to the norm-generating and norm-educating models, using a repertoire of standard mediative techniques. In the introduction, she explained the mediation process to the parties. In the story-telling stage, she elicited from each party his or her perception of the relevant facts and issues. Next, she set an agenda, urged the parties to exchange ideas and brainstorm possible solutions, aided the parties in identifying the most realistic and satisfactory options for implementation, and then distilled the common ground reached into a written care plan.

In this process, however, the mediator not only educated the parties about the relevant legal and ethical norms, but also insisted on their incorporation into the agreement. In this sense, her role extended beyond that of an educator; she became, to some degree, a safeguarder of social norms and values. She apprised the parties of relevant social norms, not simply to facilitate the parties' informed decisionmaking and provide a beginning framework for discussion; she provided information about legal and ethical norms to secure their implementation . . .

C. Identifying Paradigm Case(s) for Use of the Norm-Advocating Model

To some, norm-advocating mediation is a contradiction in terms. Yet, its growing use is undeniable. One explanation for this growth is that some disputes will be best resolved through a process which combines the informality of mediation with the reliance on legal and social norms characteristic of adjudication. These disputes often involve interconnected issues, ongoing relationships, and highly-charged disputant emotions. For these reasons, mediation's informal, communication-oriented approach offers clear benefits. However, these conflicts are ill-suited to a norm-generating or even norm-educating approach for one of two reasons. First, the conflict implicates important societal concerns, extending far beyond the parties' individual interests. Second, the conflict only involves the interests of the parties, but one party is so structurally disenfranchised that allowing her to negotiate away legal rights and entitlements would make the mediator complicit in her continued oppression . . .

Where the norm to be applied is sufficiently open-textured that it permits several equally acceptable outcomes, then the mediation shifts to a norm-generating mode. Within the open boundaries that the norm establishes, the parties are free to bring their own interests, concerns, and creative thinking to bear on the problem. Thus, the differences between norm-advocating and norm-generating mediation are not as dramatic as might be originally imagined. The differences may be framed in high relief where the norms to be applied are precise and dictate the parties follow a particular action plan. The differences fade, however, in disputes where the norms to be applied are indeterminate, leaving the parties free to decide precisely how and in what manner those norms will be given content and effect.

The norm-advocating model, then, is applicable in disputes which require application of a normative framework, but present gray areas within that framework for negotiation. It may be argued that a process that limits the options available to the parties to those congruent with pre-existing norms is too constrictive to be called mediation. However, considerable negotiation may take place in the open space which normative guidelines leave uncertain. If the mediator uses mediative techniques to help the parties reach agreement within those regions, that process should be regarded as mediation. To call it something else spawns needless confusion.

IV. Why Recognition of the Three Models — and the Divergent Role Social Norms Play in Each — Matters

As the preceding sections demonstrate, many individual practitioners and institutions utilize either the norm-educating, or norm-advocating models, or some combination. Indeed, in delineating these three models, I do not mean to suggest that they are always, or even usually, used singly. Rather, many mediators will combine these various models, depending on the nature of the dispute. A divorce mediator, for example, may employ a norm-educating model when discussing spousal support and property division. She may shift to a norm-advocating model if the parents contemplate a visitation plan that would place the child at risk. And, she may adhere to a norm-generating model when assisting the parties in how property of only sentimental value should be divided.

Despite the prevalence of the norm-educating and advocating models, academic commentators and practitioners alike tend to conceive of the norm-generating model as the authentic article and recognize the more norm-based procedures, if at all, as aberrant step-children. Both Professor James Alfini, in describing "evaluative"mediation, and Professors Craig McEwen, Nancy Rogers, and Richard Maiman, in depicting Maine's lawyer-dominated divorce mediation program, question whether these procedures represent "real mediation." Scholars and mediators Robert A. Baruch Bush and Joseph P. Folger recognize two distinct mediator orientations which they label transformative and problem-solving. Both of these approaches, however, are based on the norm-generating model. Bush and Folger's 284-page tome on the "promise of mediation" nowhere mentions social norms and their possible place in mediation practice.

In When Talk Works, researchers identified a persistent mediation mythology in which all mediation follows the norm-generating model. According to this mythology, mediators are passive actors, completely neutral with regard to the proposed outcome of the dispute, and unwilling to use social norms to constrain the disputants' settlement autonomy. Although the actual practice of the profiled mediators departed sharply from this theoretical ideal, the mediators nonetheless continued to adhere to the myths as formal virtues. Although the mediators were aware that many of their behaviors undercut and exposed the cleavage between myth and reality, this disjunction did not prompt them to question the myth's validity. This may be, as the researchers suggest, because the "mythic frame . . . gives direction and inspiration amidst uncertainty, isolation, and complexity." A concomitant explanation is simply that the norm-generating model, inspired by a communitarian vision of autonomous, self-actualizing individuals realizing mutual gains while rediscovering community norms, presents an attractive vision. While the vision may not bear a close resemblance to much that transpires in real life, it continues to command strong ideological allegiance.

But, clinging to obsolete phantasms that no longer capture a dynamic reality poses numerous dangers for a burgeoning profession. Here, I will focus on two tasks greatly hindered by the lack of an adequate theory. The first is the establishment and implementation of training and qualification standards for practitioners. The second is the creation of clear and consistent ethics codes.

[Discussion of Ethical Standards and Training omitted]

These discussions suggest that the question of whether substantive knowledge is necessary for a competent mediator can only be answered by "it depends." But this answer makes little sense according to an omnibus theory of mediation that recognizes only the norm-generating model. According to this theory, the mediator need never possess any substantive knowledge surrounding the issues in dispute; her role does not include providing information about or advocating inclusion of social norms.

Recognizing the existence of norm-based as well as norm-generating models explains why mediator familiarity with the issues in dispute may sometimes be necessary. It clarifies that mediators using a norm-generating model need process skills only; mediators using a norm-educating or norm-advocating model, however, must have some familiarity with the relevant social norms in order to employ those models effectively. This insight has implications for programs attempting to determine what sorts of academic or professional background and skills to require. Once a mediation program determines which model or combination of models is best suited to its mix of cases, then it can better fashion appropriate training and performance standards . . .

Conclusion

As the ADR revolution continues, metamorphosis remains the governing state of affairs. Although mediation observers concede that the field is not standing still, recognition of these changes is inchoate. Mediation theory remains oriented towards the traditional norm-generating process, ignoring much of what is actually practiced in the mediation "trenches."

This Article urges a reworking of mediation theory to enhance its descriptive and normative functions. Others have noted that practitioners veer between dichotomous styles. This article suggests we approach these variations by examining the mediator's relationship to, and use (or disuse) of social norms. It describes and presents examples of three separate mediation models — norm-generating, norm-educating, and norm-advocating — and suggests that each of these models may be profitably employed in different dispute contexts. Disentangling various mediation modalities according to this scheme will help explain existing practice, as well as mark the course for future growth and improvement.

The push towards professionalism poses many challenges. Determining how mediators are to be educated, trained, and perhaps certified and regulated, requires precise thinking regarding what mediators do and should do. Further, if mediators, like most professionals, are expected to obtain informed consent to their interventions, they can do so only by providing thoughtful and accurate information about the process. Further discussion and reflection is needed to close the gap between mediation theory and reality. The conceptual vocabulary suggested in this Article offers additional tools to assist in this task.

NOTES AND QUESTIONS

1.   Prof. Waldman offers an alternative framework for classifying approaches to mediation — norm generating, norm educating, and norm advocating. Do her classifications relate, in any way, to the transformative, facilitative, and evaluative approaches discussed earlier?

2.   To the extent "norm educating" and "norm advocating" models have legitimacy in family mediation, does their use suggest changes in the current ad hoc approach to training and qualifications of mediators? If so, what kind of changes? How about changes in mediator ethical standards?

3.   Prof. Waldman argues that mediating different issues — child access, child support, property distribution — requires different approaches to mediation. Do you agree? If so, what approach is best suited to financial mediation? Why?

C. IMPLEMENTING APPROACHES TO MEDIATION OF FINANCIAL ISSUES

1.   Mediating Child Support

Given the widespread use of mediation in child access cases, child support is an issue that is regularly raised in mediation. Unlike child access, however, child support formulae imposed by federal and state law places limits on parties' ability to reach their own agreements on child support. As a result, most mediators use Prof. Waldman's norm-educating or norm-advocating approach when mediating issues of child support. Child support worksheets and child support "calculators" based on state child support formulae are among the mediators' tools. Such formulae tie child support to parental income and result in the payment of a fixed sum from one parent to another usually on a monthly basis. Some mediators have attempted to approach this issue in ways that do not follow the traditional approach. The following excerpt describes one such approach.

IF THEY CAN DO PARENTING PLANS, THEY CAN DO CHILD SUPPORT[2]

33 WM. MITCHELL L. REV. 827, 828–830, 848–854 (2007)

By Stephen K. Erikson

When parents divorce or separate, they encounter the difficult task of determining child support. Since the late 1980s, mediators have been asking divorcing couples to create parenting plans instead of fighting for custody. Similar logic supports the same approach for child support. Such a shift in thinking is necessary today; the rigid application of child support guidelines can create unfair results when applied to individual divorce situations. Many states have implemented deviations from the child support formulas to address the inequities resulting from the use of these guidelines, and when these changes are evaluated as a whole they reveal that an alternate approach is necessary. This article asserts that the implementation of these deviations is necessary because current child support guidelines are based on three flawed assumptions. These deviations attempt to acknowledge and correct these flawed assumptions and, in turn, create a more fair and equitable child support system. Just as parenting plans have evolved to allow families to co-parent after divorce, states should begin to implement Child Support Plan legislation so that divorcing parents can eliminate the need to rely on statutory deviations created by the inherent unfairness in current child support guidelines.

This article examines the current approach to creating and enforcing child support guidelines and suggests a new way to achieve cooperation between divorcing and never-married parents through the use of a "Children's Checkbook" to manage the shared costs of raising the children. The three major flawed assumptions in existing child support guidelines are that the formulas assume that child support (1) must be exchanged between the parents; (2) must be tied to the amount of time a child spends with each parent, without reference to how much each parent actually pays for the child's expenses; and (3) must be a single mathematical formula. Each state has attempted to address these flaws by setting forth situations under which courts may either deviate from a rigid application of the guidelines or by adding on categories of shared expenses.

The fact that most states have created, rely on, and indeed are gradually expanding deviation procedures from statutory child support guidelines marks the beginning of a migration away from rigid formulas towards a greater use of itemizing and sharing certain categories of expenses. For this expanding list of add-ons, the parents must learn how to cooperate when managing how they will pay these expenses jointly. Currently, child support guidelines seem to view shared categories of expenses as only deviations or additions to whatever existing formula is applied. Instead, these deviations should be viewed as the core of a solution, an evolutionary change in child support law moving toward a greater emphasis on cooperation, similar to changes in custody law over the past ten to fifteen years.

More than twenty years of mediation experience demonstrates that parents can more easily and more cooperatively share the costs of raising children in two separate homes by abandoning mathematical child support formulas and reframing

---

the child support question from "how much money" the state requires them to pay or receive to "how they will share the costs" of raising their children in two homes in the future. The change is a logical extension of the movement in many states toward the adoption of parenting plan legislation, where the basic goal is focusing more on generating future cooperation between the parents. Asking a different question, together with using a joint Children's Checkbook to manage the various expenditures made on behalf of the children, creates a process that will provide both cooperative and high-conflict couples with more tools to reach consensus. This approach could dramatically change the way parents resolve the question of child support, just as reframing the child custody question dramatically changed the focus from good parent/bad parent to building parenting plans through the use of mediation — an approach which has resulted in greater flexibility of results and increased perceptions of fairness.

II. Sharing the Cost of Children Using the Children's Checkbook Allows for Creating a Child Support Plan

A. Asking a Different Question that Creates Cooperation

Mediators have long known that there is great power in asking a different question. The form of the question asked influences how the issue or dispute is defined. Professor Morton Deutsch observes that "[c]ontrolling the importance of what is perceived to be at stake in a conflict may be one of the most effective ways of preventing the conflict from taking a destructive course."

Perhaps the reason the Children's Checkbook has been successful with a variety of couples at Erickson Mediation Institute (EMI) is the fact that EMI asks a completely different question than the guidelines. While the guidelines formulas all ask a series of questions about who is the absent or less-time parent, what are the both parents' incomes, and how many children are there, the most important piece of the puzzle is left unasked. The most important piece is asking the parents what they have been spending on their children in the past and what they can afford to spend on them in the future, given the fact that they now must incur the cost of a second household. We must ask the parents how they will share the costs of raising their children in the future. In order to answer this question, we must know who will be paying for what items. Building upon Deutsch's principles, it is possible to take the typical child support question and reframe it from "how much do I have to pay in child support?" to "how can we share the costs of raising our children in the future so that it will be fair to both of us?" Thus, a mutual journey begins.

In the course of answering this question, parents will learn new methods of cooperation. They will also have failures, but they will not view the task as a contest where one side wins and the other side loses. Rather, they will begin to view the journey as a problem that must be solved. This new approach of creating a Child Support Plan welcomes and accounts for the inherent complexities that divorced and never-married parents face: they live in two separate homes, may have differing incomes, spend differing amounts of money on their children, and care for them differing amounts of time. Moreover, building a Child Support Plan acknowledges the need to allow flexibility for parents dealing with the changes in children's expenses, such as increased extracurricular or sporting activities and expenses associated with becoming a teenager . . .

Disputes in family law are poly-centric and do not always fit into neat patterns. . . . [T]the concept [of parenting plans] represents a paradigm shift in family law. "Plan" is a very different word than "award": plan is the future, award is the past; plan is collaborative, award is competitive; plan implies problem-solving, award implies a contest. The help attorneys and courts need to provide for families is to give them the knowledge and the skills to develop their own plans, not to provide "cookie cutter" plans.

To understand why we keep asking the wrong questions, it is helpful to realize that how child support is paid is a factor in limiting our ability to make this necessary paradigm shift in thinking. In order to make this shift, we must acknowledge that there are really three methods for managing child support, not just one. First, child support can be paid from the absent parent to the other, but, second, it can also be paid by buying items directly for the children, or, thirdly, it can be paid by both parents to a checkbook that is then used to buy items or to pay for expenses for the children.

First, as discussed above, the guidelines support model always puts one parent in charge of buying items for the children. This method assumes that because parents cannot live together as husband and wife, they certainly cannot raise their children together. Therefore, one parent must be in charge of the children and their care; after all, one of them is the "absent" or perhaps "more absent" parent. This method appears simple; it is the least complicated and supposedly the least conflict-producing because the parents have no interaction other than money exchanging hands. Because the guidelines say nothing about what items the child support should cover, a complex system of deviations and add-ons has evolved. Moreover, when nothing is said about what the child support covers, the following exchange is typical:

> "Son, I can't possibly buy you that new twelve-speed mountain bike you have been asking for. You'll have to speak with your father, he earns three times as much as I do." (Next time son is with dad) "Son, what is your mother doing with all of the money I send her? She gets $1,321 a month from me in child support. She should use it on you."

The second method of managing child support is for each parent to pay for items directly. Indeed, there is some statutory and case law that recognizes some parts of the Children's Checkbook principle. Parents can pay for items directly or from a checkbook; they will not necessarily always be required to have the obligor send a formulaic amount of money over to the obligee who becomes the supply sergeant because we cannot trust the other parent to cooperate. This method of direct payment of children's expenses is beginning to be used more frequently by those couples who engage in approximately equal time-sharing. In Valento, the court declared that the higher-income parent should send money to the other to help equalize the disparity in incomes. Yet the underlying assumption of the Valento case is that both parents will buy an approximately equal amount of food, clothing, and other items used by the children because the children are with each parent equally. This is also the principle of the new Minnesota Income Shares Child Support Model, effective January 1, 2007 in Minnesota. Under the new statute, there is no child support exchanged when there is equal income and equal time-sharing of the children. But in order for couples to be sure that they are each purchasing about equal amounts of child-related items, it is necessary to have some system of record keeping. One attorney familiar with couples using the checkbook reports that those who do not use a checkbook seem to have more conflict than those couples who use a joint checkbook for paying and managing shared expenses.

This second form of child support, recognized not only in Minnesota but also in other states, is to share certain children's expenses by paying these costs directly and then to adjust, reimburse, or compensate the other for fronting the costs. In the broad scheme of child support formulas, sharing payment for costs such as day care expenses or shared medical support is not the central part of the core formula computation. Paying for these items directly has been seen as add-ons or deviations. With the use of a children's checking account to create a Child Support Plan, all items that are deemed to be shared expenses are paid directly from the checkbook. Either one or both parents uses the checkbook; therefore, a third method is to pay child support to a checking account. The checkbook is then the mechanism for sharing the children's costs, much as several co-owners of a duplex may use one checkbook to track income and expenses of the operation.

B. Child Support Plan and the Children's Checkbook

Although there are a number of forms that a Child Support Plan can take, this article recommends the use of a Children's Checkbook as a tested and successful method of developing a Child Support Plan. . . .

. . . The Children's Checkbook calls for each parent to contribute monthly amounts into a joint account that is then used by each parent to pay for all the agreed upon, or court-ordered, expenses incurred on behalf of the children. It establishes support levels based on the actual needs of each family rather than a one-size-fits-all approach.

Because the amounts placed into the joint Children's Checkbook are tied to the unique and individual budget needs of the children, it allows the children to continue their standard of living as was established during the ongoing marriage. By unhooking the calculation of child support from the custody and/or visitation determination, the checkbook arrangement also solves the problem of trading days for dollars. By using a proportionate contribution (often based upon the gross incomes of the parents), the Children's Checkbook Method can also embrace another principle well established in the law: child support should be based upon the ability to pay, and in those states with an income shares model, upon the abilities of both parents to pay. Finally, and most importantly, the checkbook method enhances cooperation by scheduling periodic reviews of the budget, obviating the need for constant motions to amend.

On balance, this approach does a better job of creating fairness, allows for a simplified method of modification, and creates a written record for the parties of their shared expenses that is automatically tracked through bank statements. All of this results in better compliance and more cooperation, goals that have previously eluded legislators, jurists and commentators of the current system. Because this joint account is shared and managed by both parents, it provides the opportunity to not only create fairness, but also to involve both parents in providing for the children's needs . . .

1. Encourage Cooperation (Mutuality and Ownership of the Decisions)

Greater use of the Children's Checkbook Method will lead to more cooperation and mutuality of ownership of the final result. Child support statutes should require mediation to be the first choice. If mediation fails, the couple can always ask for a judicial ruling. This approach would begin to eliminate unhealthy conflict and positional bargaining arguments so that the child support arrangements are driven more by actual numbers and by family choices, rather than by which interpretation of a formula prevails . . .

Indeed, when parents are asked to jointly create a budget for what they believe they will spend on their children in the next twelve months, they are essentially designing their own deviations each time they decide what they can afford for their children and what they want their children to have. Jim Coogler, the Atlanta attorney widely credited with being the first to create a structured process of divorce mediation, often said to couples in the mediation room, "I want to help you create your own law of fairness." He also found in his early work with couples that when he assigned them a joint task to complete, they would engage in the joint effort and forget about their differences. When couples are engaged in the joint task of discussing fairness, and they are busy determining the amount of money they have to spend on their children, they are building trust and fairness. When couples are in the process of preparing for a temporary hearing, they are more likely to feel as if they are in an adversarial process, and are less likely to recognize that because they are aligned together for the duration of the children's minority, they must find a way to cooperate.

2. Account for Differences in Each Family's Expenditures

Child support statutes should take into account the actual specific costs of child-related expenses (sometimes referred to as 'the needs of the children'), rather than relying upon outdated or generalized national data about the average cost of raising children. In a curious backward way, the courts do take into account the cost needs of the children when a rote application of the guidelines formula to very high-income parents results in unfair and preposterous child support amounts, sometimes referred to as the "three ponies rule." If high-income parents are permitted to argue that the guidelines formulas infringe upon their right to "direct the lifestyle of his or her children," then why shouldn't all parents be permitted, and indeed encouraged, to engage in the same discussion about the level of funding that their children need or require?

3. Account for Who Pays Which Expenses of the Children

In addition to allowing each family to decide for itself the level of child-related expenses, greater use of the Children's Checkbook would also direct which parent pays for which expenses of the children. This approach can take into account differences in housing. In mediation, for example, parties will frequently decide that the one parent should stay in the family home, even though that home is quite expensive and requires a joint sacrifice to be made by both parents. It is doubtful that judges could really "deviate" enough from the guidelines in order to take into account the need for this sacrifice. This is actually a decision that must be made by the parents.

Furthermore, in order to prevent confusion and to lessen conflict, it would be helpful if all couples getting divorced took some time to discuss exactly what items and at what level of costs the recipient of child support should be expected to purchase on behalf of the children. As more and more parents are engaging in equal or near-equal time sharing and as men's and women's incomes reach more equivalency, the checkbook method assists couples in being clear and specific about how they will equally share the costs of raising the minor children.

For almost all parents who experience differing incomes, unequal time with their children, and dissimilar purchasing patterns for their children, allowing parents to clarify spending patterns through the use of the Children's Checkbook would likely reduce the number of post-decree motions to modify child support.

B. Benefits of the Checkbook Model — Desirable Goals that the New Method Accomplishes

1. No More Trading Days for Dollars

The Children's Checkbook Method disconnects the child support calculation from the custody arrangement and the problem of trading days for dollars is eliminated. In other words, it does not matter whether one parent is the visitor or the physical custody parent, or whether the parties are calling their arrangement a shared parenting plan, joint custody, split custody, sole custody, or whether the schedule is 50/50, 60/40, or 80/20 with each parent. The Children's Checkbook Method recognizes that the only expense that is really affected by changes in the schedule is the number of meals provided by each parent (and perhaps in some cases the electricity bill from kids leaving lights on and the water bill because of long showers). Otherwise, all of the other expenses remain constant and can be paid by either parent. It simply becomes a matter of determining who is going to pay for which items needed by the children and what these costs are. When they are paid through a checkbook mechanism, the real discussion can then center on what can be afforded and how much more the higher-income parent should be contributing to these expenses. In most cases where couples successfully use the checkbook method, the parents contribute to the checkbook on a proportional basis according to their gross or net incomes.

2. Both Parents Are Contributing to the Children's Expenses

The Children's Checkbook Method allows for and encourages more participation from both parents and does not allow for a slide back into the totally discretionary situation that the guidelines were determined to avoid. Just as the parenting plan approach adds much more detail to the typical one sentence custody award, the Children's Checkbook Method provides for a more comprehensive approach that also gives parents an easy record to review when modification is needed. When both parents participate in building the support plan, they are more likely to comply with the final agreement because the parents participated in designing the agreement themselves. Use of the checkbook allows for the lower- income parent to fully participate in the purchases of items for the children rather than saying, "You will just have to get that from your mother, she makes more than I do."

3. Mistrust Alleviation

Parents using the Children's Checkbook Method can readily see where the funds are being spent. There is no need to keep track of and exchange receipts because the checkbook automatically records everything for the parents. The whole system is open and transparent to both. As to the obvious concern that one person will use the checkbook approach to control or harass the other parent, many mothers (who will often take on more of the purchasing of items for the children) report that the use of the checkbook "really proves how expensive it is to raise children."

4. Easy Enforceability

Courts could take the posture of the Texas court in Bailey v. Bailey and supervise the use of the checkbook. They could also require parents to retain the checkbook for examination by the court in any dispute. But more likely, if the parents cannot maintain cooperation around the use of the checkbook . . . they will simply discontinue the method and follow the existing child support statutes in force at the time they stop using the checkbook.

5. Self-Modifying

The language used in the application of the Children's Checkbook Method suggests that parents share the total agreed-upon costs of the children through a proportional sharing of the total monthly costs based on gross income. Parents are expected to exchange income verification each year (usually W-2 statements or some other verification mechanism, such as tax returns, are sufficient). As incomes change, the pro rata contribution to the checking account will change.

NOTES AND QUESTIONS

1.   Does the existence of state imposed child support formulae help or hinder the mediation process? What are the policy reasons for adhering to fixed formulae in the mediation context versus allowing parties to make their own agreements regarding the support of their children? Should the law be different if parents agree to pay child support above the guidelines? *See, e.g., Pursley v. Pursely*, 144 S.W. 3d 820, 825 (KY. 2004)

2.   Does the Erickson article accurately describe the law regarding child support? *See, e.g.,* LAURA W. MORGAN, CHILD SUPPORT GUIDELINES: INTERPRETATION AND APPLICATION (1996) (first chapter available at www.supportguidelines.com/book/chap1).

2.   Mediating Marital Property and Alimony

A mediator makes a variety of choices throughout a mediation session depending upon the nature of the dispute. In addition, the choices made in mediation may also be affected by other issues such as the sophistication of the parties and the presence or absence of legal representation. As you read the following excerpt from a divorce mediation involving financial issues, consider the choices made by family mediator and lawyer Gary Friedman.

A GUIDE TO DIVORCE MEDIATION[3]
70–71, 78–101 (1993)
By Gary J. Friedman

I received a call from a man named Martin one afternoon. He said that he and his wife, Claire, were stuck with a disagreement they couldn't resolve and wondered if mediation could help. I told him that the intensity of their disagreement had no bearing on whether or not mediation would be workable, and that the real question was were they willing to work together to find a good solution? Martin immediately wanted to describe their situation, but I cut him off, explaining that the process would have a better chance of working if I heard the facts for the first time when we all met together, since I make it a practice not to begin a relationship with one mediation client alone. Martin seemed put off by my response, but agreed to come in with Claire.

My first impression of Claire was of an articulate, bright, sensitive woman in her late thirties. Though she looked healthy, when she walked across the room she seemed to shuffle. In the last several years, as she would tell me, she had developed headaches that had only been aggravated by medical treatment. She was now so disabled that she could no longer focus her attention for long or perform any strenuous physical activity. She had not worked for the past three years. Before that she had worked for a variety of nonprofit organizations in low-paying administrative positions. Claire still had dreams of becoming an artist but little confidence that she would be able to support herself in that effort. Martin, in his early forties, was a folk singer with enough of a following to keep him busy on weekends. He taught guitar and piano to aspiring musicians during the week.

When I begin a mediation, I usually start by attempting to I find out what brought the couple to mediation. The variety of responses to this simple question still surprises me. Some people want to tell the whole story of what happened in the marriage. Others want to reveal as little as possible. Martin and Claire were willing to give me a little background, but mainly they wanted to get right to "the heart of the problem." They were too anxious to listen carefully to an explanation of the mediation process. While it is essential in the first session to give the parties a sense of how the process works, the nonverbal creation of a warm, open atmosphere is equally important, so I was willing to postpone my explanation. The room is intended to be a place safe enough for people to say what is on their minds and in their feelings, a place where a certain level of trust can develop.

In his opening remarks, Martin got right to the point. He said that he had become increasingly disenchanted with the life he shared with Claire, and eight months before had suddenly left her to live with another woman. Martin was still living with this new woman and Claire had remained in their house. For Claire, just being in the same room with Martin was very stressful. Before we could begin to talk about what mediation was, she needed to say how hard it was for her to be there. Turning her chair toward me and away from Martin, Claire addressed me directly. It was clear that it was difficult for her to look at Martin. It was almost as if she were making an effort to shut him out of the room.

Claire: Martin's leaving was a great shock. I have been working very hard not to be victimized by my situation. I still don't understand what

---

happened. I know that I can play the role of the rejected woman and have everyone feel sorry for me — my friends do. But I don't enjoy being pitied . . .

In explaining the mediation process to Martin and Claire, I compared it to the litigation option, in which each of them would hire a lawyer. Many people automatically compare mediation to going to court, but since only a small percentage of cases are ever heard by a judge, the fairer comparison is to lawyers negotiating a resolution, There are two major differences between mediation and a negotiated settlement: the directness of the communications and the basis of the decisions reached. In negotiation the parties communicate through their lawyers; in mediation they communicate directly. In negotiation the law is the exclusive basis for their decisions; typically, lawyers negotiating with each other refer primarily to their predictions of what a court would do in trying to reach an agreement. In mediation, although the law is consulted, the primary reference points are usually the parties' personal priorities and their sense of fairness . . .

Claire's physical problems compounded her difficulty, arid I knew it would be important that in her desire to get on her own feet she not blind herself to the very real limits on her capabilities. She would have to find her own way without reacting to Martin's demands so much that she lost sight of her own needs.

Martin's motivations for beginning mediation had their own complexities. On one hand, he felt guilty that he had left Claire. On the other, he was anxious to get on with his life and was, with reason, concerned that their case could drag on indefinitely if they went the way of lawyers and courts. Yet he genuinely cared about Claire-that was unmistakable. He didn't like the situation she was in any better than she did. And Martin was vulnerable to losing sight of his own needs in this process, too. Out of his concern for Claire, he could end up in a caretaking position that would keep him from moving forward with his life.

IDENTIFYING THE BASIC DISAGREEMENTS

Two weeks later, they returned for the second session, having gathered their financial information.

> *Claire*: We bought our house three years ago for $90,000 with a down payment of $30,000, most of which came from money I saved before we married. As a result of the increase in real estate values in our area, the house is now worth about $150,000.
>
> *Martin*: There was $10,000 that came from my earnings, and I've been making the mortgage payments since we bought it.
>
> *Mediator*: When was the money for the down payment earned?
>
> *Martin*: Since we've been married.
>
> *Claire*: It's actually hard to say exactly where that money came from. Martin's books are very sloppy. I made some of that money. And even though Martin's been paying the mortgage, I've been taking care of the house.

As we explored this information, it became clear that disagreements over two separate issues had to be resolved: the house and spousal support. The specific questions regarding the house were, when would it be sold, and how would the proceeds be divided? As to support, the question was, how much would Martin pay Claire and for how long? In the middle of the session, I pointed out that the two issues were interrelated and asked them which issue they would like to work on first.

Martin: Well, I'd say the amount of spousal support is pretty well established. I've been paying the monthly mortgage, insurance, property taxes, and loan payments. And I'm willing to do it for a little longer.

Mediator: How do you *see* this issue, Claire?

Claire: I don't want to receive support from Martin any longer than I need to, but everything in my life is up in the air right now, so I don't know how long I'm going to need it.

Mediator: Is the present level of support satisfactory to both of you?

Martin: I don't mind paying what I'm paying. The question is, how long do I have to pay it?

Claire: I agree. I can get along all right with what he is paying now.

Mediator: So for you, Claire, it's hard to answer the question of how long without knowing what will happen with your career, and this depends to some extent on your health, right?

Claire: Right. But I also want to sell the house, so it will depend on that, too-on how much I get and when it sells.

Mediator: What can you tell us about your work plans for the future?

In response to this question, Claire looked at me as if she had just been assaulted, her cheeks flushed, eyes widened, an expression of shock on her face. Martin shot me a knowing glance with a hint of a smile.

Claire: Look, I'm not prying into Martin's life. Why does he get to pry into mine?

Mediator: You're uncomfortable with how we're going about this. How would you like to do it?

Claire: I don't know. I'm just sick to *death* of Martin's persistent questions about my work plans.

Mediator: Since it's you who needs the support, I think you are the one who should be defining your need here. That's why the focus is on you. But this isn't the only way of going about it. It's only Martin's strong desire to get this issue settled now that pushes us to decide the future of support. A court, for example, wouldn't require you to figure out at this point when support should end. In fact, it's probable that a judge would only set a time for review. Then at that time the judge would look at what had happened in the interim to determine whether and when spousal support should end or at least be reduced.

Claire: Listen, I know this man, and if we don't get this settled now, he will make my life miserable. I don't want to go through that.

Mediator: So you feel compelled by Martin to get this all resolved now?

Claire: Yes, but postponing the decision would be easier for me. Maybe I won't need the support for very long. I just can't tell now.

Mediator: This does set up a tension here, because to protect yourself from coming up short in case your life doesn't go as well as you hope, you need to ask for a longer period than you might actually need.

Claire: Oh, this is awful. I just don't know how to do this. [Breaks into tears]

Martin: [Looking pained] I don't either, but I think we have to have more information from you, Claire, in order to figure it out. I have told you before, I think you should talk to a career consultant and I'm willing to pay for it. That would give us a more objective basis for looking at this.

Claire: [Angrily through her tears] I've told you before and I'm going to tell you again. I'm not about to have some jerk who knows nothing about me, my life, or my values tell me what he thinks I should be doing. I've never led my life that way before and I'm not about to start now.

Martin: [Sighing in frustration] You sit there like some kind of queen. You don't have a job. You won't talk about your plans. You won't even see someone who could help you because you have too goddamn much pride.

Claire: [Enraged now] Pride! I lost that when you humiliated me eight months ago.

Mediator: Is this what you want to be talking about?

Martin: Absolutely not. What do you suggest?

Mediator: We can pursue this further to identify your disagreement more sharply and then look at what's behind it. Or we can move to other issues, which could shed some light on this one, and then return to it.

Claire: I'd like to talk about the house.

Martin: Yes, okay. I think we need to agree as to what my share of the house is worth and how I'll get paid if Claire wants to buy me out.

Claire: [Struggling to regain control of herself.] I'd agree to give you about fifteen thousand dollars or about a third of our equity, but I can't give you the money until I sell the house.

Mediator: When do you plan to do that?

Claire: I don't know. I think I might be ready to put it up for sale in the next year, but it would take about a year to sell it.

Martin: [To me] I think you'd better tell her I could force a sale of the house right now *and* receive half of the proceeds.

THE CORE OF THE MATTER

This was a very charged statement. In using the word "force," Martin was at least indirectly threatening Claire with going to court. Why would he do that? People threaten others only when they fear they will not get what they want. So they reach out for a way to exert pressure on the other person. What was it that

Martin was seeing slip through his fingers? My guess was a quick resolution-Martin wanted to get on with his new life.

But a quick fix that didn't account for the uncertainties in Claire's future ran completely counter to Claire's stated goal, which was to extricate herself from the role of victim. To be a victim, one must have a persecutor. If Claire reached an agreement without thinking through her financial future, she could end up feeling victimized by Martin after the divorce. But out of frustration or the fear that he wouldn't get what he wanted, he was trying to pressure her to conform to his desires. Both positions were understandable and each conflicted directly with the other.

Claire's Options: Claire was in a bind, but she had several options. We spent several minutes identifying and assessing each in turn. She could succumb to Martin's pressure and continue to play the victim, giving up her own needs. Only one benefit could come from this: She could feel free to blame Martin and anybody else who supported him-including me-for her failure to move on.

A second option would be for Claire to disregard Martin's desires entirely and flatly deny him what he wanted. This route had two possible outcomes: a stalemate, or Martin's concession to Claire out of guilt, fear, or frustration. With either possibility, Claire would be breaking out of her role as Martin's victim.

But neither alternative was actually in Claire's best interest. A stalemate would be counterproductive. On the other hand, if Martin agreed to her demand, she could discover that the result was not what she wanted at all, but rather an expression of her desire to keep Martin from getting what he wanted. Blocking his progress might give her a sense of power and increase her self-esteem, which would be preferable to her remaining a victim. Still, it would leave both of them unsatisfied in the long run. And in effect it would prove to be completely without value, for in operating in reaction to Martin, Claire would still be controlled by him.

A third option was for Claire to figure out what she wanted and assert her desires. Then, not only would she be likely to emerge from the process with more strength and a clearer idea of her direction, but she would have less reason to oppose Martin in his efforts to achieve his own goals. This choice would give Claire the chance to exert her power, but in a different way than a fight would do. Most of us make significant life decisions in conformity with or reaction to what others expect us to do rather than going through the difficult, confusing, and lonely process of deciding what we *really* want for ourselves. To reach that point is to feel the strength of true self-knowledge arid self-determination.

Martin's dilemma: Though Martin's suffering did not approximate Claire's, he too was trapped by the victim-oppressor pattern. *As* long as he wanted to exert control over her, he was playing into the problem. And his life was also on hold until hers straightened out. But while Claire seemed to have a pretty clear picture of their pattern of relating-she was seeing a therapist at the time, which undoubtedly helped her gain some clarity-Martin seemed much less aware of or interested in it. Claire seemed to see that the pain of aloneness could be a chamber through which she could pass to a new sense of herself. But without feeling distress analogous to Claire's that would motivate him to observe his pattern carefully and commit to the hard work of change, Martin was in danger of simply gliding into a new version of his old life.

MEDIATION AND THE LAW

As mediator, I had a delicate task to perform. Martin's last remark"I think you'd better tell her I could force a sale of the house right now" opened two central issues that had been waiting to rear their heads: my own role in the mediation process, and the role of the law. The understanding between us from the beginning was that I would remain neutral regarding their final agreement unless what they decided seemed so unfair to me that I could not in good conscience draw up the contract. Under no circumstances would I serve as an advocate for either party. If either of them found they needed the protection of an advocate, then it would be better for them to leave mediation and hire a lawyer to carry on negotiations. Still, as a human being, I could not honestly call myself a detached witness. My main role in sorting through the options and proceeding toward an agreement was to monitor the process with respect to *fairness*.

I already knew I could not let Claire agree to her first option, acceding to all of Martin's demands. That such an agreement would be unfair was as obvious to Claire as to myself. To be fair, the agreement these two finally reached would have to permit Claire to decide on and execute her plans for her life.

The agreement would also have to be measured against the law. Part of my job was to predict what the law would decide in their case so they could use that as a reference point in making their own decisions. Not only do the parties need to understand the legal context of the decisions that they are making for practical reasons, but they can also use it to develop and articulate their own sense of justice.

But the law is more than just a reference point in the mediation process. By continuing to mediate, the parties are implicitly deciding, sometimes from moment to moment, not to turn the case over to their lawyers. And throughout mediation, their understanding of the law and their decision to depart from it can be an empowering experience. But the option to stop and turn to lawyers is always present.

The trick for the mediator is to find a way to bring the law into the process without intimidating the parties into giving up their personal sense of how to resolve their dispute. I do this by trying to educate them about not merely the court decision in their case, but also the principles that would inform that decision. In that way they can measure their own sense of what's fair against the principles of justice that inform the law and society's sense of what's at stake in their dispute. I act as a neutral friend who happens to understand how a court would view their situation.

One hitch makes this job difficult for me: The law often is much less clear-cut and much more subjective than most people recognize. Judges base their decisions on their *interpretations* of the law, and lawyers can never be sure what a judge will do in a particular situation. All I could hope to give Claire and Martin was a neutral but educated guess as to how a judge would decide their conflict over the sale of their house.

This would be very delicate. As I interpreted the law, I would have to watch myself for any tendency to favor Claire in an effort to help her feel more powerful. On the other hand, I didn't want her to feel coerced by the law into going along with Martin-and thus betraying her own sense of fairness. Then we would have a double whammy to fight: her tendency to feel as if she always had to give in, and her inevitable conclusion that her personal sense of justice was in conflict with the law, a bitter notion that could weaken her further. If this happened, I would probably terminate the mediation as it would clearly be leading to a destructive end.

So it was imperative that I remain neutral in delivering the law to Claire and Martin when in fact I wasn't neutral at all. I was very much against a destructive outcome.

THE FATE OF THE HOUSE

I stepped into the mine field opened by Martin's threatening invocation of the law this way.

Mediator: So you'd like to talk about how a court would look at your situation?

Martin: At least as far as the house is concerned, I think Claire should know that I'm being very generous.

Mediator: How about you, Claire? Do you want to talk about the law now or would you rather wait until later? It's important to me that we have that discussion at some point, but only when both of you are ready.

Claire: Frankly, I'm not much interested in hearing about — the law at all.

Mediator: How come?

Claire: You said that the two of us will decide things here. We're not in court, at least not yet. If we go to court, the I'll hear plenty about the law.

Mediator: So you'd prefer not to know the law at all.

Claire: I suppose we need to hear it at some point. You did say that the agreement would not be legally solid unless we knew what the law was. Do you think we should hear it now?

Mediator: What's important to me in doing this at any time is that regardless of what the law says, neither of you gives up your sense of what's fair. And you also need to know that although I'll give you my best opinion, there is some uncertainty in the law, so I could be wrong. That's another reason why you shouldn't defer to my opinion if it differs from what seems right to you. So knowing that, do you want to hear it now?

Claire: Yes.

Martin: All I want Claire to know is that I could force a sale of the house now and get half of the proceeds.

Mediator: That's not my opinion of what the court would do. First, the question of *when* a court would order the sale would depend upon when your case came to trial, and in this county it would take at least nine months before a judge would likely hear it. It is true that at that point you could force a sale, but only if Claire couldn't make an offer to buy your share that the judge considered fair. *As* for the rest of it, it is not at all clear that a court would order the proceeds to be divided equally.

Martin: Yeah? Well, read this.

Martin pulled out of his papers a photocopy of a very recent California Supreme Court decision. I usually know the updates in the law before my clients do, but this time I was caught short. I read the published opinion carefully. The California Supreme Court had decided in a case similar to Martin and Claire's that the proceeds of the house should be equally divided when both parties had purchased the house as joint tenants even when some of the down payment came from one of the parties' alone. Martin and Claire had bought their house in this way, with $20,000 of the down payment coming from Claire's pre-marriage savings. On the surface, it seemed as if Martin was right. But as I read further and reflected, I saw substantial differences between the two cases.

> *Mediator*: Let me try to explain. For the last several years the courts here have been trying to clarify the question of how to treat a family residence when people divorce and the house is in both names. A few years ago, the law was clear. Unless you had an understanding or agreement to the contrary, if the house was in both names, you each would get half regardless of where the money came from to purchase it.

> But a couple of years ago, the legislature decided that that law was unfair and changed it to read that upon the sale of the house each of you should be reimbursed any separate money you put in for the down payment or into improvements before dividing the rest of the proceeds. Still, it's not altogether clear whether that law would be applied in your case, because at least one court has decided that this reimbursement law might violate the guarantee in the United States Constitution that no one's property can be taken from them without due process of law. Since that challenge, the courts have been distinguishing between houses bought before and after the reimbursement law was passed, using the purchase date to determine whether the new law will be applied. Since your house was bought after the reimbursement law was passed, Claire would probably be entitled to be reimbursed for her contribution. The published opinion you brought in, Martin, was based on a purchase date that preceded the reimbursement law. So reading this opinion doesn't change my mind that the reimbursement law would be applied to your situation. Before either of you reacts to what I have said, do you both understand?

> *Claire*: More or less. I've never had a lot of respect for the law, and seeing it flip-flop like that tells me that nobody has a very clear sense of what's right. So it doesn't seem very relevant to me.

> *Martin*: You've explained the law as *you* understand it, but I was given this opinion by a lawyer who told me that this was the law. So who am I supposed to believe?

> *Mediator*: That question goes right to the heart of mediation. Trust yourself after listening to everyone. Does it seem to you that what I'm saying makes more sense or less sense than what the lawyer said in interpreting the case you brought in?

> *Martin*: Frankly, neither of you make much sense to me.

> *Mediator*: What part of what I said doesn't make sense?

> *Martin*: Why would it make any difference when the property was bought?

Mediator: If you bought the property before the reimbursement law passed, you would be entitled to half of the property. But in passing the law, the legislature would, in effect, be taking away some of your property without giving you a chance to fight it. And the Constitution doesn't permit that. That's what the challenge to the reimbursement law says.

Martin: So if we bought the property in 1983 instead of 1985, then I'd be entitled to more, is that what you're saying? So the legislature took away money from me by passing the law.

Mediator: Yes, but they actually passed the law before you bought the property. So at least theoretically, if you had known the law at the time, to protect your half interest, you would have known that you had to enter into a different kind of arrangement.

Martin: But I didn't know we were going to get a divorce.

Claire: And if you had, you probably would have gotten me to sign a paper giving you half.

Martin: That's not the point.

Claire: What *is* the point here? Do you really think you're entitled to half the value of the property after I put in most of the down payment?

Martin: I never said I thought it was *right* that I get half. I only wanted you to know I was trying to be easier on you by not insisting on my legal rights.

Claire: Look, I don't need you to try to go easy on me. I just want what's fair.

Martin: Then don't put me in the position of having to support you endlessly. I want an end to this and I want it decided now.

We'd hit bedrock — support was the issue that lay under the matter of the house. However support was resolved, the house would fall into place.

THE QUESTION OF SUPPORT

Mediator: Do you want me to explain how the court would decide support?

Martin: This is the most important part to me. I don't care what the law says.

Claire: But we have to find out sometime. I am interested in knowing how long support would go on.

Mediator: If push came to shove and you decided that you *couldn't* decide at this point how long support should go on, there's little or no chance a court would decide now when support would end. The very thing that concerns you, Claire-the uncertainty of your future, particularly your work life and your health-would also concern a court. So a judge would be sure to order temporary support now and would probably set a time for that decision to be reviewed.

Martin: [Agitated] Hey, Gary, I thought you were supposed to be neutral. It seems to me you're aligning yourself with Claire, and I don't like it.

Mediator: I'm sorry you feel that way. But what I am trying to do is what I think you both asked for — to give you as clear an indication as I can about how the law would apply to your situation. I don't want either of you agreeing to something without understanding the legal context of the decision. I'm also trying to ensure that neither of you feels pushed into a decision you could regret.

Martin: Good luck, because I'm going to regret any decision that doesn't settle everything *right now.*

Mediator: That's clear enough to me. And if Claire agrees to that, too, then there will be no problem. But if Claire doesn't want that, it's important that both of you realize that on the issue of support, she has the legal power to put off deciding the question. You could get a court to decide the question of the amount of temporary support almost immediately, but not the termination date.

Martin: I think that stinks.

Mediator: How come?

Martin: Because we don't have kids. There's no reason in the world we should have to continue to be bound together financially. I need to know when I can quit sending Claire money, and I need to know it *soon.*

Martin had nailed it. In the matter of support, I was once more in danger of becoming Claire's advocate. Martin already felt alienated. The only thing worse would be if Claire began to perceive me as her advocate and fell back into a passive role, leaving me to deal with Martin. For me to play Claire's advocate would be implicitly suggesting that she was too weak to protect herself and robbing her of the chance to stand up for herself against Martin, thus sabotaging the whole mediation process.

Yet there was also the opposite danger that Claire would continue to play the victim by capitulating to Martin's wishes. That could spell disaster not only for Claire but for Martin as well: If she caved in now, she could go to court later to have the mediated agreement overturned on the grounds that she had been unaware of her legal rights or pressured into the agreement at the time. I realized that although it was necessary for both to understand Claire's legal rights, by emphasizing what a court would do, I might be inadvertently encouraging them to view such a conclusion as the "right" one, even if neither saw it as the best.

To add one further twist, if my effort to ensure that Claire understood her legal rights resulted in her agreeing not to exercise those rights, then the conversation we were having now would probably jeopardize the possibility of her chances of having the agreement overturned at a later date. From that perspective, it could be said that what I was doing now was more in Martin's interests than Claire's.

This kind of step-by-step analysis is absolutely imperative to my remaining in the middle. With the momentum of the conflict constantly propelling the two disputants toward confrontation, an important part of my role is to define the disagreement precisely. The delicate part is remaining objective while still being empathetic enough that both parties feel I understand them and care about what happens.

Deciding whether a person whose position is favored by the law is personally strong enough to stand up for his or her position in the mediation process is one of the most difficult assessments I need to make. With Martin and Claire, I was concerned about Claire's victim history and the very real obstacles she would face in her effort to become self-supporting. Her way out of the victimization pattern would be to articulate her needs for support precisely. It was essential that if she agreed to a termination date for spousal support she do it because it felt right to her and not because she was intimidated by or wanted to conciliate Martin. It was equally important that the date, if she gave one, be realistic, and that she would be able to manage or have contingent plans for surviving financially after support ended. I certainly did not want to be an agent of Claire's self-destruction.

For Claire to independently agree on a realistic date for termination of support could be an extraordinarily liberating and powerful act, a way of declaring her own independence and autonomy. So it might well be in her own best interests to do the very thing that Martin wanted her to do. I hoped that by my injecting the law, Claire would feel enough power to decide how much money she could realistically expect to earn and when she could become self-supporting.

Although it was not clear to Martin yet, the worst thing that could happen at this point would be for Claire to succumb to his pressure on a termination date and thus remain dependent not only in her own eyes but in the eyes of a judge. That would keep both of them locked into their old pattern. The key to Claire's liberation would be Claire herself, and that is why it was so important for me to avoid a position where I was perceived as her advocate. Turning the spotlight on Claire was what we all needed to create the hoped-for balance between us.

Mediator: [To Claire] What is your view of this?

Claire: Frankly, I have mixed feelings. I know that if I don't agree to a specific date I'll pay the price of Martin's resentment. I don't want that. I know that we'll probably not be friends, and I'm not sure I would want that even if Martin did. But I sure don't want him to get any angrier.

But I also think that it would be helpful to me to be able to cut the cord that connects me to him. I need to do that for my *own* good. I don't *want* Martin to take care of me-he was never particularly good at it anyhow, and it's not really worth it to me to have to count on him. He'd always be hassling me about getting a job or a better job. I know that whatever I decided to do wouldn't be good enough for him, and I don't want to have to answer to him any more in my life. I've had enough of that. Still, I have to be sure that I'm going to be able to make it financially. And I just don't know what's going to happen in that regard. Some days I think I can do it. Others I feel lucky to be able to get out of bed.

Mediator: So what you would like is to have enough support from Martin to get you through this transition. It would make sense, I think, to look at various possibilities of what might happen: What's the worst that could happen to you? What's the best?

Claire: I'm not sure I want to do that. What I know is that I'll probably sell the house within the next year and buy a smaller place. I'll have to pay some taxes if I do that, but it would still give me some cash. If I knew I could count on the money from the house sale and have help from Martin *until* it sold, well-I guess I'd probably be willing to give up support beyond that point.

Martin: [Bursting out] That would leave me with nothing!

Claire: No, you'd still have your health, your business, and your relationship with what's-her-name. And that's a hell of a lot more than I can say for myself.

Martin: I wouldn't even get back the money that I've put into the house. And I've been paying the mortgage since we bought it.

Claire: I know that, but look; you say you want me to be financially independent. If you really don't want me knocking on your door, you have to give me a head start.

Martin: I'd be totally screwing myself if I agreed to this.

Mediator: How so?

Martin: The house is the only asset I have in the world outside of my paycheck. I don't even have any money in savings. Besides, she'd never get anything like this in court.

Mediator: That's true. And you wouldn't get the termination date. I think from your point of view, Martin, the question is really how important it is to you to get a termination date. I imagine that neither prospect at the moment is appealing: giving up your whole nest egg or paying out support indefinitely.

Martin: You're damn right.

Mediator: But you might consider that there are some real advantages to you in Claire's proposal. I would suggest that you sit with it a bit before you decide.

We ended the session on that note. Martin's impatience and sense of urgency were signals to slow down the process. I was afraid that he might now make a decision that he would later regret, so I was glad that our time was up before he had an opportunity to decide. When the parties are moving quickly toward a solution, my function often is to slow things down. If people have an opportunity to deliberate, their feelings frequently shift. Time is an important test of the solidity of a decision. I was not surprised when Martin came into the next session with a variation on Claire's proposal.

Martin: Here is what I am willing to do. I'll give up all of my interest in the house if you give up support. And I'll lend you $750 a month between now and when the house sells, if you pay me back with interest out of the sale proceeds.

Claire: Hell, no! I'm not about to pay you a dime of interest. You're not a bank. And *no*, I don't like the idea of the support money being a loan.

Mediator: Why doesn't this seem fair to you?

Claire: Damn it, he's acting as if we were never married.

Martin: What do you mean? I don't go around giving away my property, everything I have, to my business associates, you know. Giving up my share of the house is a huge concession. It's $45,000. [This was based on the house's present value of $150,000, reduced by closing costs and the mortgage balance of $60,000, divided by two.]

Claire: [Slowly] It's actually more like $25,000, if we followed the law. And I assume I'll be paying the taxes on the gain. That could cost $15,000. I do appreciate your being willing to give up your interest in the house, but making the other money a loan with interest feels awful.

Martin: Then get the money someplace else. [Long silence] Okay, look. I'll give you the $750 a month without interest, if that will make you feel better, but I want that money back. I've already been paying you for the past eight months.

Claire: Okay. [Strongly] But we'll only make the loan retroactive to four months ago and I want you to get all of your stuff out of the house within the next week.

Martin: Consider it done.

Claire: And I don't want *her* coming over to help you, either!

Martin: Yeah, all right.

DOUBLE CHECK

Claire got up and walked over to the window with her back to both of us. Martin seemed to sink deeper into his seat and breathed a sigh of relief. They had an agreement, but I still wasn't sure if it was mutually fair or realistic. I needed to find out.

Mediator: We need to be sure that this agreement is going to work for both of you, not just now but in the long run. So I need to ask you some questions to check that out. My main concerns are with you, Claire. [Claire shot me a look as if I were intruding on her.] What happens to you if your life doesn't work out as you hope? What happens if you don't get better, or if you get worse?

Claire: I'm not worried about the medical bills. They're covered by my insurance.

Mediator: But how will you pay your expenses?

Claire: I don't know. I guess I'll be okay until the house sells with Martin lending me the money. And then when the house sells, I'll have that money to live on. That will be at least fifty or sixty thousand dollars after I pay Martin back and pay taxes, the mortgage balance, commissions, and closing costs. And after that, I don't know. I might rent a house for a while or buy a smaller place. I guess I don't think that should be Martin's problem. But I'd still feel better if the money he gives me until the house sells isn't a loan.

Martin: It has to be a loan to give you incentive to sell the House quickly.

Claire: [Snapping] You back off. It's hard enough dealing with Gary's questions.

Mediator: And what happens if you can't sell the house for a long time? Or if you run through the house sale proceeds before you get a job?

Claire: I don't think that'll happen, but if it does, I don't think Martin should have to help me just because he's obligated to.

Mediator: Do you think he would help you if he weren't obligated?

Claire: Maybe, but it's not healthy for me to think that way. I need to think positively. I know what you're getting at, but I think that what he proposes, but without the interest, is reasonable. I think it'll work.

Mediator: You sound only half-convinced.

Claire: Maybe sixty percent.

Mediator: Is that enough to make an agreement?

Claire: Yes, I think it is.

Mediator: That's going to feel better or worse in the few weeks between now and when you sign the agreement. I don't want you to sign it if it feels worse, or even if it doesn't feel better.

Martin: What about me? I'm giving up all my property.

Mediator: I think that when you have this agreement reviewed by your lawyer, that person will advise you that you've probably done better financially than if you were *to* go to court. Under a judge's decision, your obligation to pay support would be open-ended and Claire would also be entitled to half of the value of your business, whatever that amounted to. Since you don't have any savings to fall back on in case you get sick and can't work, this is a big consideration. It's also true that if Claire were to remarry quickly, then from an economic standpoint you'd have paid more than you are legally obligated because support would end upon her remarriage.

Martin: That's right. And I've been paying the mortgage since we separated. Except for the mortgage, we're now debt-free. And-I didn't mention this earlier because I didn't want to ruffle Claire's feathers-but if she gets into trouble, her mother would help her out.

Claire: I told you to *back off*. You know how hard she is to deal with. If that's what you need to say to yourself to assuage your guilt about what you've done to me, then say it, but it's not true. My mother doesn't have the money to support me, and she wouldn't do it even if she had it.

Mediator: [To Martin] *As I* implied, Claire's lawyer is probably going to discourage her more strongly from accepting these terms than yours will you.

Martin: That would ruin all the work we've done to get to this point.

Claire: I know it. Martin, I know I'll stick to this agreement if you agree that I don't have to repay you the money you are lending me.

Martin: I won't do that. It's too open-ended, and I need to get something out of the house sale.

Claire: All right. I guess I'll go along with it.

Was this the victim operating again? How did Claire really feel about the agreement? I wasn't sure. Sometimes she seemed to be solidly advocating her position, and other times, not. It was a borderline situation for me. Whether I would draw it up was my next decision-I had been clear from the beginning that I would not draw up an agreement that I felt was unconscionable.

On the one hand, it seemed that Martin had won. Claire had given up support-so in the one area they disagreed upon most strongly, she had given in. On the other hand, she would be getting at least $25,000 to $30,000 or more in exchange for the right to any support and whatever interest she would have had in Martin's business. She undoubtedly would have gotten more money if she had had a lawyer negotiate for her, or at least the security of knowing that she could look to Martin for support, but she would be free of any scrutiny of her life by a judge or Martin. It also appeared to me that during the process, she had moved away from her place of victimization and toward a position of strength. If her health held out and she landed on her feet, I concluded, this would work well. If not, she could end up regretting this agreement. I didn't know whether we were finished or not, but drew up the agreement feeling that this was not so unfair that I would inject my opinion. And it was clear to me that they both understood what they were doing. It had taken us four sessions to reach this point.

When I sent Claire and Martin each a draft of the agreement to review with their consulting lawyers, and they sent me back copies marked up with minor changes, Claire enclosed a note saying that she was relieved it was over and that the agreement felt right to her, even though she felt under pressure to sell the house quickly. Her lawyer did not support the agreement, but that hadn't changed her willingness to commit to it.

A few months later, I ran into Claire. She looked wonderful, happy, and healthy. When she saw me, she came right over. "It all worked out well," she said. "Selling the house felt like getting rid of a great burden, and I never would have done it if I hadn't had to. As it turned out, the week after we signed the agreement, I got an offer on the house for $15,000 more than we thought it was worth, so I didn't have to borrow any more money from Martin. And I found a job designing greeting cards. It gives me a chance to be creative, the hours are flexible, and the pay's not bad." Then, looking at me, she winked. "And you know, my headaches have almost gone away."

NOTES AND QUESTIONS

1. Which approach or mix of approaches did mediator Gary Friedman use in the "Claire and Martin" mediation? Are these examples of transformative, facilitative, or evaluative mediation? How about examples of norm generating, norm educating, or norm advocating? Was the mediator's approach(es) "appropriate" and "effective" given the circumstances of these parties?

Chapter 6

LEGAL REGULATION OF FAMILY MEDIATION

A. INTRODUCTION

The flexibility of mediation is in stark contrast to the procedural, substantive, and evidentiary boundaries of litigation. This is not to say that legal regulation does not have an impact on the conduct and framework for mediation. To the contrary, the interaction between law and family mediation can be subtle, complex, and profound.

This Chapter will explore an aspect of this large issue: in what ways is family mediation regulated by legislatures, court rules, and judicial decision-making?

B. COURT-CONNECTED MEDIATION

In the last two decades, nearly every state has enacted statutes or rules establishing court-connected mediation of family disputes. In designing these programs, each state or jurisdiction has to resolve a number of issues:

a. Which categories of cases will be referred for mediation;
b. Whether the statute provides for exceptions of cases within these categories when certain facts are present in a case;
c. Whether courts will mandate all cases for mediation, whether they have discretion to determine whether mediation will be ordered in a particular case, or whether mediation occurs only by consent of the parties;
d. Who will pay for mediation.

The first reading describes how one jurisdiction — California — resolved these issues and highlights some of the challenges faced in public sector mediation. The chart that follows the reading provides an overview of family mediation statutes throughout the country. As you learn more about California's family mediation program and other family mediation statutory schemes, think about the choices they make on issues such as case selection, voluntariness, and costs, and consider whether these choices impede or facilitate the goals of family mediation.

HISTORICAL CONTEXT FOR COURT-CONNECTED MANDATORY FAMILY MEDIATION[1]

From DIVORCE AND FAMILY MEDIATION 399–400, 404, 406–414 (Jay Folberg, Ann L. Milne & Peter Salem, Eds.) (2004)
By Isolina Ricci

[Mandatory Mediation]

. . . A court-based family mediator in a mandatory program has the opportunity to work with a broad client base representing a wide range of issues and circumstances. Court mediation clients can include parents who were never married to one another, stepparents, grandparents, guardians, as well as currently married and formerly married parents. In California, a state where no ethnic group is in the majority, court mediation clients come from many different ethnic, cultural, economic, and educational backgrounds . . . Non-Hispanic white clients are in the minority, and a significant number of clients do not speak English. The court mediation staff, however, is predominately non-Hispanic white and speaks only English. Unfortunately, certified interpreters for family court are often in short supply.

Custody and visitation disputes are often embedded in families' difficulties with their environment and with personal and interpersonal functioning. These nonlegal issues often need to be addressed in mediation in parallel with the legal issues, in order to aid the family in developing a better environment for child rearing. Research on families using court-based mediation in California identifies the many challenges faced by these parents and their children.

- In 44% of the families, there was either a current or a previous domestic violence restraining order.
- In 41% of the families, children have witnessed violence in their homes.
- In 67% of the families, parents expressed serious concerns about their children's well being, especially their emotional adjustment.
- In 39% of the families, parents raised concerns over their children's safety.
- In 25% of all cases, families had been investigated by Child Protective Services at one time.
- In 59% of the mediation sessions, one or more serious issues were raised, including domestic violence, substance and alcohol abuse, maligning the other parent, harassing the other parent, and stalking (Center for Families, 1996, 2001a).

A court mediator, therefore, must be skilled in assessing the family's circumstances as well as addressing allegations and counter allegations by mediation clients about illegal or dangerous behavior . . .

When mediation is court based or court connected, the standards of practice for mediation extend beyond mediators and mediation participants to include the court

---

[1] Copyright ©2004. Reprinted with permission.

itself. Courts, rather than their mediators, are now ultimately responsible for the quality and scope of their mediation programs and the competency of their mediators. A mandate that requires mediation carries with it an obligation for accessibility and consistency of service across jurisdictions. The history and customs of a jurisdiction or an individual court, while important, should not override the intentions of statewide statutes or standards. Furthermore, since mediation as a discipline differs from that of court management as well as that of the bench, there are often competing principles at work. Mediation requires adequate preparation and time for deliberations and negotiations. The principles of court management, in contrast, may emphasize efficiency and a speedy case resolution. Standards of practice are therefore necessary to clearly articulate principles and boundaries for mediation that will cut across the different disciplines by setting requirements for the court as well as for the mediators. Hence, statutes, rules of court, and codes of ethics for the conduct of mandatory programs and for the certification of mediators may become quite detailed.

*   *   *

When mediation is mandatory and court based, its purpose may be defined in a court rule as well as in statute. In California, the purpose of mediation is more than the facilitation of a self-determined agreement on child custody or visitation. It is marked by a focus on the child's "best interests," a term that is defined by law. The California standards of practice, which extrapolate on the law, provide an extensive list of expectations for the active involvement of the mediator. For example, although mediators are expected to assist the parties in developing a written parenting plan without injecting any undue influence or personal bias in the discourse, the mediator's role (as defined below) may become directive, even in a "confidential" model. The California court-based mediator is expected to facilitate the development of a parenting plan that "protects the health, safety, welfare and best interest of the child and that optimizes the child's relationship with each party." The mediator is charged with aiding the parties to create an agreement that addresses each child's current and future developmental needs. This agreement should ensure the child's frequent and continuing contact with both parents, as long as this arrangement is in the best interests of the child.

. . . In addition to issues of custody and access, the mediator's role is to facilitate the family's transition and to reduce acrimony that may exist between the parties by helping them improve their communication skills. The mediator is directed to focus on the child's needs and areas of stability, to aid the family to identify its strengths, and to refer, when needed, to local counseling or other services.

. . . Most mandatory statewide programs provide court-based mediators or have panels or lists of court approved private mediators that meet the state's formal qualifications and certification requirements. Litigants in some states are required to pay either for court-connected or private mediation services, unless payment would pose a hardship. California law, on the other hand, requires the courts to provide mediators free of charge.

State law may limit the scope of court-based mediation to issues of custody, visitation, and other issues that pertain solely to children and parenting. Private mediators, in contrast, may have the flexibility and freedom to mediate all issues, unless the court has referred a case to them for a specific reason. Court-connected mediators or other certified private mediators must usually meet pertinent statutory requirements and standards of practice, including those for eligibility, education, experience, supervision, ongoing training, and continuing education in specified areas.

Many states do not have formal criteria for private-sector mediators, even those who receive referrals from the court. In these states, a private mediator may choose to meet all of the same requirements as a court mediator but is not bound to do so. If unschooled in what to expect in mediation, a potential client may not be aware of what constitutes a competent mediator, whether or not certification or qualifications are required, or what they have a right to expect from the mediation process. Clients, then, must rely on the training and experience of the private-sector mediator they select and on the accuracy of the orientation, education, or information they are given regarding mediation.

Unlike court-based mediators, private mediators are not usually supervised. They rarely are subject to formal performance reviews or disciplinary action but may sometimes have actions taken against them by clients who attempt to sue or file complaints with their licensing boards. It is important to note that for a private practitioner there is no built-in economic incentive to provide efficient services, especially when a couple has generous financial resources. Couples unaware of the terms of the state or local mandate may not question attending regular mediation sessions for 6 or 8 months, assuming that long-term negotiations are expected by the state mandate. Although national professional organizations and mediators upholding their national standards have made impressive strides in addressing issues such as these, most of the attention has been centered not on the private practitioner but on the court mediator. Although court-based mediation is less flexible and more abbreviated than private mediation, it currently may be more accountable to the public than is private mediation.

Court based mediators are required to understand and uphold the foundations of law, ethics, and principles that are set forth in statutes, Rules of Court, and the Court's Code of Ethics. They must be especially conversant with legal practices and the local legal conventions, because they are representatives of the legal system. In California, court mediators must have, at a minimum, a master's degree in a behavioral science, 2 years of prior mediation experience, knowledge of the court system, family law procedures, community resources, as well other areas beyond the practice of mediation. Most court mediators are licensed mental health professionals with over 5 years of court experience, and 44% have more than 10 years experience. Most of these child-custody mediators also have other duties, primarily guardianship mediation, partial and full custody evaluations, and special procedural responsibilities in cases involving domestic violence. A court-based mediator in a mandatory mediation program, therefore, usually has expertise far beyond the scope of the traditional clinical training provided for private mediation . . .

[The "Confidential" and "Recommending" Models of Mediation]

Few subjects in mediation have sustained the intense polemic as has the debate about whether or not mediators should make recommendations to the court. The controversy, not unique to family mediation, usually centers on the varied philosophies of mediation, the degrees of self-determination, mediator neutrality, the degree to which the circle of confidentiality is extended, child and victim safety issues, the balance of power between parties, and the participants' needs for and trust in the process itself. The recommending mediation model is not limited to California; variations are found in other court settings and may be referred to as "open" or "evaluative" mediation.

Both the recommending and confidential models of mediation are utilized in California courts. The majority of mediation programs provide recommending mediation, but nearly half of the mediations conducted in the state are in courts that use confidential models of mediation. Two important distinctions should be made about these models. First, *recommending* and *confidential* are umbrella terms for a number of individualized programs that process cases somewhat differently. Second, a court can change from a recommending to a confidential mediation model at will. The bench and court administration may decide to shift models to accommodate changes in court philosophy or to respond to what it believes are the changed needs of the litigants. Third, some courts use both models. Of interest is the reaction of mediation clients to each model. With some exceptions, clients give both models high marks, with most clients stating that they would recommend the process to their friends.

Both approaches to mediation must follow the principles set forth in the Rule of Court and statutes. For example, if there are five issues to be addressed in mediation and four of them are settled by agreement, mediators in both models are required to write out the agreement on the four issues either as a Parenting Plan that is attached to the court order or written as a stipulation on a court-order form. Mediators in both models may recommend further action to the court, as described in the statutes and the Rule of Court. For example, the mediator might recommend that the court appoint an attorney for the child or that a child custody evaluation be conducted. In both models, the attorneys are intended to have sufficient time to review the outcome of mediation and to confer with their clients prior to a settlement conference or a court hearing. However, mediators approach the resolution of the unresolved issue differently.

In a confidential model, the mediator makes no recommendation as to the preferred outcome of any unresolved issues, either verbally or in writing. Instead, the mediator notes the remaining issues to be addressed and forwards it to the court for further assignment, or the case may proceed to a settlement conference. The attorneys receive a copy of both the agreement and the document that states which issues remain in dispute. The mediator does not suggest solutions or resolutions to the outstanding issues but may recommend a brief assessment, an investigation, an evaluation, or the appointment of an attorney for the child if the circumstances warrant. The matter may also be returned to the court in order to schedule a contested hearing.

In contrast, under the recommending model, mediators may be asked to make a recommendation regarding the unresolved issues in a written report to the court for the judge's perusal. Courts that use the recommending approach are required to advise their clients prior to the beginning of mediation that if and when their negotiations reach an impasse, the mediator may carry out a dual role of mediator and evaluator. Mediation participants are to be told about this dual role in written materials, again in the orientation sessions, and again by the mediator at the beginning of the session. If the negotiations reach an impasse, the mediator informs the parties of his or her shift in role. If issues still remain after further discussion, the mediator may elect to terminate the mediation and begin the recommendation process or refer the case back to the court for further deliberations or evaluation.

If the case warrants further investigation due to allegations of substance abuse, child abuse, psychological problems, or neglect of the child's educational needs, the mediator may also obtain signed releases from the parents to collect information from other sources such as day-care providers, teachers, doctors, therapists, agencies such as Child Protective Services, or services connected to social welfare or mental health. In jurisdictions where the court either encourages or requires mediators to collaborate on case out-comes with Social Services, the law regulates any information received by the mediator. Since the recommending process is not detailed in the California Rule of Court for mediation, some courts structure their recommendation process by following the laws regulating child custody investigations and evaluations and the Rule of Court for "partial" child custody evaluations. The child custody evaluation Rule of Court applies to all practitioners, both in the public and private sector, who conduct any child custody evaluation. A *partial* evaluation is defined as an "examination of the health, safety, welfare, and best interest of the child that is limited by court order in either time or scope." This rule requires that a recommendation include "data collection and analysis that allow the evaluator to observe and consider each party in comparable ways and to substantiate interpretations and conclusions regarding each child's developmental needs, the quality of attachment to each parent and that parent's social environment; and the child's reactions to the separation, divorce or parental conflict." This rule also states that any recommendations made to the court must be made only for parties who have been interviewed and evaluated.

Clients receive their recommendation from the mediator in a variety of ways. Some courts make the recommendations available a number of days before court. Other courts provide the parties with the mediator's recommendations only a day or two before the hearing; some courts, on the day of the hearing. The mediator may meet with the parties after the information gathering has been completed but before a recommendation is made. The mediator calls this meeting so that the parents can be informed of the reports the mediator has collected from different contacts. Sometimes the new information clarifies matters for the parents, and they negotiate and reach agreement on most or all of the issues prior to their court hearing. In other courts, the mediator may have no further contact with the family. At the hearing, the mediator's recommendation, along with other evidence, is considered by the judge. In some instances, the judge may consider the recommendation to fashion a final order, but in many other cases, the recommendation is considered for a temporary order pending further deliberation or until the next mediation appointment. Although the judge may or may not use the mediator's recommendation in rendering a judgment, the common belief is that a judicial officer always reviews the mediator's recommendations. When a mediator makes a recommendation, the mediator may be called to testify before the court.

An Example of Mediation with Low Risk to the Child

Stanley and Sara are divorced parents disputing a schedule change and have come to the court for mediation. Stanley wants 3 more hours of time with his sons, ages 6 and 7, twice a month. Sara thinks that this additional time would disrupt the boys' school night schedule and is standing firm on her position. Prior to the mediation session, the parents will receive detailed information on mediation and other related topics and will be expected to attend an orientation class and probably a parent education class. Stanley and Sara will be expected to complete an intake form that elicits a social history and attempts to screen for serious problems, including family violence. Their case appears to be a straightforward dispute that presents no undue risk to the child or to a possible victim.

The mediation session with Stanley and Sara lasts 2 hours, during which they reach an agreement. Typically, sessions last 11/2-3 hours, and couples attend just one session. (However, some couples may attend up to six sessions, but rarely more.) When the mediation results in an agreement, the agreement is put in writing and submitted for review by the parties and their attorneys. For example, in one large court that uses a confidential model of mediation, the agreement is written up on a court-order form and the parties are given 20 days to reconsider. If they do not submit any objections in writing during that time frame, the court order goes forward. If objections are raised, the parties are expected to return for further mediation, or the judge may hear the case. In some other courts, the parties pick up their agreement after their mediation, sometimes on the same day. In other courts, the agreement is sent by mail.

At the end of the mediation or several weeks later, clients may be asked to fill out a client form registering their level of satisfaction with the mediation and the mediator. In some courts, the parties may agree to return to mediation after several months to discuss how the plan is serving the children or to aid the parents with its implementation.

An Example of a Mediation When a Question of Risk Exists

Because California mediation programs do include cases with issues or incidences of domestic violence, the following example is included to illustrate how such a mediation process can be used to aid the family and protect the alleged victim and children. Linda has filed for divorce and full custody of their two children, ages 9 and 11, stating that Mike, the children's father, is abusing alcohol and has slapped her on several occasions over the past 3 months. Mike contends that Linda abuses painkillers and is a poor parent. Linda has a temporary restraining order in effect, issued by the family court, which includes a "stay away" order from the family home. Mike asserts that he will dispute the temporary restraining order and contests Linda's request for full custody.

The presence and terms of a temporary restraining order severely restrict what can be negotiated in mediation. For example, although custody is an issue with Linda and Mike, it cannot be negotiated in mediation because of the restraining order and the allegations of violence. A restraining order is issued by the court on behalf of the person who is asserting the allegations (i.e., the protected party). The order restrains certain actions by the alleged batterer. The mediation process cannot be used to dismiss any restraining order or to negotiate the issue of violence. In this case, mediation may be useful in other ways. For example, the mediator can assist with immediate needs, such as safety planning and possibly a temporary supervised visitation arrangement, and can determine whether he or she will want to interview the children. Mediation can also help by providing referrals to community resources that specialize in serving families with issues of domestic violence.

When Linda fills out the mediation service intake form, she notes the incidents of violence and the restraining order and alleges Mike's alcohol abuse. She also states that she is in poor health and jobless. When violence is an issue, the victim or threatened party can request separate mediation sessions at separate times. When there is a temporary restraining order that includes a "stay away" order, separate sessions may be required. Like Stanley and Sara, Linda and Mike will be expected to attend a parent education or orientation program prior to mediation. However, because of the temporary restraining order, Linda will attend a separate session at a different time from Mike's session. Linda could also request the presence of a support person in the mediation session.

Linda and Mike meet with the mediator separately on different days to reduce the possibility of stalking. Information regarding the day and times of their appointments is kept confidential. The mediator isolates the issues in individual sessions with each of them and aids them in exploring their options. Over the course of the mediation process, the parents do agree to supervised visitation so that the children can see their father during the course of the restraining order. The mediator meets with the children. She observes that they appear anxious and want to talk about the slapping incidents, their father's absence, and their mother's illness.

In a confidential model, the mediator usually writes up the issues on which the parties agree, than itemizes the remaining issues in dispute without making any recommendation as to their resolution. In this case, the mediator could recommend referrals to community services or interventions to address the violence, the children's needs, and the mother's ill health. These recommendations could even include recommending an attorney for the children or a full custody evaluation. This memo is sent to the parents and their attorneys (if they have counsel). The memo is the basis for their further deliberations and possibly a settlement conference. However, since there are issues of risk, Mike and Linda will probably be referred first for a family assessment process with a different mental health professional.

In some family courts that use recommending models, the mediator is the court's primary resource for neutral information regarding risk factors and children's needs. For example, in one court, the mediator would prepare a confidential report to the judge that listed first the parents' mutual agreements, followed by a narrative about the unresolved issues. Finally, the report would list any recommendations reached by the mediator after his or her discussions with collateral contacts-including, when necessary, a recommendation for a psychological evaluation, specialized information from a doctor or therapist, or a restraining order. The mediator may be more likely to conduct an assessment or brief investigation under the label of a *recommendation* when the court does not have separate child custody assessment or evaluation resources and when parents do not have legal representation or the resources for private evaluation services. For cases with these complex circumstances, the mediator should be cross-trained to carry out both assessment and mediation functions.

If Linda and Mike's agreement for supervised visitation becomes a court order, the mediation program should aid them in enrolling for this service. The court may also provide Linda and Mike with follow-up sessions or case management services with the mediator or a court counselor . . .

The Economics of Mandatory Mediation

When decision makers are charged with constructing a funding base for mandatory mediation, a key question to explore is whether it is ethical or appropriate to charge citizens for a mandated service. Many courts have answered "Yes," whereas others, such as those in California, have answered "No."Depending on the state and jurisdiction, mediation may be free; may be fee based, computed on a sliding scale in relation to the client's ability to pay; or it may be based on the full fee customarily charged by private mediators. Adequate financial support for a court-based mediation program is essential but not always forthcoming. Furthermore, the source of financing can shape a mediation program model and determine who can use the service.

If permitted, courts can obtain some or most of the needed funding by charging fees for the services they provided. Courts can also expect litigants to find their own private mediators and negotiate their own fees. When court-based mediation is free to the client, however, the court takes on the full responsibility of funding the program. The court can provide this free service at the court, using court staff trained as mediators, or it can contract with outside providers. Compensation for outside court-connected providers also varies. Some courts offer their contractors a flat fee for each mediation they conduct, whereas others offer a set hourly rate. Contracting for services can release the court from overhead costs of providing an in-house service, because mediators on contract usually conduct the sessions in their own private offices. Although the use of contract mediators is common, the trend in California has moved toward more in-court staff. This shift may be due to the higher level of risk inherent in conducting mediations without access to secure offices and security personnel, the desire to have expert staff in residence, as well as the court's desire to provide greater oversight and accountability.

Unless client fees cover all program costs, court-based mediation programs must compete with other worthwhile programs for local and state resources. Mandatory mediation programs are not automatically exempt from this competition because of their mandate, unless they have a protected and adequate funding stream. All court-based services experience both the constraints and benefits of being part of a court, including the court's level of success in procuring adequate funding for its operations.

Access to Different Mediation Models

Different funding and fee models can heavily influence variations in mediation services. In many jurisdictions, there are differences in the duration of mediation, the issues that can be mediated, the availability of appointments, and the level of compliance by the mediators and the programs to existing rules or standards of practice. A court-based mediation may be completed in one or two sessions for several reasons: (1) mediation may be limited to custody and visitation disputes, (2) parents may wish to negotiate only one or two issues rather than a full parenting plan, or (3) the court does not have the resources to provide more than one or two sessions. Private mediation, on the other hand, (1) addresses a wide range of issues, (2) often attracts clients who seek to develop a full parenting plan, and (3) offers the potential for ongoing mediation sessions. Courts, unlike private practitioners, typically do not have the freedom to offer evening or weekend appointments, and their mediators must follow state standards. Private mediators may offer a wide variety of appointment options, may not be required to follow standards of practice, and are usually sole proprietors or in practice with one or two partners.

Both systems of providing mediation, although different, can be both useful and helpful. However, the different models are not equally accessible to all citizens. The private mediation model is out of the reach of less financially endowed clients, whereas the court-based model is open to all. In short, a litigant's access to different mediation models is usually determined by the ability of the litigant to pay for the service.

Mandatory mediation should be characterized by consistency and fairness of service delivery to citizens of all incomes. As a rule of thumb, if the population using court-based mediation reflects the economic composition of the community, then an egalitarian mediation system has probably been achieved. However, if a court-based mediation program serves a disproportionate number of citizens who are near or below the poverty line, as is the case in so many California courts, then a dual system may exist. When evaluating mandatory mediation, important questions to include are "Do clients have choices between systems of mediation?" and "Are the indigent limited to the court model while the affluent have a choice of models?" . . .

NOTES AND QUESTIONS

1.   The author notes that there is "intense polemic" about the choice between a "recommending" or "confidential" model. What, in your view, is the better choice? Are there certain issues in family mediation that should be subject to a mediator's "recommendation" or, conversely, should be kept confidential?

2.   Whether a court-connected mediator is in a "confidential" or "recommending" jurisdiction, what "style" of mediation do you think the California scheme contemplates?

3.   How about "mandatory mediation"? Does a particular style comport with a "mandatory mediation" jurisdiction such as California or do you believe that a range of styles can be effective?

4.   The preceding article acknowledges the possibility of parties turning to "private mediation" and that such mediation is not subject to the legal strictures to which court-connected mediators are subject. Does this accord with what, in your view, is sound public policy? Does this fact put those who can afford private mediation at a disadvantage or vice versa? What issues related to socioeconomic status does such a structure bring into play?

5.   Do you believe that court-connected mediation generates additional incentives for agreement? If so, how do you believe such incentives comport with the goals of family mediation. Would the incentives vary depending on whether the jurisdiction is "mandatory" or "discretionary," or "confidential" or "recommending"? *See* Marian Roberts, *Systems or Selves? Some Ethical Issues in Family Mediation*, 10 Med. Q. 3, 15 (1992).

NOTE: MEDIATION TRENDS: A SURVEY OF THE STATES[2]
39 FAM. CT. REV. 431 (2001)
Student Note

MEDIATION CHART OF THE STATES

State	Attendance [1]	Exceptions [2]	Parties Pay for Mediation [3]
Alabama	Discretionary	Domestic abuse allegations by Victim	Yes
Alaska	Discretionary	Domestic abuse allegations/ protective order	Yes, unless indigent
Arizona	Discretionary, except custody disputes	Undue hardship	Yes
Arkansas	Discretionary	Not listed	Yes
California	Mandatory	Not listed	No
Colorado	Discretionary	Physical or Psychological abuse allegations	Yes
Connecticut	Discretionary	None	Not listed
Delaware	Mandatory	Domestic abuse allegations	Not listed
District of Columbia	Discretionary	Court's discretion	Not listed
Florida	Mandatory	Domestic abuse allegations	Apportioned
Georgia	No statute	No statute	No statute
Hawaii	Mandatory	Domestic abuse allegations or restraining order	Not listed
Idaho	Mandatory	Not listed	Not listed
Illinois	No unified statute/ local circuit is discretionary	Domestic abuse allegations	Yes
Indiana	No statute	No statute	No statute
Iowa	Discretionary	Domestic abuse allegations	Yes
Kansas	Discretionary	None	Yes
Kentucky	Mandatory	Good cause	Yes
Louisiana	Discretionary	Domestic abuse allegations	Yes
Maine	Mandatory if children are involved	Can be waived for extraordinary causes	Not listed

State	Attendance [1]	Exceptions [2]	Parties Pay for Mediation [3]
Maryland	Discretionary	Sexual or physical abuse allegations	Yes
Massachusetts	No unified statute	No statute	No statute
Michigan	Discretionary	Good cause	Yes
Minnesota	Discretionary	Physical or sexual abuse allegation	Free, low cost
Mississippi	No statute	No statute	No statute
Missouri	No unified statute	Not listed	Yes
Montana	Discretionary	Abuse allegations	Yes
Nebraska	Discretionary	Not listed	Not if court ordered
Nevada	Mandatory	Domestic abuse allegations	Yes
New Hampshire	Discretionary	Domestic abuse allegations	Yes
New Jersey	Discretionary	Domestic violence allegations	Yes
New Mexico	Discretionary	Not listed in some districts	Yes
New York	No statute	No statute	No statute
North Carolina	Discretionary/ mandatory in child custody and visitation	Domestic abuse allegations/ substance abuse/ undue hardship	Varies
North Dakota	Discretionary	Domestic abuse allegations	Yes
Ohio	Discretionary	Not listed	Varies
Oklahoma	Discretionary	Domestic abuse allegations	Yes
Oregon	Discretionary	Cannot mediate custody issues with property division/spousal and child support	Yes
Pennsylvania	Mandatory in McKean County; No unified statute	Domestic violence	Not listed
Rhode Island	Discretionary	Not listed	Not listed
South Carolina	No statute	No statute	No statute
South Dakota	Mandatory	Determined by the court	Yes
Tennessee	Discretionary	Domestic violence	Not listed
Texas	No statute	No statute	No statute
Utah	Mandatory	Cohabitant abuse	Yes
Vermont	No statute	No statute	No statute
Virginia	Discretionary	History of family abuse	Yes

State	Attendance [1]	Exceptions [2]	Parties Pay for Mediation [3]
Washington	Mandatory in two counties	Good cause showing	Yes
West Virginia	No statute	No statute	No statute
Wisconsin	Mandatory	Domestic abuse allegations	Yes
Wyoming	No statute	No statute	No statute
[1] Attendance is defined as how the parties opt into the mediation process; sometimes, they enter mediation by choice, and other times, they are required by court order or statute to attend.			
[2] Exceptions refer to what reasons, if any, prohibit parties from using mediation.			
[3] This column refers to who is responsible for the costs of mediation proceedings.			

QUESTION

Do you find this chart surprising? If so, why?

C.   FAMILY MEDIATOR QUALIFICATIONS

For many years, the mediation profession was largely unregulated. As states enacted legislation establishing court-connected mediation, issues surrounding mediation qualifications came to the fore. The reading below identifies the primary issues to be resolved in deciding who may mediate family law cases. As you read this section, consider what qualities would make one an effective and competent family mediator. Do these qualities vary depending upon the case being mediated? If so, how?

NOTE: A SURVEY OF DOMESTIC MEDIATOR QUALIFICATIONS AND SUGGESTION FOR A UNIFORM PARADIGM[3]
16 Ohio St. J. on Disp. Resol. 1, 1-37 (2000)

At first glance, a nationwide statutory survey reveals some consistency among the fifty states relative to qualifications for mediators of domestic disputes. Though seemingly harmonious, the various statutory qualifications are hardly uniform. A moderate minority of states affords no statutory treatment for domestic mediator qualifications. Conversely, a large majority address domestic mediator qualifications within each state's respective body of statutory laws, with varying degrees of regulation. Additionally, among those states with statutory qualifications, the rather ubiquitous classification of domestic disputes is often further distinguished, with some states regulating qualifications for mediators in child custody or visitation disputes as well as marital dissolution or divorce. What follows is a summation of the predominant specifications recurrent in those states prescribing statutory domestic mediator qualifications.

A. *General Knowledge Requirements*

Under this rather broad category, statutory qualifications generally require mediators to possess basic knowledge of court procedures, family law issues, and an awareness of other resources in the community offering assistance for domestic matters. Typical among statutes that follow this rubric is Michigan's statute governing "domestic relations mediation." The statute reads: "A domestic relations mediator who performs mediation under this act shall have all of the following minimum qualifications: . . . (b) Knowledge of the court system of this state and the procedures used in domestic relations matters [and] (c) Knowledge of other resources in the community to which the parties to a domestic relations matter can be referred for assistance." California has expanded on these general knowledge qualifications and requires its mediators to have knowledge of "adult psychopathology and the psychology of families, and child custody research sufficient to enable a counselor to assess the mental health needs of children."

B. *Degree Requirements*

Only six states mandate degree requirements for domestic mediators. All of these states require, at minimum, a bachelor's degree, with some states calling for graduate degrees. Missouri, a state with specialized graduate degree requirements, obligates its mediators to have a graduate degree in the fields of "psychiatry, psychology, social work, counseling, or other behavioral science"substantially related to marriage and family interpersonal relationships. Similarly, Michigan requires its domestic mediators to possess a master's degree in counseling, social work, or marriage and family counseling, in the absence of a license or limited license to engage in the practice of psychology. Two states, North Dakota and Ohio, waive the graduate degree requirement in favor of a bachelor's degree if coupled with experience with family services or counseling.

C. *Professional License Requirements*

Another recurrent requisite qualification for domestic mediators in some states is that of a professional license or professional certification. Typically, statutes in this genre require domestic mediators to hold a license or certification as an attorney, psychiatrist, psychologist, social worker, or family counselor. Louisiana, for example, requires its domestic mediators to hold a license or certification as an attorney, psychiatrist, psychologist, social worker, marriage and family counselor, or clergyman. In the absence of similar professional requirements to those stated above, applicants for certification as a "family and dissolution of marriage mediator" in Florida, must be certified public accountants licensed to practice in any U.S. jurisdiction. Additionally, one state, Idaho, in child custody and visitation disputes mandates mediator membership in the Academy of Family Mediators, or other national organization with equivalent standards, in the absence of previously mentioned professional qualifications.

D. *Experience*

A few states obligate mediators to possess past experience prior to engaging in domestic mediation. Generally, these states compel experience as a practicing professional, usually in the fields of counseling, family law, or alternative dispute resolution. The majority of states within this group require at least 3 years of the particular statutorily prescribed experience. Also, of note, two states, Utah and Wisconsin, allow domestic mediators to alleviate a statutory training hour minimum with relevant professional experience.

E. *Hours of Mediation Training*

Many states require applicants to have completed a minimum number of hours of training in order to become qualified domestic mediators. There is little uniformity among states, as these requirements take a variety of forms. Generally, however, states require between 20 and 40 hours of training for domestic mediators. Within some of these states' respective requirements, however, requisite numbers of hours are to be specifically apportioned among express areas of training. One such state is Idaho, which requires its child custody and visitation mediators to have completed at least 60 hours of training, 20 of which shall be in the field of child custody mediation, which includes: conflict resolution; psychological issues in separation, divorce, and family dynamics; domestic violence; issues and needs of children; mediation processes and techniques; and family law, including custody and support. The remaining 40 hours of mediation training shall be in the following components, at least 30% of which shall be in the field of practicing mediation skills: information gathering, mediator relationship skills, communication skills, problem solving skills, conflict management skills, ethics, and professional skills. In addition to initial training, a small minority of states requires domestic mediators to complete supplementary hours of continuing education subsequent to being certified, in order to maintain status as a certified domestic mediator.

F. *Observation or Participation with an Experienced Mediator*

Observation of participation with an experienced mediator is another condition incumbent upon mediators of domestic disputes seeking certification in some states. Typically, in addition to other qualifications, these states require an applicant to have performed a minimum number of hours of mediation with an "experienced" mediator. Georgia, a state requiring no hourly minimum, does, however, mandate mediation with an experienced mediator in at least five mediations, as well as two such mediation experiences in divorce or custody proceedings.

G. *Miscellaneous Qualifications*

A distinct minority of states, in addition to the major themes discussed previously, impose rather unique requirements upon prospective domestic mediators. For instance, two states, Florida and North Dakota, oblige domestic mediators to be possessed of "good moral character,"the exegesis of which is absent within the respective statute. Another state with such a multifarious requirement is Ohio, which requires its domestic mediators to possess "appropriate liability insurance." In its statute governing mediation of child custody matters, Alaska's sole requirement is that if the mediator determines there has been domestic violence, the mediation should be provided by mediators trained "in a manner that protects the safety of the victim and any household member, taking into account the results of an assessment of the potential danger posed by the perpetrator and the risk of harm to the victim."

Worthy of mention are two local rules from the California Rules of the Court. Adopted in two respective superior court jurisdictions, these rules summarily require that in domestic matters the Superior Court shall appoint a mediator or evaluator whose skills, training, and background are best suited to the particular needs of the family in the present dispute.

NOTES AND QUESTIONS

1. In light of your reading, draft your own statute setting forth requisite qualifications for family mediators. In so doing, consider the following questions:

- Do you think additional qualifications should be required for subcategories within family disputes, such as child access mediation or financial issues?
- Should private mediators be subject to qualification requirements as well as mediators acting under the auspices of courts?
- Do more rigorous qualifications reduce the number of qualified mediators, thereby limiting the availability of family mediation particularly to those who cannot afford private mediators?
- Should there be continuing mediator education requirements or continuing assessments of the skills of mediators?
- Should there be a mechanism for prohibiting previously qualified mediators in light of certain misconduct from mediating?

2. Some have argued that by training and temperament, lawyers are *not* well suited to be mediators. *See* Leonard Riskin, *Mediation and Lawyers*, 43 Ohio St. L.J. 29, 57–59 (1982); Jean Sternlight, *Lawyers' Representation of Clients in Mediation: Using Economics and Psychology to Structure Advocacy in a Nonadversarial Setting*, 14 Ohio St. J. Disp. Resol. 269, 315 (1999). Do you agree? Why or why not?

3. The Model Standards of Practice for Family and Divorce Mediation, included as Appendix C and discussed in detail in Chapter 10, represents a consensus among family mediators, although, as a consensus, its principles are often general and short on details. Standard II describes what a family mediator needs in order to be "qualified by education and training to undertake the mediation." Review this Standard in the Appendix. Does this advance your thinking about appropriate qualifications for family mediators?

D. JUDICIAL REGULATION OF AGREEMENTS IN FAMILY MEDIATION

Another context in which family mediation is subject to legal regulation is when courts are asked to intervene to enforce or set aside a mediated agreement. The material that follows explores these issues.

1. Enforcement of Agreements Relating to Finances

The following case highlights the relationship between mediated agreements and court orders and illustrates principles courts will consider in determining whether an agreement is subject to the court's enforcement powers.

CLOUTIER v. CLOUTIER
814 A.2d 979 (Me. 2003)

I. BACKGROUND

Lorenzo and Dawn Cloutier were married on August 29, 1987, and three children were born to the marriage. Early in their marriage, they purchased land in Greene and built a house on it. At the time of the divorce, the house was valued at approximately $80,000, and the Cloutiers owed $61,000 on the mortgage. Lorenzo's father, Wilfred, gave the Cloutiers $25,000 to purchase the land and build the house. Wilfred provided for the $25,000 with a home equity line of credit from the Rainbow Credit Union secured by his own home. In return, the Cloutiers signed a promissory note in favor of Wilfred for $25,000 plus interest.

At the time of the trial, Lorenzo was employed at L.L. Bean as a team leader in technology services with an approximate salary of $38,667. Dawn worked at Mid-State College as an accountant and earned approximately $20,400. The house has an apartment attached to it that creates $125 a week in rental income.

Dawn filed a complaint for divorce in September of 2000. On December 11, 2000, a case management officer (Carlson, CMO) issued an interim order that placed the children's primary residence with Dawn at the marital home. As a result of a mediation at which both parties were represented, the Cloutiers signed a "points of agreement" form that resolved the majority of the issues in dispute. Among the matters agreed upon was an arrangement for their home to be sold and for the proceeds to be used to satisfy certain debt. The agreement was never incorporated into a court order. Immediately after the mediation session, the CMO held a pretrial conference. In its pretrial order, the CMO listed only a few matters remaining in dispute, including allocation of pension benefits, personal property and debt, and coverage of medical insurance for Dawn.

The District Court began the trial on the 2nd of August. At the beginning of trial, Dawn requested that the court disregard the mediation agreement and award sole possession of the home to her. Initially, the court declined to disregard the agreement and precluded real estate from becoming an issue. As the evidence developed, however, the court concluded that the issue of the disposition of the real estate was intricately intertwined with the resolution of the matters remaining in dispute. Therefore, the court postponed the hearing until October 16 to allow each party to gather more evidence of their financial situations. The court specifically stated at the August 2 hearing and in the resulting order that disposition of the real estate would be an issue to be resolved at the October hearing. Lorenzo objected to the court's ruling and the court overruled this objection. The parties returned to trial on October 16, and the court ultimately awarded the home and all rental income to Dawn. After the court denied Lorenzo's motion for further findings of fact, he appealed the divorce judgment.

II. DISCUSSION

Lorenzo argues that the trial court erred when it awarded the home and rental income solely to Dawn and disregarded the mediated "points of agreement," which included a different disposition of the real estate . . .

The question presented is whether, and under what circumstances, a judge may set aside a pretrial agreement between parties to a divorce and award an item of property in contravention of that agreement. Preliminarily, we note that the nature of the proceeding is important to the analysis. This is not a general civil matter where the parties are ordinarily free to enter into any agreement so long as it is not coerced. Rather, this is a family matter, where the court is called upon to exercise its authority in equity, and may be required to act as parens patriae if children are involved. Thus a pretrial agreement between parties to a divorce may be treated somewhat differently than a settlement in a civil suit.

Further, the fact that the pretrial agreement was entered into in the context of a court mandated mediation does not give the agreement the imprimatur of a court order. A family matter agreement does not become an order of the court until it is presented to and approved by the court. As is often the case in the progression of divorce proceedings, the mediated partial agreement between the Cloutiers had not been presented to and approved by the court or a CMO prior to trial. Therefore, the agreement in this case was not enforceable as a court order.

Nonetheless, an agreement reached prior to trial does represent a method by which the parties may identify matters that are not disputed and by which the parties may be assured that those matters will not be the subject of litigation. Thus, in the normal course, the court should honor an agreement reached by the parties. This assures that mediation is an effective tool for dispute resolution, and prevents the parties from unilaterally reopening matters that have been resolved. Therefore, ordinarily, when the parties have agreed to the resolution of some or all of the matters previously in dispute, the court will not address those matters at any trial on the remaining disputed issues, and will not, without more, allow the agreed upon matter to be litigated.

When the court, acting within its discretion, concludes that there is a basis for setting aside an agreement that has not been incorporated in a court order, however, it may do so.

Because the court will not set the agreement aside without cause, we address several factors that may be considered in making the decision to enforce or set aside a pretrial agreement. The court should consider, among other things, whether the parties have agreed to set aside the agreement; whether leaving the agreement in place would result in a significant inequity; whether there has been an unanticipated and substantial change in the parties' circumstances since the creation of the agreement; whether the court can resolve the matters not contained within the agreement in a reasonable manner in light of the parties' agreed upon resolution of the settled matters; and what affect the enforcement or setting aside of the agreement would have on the best interests of the children.

Once the court determines that an agreement must be set aside, there may be delay in resolving the entire matter and there may be further expenses or detriment to the children inherent in returning an issue to disputed status. Thus, in determining whether to reopen a previously agreed upon matter, the court should consider whether the expense and delay occasioned by setting the agreement aside is outweighed by the importance of the issue to be returned to litigation.

In the context of the Cloutiers' disputes regarding the allocation of their debt, particularly regarding the debt related to the marital home, the court did not exceed the bounds of its discretion in setting aside the parties' agreement to sell the home. The court had ample reason to conclude that selling the Cloutiers' home and dividing the profits would be manifestly unjust. The court was concerned that the Cloutiers' equity in the home was not nearly enough to pay off any of their large debt. Since this was the home in which the children have always lived, one of the main reasons for allowing Dawn to retain the house was to keep the children in their current school district. Further, Dawn's ability to pay for alternative housing, in relation to Lorenzo's, was insufficient. Given the limited benefit that selling the house would have had on the debt and the substantial detrimental effect it would have had on the children, the court acted well within the bounds of its discretion when it set aside the parties' agreement to sell the marital home . . .

IN RE MARRIAGE OF MARY JUANITA BANKS AND KENNETH WAYNE BANKS
Court of Appeals of Texas, Texarkana
887 S.W.2d 160 (1994)

BLEIL, Justice.

Mary Banks appeals from the final judgment entered in her suit for divorce . . . At issue is whether the trial court erred in granting the motion for summary judgment filed by Kenneth Banks and Acme Bag Manufacturing, Inc., and further erred in awarding attorney's fees to Kenneth Banks and Acme. We find no error except insofar as the trial court provided that attorney's fees might be recovered from the proceeds of the sale of the parties' homestead. We modify the judgment to delete that provision and, as modified, we affirm.

Mary Banks was the petitioner for divorce. Kenneth Banks and his business, Acme Bag Manufacturing, Inc., were co-respondents. The trial court referred the case for mediation and, as a result of the mediation, Mary Banks, Kenneth Banks, and their attorneys signed a document entitled "Rule 11 Stipulation and Settlement Agreement" on June 28, 1993. The agreement addresses the issues of conservatorship and support of the Bankses' daughter and division of the community estate. Mary Banks filed a notice of repudiation and motion to set aside the agreement on July 9, 1993, and filed an amended notice on July 16, 1993 . . . Mary Banks . . . alleged that she was the victim of fraud, duress, or undue influence that caused her to execute the agreement. . . .

A party who has reached a settlement agreement disposing of a dispute through alternative dispute resolution procedures may not unilaterally repudiate the agreement. If voluntary agreements reached through mediation were nonbinding, many positive efforts to amicably settle differences would be for naught. In order to effect the purposes of mediation and other alternative dispute resolution mechanisms, settlement agreements must be treated like other contracts reached after arm's length negotiations.

No party to a dispute can be forced to settle the conflict outside of court; but if a voluntary agreement that disposes of the agreement is reached, the parties should be required to honor the agreement. In the order granting the summary judgment motion, the trial court recognized that the parties were not required to enter into an agreement, but properly held that, once they did, they were held to the agreement pursuant to section 154.071 of the Civil Practice and Remedies Code . . .

Mary Banks alternatively contends that summary judgment was improper because genuine issues of material fact exist concerning fraud, duress, and undue influence exerted on her at the time she executed the agreement. These grounds are alleged in her first amended original petition. She included these allegations in an affidavit attached to her response to the summary judgment motion, too, but the trial court found that the allegations were conclusory and did not set forth facts supporting her claims. A summary judgment is proper only when the movant establishes that there are no genuine issues of material fact and that he is entitled to judgment as a matter of law.

In her affidavit, Mary Banks asserted that she was in a highly emotional state at the time she engaged in the mediation proceedings and signed the agreement; her attorney failed to inform her of the law of reimbursement; she was manipulated into signing the papers and did not feel she had the right to refuse and believed she was without an ally or advocate; she was told that the judge was a "50/50 Judge"; the mediator told her attorney that it would cost each law firm $50,000.00 to go forward with the case and she felt financially threatened by this amount of attorney's fees; and she was induced to enter the agreement by duress or fraud. Mary Banks' statements that she was induced to sign the agreement by fraud and duress are merely legal conclusions and are insufficient to raise a fact issue. The failure of her attorney and accountant to inform her about the law of reimbursement is not an act of misconduct attributable to her husband, his attorney, Acme, or its attorney. Likewise, the statements of the mediator regarding the estimated amount of legal fees if the case proceeds are not attributable to Kenneth Banks, his attorney, or his business.

Understandably, Mary Banks was distressed and under much pressure, for divorce is not an emotionless proceeding. But nowhere in her affidavit does Mary Banks raise a fact issue concerning how her ex-husband or anyone for whom he is responsible exerted duress or undue influence that caused her to enter into an agreement she otherwise would not have made.

We modify the judgment to set aside the provision that the attorney's fees may be recovered from the sale of the homestead and, as modified, we affirm the trial court's judgment.

VITAKIS-VALCHINE v. VALCHINE
District Court of Appeal of Florida, Fourth District
793 So. 2d 1094 (2001)

STEVENSON, J.

This is an appeal from a final judgment of dissolution which was entered pursuant to a mediated settlement agreement. The wife argues that the trial court erred in affirming the recommendations of the general master and in denying her request to set aside the settlement agreement on the grounds that it was entered into under duress and coercion. We affirm the order to the extent that the trial court concluded that the wife failed to meet her burden of establishing that the marital settlement agreement was reached by duress or coercion on the part of the husband and the husband's attorney. The wife also alleges that the mediator committed misconduct during the mediation session, including but not limited to coercion and improper influence, and that she entered into the settlement agreement as a direct result of this misconduct. For the reasons which follow, we hold that mediator misconduct can be the basis for a trial court refusing to enforce a settlement agreement reached at court-ordered mediation. Because neither the general master nor the trial court made any findings relative to the truth of the allegations of the mediator's alleged misconduct, we remand this case for further findings.

Procedural background

By August of 1999, Kalliope and David Valchine's divorce proceedings to end their near twelve-year marriage had been going on for one and a half to two years. On August 17, 1999, the couple attended court-ordered mediation to attempt to resolve their dispute. At the mediation, both parties were represented by counsel. The mediation lasted seven to eight hours and resulted in a twenty-three page marital settlement agreement. The agreement was comprehensive and dealt with alimony, bank accounts, both parties' IRAs, and the husband's federal customs, postal, and military pensions. The agreement also addressed the disposition of embryos that the couple had frozen during *in vitro fertilization* attempts prior to the divorce. The agreement provided in this regard that "[t]he Wife has expressed her desire to have the frozen embryos, but has reluctantly agreed to provide them to the husband to dispose of."

A month later, the wife filed a *pro se* motion seeking to set aside the mediated settlement agreement, but by the time of the hearing, she was represented by new counsel. The wife's counsel argued two grounds for setting aside the agreement: (1) coercion and duress on the part of the husband, the husband's attorney and the mediator; and (2) the agreement was unfair and unreasonable on its face. The trial court accepted the general master's findings which rejected the wife's claim on both grounds. On appeal, the wife attacks only the trial court's refusal to set aside the couple's settlement agreement on the ground that it was reached through duress and coercion.

Third party coercion

As a general rule under Florida law, a contract or settlement may not be set aside on the basis of duress or coercion unless the improper influence emanated from one of the contracting parties-the actions of a third party will not suffice. In this case, the record adequately supports the finding that neither the husband nor the husband's attorney was involved in any duress or coercion and had no knowledge of any improper conduct on the part of the mediator.

Because there was no authority at the time holding that mediator misconduct, including the exertion of duress or coercion, could serve as a basis for overturning the agreement, the general master made no findings relative to the wife's allegations. The mediator's testimony was presented prior to that of the wife, and, consequently, her allegations of potential misconduct were not directly confronted. Here, we must decide whether the wife's claim that the mediator committed misconduct by improperly influencing her and coercing her to enter into the settlement agreement can be an exception to the general rule that coercion and duress by a third party will not suffice to invalidate an agreement between the principals.

The former wife's claims

The wife testified that the eight-hour mediation, with Mark London as the mediator, began at approximately 10:45 a.m., that both her attorney and her brother attended, and that her husband was there with his counsel. Everyone initially gathered together, the mediator explained the process, and then the wife, her attorney and her brother were left in one room while the husband and his attorney went to another. The mediator then went back and forth between the two rooms during the course of the negotiations in what the mediator described as "Kissinger-style shuttle diplomacy."

With respect to the frozen embryos, which were in the custody of the Fertility Institute of Boca Raton, the wife explained that there were lengthy discussions concerning what was to become of them. The wife was concerned about destroying the embryos and wanted to retain them herself. The wife testified that the mediator told her that the embryos were not "lives in being" and that the court would not require the husband to pay child support if she were impregnated with the embryos after the divorce. According to the wife, the mediator told her that the judge would *never* give her custody of the embryos, but would order them destroyed. The wife said that at one point during the discussion of the frozen embryo issue, the mediator came in, threw the papers on the table, and declared "that's it, I give up." Then, according to the wife, the mediator told her that if no agreement was reached, he (the mediator) would report to the trial judge that the settlement failed because of her. Additionally, the wife testified that the mediator told her that if she signed the agreement at the mediation, she could still protest any provisions she didn't agree with at the final hearing-including her objection to the husband "disposing" of the frozen embryos.

With respect to the distribution of assets, the wife alleges that the mediator told her that she was not entitled to any of the husband's federal pensions. She further testified that the mediator told her that the husband's pensions were only worth about $200 per month and that she would spend at least $70,000 in court litigating entitlement to this relatively modest sum. The wife states that the mediation was conducted with neither her nor the mediator knowing the present value of the husband's pensions or the marital estate itself. The wife testified that she and her new attorney had since constructed a list of assets and liabilities, and that she was shortchanged by approximately $34,000-not including the husband's pensions. When asked what she would have done if Mr. London had told her that the attorney's fees could have amounted to as little as $15,000, the wife stated, "I would have took [sic] it to trial."

Finally, the wife testified that she signed the agreement in part due to "time pressure" being placed on her by the mediator. She testified that while the final draft was being typed up, the mediator got a call and she heard him say "have a bottle of wine and a glass of drink, and a strong drink ready for me." The wife explained that the mediator had repeatedly stated that his daughter was leaving for law school, and finally said that "you guys have five minutes to hurry up and get out of here because that family is more important to me." The wife testified that she ultimately signed the agreement because

> [I] felt pressured. I felt that I had no other alternative but to accept the Agreement from the things that I was told by Mr. London. I believed everything that he said.

Court-ordered mediation

Mediation is a process whereby a neutral third party, the mediator, assists the principals of a dispute in reaching a complete or partial voluntary resolution of their issues of conflict. Mandatory, court-ordered mediation was officially sanctioned by the Florida legislature in 1987, and since then, mediation has become institutionalized within Florida's court system. *See* Ch. 44, Fla. Stat. (2000). All twenty judicial circuits in Florida utilize some form of court-connected mediation to assist with their caseloads. The process is meant to be non-adversarial and informal, with the mediator essentially serving as a facilitator for communications between the parties and providing assistance in the identification of issues and the exploration of options to resolve the dispute. Ultimate authority to settle remains with the parties. Mediation, as a method of alternative dispute resolution, potentially saves both the parties and the judicial system time and money while leaving the power to structure the terms of any resolution of the dispute in the hands of the parties themselves.

Mediation, pursuant to chapter 44, is mandatory when ordered by the court. Any court in which a civil action, including a family matter, is pending may refer the case to mediation, with or without the parties' consent. Communications during the mediation sessions are privileged and confidential. During court-ordered mediation conducted pursuant to the statute, the mediator enjoys "judicial immunity in the same manner and to the same extent as a judge." The mediation must be conducted in accordance with rules of practice and procedure adopted by the Florida Supreme Court.

Comprehensive procedures for conducting the mediation session and minimum standards for qualification, training, certification, professional conduct, and discipline of mediators have been set forth by the Florida Supreme Court in the Florida Rules for Certified and Court Appointed Mediators, Rule 10 . . . One of the hallmarks of the process of mediation is the empowerment of the parties to resolve their dispute on their own, agreed-upon terms. While parties are required to attend mediation, no party is required to settle at mediation.

> (a) **Decision-making**. Decisions made during a mediation are to be made by the parties. A mediator shall not make substantive decisions for any party. A mediator is responsible for assisting the parties in reaching informed and voluntary decisions while protecting their right of self-determination.

Fla. R. Med. 10.310(a). The committee notes to the rule provide in part that while mediation techniques and practice styles may vary from mediator to mediator and mediation to mediation, a line is crossed and ethical standards are violated when any conduct of the mediator serves to compromise the parties' basic right to agree or not to agree. Special care should be taken to preserve the party's right to self-determination if the mediator provides input to the mediation process.

In keeping with the notion of self-determination and voluntary resolution of the dispute at court-ordered mediation, any improper influence such as coercion or duress on the part of the mediator is expressly prohibited:

> (b) **Coercion Prohibited.** A mediator shall not coerce or improperly influence any party to make a decision or unwillingly participate in a mediation.

Fla. R. Med. 10.310(b). Likewise, a mediator may not intentionally misrepresent any material fact in an effort to promote or encourage an agreement:

> (c) **Misrepresentation Prohibited**. A mediator shall not intentionally or knowingly misrepresent any material fact or circumstance in the course of conducting a mediation.

Fla. R. Med. 10.310(c).

Other sections of Rule 10 address the rendering of personal or professional opinions by the mediator, and one section specifically provides that

> A mediator shall not offer a personal or professional opinion as to how the court in which the case has been filed will resolve the dispute.

Fla. R. Med. 10.370(c). Under this section, the committee notes caution that while mediators may call upon their own qualifications and experience to supply information and options, the parties must be given the opportunity to freely decide upon any agreement. Mediators shall not utilize their opinions to decide any aspect of the dispute or to coerce the parties or their representatives to accept any resolution option.

The question we are confronted with in this case is whether a referring court may set aside an agreement reached in court-ordered mediation if the court finds that the agreement was reached as a direct result of the mediator's substantial violation of the rules of conduct for mediators. We believe that it would be unconscionable for a court to enforce a settlement agreement reached through coercion or any other improper tactics utilized by a court-appointed mediator. When a court refers a case to mediation, the mediation must be conducted according to the practices and procedures outlined in the applicable statutes and rules. If the required practices and procedures are not substantially complied with, no party to the mediation can rightfully claim the benefits of an agreement reached in such a way. During a court-ordered mediation, the mediator is no ordinary third party, but is, for all intent and purposes, an agent of the court carrying out an official court-ordered function. We hold that the court may invoke its inherent power to maintain the integrity of the judicial system and its processes by invalidating a court-ordered mediation settlement agreement obtained through violation and abuse of the judicially-prescribed mediation procedures.

"Every court has inherent power to do all things that are reasonably necessary for the administration of justice within the scope of its jurisdiction, subject to valid existing laws and constitutional provisions." *Rose v. Palm Beach County*, 361 So.2d 135, 137 (Fla.1978). In a variety of contexts, it has been held that the courts have the inherent power to protect the integrity of the judicial process from perversion and abuse. While the doctrine of inherent power should be invoked "cautiously" and "only in situations of clear necessity," we have little trouble deciding that the instant case presents a compelling occasion for its use.

We hasten to add that no findings were made as to whether the mediator actually committed the alleged misconduct. Nevertheless, at least some of the wife's claims clearly are sufficient to allege a violation of the applicable rules. On remand, the trial court must determine whether the mediator substantially violated the Rules for Mediators, and whether that misconduct led to the settlement agreement in this case.

AFFIRMED in part, REVERSED in part, and REMANDED.

NOTES AND QUESTIONS

1.   Compare *Cloutier, Banks,* and *Vitakis-Valchine.* In what ways, legally or factually, are they distinguishable? In what ways, legally or factually, are they similar?

2.   To what extent do you believe procedural issues played a role in these decisions? Do you believe the courts would have come out differently if, for example, Mary Banks' allegations in her motion for summary judgment were not "conclusory"?

3.   What legal bases do these decisions set forth for setting aside a settlement agreement in divorce? Do you agree with any of them? If not, what legal test or tests would you propose? What facts would you consider crucial in analyzing your tests?

4.   How do these decisions draw distinctions between a "family matter" and "a general civil case" in terms of judicial scrutiny of mediated agreements? Do you believe this distinction is justified? Why or why not? Are there other "civil cases" that you believe warrant as much scrutiny as family matters?

5.   Should all "family matters" with mediated agreements be equally subject to judicial scrutiny? If not, which types should be subject to higher or lower scrutiny?

6.   We will explore the role attorneys play in family mediation in detail in Chapter 11. At this stage of your understanding of family mediation, however, how does representation of parties in these cases affect the court's decision? Do you agree with the decisions on this score?

2.   Enforcement of Agreements Relating to Custody and Visitation

Many of the benefits attributed to child access mediation result from the power given to the parties, rather than the court, to make agreements about the care of their children. As you read the following excerpt from a custody decision, consider whether it is ever appropriate for a court to overrule a mediated agreement when neither party is alleging unfairness or, for other reasons, seeks to set aside the agreement. How does the fact that the agreement relates to child access affect your answer?

WAYNO v. WAYNO
District Court of Appeal of Florida, Fifth District
756 So. 2d 1024 (2000)

This is an appeal from a judgment in a marital dissolution case. We find no error but write to address one point. Appellant asserts the court was bound to accept and ratify by judgment the mediated settlement regarding child custody once the court had granted its approval in accordance [with *rule 12.740(f)(2), Florida Family Law Rules of Procedure*:

(2) After the agreement is filed, the court shall take action as required by law. When court approval is not necessary, the agreement shall become

binding upon filing. When court approval is necessary, the agreement shall become binding upon approval. In either event, the agreement shall be made part of the final judgment or order in the case.

We disagree with appellant's assertion. The court had not heard evidence before its approval and granted the approval before rendering final judgment. It is axiomatic that only the court can be the final authority regarding child custody and child support and those issues can always be subject to review based on the evidence and, after judgment, upon a showing of a material change in circumstances. It goes without saying that the best interest of the child is the overriding factor to be considered. Even though the judge found in this case that a change in circumstances had occurred, that is not the guiding principle. Although the rule does not explicitly require it, it is at least implicit in the rule and certainly the better practice for the judge to not approve either custody or support before being fully informed about the welfare of the children. Thus, approval should be withheld in those issues until final judgment, or, if not, then the withdrawal of approval must be fully available until judgment. Therefore, the judgment is affirmed.

AFFIRMED.

CONCUR: Cobb, J., concurring specially.

I concur with the majority opinion. A trial judge has inherent authority to alter or rescind interlocutory orders prior to entry of final judgment. *Young v. Young, 65 So. 2d 28 (Fla. 1953); Whitaker v. Wright, 100 Fla. 282, 129 So. 889 (1930).* This authority certainly extends to a court's interlocutory approval of an agreement involving custody of children entered at a point in the case where the evidence has not been presented to the trial court. If this traditional concept is to be abrogated in custody cases, it should be done in a much clearer fashion than the provisions of Family Law Rule 12.740(f) (2). n1 I would construe that rule as providing that the interlocutory approval of a custody mediation agreement becomes final (and therefore no longer subject to rejection by the trial court) only at the time that agreement is made part of the final judgment, as is required by the rule. Thereafter, alteration of the custody provisions of the final judgment would be subject to change only upon a showing of a material change of circumstances. To construe the rule as does the dissent presents a trap for the unwary and well-intentioned trial judge, and seriously interferes with his obligation to protect the best interest of the child in a custody dispute.

DISSENT: Sharp, W., J., dissenting.

I respectfully disagree and would reverse this case. In my view, the trial judge erred when he changed the primary parental residency of the parties' daughter, after having approved the parties' mediation agreement which provided for primary residency to be with the former wife for the parties' daughter, and primary residency for the parties' son to be with the former husband. In my view, the majority opinion strips the new Family Law Rule of Procedure 12.740 of any effectiveness, or relevance, and if the majority opinion is to prevail in these cases, the rule needs reconsideration and redrafting.

Rule 12.740 provides for mediation of contested family matters in dissolution cases. If the parties reach an agreement through mediation, concerning any matter or issue, including legal or factual issues to be determined by the court, the agreement shall be reduced to writing, signed by the parties or stipulated to, and if not objected to by counsel timely under the rule, it is filed with the court by the mediator. The issues of parental responsibility and primary residence were subjected to mediation in this case and the parties arrived at a formal settlement. The settlement was then presented to the court, pursuant to rule 12.740(f) (2).

Subdivision (f) (2) provides that after the agreement is filed by the mediator with the court, it becomes binding on the parties, if no court approval is required. But if court approval is necessary, "the agreement shall become binding upon approval. In either event, the agreement shall be made part of the final judgment or order in the case." We could find no case which discusses what kinds of settlement agreements necessitate court approval, but in any event in this case, the court *did* approve the mediated settlement agreement.

However, at the trial of this dissolution case, the court took the position that it was not bound by the court-approved settlement of the child custody issues. Seemingly, it recognized some difficulty with this position when it declared there had been a substantial change in circumstances since the settlement had been approved. However, it is clear from the testimony given by the two psychologists who testified in this case, which the trial court relied upon expressly as creating a change of circumstances that nothing in fact had changed concerning the parties' circumstances since the mediation agreement had been approved.

As to whether there had been a change in the parties' circumstances, Dr. Olsen was asked and answered the following questions:

Q. Do you know of anything or have you learned of anything since that occurred since May of 1998, May 21st of 1998, which would constitute a substantial change in circumstances which would require this Court to overturn that mediation agreement?

A. No. I think these patterns have been going on, A, for a long time in the marriage and, B, have been escalated the whole time they've been living in the house but estranged. So nothing knew [sic] that I can see has occurred from May to the time that I evaluated them.

Q. You don't know of any emergency situation that would require a change?

A. No, I don't.

Similarly, when asked about a change in circumstances, Dr. Conic testified:

Q. Regardless of whether you've done a custody evaluation, do you know and/or have you learned from your therapy sessions with Donna and Tommy and the children of any substantial change in circumstances which has occurred since May 21st, 1998 that would require a change of that agreement?

A. I don't know of any.

Even the former husband was unable to identify what emergency circumstances or change of circumstances had occurred since he signed the settlement agreement that would justify modification. He said: "Well, I think the most important thing is that Donna has failed to include her daughter, who she is petitioning the court for custody of, in her week-end activities and in her afternoon activities." He failed to tie this behavior to post-settlement behavior as opposed to his former wife's behavior prior to the settlement. Further, as measured by typical change of circumstances cases justifying a change in child custody, this testimony is clearly insufficient to meet that difficult burden.

Dissecting this case to what actually occurred and bypassing the legalese, the trial judge in this case erroneously allowed the former husband to try the issue of child custody in the dissolution case despite the mediated court-approved settlement of this issue, where the former husband neither pled nor proved a substantial change in circumstances and having heard the testimony. The court decided the custody issued *do novo*. This may be proper in cases involving settlement agreements between parties, which have not been court approved. But this is not such a case.

The question in this case is whether a court-approved settlement agreement mediated pursuant to the Florida Family Law Rules is entitled to the same kind of finality as settlement agreements incorporated in final judgments.

In my view, the rules suggest that mediation agreements, after being filed and particularly after being court-approved, are entitled to be treated as final determinations of the issues covered. If not, there is very little incentive for parties to engage in mediation, in the first place. Why should they go to the trouble and expense to mediate if the issues resolved can be freely retried in the dissolution case by a party, belatedly unhappy with the mediated settlement? Parties should be encouraged to mediate family law disputes, and when the process is followed and the agreement is approved by the court they should be bound by their agreement. Otherwise the mediation process is an exercise in futility.

In Trowbridge v. Trowbridge, 674 So. 2d 928, 931 (Fla. 4th DCA 1996), the fourth district explained:

Mediation settlement agreements differ from traditional prenuptial and postnuptial agreements. Typically, the parties enter into prenuptial and postnuptial agreements without court supervision. Mediation agreements are reached under court supervision, before a neutral mediator. The mediation rules create an environment intended to produce a final settlement of the issues with safeguards against the elements of fraud, overreaching, etc., in the settlement process.

NOTES AND QUESTIONS

1. *Wayno* is explicitly about custody and visitation. Do you believe such cases should be scrutinized differently from those involving purely financial issues? How about cases that raise both kinds of issues?

2. *Wayno* as well as *Cloutier, Banks, and Vitakis-Valchin* implicate contradictory public policy concerns. What are these concerns? Do you believe the *Wayno* dissent has balanced them appropriately? Why or why not?

3. Compare *Cloutier, Wayno, Banks and Vitakis-Valchin* in terms of the allegations justifying setting aside the mediated agreement. In light of this contrast, do you agree or disagree with the court's reasoning in each case?

E. SPECIAL LEGAL ISSUES IN FAMILY MEDIATION INVOLVING LESBIAN, GAY, BISEXUAL AND TRANSGENDER PARTICIPANTS

Family mediation can, of course, involve lesbian, gay, bisexual, or transgender participants. It is worth considering the special legal issues facing such participants and the impact this might have on mediation.

The "shadow of the law" can be a distinct shadow indeed when dissolving LGBT relationships. Consider the following overview of this situation.

MOVING FORWARD TOGETHER: THE LGBT COMMUNITY AND THE FAMILY MEDIATION FIELD[4]
6 Pepp. Disp. Resol. L.J. 296–99 (2006)
By Mark J. Hanson

A. The American Legal System's Hostility to LGBT Interests

. . . When a LGBT couple ends their relationship, they need to be able to address many issues such as distribution of assets, calculation of possible spousal support, and, if the couple has children, figuring out the child custody arrangements. Yet, for most of recent history, LGBT couples were unable to access state courts to dissolve their relationships because state courts have refused to recognize their relationships.

States such as Vermont do allow LGBT couples access to its courts to dissolve their civil unions. However, other states have refused to dissolve LGBT relationships. Dissimilar state laws are currently creating legal havoc. In one instance where a LGBT couple legally married in Vermont sought to dissolve their civil union in a Georgia state court, the Georgia state court refused to recognize their civil union. As a result, the Georgia state court refused to allow the LGBT couple access to its state court functions in order to resolve issues related to their breakup. In many states, the vast legal framework of family law that deals with dissolving relationships has long been inapplicable to LGBT couples.

Even if LGBT couples had access to the state courts, there have been many reasons why the LGBT community has avoided using those courts. First, LGBT couples have stayed away from the state courts due to ostensibly homophobic judicial decisions that have either derided or belittled the LGBT community. One recent example of such a homophobic sounding court decision came from the Supreme Court of Alabama, which stated that homosexual behavior "has been, considered abhorrent, immoral, detestable, a crime against nature, and a violation of the laws of nature and of nature's God upon which this Nation and our [Alabama's] laws are predicated." Ex Parte H.H. 830 So.2d 21, 26 (Ala. 2002). Homophobic decisions also exist in child custody cases, where courts have refused to grant custody or joint custody to a LGBT parent because of fears: that the child would be molested; the child will become gay; the LGBT parent is mentally ill because they are gay; the child might contract HIV; or the child might be overly exposed to harassment and/or stigmatization because of having a gay parent. Moreover, the LGBT community has experienced instances of outright and overt

---

[4] Copyright ©2006. Reprinted with permission.

hostility by court officials; in one such case, a court official stated it was unbecoming to shake the hand of a lesbian. LGBT couples have also avoided the court system in order to maintain their privacy. LGBT couples fear being "outed," with the potential ramifications of being discriminated against either at work or within public society.

However, sometimes LGBT couples cannot avoid the court system. One such instance is child custody and visitation suits, which are the most frequently litigated controversy involving sexual orientation. These child custody cases can be especially emotional for LGBT couples when they have to overcome obstacles such as adoption, surrogacy, or donor insemination in order to have children.

LGBT couples must keep potential litigation in mind and plan in advance. In many cases, one of the LGBT partners may have the status of being a non-adoptive or non-biological parent. A prudent course of action for the non-adoptive non-biological LGBT parent would be to adopt the child as his or her own, or seek to have the birth certificate amended. The stakes are high if this is not accomplished. For instance, the United States Supreme Court decision Troxel v. Granville stated that the Court would avoid extending parental rights to non-parents. Many courts treat a non-adoptive, non-biological LGBT parent as a non-parent or, using a commentator's term, a "legal stranger." Troxel and many courts instead give a custody preference to the biological parent. The only way a non-adoptive, non-biological LGBT parent can be granted custody is if he or she can achieve standing as a parent. The requirements of such standing vary state by state. Additionally, the court must also determine what is in the best interests of the child.

Non-adoptive, non-biological LGBT parents have used many arguments to obtain custody. Some LGBT parents have argued that custody and visitation statutes should be interpreted broadly to include LGBT parents, and some states do interpret existing statutes in such a manner. States such as Maryland, Minnesota, and New Jersey allow a non-adoptive, non-biological LGBT parent to gain custody or joint custody if they can prove they had a "parent-like" relationship with the child. If the non-adoptive, non-biological LGBT parent can prove the required link, a possibility exists that LGBT parent could be granted custody or joint custody. However, there is no guarantee that a state court will find this established link.

Alternatively, the non-adoptive, non-biological LGBT parent can seek to be a "psychological parent." This may allow the LGBT parent to obtain visitation privileges. If a trial court judge rules against the LGBT parent, the decision will likely stand because wide deference is given to state trial courts on family law issues. Many states do not even grant a third-party LGBT parent any standing in order to gain custody. Frequently, non-adoptive, non-biological LGBT parents have been at the mercy of the courts. Because of the negative legal biases against LGBT couples and parents within the American legal system, the LGBT community has long turned to mediation as a preferred way to settle family disputes.

NOTES AND QUESTIONS

1.   Given the legal framework that Hanson sketches out, what general advantages do you see to mediation for LGBT participants? How about disadvantages? Write a list of both.

2.   Examine the list you have written. Could you contemplate one party viewing any of these advantages as disadvantages? Vice versa? If so, which ones?

3.   We will be considering issues relating to "power" issues in mediation in Chapter 8. Even prior to that discussion, do you have ideas as to what extent, if any, the legal framework or lack thereof "empower" one party in LGBT family mediation? Is this any different from how law might empower one party in a mediation involving heterosexual participants? If so, how generally and specifically?

4.   Should mediators who facilitate LGBT disputes have any special qualifications? Would mediators who are themselves LGBT be particularly appropriate?

5.   Are LGBT mediations substantially different from mediations involving heterosexuals? The range of family dynamics, the nature of conflicts within relationships, parenting issues, and financial arrangements might well be no different from those mediators encounter with heterosexual participants. Although we are not aware of studies examining this issue, anecdotal evidence suggests there is disagreement among mediators who specialize in LGBT mediations about this question.

Chapter 7

MEDIATING OTHER FAMILY CONFLICTS

A. INTRODUCTION

"Family mediation," while often conceived of as involving divorce and child access, can encompass many other disputes in which family dynamics play a part. The concepts and practical applications that we have been exploring often apply in these types of disputes, although each has its own distinctive qualities.

This Chapter will offer an overview of these disputes. Coverage is necessarily brief and something of a "grab bag," but this is not intended to dismiss the significance of the growing use of mediation in these and other types of disputes in which families are involved.

B. CARE OF INFIRM FAMILY MEMBERS

A range of wrenching issues face families who have ill or aging family members. As the population ages, these situations are, unfortunately, becoming increasingly common. They generally fall into two general categories: 1) end of life decisions and 2) guardianship cases.

1. End of Life Decisions

Situations involving family disputes are no doubt familiar through the intensely publicized case of Terri Schiavo, but, of course, many less heralded situations face families. Sometimes these disputes arise between physicians and family members, while others are among family members. Both may implicate family dynamics, but the latter is more likely to do so. Consider the situation in the following excerpt.

MEDIATING LIFE AND DEATH DECISIONS[1]
36 Ariz. L. Rev. 821, 830–831, 836–838, 873–874 (1994)
By Diane E. Hoffman

. . . Joseph R. is a 75 year old male with a history of chronic emphysema who suffered a massive stroke while hospitalized for breathing difficulties. As a result of the stroke, he was initially unable to breathe on his own and experienced considerable loss of brain function. He was supported on a ventilator, underwent surgical drainage of intraventricular cerebrospinal fluid and then placement of a permanent shunt, was weaned from the ventilator but required a tracheostomy tube. He developed a pneumonia and was being given IV (intravenous) antibiotics to treat the infection. His other medical conditions included diabetes, hypertension, and chronic bronchitis.

The patient's family, his 49 year old son, who is an engineer, and his 42 year old daughter, who is a nurse, disagree about the appropriate course of treatment for him. The daughter wants the attending physician to stop treating the patient with antibiotics and wants only tube feeding and hydration administered. The son disagrees. He bases his decision on the attending physician's remarks that the pneumonia is reversible and would routinely be treated. If the antibiotics are discontinued the patient will likely die from the pneumonia. If the pneumonia is treated, the patient may live more than six months, although he will suffer from the residual effects of the stroke, i.e., diminished mental capacity, and from his other chronic conditions.

In an interview with the chair of the institution's ethics committee, the patient's daughter stated that it seemed to her that the patient was only going "downhill all the way." In particular, she remembered her 19 year old nephew who twice suffered a cardiac arrest and each time was "saved" only to become "blind, demented, and comatose." That, the daughter related, was thought by the patient to be a terrible outcome and something that he wanted to avoid for himself. The patient's son, however, remembered that when their mother died, their father did everything to keep her alive despite the fact that she was bedridden and senile.

The daughter had cared for the father during the previous year in her home and felt that she should make this decision. The son, although close to his father as a younger man, had not seen his father much during the past six years as he had moved across the country to take a new job . . .

In the case of family disputes, disputing parties can include spouses, adult children where the patient has more than one child, a spouse and a child, a spouse and a parent, a parent and a sibling, some other combination of individuals related to the patient, or disputes between blood relatives and domestic partners. . . .

What makes disputes among family members unique is the historical relationship of those individuals. Family disputes often come "wrapped in a thick gauze of past relationships." These relationships also tend to be ongoing and are often interdependent. Each family is unique but typically has an established pattern of relating wherein the individuals take on certain roles. These roles, in terms of dominance and dependence are likely to play themselves out in the context of health care decision-making.

---

[1] Copyright ©1994. Reprinted with permission.

For example, there may be power issues at play. Certain family members may have dominated family life years ago and want to continue in that role, e.g., "mom would have wanted me to speak for her, not you." Others may now resent that domination and attempt to assert their more recent status within the family or relationship with the patient, e.g., "I was a better daughter than you, I cared more about mom, you were never good to mom, you never visited mom while she was in the nursing home," etc. The case of Joseph R. has some of these elements. The patient's daughter seems resentful of the fact that her brother has not participated much in the care of their father or even visited him much during the past six years and now wants to participate in the decision about their father's treatment . . .

The case of Joseph R. seems to have most of the attributes of the "paradigm" case for mediation. It is likely that the parties — Joseph's 49 year old son and 42 year old daughter — would be willing to mediate their disagreement and, in fact, may prefer it to the "intervention" of an ethics committee. As brother and sister they have an "ongoing" relationship and they probably see this as a private family matter and may be reluctant to disclose these private matters to the scrutiny of a committee of "strangers." Both parties also seem to be "competent" to negotiate. Although they are both dealing with the possible death of their father, the facts indicate that Joseph has been ill for a number of years — his illness was not sudden. Also, it does not appear that there is a significant power imbalance between the parties. Although the son is older, there is no indication of a history of dominance on his part and although the daughter may be somewhat more knowledgeable of the medical issues, given her nursing background, both parties appear to be well educated. There may be some underlying emotional issues influencing their positions, i.e., guilt on the part of the son for not being around more for his father during his illness, and resentment on the part of the daughter towards her brother, yet neither party appears to have any overriding conflict of interest that would prevent him or her from acting in the best interest of their father. Although it may seem fairly narrowly defined, the resolution of the case also does not necessarily rely on a choice between two mutually exclusive options — treatment with antibiotics or no treatment with antibiotics. The options can be expanded to include other types of treatment, e.g., CPR if the patient has a cardiac arrest, ventilatory support if the pneumonia does not respond to the antibiotics, artificial nutrition and hydration, etc.

As mentioned, the Joseph R. case has a host of emotional issues that need to be addressed between the two parties. It is not a case that is purely ethical or legal. Finally, a norm centered approach to the case will not necessarily lead to a single, best outcome. Both results advocated by the parties, treatment and no treatment, are justifiable on ethical or legal grounds. Both ethical and legal norms would support the son and daughter as appropriate decision-makers in this case and there is evidence to support a conclusion that providing or withholding of the antibiotics is consistent with what the patient would have wanted or is in his best interests.

NOTES AND QUESTIONS

1.   This excerpt does not fully detail how exceptionally careful the author is to argue that mediation must be used with extreme care in these cases, and, in many instances, it should not be used at all. How does she define the "Joseph R." as a case that is appropriate for mediation? What sorts of cases, given her analysis, would not

be appropriate for mediation? Does the litigation alternative offer a more effective way to resolve conflicts in this area than mediation?

2.   Institutional "ethics committees" are important entities in reaching decisions about medical care. The author argues that such committees should, in appropriate cases, be involved in mediation, even to the extent in participating in the mediation itself. Is this a departure from "traditional" norms of mediation appropriate in these cases? In one famous case involving Karen Ann Quinlan, the New Jersey Supreme Court held that the concurrence of the hospital ethics committee was necessary before Quinlan's feeding tube could be removed. Matter of Quinlan, 70 N.J. 10 (1976).

3.   One aspect of this type of mediation is its legal and, equally important, moral dimension. The morality of end of life decisions is, of course, hotly contested in public discourse and may strike at the core of individual values, whether religious or not. Can such differences be mediated? Consider the famous case of Terri Schiavo, which involved a dispute between Schiavo's husband, who wanted her feeding tube removed, and her parents, who did not. The case was litigated but never mediated. Is it in society's interest to privately mediate such disputes or are there advantages to a public adjudication through the courts? For discussions of this issue, see Judith D. Moran, Families, Courts and the End of Life: Schiavo and Its Implications for the Family Justice System, 46 Fam. Ct. Rev. 297 (2008); Robert M. Shafton, Family Meltdown or Mediation? Schiavo Converges Private and Public ADR Needs, 23 Alternatives to High Cost Lit. 77 (2005).

4.   To what extent is end-of-life mediation similar or different from family mediation as conventionally understood?

2.   Guardianship

MEDIATION: A TOOL FOR RESOLUTION OF ADULT GUARDIANSHIP CASES[2]
14 Nat'l Ass'n of Elderlaw Attorneys Q. 4, 6–7 (2001)
By Susan Butterwick & Penelope A. Hommel

Robert Jones is concerned that his sister, Linda Smith, a single working mother, is not giving their mother, Mary Jones, the care she needs and is wasting her assets. Mary Jones has lived in Linda's home for a year.

Take One — without mediation:

Robert files a petition requesting that he be appointed guardian of his mother. Mary and Linda are angry and upset at this action. The matter escalates into litigation in which harsh accusations are exchanged. The judge appoints a third party non-relative as guardian. The guardian moves Mary into an adult care home. All parties end up angry and hurt.

Take Two — with mediation:

The parties meet with a mediator who helps them identify needs and issues. They recognize that Mary enjoys living with Linda, but she is lonely while Linda is at work. They acknowledge that Mary is confused about her finances and Robert is willing to help. With the mediator's help, they agree that Mary will continue to live with Linda; Robert will help Mary with her bills, and Mary will attend a senior center during the week. They agree to meet in three months to review the situation. The parties end up understanding and respecting each other's concerns. And, an unnecessary guardianship is avoided . . .

Mediation can save time in the long-run in cases where the legal issues presented in the petition or motion are not the underlying issues causing the family turmoil and dissension. Complicated family dynamics can be extremely difficult and time-consuming for courts and attorneys to try to unravel and find an equitable solution that meets the needs and interests of the proposed ward as well as other parties. Mediation allows the parties to discuss the underlying interests and needs in a way that more fully addresses some of the real "sticking points" that can make court hearings contentious and sometimes lead to violation of court orders and further hearings. Mediation can also result in a more thorough, personalized, and specific plan that better addresses underlying issues and needs than a court can craft. In the long-run, the more specifically these underlying needs and issues can be addressed at the beginning, the more time is saved in repeated court hearings and even litigation later on, when difficulties arise in contentious cases or in cases involving difficult family relationships . . .

[C]ases [can begin] where disputes arise at the time an initial petition for guardianship is filed. Typically the respondent feels s/he is able to make his or her own decisions and does not need a guardian because a less restrictive alternative is available. Or, the respondent may contest the petition on the grounds that the guardian's powers should be limited, or that someone other than the petitioner should be named guardian. Of course, other interested parties may also raise any of these issues.

Other disputes arise after a guardian has been appointed. These issues, raised either by the ward or by another interested party, may involve accounting for expenditures by the guardian, the need to continue the guardianship, a petition to terminate, limit, or expand the guardian's powers, a petition to remove the guardian and substitute another, or a challenge to an action or proposed action of the guardian.

Disputes may also arise in advance of, or in anticipation of, the filing of a guardianship petition. Issues in these "pre-petition" situations may include such things as whether the person needs a surrogate decision maker (a guardian, conservator, or power of attorney) and who that person would be, what medical care decisions should be made, whether the person needs a change in living arrangements and care facilities, other issues involving autonomy, independence, safety, and decision-making, and how money will be invested or spent and by whom. Often, legal issues are not the ones causing the turmoil, and the parties in mediation may focus on quite different issues from those that would be argued in a legal case or court proceding. Even when there are no contested legal issues, family disputes may need to be addressed in order to preserve family relations or avoid future litigation.

Cases that are inappropriate for mediation are those where domestic abuse or substance abuse are involved, or where an emergency decision is needed by a court, the parties exhibit volatile or extremely hostile behavior, or when the possibility of coercion or intimidation of a vulnerable party exists. The personal presence of the alleged incapacitated person or ward may not be appropriate if the person is too incapacitated to take part in the mediation and understand and voluntarily make or keep agreements. In such circumstance, nevertheless, mediation may be helpful for the other parties — family members, caregivers, other support persons, who may disagree among themselves over the best course to follow for an incapacitated person.

NOTES AND QUESTIONS

1.   Yet again family dynamics are at play in these situations. Nevertheless, there is a unique element here: decisions to be reached in mediation are, by definition, about an individual — the "ward" or "alleged incompetent person" — who may or may not be present in the mediation and may be incompetent. Indeed, the determination this individual's competence is often the sole or primary issue of mediation. Does this strike you as appropriate for mediation? Should there be additional participants in these mediations?

2.   The Model Rules of Professional Conduct define "diminished capacity" as caused by "minority, mental impairment, or some other reason." MODEL RULES OF PROF'L CONDUCT R. 1.14. As a matter of law, parents or others involved in family mediation are guardians of minors. Does child access mediation have similar characteristics to guardianship mediation? Why or why not?

3.   As with end of life mediation, expert medical opinion seems to be crucial in guardianship mediation. Should physicians or mental health professionals be formally included in such mediation? If so how? What alternatives might there be?

C. TRUSTS AND ESTATES

Most issues surrounding estate planning and administration involve family issues in one form or another. Obviously the vast majority of estate planning and administration matter are straightforward and/or generate no controversy, but this is not always the case.

The growth of mediation in this area falls into two categories: 1) anticipating conflict through mediation clauses in estate planning documents; 2) employing mediation to resolve disputes surrounding estates whether or not estate documents contain a mediation clause.[3]

Mediation in the context of trusts and estates, as with other matters we have been exploring, typically involves family dynamics. Most will disputes are among family members. Some family members might resent their share of an estate given additional burdens associated with the care of an aging testator. Sometimes shares of an estate claimed by a second or subsequent spouse will lead to conflict among other family members. Moreover, as discussed in the next section, disputes

---

[3] For an excellent overview of the role in mediation in estate planning and disputes, see Roslyn L. Friedman & Erica E. Loard, *Using Facilitative Mediation in a Changing Estate Planning Practice*, 32 EST. PLAN. 15 (2005).

generated by the transfer of family businesses can raise delicate issues about succession and control among families.

The risk of such disputes has made the inclusion of mediation clauses in wills more common, and this, and the advantages of mediation after such disputes arise whether or not a mediation clause is in a will, should be obvious:

- Litigated will contests are time consuming and expensive, which both dissipates resources of parties who might share in the estate and delays the dispensation of shares of the estate.
- Remedies available through litigation are uncertain and unlikely to satisfy family members in conflict.
- Litigation is more likely to drive siblings apart, thereby generating resentment that might permanently damage family relationships.
- Will contests may, at bottom, be driven by longstanding issues with relationships within families, and mediation might allow venting and airing of grievances which has the potential to address underlying causes of conflict.

It is important to note that estate conflicts need not involve large sums of money. Financial value is not always related to the intensity of conflict. For example, jewelry or family heirlooms might generate passionate conflict despite their monetary value being modest. Continuing resentments and conflict might lead to lasting or even irreparable conflict among family members, with, once again, mediation offering the promise of resolving issues productively. Indeed, depending on the items at issue, their "value" in a monetary sense might make litigation not feasible, and, thus, mediation might be the only plausible means of conflict resolution.

D.   FAMILY BUSINESS DISPUTES

It is common for organizations to arise and continue to be "family businesses," that is, businesses which are substantially or entirely controlled within a family. These businesses can range from the proverbial "mom and pop" store to multinational corporations. While disputes among family members involved in the same business can happen at any time, such disputes commonly arise as founders of businesses age or die and spouses, siblings, or other relatives dispute management or ownership. At least in terms of the commercial dimension of these disputes, business leadership, at the surface, appears to be the primary issue for resolution.

Nevertheless, passion and emotion generated by such disputes can be extraordinarily high. While disputes about business organizations may, at first blush, be solely about money, particularly in comparison with divorce or child access disputes, this is usually not the case. Simmering tensions and conflicts within family relationships overlap with business considerations. Such disputes thus have a close relationship with family mediation as more commonly understood: they involve conflict laced with emotion generated by longstanding family dynamics where the preservation of the relationship (as in child access) is crucial to a durable and successful resolution. There is the additional interest in privacy which can be driven by a desire not only to avoid airing embarrassing personal issues, but also to minimize or eliminate the impact that a public airing of family "dirty laundry" can have on the business itself. Of course, divorce can also involve complex financial business and financial considerations. These many parallels with family mediation have led some mediators to "specialize" both in divorce and in family business disputes. Successful mediation of these disputes does require the mediator to have some expertise in financial matters, particularly in the context of businesses.

Another aspect of mediation involve family business disputes is how mediation can involve a range of family members or others who might not be formal "parties" in litigation. This might enhance the quality of the path to resolution and the durability of any resolution that might be reached.

Lawyers play a distinctive role in family business disputes. It is highly likely that disputants in this type of conflict have resources and thus almost always have retained an attorney, particularly a lawyer with some experience in litigating general business disputes. While no research and little scholarship have been devoted to this area, some evidence suggests that such lawyers still embrace mediation as preferable to litigation, albeit typically after litigation has been commenced.[4] Lawyers might have a tendency to veer towards evaluative mediation — a commonly employed style in general business mediation — although mediators who are involved in family disputes can engage in the full range of styles, including transformative mediation.

---

[4] James John Jurinski & Gary A. Zwick, *How To Prevent and Solve Operating Problems in Family Business*, 47 Prac. Law. 37 (2001).

Chapter 8

THE "POWER CRITIQUE" AND FAMILY MEDIATION

A. INTRODUCTION

Commentators and practitioners of family mediation often grapple with the challenges of how to address "power differentials" among parties. Early proponents highlighted mediation's promise as a dispute resolution tool especially suited to disputes where one party is less powerful. Other commentators, focusing on the informality and privacy of mediation, have developed a "power critique" which questions the suitability of mediation for certain groups of people or as a means to resolve classes of disputes.

This Chapter will examine "power" and family mediation at several levels. One set of issues plays out prior to and in specific mediation sessions: preexisting power dynamics might exist between the parties and mediation sessions themselves might have aspects that enhance the power of one party or another. We will also examine how power develops or is enacted at a family mediation session — a complex and critical topic in and of itself.

A second issue is the extent to which, if at all, a family mediator has a role to play in somehow "equalizing" or at least minimizing such power disparities. The tension between such a role for a mediator, if it is appropriate at all, and a mediator's status as a "third party neutral" is a significant challenge in family mediation.

A third issue is whether, as a matter of public policy, certain situations by their nature generate such substantial power disparities that mediation should not be an appropriate means to resolve such disputes. The classic example often given of such a circumstance is domestic violence, which we will explore in Chapter 9, but some commentators have gone further and argued that the mediation process itself tends to disfavor women. These debates often focus on family law mediation. We will examine arguments for and against such critiques and review legislative responses that seek to take these critiques into account.

B. THE ELEMENTS OF POWER

The term "power" often obscures as much as it reveals. While the abstract philosophical and political implications of the term need not detain us, the details of how power manifests itself in family mediation is a crucial issue that warrants sustained examination.

Power in family mediation, in its broadest sense, means the ability of one party to exert influence to achieve a desired end. While power usually has negative connotations and appears to be inconsistent with the spirit and process of mediation, this does not need to be the case. Such influence, for example, can be exerted for the good of both parties, or for children, or for the process. Moreover, it is seductive to reduce power to a ledger where one party has all of it and the other party has none of it. While there are certainly instances of very large and significant disparities of power, a closer examination of circumstances often reveals that there are, at least potentially, sources of power on the part of both parties. Moreover, as addressed in more detail below, power tends to be fluid in family mediation and to be allocated in complex ways. An appreciation of this complexity is central to success both as a mediator and as an attorney in family mediation.

1.   Preexisting Power Differerentials Between Parties Prior To Family Mediation

Family mediation, like any process of dispute resolution, occurs in real time between real people who have real circumstances and a real history of interactions. The intimacy that has usually existed between parties previously and its subsequent disintegration might well heighten the intensity and impact of all of these details, which, in turn, might generate "power" in favor of one party or another.

Here is a partial list of potential sources of power that parties to family mediation might possess:

- Physical power: There might be history of threatened or actual physical violence in a marriage.

- Emotional power: Marital relationships may be characterized by emotional abuse through words or actions.

- Financial power: One spouse might command greater compensation, or real or personal property, or have ready access to financial resources through extended family or contacts. In addition, financial power might be exerted through knowledge: one spouse might have exclusively or primarily handled family finances, or have far greater knowledge of financial matters in general.

- Interpersonal style: It is common to describe human beings in terms of their willingness and ability to pursue needs and wants. Some people, for example, might have "strong personalities," or "be aggressive" or "forward." In contrast, others might be "timid," or "retiring," or "soft-spoken." These terms do not necessarily mean that individuals who exhibit individual characteristics are successful or unsuccessful in getting what they want. For example, a person who is soft-spoken but determined and diplomatic might be more likely to achieve desired ends than an aggressive, impetuous person. Moreover, as with much else, success or failure depends upon a particular context. That said, these personality types, interacting over time in a relationship, might describe longstanding power differentials between parties prior to and at the mediation.

• Custody or possession: The old saw that "possession is nine-tenths of the law" has particular meaning in family mediation. One party might currently have sole custody of children, or of a home, or of personal property. Such possession might generate power in favor of the possessor.

2.   Power Differentials at the Mediation Session

While the above list describes power differentials prior to the mediation sessions, these, of course, may manifest themselves in the family mediation itself. There are other power differentials, however, that tend to tie to the mechanics and process of mediation, although they might flow from the differentials we have already described.

• One party is represented and one party is not. As discussed more fully below, the existence of an attorney for only one side introduces a power differential. Even if the attorney does not attend the mediation, the represented party has far greater access to an expert source of information about judicial proceedings, each party's legal rights and remedies, and the parties' chances of success in court. If the attorney actually attends the mediation, there might power in terms of greater numbers or of the voice of a trained advocate speaking on behalf of one party. The represented party might also be less willing to work towards a resolution in the mediation, for the prospect of a judicial proceeding might be less daunting when represented by a lawyer.

• Time. In the famous words of Andrew Marvell, "If there were but world enough and time . . . " Parties to family mediation might well inhabit worlds characterized by different time constraints. A spouse, for example, who earns an hourly wage, or who has a significant commute to work, or who has primary or exclusive child care responsibilities might not be in a position to devote substantial time to mediation. This, in turn, might motivate that spouse to simply get the mediation process over with quickly. In such a situation, the other spouse can use time to generate leverage to his or her advantage.

• Location. The location of the mediation might generate sources of power. The location might be in a setting familiar to one party and not to the other (say, at the office of a lawyer representing one party) or the location may be more convenient to one party than to another.

• The Law. All jurisdictions, of course, have detailed family law statutes that address the dissolution of marriages and issues of custody and visitation. Although, as with much else in adjudication, questions usually arise as to the "facts" that would generate a judicial decision going one way or another, sometimes a party has relatively clear legal rights or advantages under the law that could then become a source of power in mediation.

- The Mediator: The gender, race, or ethnicity of the mediator may have an impact on the power balance between the parties to the mediation.

3. Does Mediation Itself Preserve Preexisting Power Imbalances?

Proponents of mediation have argued that it has many advantages over litigation for all disputants, including women, people of color, immigrants and the poor. They argue that the hierarchical, "winner takes all" approach of the dominant adversary system further disempowers and silences the less powerful. The delays, expense, complexity and inflexibility of litigation make it particularly ill suited to resolving family disputes. Mediation, on the other hand, with its emphasis on listening, relationships, and problem solving has greater potential to "heal" and "hear" all voices. Further, some claim that mediation's focus on permitting participants to express emotions and articulate needs may be better suited to women than men. Its procedural informality, lack of reliance on substantive rules of law and lower cost might make it more accessible to those who cannot afford lawyers and are not well versed in the American justice system.

Other scholars maintain that mediation is most inappropriate, even dangerous, when it involves family disputes involving couples where one party is less powerful than the other. They argue that, among other things that mediation's lack of formal procedures, confidential, private setting, focus on the parties' "needs" rather than "rights" under substantive family law, and lack of meaningful review of both the process and outcome of mediation create a setting where the more powerful dominate and bias and prejudice are unchecked.

C. DOES FAMILY MEDIATION TEND TO DISFAVOR WOMEN?

Some commentators have argued that mediation itself tends to disfavor women. Family mediation often involves a woman and a man[1], and thus most of this debate centers on how family mediation affects women. The following excerpt is from perhaps the most prominent of these critiques. As you read this excerpt, consider whether and why you are or are not convinced by the author's arguments.

---

[1] Of course, mediation involving same-sex couples is common and an important topic in and of itself. We explored such mediations in Chapter 6.

THE MEDIATION ALTERNATIVE: PROCESS DANGERS FOR WOMEN[2]

100 Yale L.J. 1545, 1555–1581 (1991)

By Trina Grillo

. . . The good woman: She comes into mediation ready to be cooperative. She does not deny her feelings, but does not shift them onto her children. She realizes her problems are her problems, that she should not use the children as a way of solving them, and that it is critically important that her husband stay involved in the lives of the children. She does not play victim, but realizes what she is entitled to and insists on it calmly. She is rational, not bitter or vengeful, and certainly not interested in hurting her husband. She understands that she played a role in whatever harms he inflicted on her, since in a family no one person is ever at fault.

The bad woman: She is bitter and wants revenge for things that have happened to her in the past. She fights over the most trivial, petty things. She is greedy and ready to sacrifice her children as a tool against her husband. She is irrational and unwilling to compromise. When a specific, focused response is called for, she responds by bringing up a completely unrelated matter. It is hard to keep her on track. She keeps venting her anger instead of negotiating constructively . . .

Persons in the midst of a divorce often experience what seems to them a threat to their very survival. Their self-concepts, financial well-being, moral values, confidence in their parenting abilities, and feelings of being worthy of love are all at risk. They are profoundly concerned about whether they are meeting their obligations and continuing to be seen as virtuous persons and respectable members of society. They are especially vulnerable to the responses they receive from any professional with whom they must deal. Against this backdrop, mediation must be seen as a relatively high-risk process . . . The parties do generally not understand its norms in advance, with the result that the parties are extremely sensitive to cues as to how they are supposed to act; they will look to the mediator to provide these cues. Mediators are often quite willing to give such cues, to establish the normative components of the mediation, and to sanction departures from the unwritten rules . . . These sanctions might be as simple as criticizing the client for not putting the children's needs first, or instructing her not to talk about a particular issue. That these informal sanctions might appear trivial does not mean they will not be as influential in changing behavior as sanctions that might on their face appear more severe.

. . . The informal law of the mediation setting requires that discussion of principles, blame, and rights, as these terms are used in the adversarial context, be deemphasized or avoided. Mediators use informal sanctions to encourage the parties to replace the rhetoric of fault, principles, and values with the rhetoric of compromise and relationship. For example, mediators typically suggest that the parties "eschew the language of individual rights in favor of the language of interdependent relationships." They orient the parties toward reasonableness and compromise, rather than moral vindication. The conflict may be styled as a personal quarrel, in which there is no right and wrong, but simply two different, and equally true or untrue, views of the world.

. . . [T]he reluctance to discuss principles is based on the view, held by most mediators, that . . . all parts of the family are equally implicated in whatever happens within it. Each part of this system is simultaneously a cause for, and an effect of, all the other parts . . . Under this approach, "the mediator can view the interactional system between the husband and wife in such a way that each spouse's behavior appears perfectly complementary to that of the other spouse and the concepts of reasonable and unreasonable no longer apply."

Although this systems approach can be a useful one in understanding how families and other social organizations work, it has some serious shortcomings. Most critically, it obscures issues of unequal social power and sex role socialization. Structures within the nuclear family are viewed in isolation from outside social attitudes and forces. Thus, a person who has been a victim of violence can be seen as deserving her fate because of her self-defeating patterns of behavior and participation in cyclical negative interactions with her spouse. In this manner, the family systems approach imposes a value-free universe. It does not leave room for the situation in which one parent is complying with the legitimate expectations of society and the other is not . . .

Moreover, an unrefined family systems perspective can deprive a divorcing spouse of the opportunity to appear virtuous in society's eyes and her own. No matter how much she struggles, her good works are for naught so long as she is connected to someone who is acting irresponsibly. To the extent mediation incorporates such a family systems perspective, the spouse who is doing "good work" must bear the burden of the other spouse's noncompliance . . .

Kenny had spent ten days with his father Jerry and was scheduled to return to his mother on a flight arriving on Thanksgiving afternoon. That morning, Jerry called Linda[, Kenny's mother and Jerry's ex-wife,] and told her that flying was expensive, and that he was returning to his ex-wife's area at Christmas anyway. He said he intended to keep Kenny with him until then; Kenny's stepmother would care for Kenny at their home. Linda, her Thanksgiving dinner in the oven and relatives scheduled to arrive, thought of going herself to pick up Kenny or going to court, but decided that the worst thing for Kenny would be a custody battle.

When Kenny returned at Christmas, his behavior was odd; for the first time in his life he was violent and aggressive toward other children. Upon questioning Kenny, Linda discovered that he had not been cared for by his stepmother during the day as promised, but had instead been sent to unlicensed daycare where the teacher had regularly used corporal punishment, to which Linda was passionately opposed and to which Kenny had never before been subjected.

In mediation, Linda asks that she be given primary custody of Kenny. She says that Jerry has been untruthful, unreliable, and has risked Kenny's emotional and physical well-being. She tries to argue that such a young child needs one home base, and that should be her home since she was effectively his sole parent for most of his first three years of life. The mediator does not allow her to make these points. Instead, she says that the past is not to be discussed; rather, they must plan together about the future. She says that whether Jerry participated in Kenny's life for his early years is irrelevant; he is here now. The Thanksgiving situation is past history, and she is sure that they both have complaints about the past. Blaming one another is counterproductive. The mediator tells Linda that she must recognize that the parent who has the child is responsible for choosing daycare. Linda must learn to give up control.

The chief means by which mediators eliminate the discussion of principles and fault is by making certain types of discussion "off-limits" in the mediation . . . It is typical for mediators to insist that parties waste no time complaining about past conduct of their spouse, eschew blaming each other, and focus only on the future . . .

In Linda's case, the questions of whether Jerry had been remiss in not returning Kenny or in secretly placing Kenny in an inadequate childcare situation were ruled irrelevant by the mediator. The mediator did not permit discussion of these issues because reaching an agreement was paramount, and because, under family systems theory as interpreted by the mediator, Jerry could not be at fault — Linda and Jerry were equally responsible for everything. That Jerry had virtually disappeared, leaving Linda to struggle to raise her son alone, and that Jerry had not kept his word about returning Kenny after his visit were simply not proper subjects of discussion. There was nothing Linda could say to introduce these concerns into the dialogue. Further, she could not refer to the past to demonstrate she was a responsible and loving parent. Her attempts to protect her son were labeled as controlling.

. . . A woman I knew only vaguely from my daughter's school called me, her voice shaking, and asked me if I could mediate her case. I said that I could not, but would be glad to talk to her and refer her to other mediators. She told me that her husband had told her two days previously that he was leaving her and intended to marry someone else. He told her he wanted to have the divorce mediated and wanted joint custody of the children. He told her she would have to start looking for a job right away. He also told his wife that it would hurt the children if he and she were angry at each other, and that he wanted to retain a friendly, cordial relationship and have a rational, peaceful divorce. She cried into the phone that she felt terrible that she was unable to be rational, and that although she was trying hard to be mature, she still had these angry feelings. She still wanted to blame him, although she realized, she said, that nothing is ever black and white, and no one is at fault when a marriage breaks up . . .

One adverse consequence of de-emphasizing discussion of principle and fault is that some persons may be discouraged from asserting their rights when they have been injured. Even more troubling, some persons may cease to perceive injuries when they have been injured, or will perceive injuries but those injuries will remain inarticulable, because the language to name them will not be easily available. My acquaintance . . . did not trust her sense that she had been injured, treated in a way that human beings ought not to deal with each other. She did not have the support of a clear set of legal principles to help her define her injury; rather, she had been exposed to a discourse in which faultfinding was impermissible, so that she ended up unable to hold her husband responsible for his actions, and instead felt compelled to share his fault. To the extent that there is something to be gained by the assertion of rights, especially for women and minorities, this is unacceptable . . . Both the current state of divorce law and the reigning model of mediation were operating to keep her in a position in which she tried not to blame others and, in the process, lost herself . . .

Context is also destroyed [in mediation] by a commitment to formal equality, that is, to the notion that members of mediating couples are, to the extent possible, to be treated exactly alike, without regard for general social patterns and with limited attention to even the history of the particular couples. Thus, it becomes close to irrelevant in determining custody that the mother may have been home doing virtually all the caretaking of the children for years; she is to move into the labor market as quickly as possible. It is assumed that the father is equally competent to care for the children. In fact, it frequently is said that one cannot assume that a father will not be as competent a caretaker as the mother just because he has not shown any interest previously . . .

In mediation, insistence on this sort of formal equality results in a dismissal of the legitimate concerns of the parent who is, or considers herself to be, the more responsible parent . . . The insistence of a mother that a young child not be permitted to stay overnight with an alcoholic father who smokes in bed might be characterized as the mother needing to stay in control. Or the mediator might suggest that it is not legitimate for one party to assume that the other party will renege on her obligations, simply because she has done so in the past. In the example above, once Linda was in mediation, she was treated exactly equally with Jerry even though their past parental performance had been dramatically different . . . By defining the process as one in which both parties are situated equally, deep, heartfelt, and often accurate concerns either are not permitted to be expressed or are discounted . . .

All too often mediators stress the need for women to become economically independent without taking into account the very real dollar differences between the male and female experience in the labor market. While gaining independence might appear to be desirable, most jobs available for women, especially those who have been out of the labor market, are low paying, repetitious, and demeaning. Studies show that women in such dead-end jobs do not experience the glories of independence, but rather show increased depression . . .

Linda had taken a low-paying job in a childcare center so that Kenny could be with her while she worked. Jerry continued to work the chaotic schedule required by the railroad. After determining that Linda and Jerry would share custody of Kenny, the mediator asked Jerry what schedule would work for him. Jerry said that he could not be tied down to a particular schedule because his job on the railroad required him to be available at short notice and out of town for long periods of time. When Linda protested that both she and Kenny needed a predictable schedule, and that she had spent her entire married life at the mercy of the whims of his employer, the mediator smiled sympathetically and said, "I guess you didn't get to divorce the railroad after all" . . .

Mediators . . . are as likely as others in society to assume that women's work commitments are secondary to those of men, and to give more credence to the work obligations and ambitions of fathers. Women may be encouraged in mediation not to think of themselves as ideal workers so that they will be able to take on primary responsibility for the children . . . [T]he mediator expected Linda to be flexible and work around Jerry's schedule, even though the same flexibility was not required of Jerry. Thus, the "equality" that prevailed to give Jerry equal control did not require equal responsibility of him . . .

Women undergoing a divorce, especially ones from nondominant cultural groups, are particularly likely to be harmed by having their anger actively discouraged during the dissolution process. Women have been socialized not to express anger, and have often had their anger labeled "bad." A woman in the throes of divorce may for the first time in her life have found a voice for her anger. As her early, undifferentiated, and sometimes inchoate expressions of anger emerge, the anger may seem as overwhelming to her as to persons outside of it. And yet this anger may turn out to be the source of her energy, strength, and growth in the months and years ahead. An injunction from a person in power to suppress that anger because it is not sufficiently modulated may amount to nothing less that an act of violence . . .

Some mediation literature suggests that mediators should proceed by discouraging the expression of anger. This literature evinces a profound lack of respect for the anger that divorcing spouses feel . . . Even when mediation literature does approve of bringing anger into the process, it often recommends doing so in a way that subtly undercuts the legitimacy of the anger. Mediators are encouraged, where necessary, to permit parties to "vent" their anger, after which the parties can move on to discuss settlement. This view does not take anger seriously enough. Because it treats expressed anger as having no long-range impact on the party who is exposed to it, it is not necessarily seen as objectionable to require one party to be present and endure the other party's "venting" — even where the party enduring the venting has been the subject of abuse in the marriage.

[E]qually critically, the view of anger as something to be "vented" does not take anger seriously as a path to clarity and strength. Anger that is merely vented has lost its potential to teach, heal, and energize; it is ineffective anger, anger that "maintains rather than challenges" the status quo . . .

It is considered unfeminine to be angry, even angry with good reason: "From birth, the parent's awareness of the child's sex . . . organizes and directs that parent's response to the child's expression of anger, rebelliousness and protest. Despite changes brought about by the recent feminist movement, expressions of anger and aggression are still considered 'masculine' in men, and 'unfeminine' in women" . . .

We carry with us two powerful images of female ways of dealing with aggression. The first image is of the "nice lady" or peacemaker: a woman who, "in situations that might realistically evoke anger or protest . . . stays silent — or become s tearful, self-critical or 'hurt.' " Women serving this image are vulnerable to victimization and "share deep unconscious anxieties about 'fighting' which interfere not only with their ability to express anger, but with their capacity to be adaptively self-assertive and competitive as well." But under the "nice woman" exterior is much unconscious rage, which, because direct experience of it is forbidden to women, may be experienced as depression, hurt or guilt. "The amount of creative, intellectual and sexual energy that is trapped by this need to repress anger and remain unaware of its sources is simply incalculable."

The second image imposed on women is that of the "bitch." Bitchiness, descriptive of women who express anger with ease, is characterized by "ineffective fighting, complaining, and blaming that leads to no constructive resolution." This image is forced on women "when intra-psychic and cultural pressures combine to inhibit the direct and appropriate expression of legitimate anger and protest." The alternative presented is not to express anger at all. The "bitch" is willing to experience her anger and communicate it in some sense, but may "get stuck in a pattern of ineffective fighting, complaining and blaming that only preserves the status quo"; she may "unwittingly protect others" at her own expense.

Neither of the alternatives traditionally available to women allows a woman to use her anger to clarify and strengthen herself and her relationships. Rather, both alternatives force her to deny, displace, internalize, or fear it . . .

[A]t the time of divorce, all women must cope to some degree with being alone, physically, economically, and for all to see, sometimes for the first time in their lives. They must deal with a painful and permanent loss of connection when, for some, the experience of connection has been the hallmark of their lives. At this vulnerable moment, they may be told in a child custody mediation that their anger is not legitimate. This is a message that their worst fears are true: "You are, indeed," they are told, "threatening your own children by expressing your anger." . . .

NOTES AND QUESTIONS

1. Are you convinced by some or all of Grillo's points? If you are convinced, which ones and why?

2. One possible response to Grillo's argument is that the situations she describes are examples of "bad" mediation. For example, in *In Defense of Mediation*, 33 Ariz. L. Rev. 467, 468 (1991), Joshua Rosenberg argues:

> Professor Grillo's stories tell about mediators who appallingly misapply family systems theory; mediators who dismiss as irrelevant important family history; mediators who make unsubstantiated assumptions that one parent is or is not an appropriate caretaker; mediators who make their own "determinations" and rulings rather than let the parties decide with respect to child custody; mediators who make parties feel guilty and bad about themselves; and mediators who are rude, insensitive, stupid, or otherwise incompetent. I do not doubt that such mediators exist. Similarly, some physicians have raped and murdered their patients, judges have knowingly sentenced innocent men to death, presidents have lied and cheated, and schoolteachers have exhibited racial bias to their students. Nonetheless, we require parents to subject their children to both school and medical care, and we are all required to live according to rules established by politicians and courts. We do not judge these necessary aspects of our everyday lives by focusing only on various worst case scenarios.

Do you agree? Or, to put the matter somewhat differently, if you were the mediator in Linda and Jerry's mediation, or in the scenarios Grillo describes, would you or could you have handled the mediation differently? If yes, how would you have done so? For a list of "power balancing" techniques mediators can employ that may address some of these issues, see Michael Lang, *Understanding and Responding to Power in Mediation*, in Folberg, DIVORCE AND FAMILY MEDIATION 209–224 (2004); Diane Neuman, *How Mediation Can Effectively Address the Male-Female Power Imbalance in Divorce*, 9 Mediation Q. 227, 229 (1982).

3.   Even if you agree that Grillo chooses only examples of "bad mediation," does this fully answer Grillo's argument? After all, not all mediators are equally skilled or sophisticated, and an implication of Grillo's argument is that an "informal" process like mediation carries particular "risks" that are not present in judicial proceedings. Then again, not all judges are equally skilled or sophisticated either. Is there something about mediation that makes this more worrisome? Less worrisome? Are there specifics about a particular mediation or the circumstances leading up to it that would make a difference to you in answering these questions? *See, e.g.,* Robert Rubinson, *A Theory of Access to Justice,* 29 J. Leg. Prof. 97, 154–60 (2005) (exploring the advantages and risks of good and bad mediating and judging, and proposing a mediation alternative that minimizes these risks).

4.   The crux of many of Grillo's arguments is that litigation is a more effective means than mediation for women to vindicate their rights, express their anger, and transcend social stereotypes. Do you agree with these conclusions? For a different view on the potential of the adversary system to address the needs of women and minorities in resolving disputes, see Carrie Menkel-Meadow, *The Trouble with the Adversary System In A Postmodern, Multicultural World,* 38 Wm. & Mary L. Rev. 5 (1996).

5.   An interesting aspect of the debate about mediation and its impact on women is that although the discussion is usually framed as being about "mediation" generally (see, for example, the titles of the Grillo and Rosenberg articles), the details of the argument almost always involve family mediation. Is there something about family mediation that poses particular risks for women? Are these risks, to the extent they are present, also present in family law litigation? If so, are they present to the same degree? Compare Richard Delgado et al., *Fairness and Formality: Minimizing The Risk of Prejudice In Alternative Dispute Resolution,* 1985 Wis. L. Rev. 1359, 1402 (arguing the mediation's privacy and informality promote free expression of prejudice and bias making it particularly dangerous for mediation of issues that touch "a sensitive or intimate area of life" such as "intra familial disputes") with Ann Milne, *Mediation — A Promising Alternative for Family Courts,* 1991 Juv. & Fam. Cts. J. 61 (1991) (arguing that mediation is particularly well-suited to resolving disputes among family members because agreements, rather than a public adversarial proceeding, are less destructive to family relationships, particularly parent-child ties).

6.   As we have seen, when resources permit, it is not unusual for two mediators — typically a woman and a man — to "co-mediate" family law matters. Do you see such co-mediation as a means to minimize Grillo's concerns? *See, e.g.,* Isabelle Gunning, *Diversity Issues In Mediation: Controlling Negative Cultural Myths,* 1995 J. Disp. Reso. 55, 88–90 (arguing for greater mediator intervention to combat cultural bias but suggesting that the benefits and practicality of matching mediator and disputants' gender, race or ethnicity are limited). How about the presence of attorneys for one or both parties? The risks of mediation for unrepresented parties are discussed more fully below.

7.   Many social scientists have noted that human beings often identify with a range of socially recognized categories apart from gender, including race, ethnicity, age, religious affiliation or non-affiliation, professional status, geographic origin, and many others. *See generally* Robert Rubinson, *Constructions of Client Competence and Theories of Practice,* 31 Ariz. St. L.J. 121 (1999) (exploring the impact of social assumptions about the elderly and other social groups on members of those

groups and on others who interact with them). To what extent do Professor Grillo's arguments apply to categories combined with gender, such as, say, an African-American woman? Does it matter if the woman is part of a biracial couple where the man is white? What about when a woman is white and a man is African-American? How does wealth or poverty affect the power balance between men and women? Does the power balance continue to exist if a woman has greater access to economic resources than a man?

8.   Research on mediation and the impact of power imbalance is mixed. The research looking at gender differences in family mediation tends to show different results depending upon a number of factors including the type of issues mediated (custody vs. financial issues), whether process or outcomes are being examined, and whether the parties have experienced both litigation and mediation. For a summary of some of the research regarding gender and mediation, see J. FOLBERG, A. MILNE & P. SALEM, DIVORCE AND FAMILY MEDIATION 456–57 (2004) (citing studies that showed, among other things, that women were more satisfied with the process of mediation than men but less satisfied with the outcome of mediation than men; another study showed that men were less satisfied than women with litigation outcomes as compared to mediation outcomes).

D.   *PRO SE* LITIGANTS

Unrepresented parties present a particular challenge in family mediation. Recent statistics from state courts across the country demonstrate that family law cases constitute 25% of trial court civil dockets. NATIONAL CENTER FOR STATE COURTS, EXAMINING THE WORK OF STATE COURTS: A NATIONAL PERSPECTIVE FROM THE COURT STATISTICS PROJECTS 33 (2006). The majority of such cases involve one or both parties who do not have counsel. Robert Rubinson, *A Theory of Access to Justice*, 29 J.L. Prof. 89, 114–15 (2004–2005). Some family mediation rules exclude cases with unrepresented parties from mandatory mediation but most do not. This section will explore the "*pro se* phenomenon" in family law, the issues it raises for fair and appropriate use of family law mediation, and the impact mediation has had on redressing traditional inequalities in access to justice based on parties' financial resources.

1.   Family Mediation and Access to Justice Issues Generally

The impact of the rise of family mediation on low-income parties remains a contested issue. Some commentators hail the development, arguing that family mediation provides a greater quality of dispute resolution than litigation. Others argue that family mediation, particularly given the limited resources of court-annexed programs where most low-income parties will mediate, presents grave risks to low-income parties.

A primary basis for the argument that mediation provides greater access to family dispute resolution is that it is less costly than litigation. Research supports this claim in cases where the mediation is successful. JESSICA PEARSON, FAMILY MEDIATION: A REPORT ON CURRENT RESEARCH FINDINGS: IMPLICATIONS FOR COURTS AND FUTURE RESEARCH NEEDS, 53–75 (1994). But commentators have raised concerns about the impact of cost on mediation. The first concern is about the risk that mediation will become justice "on the cheap" for the poor. While the "second class" justice concerns usually focus on court-ordered mediation versus litigation, there is growing concern that vast differences in quality may develop between private, voluntary mediation and public, court ordered mediation. To the extent parties have resources, they will tend to choose their own mediators and opt out of court-based programs. The remaining cases sent to mediation from the ever expanding family law docket will be predominately poor, unrepresented litigants who have no choices and will experience the mediation equivalent of the "mass justice" of low-income courts. *See* Robert Rubinson, *A Theory of Access to Justice*, 29 J. Legal Prof. 89 (2005).

A second concern about costs and access to justice is that mediation for which litigants have to pay can add to the costs if it is a prerequisite to litigation or perceived as such. As one commentator has put it:

> Programs mandating or encouraging divorcing parties to mediate and pay for the service raise significant legal and policy questions concerning access to justice. Mandatory referral schemes, in which divorcing parties are ordered to attend mediation and pay the costs, are certainly effective in increasing the use of mediation while holding down court expenditures. If mediation is not voluntary, and parties are required to attend and are obligated to pay the mediator, constitutional due process and equal protection issues may be implicated. Further, as a practical matter, parties may be denied access to adjudication of their cases because they lack the funds to pay for the prerequisite mediation. Particularly in divorce cases, when partners are setting up two households on the same income that formerly supported only one, money is tight. Divorcing parties who are mandated to use and pay for mediation services may be unduly pressured to settle on unacceptable terms because they cannot afford to pay lawyers' fees for trial or further negotiation, in addition to the fees they have been forced to spend for mediation.

Carol J. King, *Burdening Access To Justice: The Cost of Divorce Mediation On The Cheap*, 73 St. John's L. Rev. 375 (1999). *See also* Craig A. McEwen and Laura Williams, *Legal Policy and Access to Justice Through Courts and Mediation*, 13 Ohio St. J. on Disp. Resol. 865 (1998). Some states waive costs for indigent litigants, have a sliding scale fee system or excuse parties who cannot pay from mediation requirement. *See, e.g.*, Colo. Rev. Stat. Ann. § 13-22-311(1) (2000) (party can be excused for a compelling reason including costs of mediation and lack of success in previous mediation).

2.   The *"Pro Se* Phenomenon" In Family Law

Legal needs studies conducted nationwide over the last decade reveal that (1) from 50–80 percent of the poor eligible for free legal assistance for domestic problems are not able to obtain such assistance and (2) in about half of all domestic proceedings, one or both parties are not represented by a lawyer. While some contend that the numbers of unrepresented litigants are much lower in contested cases, few dispute that unrepresented litigants continue to be a major presence and challenge for courts hearing family disputes. And while some may choose to represent themselves in family law cases, the majority of unrepresented litigants appear to forgo a lawyer because they cannot afford one and cannot obtain free legal assistance.

There is currently no "right to counsel" for family law cases despite some litigation urging courts to recognize such a "Civil Gideon" right. Nevertheless, much has been done in the last decade to assist unrepresented litigants in litigation: standardized domestic relations forms, telephone hotlines, and courthouse pro se clinics providing limited legal information and advice and law libraries on the Internet.

But courts and legislatures have paid less attention to the unrepresented litigant in mediation. This issue is especially crucial when mediation is "mandated" or "referred," as it often is in family law matters. Do these unrepresented parties need special assistance while participating in mediation? Is access to mediation a solution to the "*pro se* phenomenon" in family law? The role of mediation in providing access to justice for unrepresented litigants is much debated.

Some proponents of mediation have argued that one of its principle benefits for unrepresented parties is that it improves access to family dispute resolution. Without complex rules of procedure and evidence and governing substantive law, parties can navigate the process of mediation themselves. Under this conception of family mediation, lawyers have little or no role. Mediation, therefore, is less costly than litigation and produces results more quickly. Other commentators believe that family mediation programs, as they are currently designed, create dangers for *pro se* litigants. They argue that lawyers are important to ensuring fairness of both the process and the results of mediation. Others have raised concerns about whether mediation, when it is mandatory, makes the process more rather than less costly. The following materials examine these debates.

a.   Benefits of Family Mediation for Unrepresented Litigants

Proponents of family mediation have identified a number of ways in which mediation is superior to litigation for divorce, custody and other intrafamily disputes. One claim is that the mediation alternative improves access to dispute resolution for the participants by giving parties the opportunity to resolve disputes with fewer costs. The process is simple, communication is direct and the formalities of court are discarded. Parties have more control over the process and can arrive at resolution of their disputes more quickly and without substantial time spent in court proceedings away from work and other responsibilities. *See, e.g.*, FORREST MOSTEN, THE COMPLETE GUIDE TO MEDIATION: THE CUTTING EDGE APPROACH TO FAMILY LAW PRACTICE 60 (American Bar Association 1997); WAYNE D. BRAZIL, WHY SHOULD COURTS OFFER NON-BINDING APR SERVICES (arguing that the poor should have access to court-sponsored alternative dispute resolution and not be "relegated" to the delays and expense of the adversarial system).

The primary basis for the claim that family mediation is less expensive than litigation is that the relative simplicity of the mediation process makes attorneys either unnecessary or relegates them to a very limited role. Indeed, some commentators believe allowing traditional attorney participation in the mediation process is harmful to the process:

> The primary advantage of the mediation model over litigation is that it is less restricted by rules of procedure or substantive law and by assumptions, either judicial or statutory, that dominate adjudicatory proceedings. Mediation does not place an emphasis on determining rights

or faults, or who wins or loses because of a particular rule, and the agreement the parties reach is neither governed by nor sets precedent. Instead the goal is to establish an atmosphere of communication and compromise with the ultimate authority for the agreement residing with divorcing couple.

For mediation to succeed as a profession and to reach its highest objectives, advocacy has no place in any part of the process. For outside counsel to advocate a client's interests contradicts the very essence of mediation and can produce inequitable results.

Mark Rutherford, *Lawyers and Divorce Mediation: Designing The Role of "Outside Counsel,"* June 1986 Mediation Q. 18, 20, 27.

b.   Dangers of Mediation for Unrepresented Litigants

Others argue that participating in mediation without a lawyer, especially if the other side is represented, puts parties at great risk of unknowingly waiving rights and entering into agreements that are unfair and unjust. One scholar describes his view of the potential harm for unrepresented litigants in court sponsored mediation programs.

AND JUSTICE FOR ALL — INCLUDING THE UNREPRESENTED POOR: REVISITING THE ROLES OF THE JUDGES, MEDIATORS, AND CLERKS[3]
67 FORDHAM L. REV. 1987, 2006-11 (1999)
By Russell Engler

[T]he legal system has erected barriers that hinder the ability of unrepresented litigants to obtain the assistance necessary to make informed choices about their cases. The rules primarily prohibit clerks, mediators, and other court players from giving legal advice to unrepresented litigants. In theory, the prohibition is intended to protect the unrepresented litigant from receiving legal advice from someone not qualified to give such advice. In practice, however, the prohibition deprives the unrepresented litigant of the opportunity to obtain legal advice throughout the course of the proceeding. She is forced to make choices at every turn without understanding either the range of options available or the pros and cons of each option.

Despite being deprived of the opportunity to make informed choices, the unrepresented litigant is deemed to be an informed, rational actor. Most cases settle, usually under pressure from the court. Where the unrepresented party faces a represented one, additional settlement pressure comes from the opposing lawyer.

These consequences are devastating for unrepresented litigants. Settlement agreements routinely involve the waiver of significant rights by unrepresented litigants. Unrepresented litigants appearing before mediators suffer a similar fate, after being deemed to have made an informed choice to participate in mediation in the first place. Where cases do not settle, unrepresented litigants also routinely forfeit important rights due to the absence of counsel.

---

* * *

Courts, including those with significant numbers of unrepresented litigants, have increasingly turned to mediation as a means of docket control. In some settings, mediation is mandatory. More often, the mediation is labeled voluntary, but often appears to be mandatory to the uninformed litigant.

Despite the varying contexts for court-connected mediation, standard restrictions govern the mediator's role. As with clerks, mediators are prohibited from giving legal advice.

Mediators also must remain "impartial" and/or "neutral" and are required to be "fair." A 1997 Florida advisory opinion illustrates the devastating effect these seemingly innocuous rules can have on the outcome of cases involving unrepresented litigants. A mediator initially asked:

> Is a mediator who becomes aware that a plaintiff in a wrongful death action is making no claim for loss of consortium, which claim would appear to the mediator to be appropriate under the circumstances, bound to inform that party of this matter?

The panel replied that "it is the opinion of the panel that it is an ethical violation for a mediator to give legal advice to a party." The mediator asked whether he could tell the plaintiff of the right to make a claim without advising as to whether the claim should be made, and also whether he could ask why the claim was not being made. He inquired further as to how he could ascertain whether a party "does not understand or appreciate how an agreement may adversely affect legal rights or obligations" and how he might "assure that the plaintiff understands the legal consequences" of the agreement.

The Advisory Panel emphatically responded that the prohibition against giving legal advice barred the mediator from informing the plaintiff of the right to make a certain claim, or even to ask why a claim was not being made, regardless of whether the mediator is an attorney. The mediator's approved course of action is to "advise the participants to seek independent legal counsel." With respect to whether the parties are competent to enter into negotiations, the panel recommended that the mediator ask questions such as "Have you consulted legal counsel? Do you wish to? Do you feel comfortable that you have considered all possible legal rights and responsibilities in this situation?"

The mediator may encourage the unrepresented party to seek counsel or may terminate the mediation if he determines that one party is not competent to participate. Otherwise, he must attempt to mediate. Since efforts to inform an unrepresented litigant that the agreement entails the waiver of certain rights apparently amount to impermissible legal advice, the mediator must simply watch silently while the unrepresented litigant's rights are waived.

From a mediator's point of view, the role described in the Florida decision flows naturally from the concept of mediation, a process voluntarily selected by the parties as a means of dispute resolution different from an adversarial trial. From an unrepresented litigant's point of view, however, the effect of the rules can be devastating. The pressure exerted by courts to send cases to mediation and the lack of explanation of the mediation process raise serious questions about the "voluntary" nature of the decision to mediate. Once in mediation, the pressures on mediators to obtain settlements are immense. With a large number of unrepresented litigants, this pressure guarantees that mediators will rarely, if ever, exercise the option to terminate the mediation due to the incapacity of an unrepresented litigant to participate. The mediation will proceed, with the mediator pressing for an agreement, and prohibited from protecting the unrepresented litigant from waiving significant rights. In mediated settlements, the routine waiver of rights by unrepresented litigants flows from presumptions that the choice to mediate is voluntary and informed; that the litigant has a realistic opportunity to obtain counsel and chooses to forego counsel; that the litigant has access to independent advice; and that the litigant appears in mediation aware of her legal rights and capable of participating in mediation.

In theory, judges could provide a check on the dangers identified above in mediation, because mediated agreements are usually sent to them for approval. In reality, judges typically rubber-stamp agreements reached in mediation.

NOTES AND QUESTIONS

1.   Despite their belief that reaching an agreement in the presence of a mediator presents fewer risks for unrepresented litigants than negotiating with the other party or, worse, the other party's lawyer, mediation scholars Professors McEwen, Rogers and Maiman argue for an "opt out" provision for unrepresented parties in family mediation statutes:

> Still, the research provides little guidance about whether the greater prospect of unfairness for pro se litigants argues in favor of giving those litigants an opportunity to "opt out" of mandatory mediation. The pro se party who opts out would be left to his or her own devices. Because the most likely alternative to mediation is negotiation, those who opt out would presumably face negotiating with the other party's lawyer or directly with the other party. If they are not permitted to opt out, however, the "regulatory" approach is not likely to assure fair mediation. Furthermore, the regulation is likely to be costly for the bulk of the mediation parties who have lawyers. Thus, an "opt out" provision for pro se parties may be the best alternative for the present.

Craig McEwen et al., *Bring in the Lawyers: Challenging the Dominant Approaches to Ensuring Fairness in Divorce Mediation*, 79 Minn. L. Rev. 1317 (1995).

Do you agree or disagree?

2.   Only a handful of family mediation statutes or rules currently address the need for representation during court-ordered family mediation. *See, e.g.*, Ala. Code § 6-6-20 (Supp. 2004) (any party not represented by an attorney may be assisted in mediation by a person of his choice); Cal. Fam. Code § 3170–3185 (mediator may recommend to court that counsel be appointed for child in custody mediation); Mich. C.R. 3.216(D)(3)(c) (cases may be exempt from mediation if one or both parties are unable to negotiate for themselves at mediation). Some statutes recognize the particular need for representation in certain cases such as cases where there has been family violence. *See, e.g.*, Del. Code Ann. 13 § 711A (mediation prohibited in cases where court has made a finding of domestic violence unless victim requests it and is represented by counsel).

Which, if any, of these statutory schemes seem to you most appropriate? Should statutes and rules simply prevent court-ordered family mediation where one party is unrepresented?

Chapter 9

FAMILY VIOLENCE AND MEDIATION

A. INTRODUCTION

Perhaps no question has engendered as much controversy in family mediation as the issue of whether mediation is appropriate in cases involving family violence. Most would agree that mediating custody and visitation decisions where one parent has engaged in child abuse or intimate partner violence raises issues that require special treatment in mediation. Some argue that mediation should never happen when there are allegations of child abuse or domestic violence. Others feel, given appropriate protections, mediation is an acceptable or even preferred alternative to litigation. As with many such questions, the answer depends on a deeper examination of the circumstances in each case. What do we mean by domestic violence or child abuse in this context? How do lawyers or the court screen for it? Once family violence is identified, what steps should be taken to protect parties and preserve the benefits of the mediation process?

The Chapter begins with a primer for identifying intimate partner violence. Later excerpts address the complex question of appropriate mediator response when domestic violence is present in a couple or family that is court-referred or seeks out private mediation. Finally, the special circumstances of child abuse are briefly addressed.

B. WHAT IS DOMESTIC VIOLENCE?

SCREENING FOR DOMESTIC VIOLENCE: MEETING THE CHALLENGE OF IDENTIFYING DOMESTIC RELATIONS CASES INVOLVING DOMESTIC VIOLENCE AND DEVELOPING STRATEGIES FOR THOSE CASES[1]

39 COURT REVIEW 4, 4–6 (2002)

By Julie Kunce Field

Domestic violence is a pattern of assault and coercion, often including physical, sexual, and psychological attacks, as well as economic coercion, that adults and adolescents use against their intimate partners. The key factor characterizing domestic abuse is one partner's need to control the other. The most recent, reliable and comprehensive studies of violence find that:

- Women are more likely than men to be victimized by intimate partners; women are harmed more severely in those assaults; and males who are victims of assault are generally assaulted by other males.
- More than 50% of abusers will be abusive of their partners in a subsequent relationship.
- Nearly 100% of children in violent homes hear or see the abuse.
- False allegations of domestic violence occur infrequently, and there is in fact a significant *underreporting* of domestic violence.
- Consequently, the great majority of cases where there is domestic violence will have female victims and male perpetrators.

The Family Violence Preservation Fund has identified five central characteristics of domestic violence:

1. Domestic violence is learned behavior.

Domestic violence perpetrators use domestic violence because it works: it serves to maintain power over the battered woman and to cause her to do what the batterer wants. Domestic violence is learned behavior that batterers perfect through observation, experience, reinforcement, culture, family, and community. The batterer learns what works, and what doesn't, to cause his victim to do his will.

2. Domestic violence typically involves repetitive behavior encompassing different types of abuse.

The key factor characterizing domestic abuse is one partner's need to control the other. The methods of control include using economic abuse, isolation, intimidation, emotional abuse, and sexual abuse. Children become pawns that the abuser may use to continue his control over his partner's actions. Each method of control may be enforced — and reinforced — with the use or threat of physical violence.

---

[1] Copyright ©2002. Reprinted with permission.

3. The batterer — not substance abuse, the battered woman, or the relationship causes domestic violence.

Rarely do substance abuse, genetics, stress, illness, or problems in the relationship cause domestic violence, though these conditions are often used as excuses for the violence, and they may exacerbate violent behavior.

4. Danger to the battered woman and children is likely to increase at the time of separation. . . .

Notably, leaving the home or the relationship breaks all of the universal rules of batterers. So, far from guaranteeing safety, when the battered woman attempts to leave, the violence against her and the children is likely to increase. To the batterer, leaving or attempting to leave can represent his ultimate loss of control over his victim and can lead to lethal violence.

5. The victim's behavior is often a way of ensuring survival.

The conduct of domestic violence victims may sometimes seem counterintuitive — the victim fails to leave the situation, even though it may objectively appear to be intolerable. Her failure to leave doesn't necessarily indicate a lack of desire to do so, but rather that she is afraid, doesn't have resources, fears that he will become lethal if she leaves, or for some other reasons, leaving is not a viable option.

C.   IS IT APPROPRIATE TO CONDUCT MEDIATION IN THE PRESENCE OF DOMESTIC VIOLENCE?

The following excerpt recognizes the complexity embedded in the question: Should domestic violence cases be mediated? Rather than taking a rigid position on one side of the debate, Prof. Ver Steegh undertakes the challenging task of identifying when mediation should never be used, when it might be the best alternative and the many cases that fall between these ends of the spectrum. She provides an analysis of factors that are particularly relevant to this decision making. In this way, she provides mediators, lawyers, and most importantly, domestic violence survivors, the tools to make informed decisions about whether to participate in mediation and what to expect from the mediation process.

YES, NO, AND MAYBE: INFORMED DECISION MAKING ABOUT DIVORCE MEDIATION IN THE PRESENCE OF DOMESTIC VIOLENCE[2]
9 Wm. & Mary J. Women & L. 145, 180–81, 184–86, 195–98 (2003)
By Nancy Ver Steegh

Although mediation provides a desirable alternative for many families, there are serious concerns about its use in cases of domestic violence. Some of these concerns arise from the mediation process itself and others stem from the varying quality of the conducted mediation.

---

[2] Copyright © 2003. Reprinted with permission.

A. Reasons Why Mediation Might Never Be Appropriate

1. Is Mediation Too Private?

Privacy and confidentiality are critical aspects of the mediation process. Both are necessary to encourage full disclosure and candid problem solving. Some women's advocates, however, are troubled by the private nature of mediation. After years of working to have domestic violence dealt with as a crime, they see mediation as potentially returning the issue "back into the shadows." Because criminal prosecution sends a public message to the abuser that his behavior is unacceptable, advocates fear that the abusers in mediation will not be held accountable for the abuse. Similarly, they fear that if these cases are removed from the courts, new favorable legal precedents will not be established. Two factors mitigate these concerns. First, divorce mediation need not supplant the use of the criminal system. If an abuse survivor chooses to do so, she can file criminal charges, pursue a protective order, and mediate the divorce. Use of the criminal courts is not an exclusive remedy. Second, a growing body of evidence suggests that applying criminal sanctions may not deter further abuse. Rather, in some cases, criminal charges have been correlated with an increased likelihood of a recurrence of abuse. Consequently, each victim must make an individual assessment of whether the abuser will be deterred from further violence by criminal prosecution. Either way, she could proceed with mediation . . .

b. The Problem of Power Imbalance in Cases of Domestic Violence

In cases where domestic violence has taken place, there has already been a severe abuse of power and the consequent power imbalance can make mediation impossible. Barbara Hart argues that cooperation between spouses when domestic abuse had occurred is "an oxymoron." Others agree that especially where there has been a culture of battering coupled with severe abuse, the power imbalance is too great to be overcome in mediation. Victims may fear retaliatory violence if they disagree with the abuser, thus making negotiation impossible.

. . . Research does bear out some of these concerns. A 1995 study found that abused women perceive themselves as having less power than women who have not been abused; they were more likely to think that the abuser could "out-talk" them, had "gotten back at them" previously, and said they were afraid to "openly disagree" for fear of retaliation. Interestingly, the authors also made some contrary discoveries as well.

However, there were no significant differences for abused and nonabused women on four personal empowerment items: (a) giving in just to stop dealing with the abuser, (b) feeling guilty for asking for the custody and visitation that they wanted, (c) perceived ability to speak up for themselves about custody and visitation wishes, and (d) getting what they wanted in disagreements.

Other studies report that abuse survivors are able to negotiate effectively and are not at a disadvantage in mediation because of power imbalances. These favorable findings may be related to the mediator screening for abuse and carefully monitoring relative power levels.

Despite the contrary indications found in the research, power imbalance is an important consideration in deciding whether mediation is appropriate. The extent of the problem varies with the individual couple. As discussed previously, women who are dealing with ongoing and episodic male battering or psychotic and paranoid reactions as defined by Johnston and Campbell, may have more difficulty mediating. Similarly, women suffering from "battered women's syndrome" or PTSD may have difficulty standing up for themselves. However, some abuse survivors are able to state their own needs and problem solve effectively. . . .

Each couple differs with respect to power imbalance and relative power levels may change throughout the relationship. The power imbalance inherent in domestic violence will render some abuse survivors unable to mediate. However, this assumption cannot be made for all couples who have had violent incidents. Capacity to mediate can only be assessed on an individual level. However, if the couple and the mediator proceed with the mediation, the mediator needs to remain especially alert for power imbalances and be prepared to deal with them. In addition to viewing each couple as unique when deciding whether the mediation process is appropriate, it is important to ask, as Folberg and Milne do, "Compared to what?" . . .

Mediation Triage

As noted previously, mediation should never proceed against the wishes of the abuse survivor. However, even when the victim wants to mediate, there are some conditions under which many mediators will not agree to mediate. For this reason, the Model Standards specifically state that some domestic violence situations "are not suitable for mediation because of safety, control, or intimidation issues."

Experts agree that some categories of domestic violence cases should never be mediated. Erickson and McKnight find mediation inappropriate when (1) the abuser discounts the victim and refuses to acknowledge how his behavior affects her, (2) abuse is ongoing between mediation sessions, (3) either client is carrying a weapon or attempts to mediate while drinking or using drugs, or (4) either party continues to violate the mediation ground rules.

Linda Girdner writes that cases should be excluded from mediation when abuse and/or control are central to the relationship to such an extent that the parties are unable to differentiate their interests, the abuser does not accept responsibility for his behavior, and the victim fears retribution. These conditions render the couple unable to negotiate. In addition, Girdner cautions against mediation when weapons are involved and/or the abuser has fantasies of killing the victim and children or committing suicide. These exclusions are similar to those recommended by Johnston and Campbell. In a similar vein, Elizabeth Ellis suggests that mediation may go forward if the violence has been brief, was instigated by the wife, and/or began only after the separation.

Because abuse can differ widely in "form, duration, and severity," the existence of violence creates a red flag for the mediator signaling a need for a closer look at the victim's ability to negotiate and the level of the abuser's denial and control.

If there has been abuse but the identified prohibitions are absent, mediation might proceed, but only under stringent conditions. These include use of a specially trained mediator, a specialized process, and agreed upon safety protocols.

Context and Making Informed Decisions

The abuse survivor is more familiar with her situation than anyone. Consequently, all process decision-making should start and end with her. She will have the best information on the following topics and should consider the following questions.

The Abuse. As discussed previously, there is a continuum of abuse and the experience of each victim is unique. What is the history with respect to the severity, frequency, and amount of abuse? How recently has the abuse occurred? Is there a pattern? Is there a culture of battering with systematic domination and control by the batterer?

Immediate Safety Issues. The abuse survivor cannot make any decisions until she is safe. Has the couple separated? Is the abuse ongoing? If so, referrals should be made to community resources and the victim should consider pursuing a protective order and/or pressing criminal charges.

Status of the Abuse Survivor. Is she ready and able to make decisions? What does she want to happen? Is she interested in counseling? Does she need medical treatment for PTSD?

Likely Behavior of the Abuser. The abuse survivor is usually very knowledgeable about how the abuser is likely to respond to a protective order, criminal charges, and/or mediation. The point of this discussion is not to put his needs before hers, but to anticipate and avoid future abuse.

Need for Future Contact. If the couple has children, especially young ones, there will be some form of future contact that must be carefully structured.

Resources. What resources does the victim have? Can she afford to be represented by an attorney? Is she connected to an advocate or other support system? Are there other time and cost issues?

All of these factors can point in different directions and this makes decision-making difficult. For example, if the abuse survivor is seriously traumatized, has no children, and can afford an attorney, she may elect to proceed through the court system. On the other hand, if the abuse has been less severe and only took place around the time of the separation, if she has small children, and if she cannot afford an attorney, exploring mediation might make sense. Most abuse survivors will fall between these two scenarios and their decisions will be more complex.

Beyond individual considerations, divorce process decisions must be made within a larger context. Ideally the abuse survivor should have access to information about the quality and approach of the court system as well as the particular mediation process. Whatever process is chosen, state law will inform the ultimate outcome. The abuse survivor should be aware of whether the law provides a rebuttable presumption against custody awards to batterers or whether custody decisions are made in accordance with the "best interests" standard. The survivor might also want to consider whether joint custody is the norm.

If the abuse survivor enters the adversarial system, she should know whether the judge is likely to be informed about domestic violence issues. If she enters mediation, she might consider whether she will have access to a mediator or co-mediators who are experienced and specially trained to mediate domestic violence cases. The survivor should also learn whether the mediation will cover all topics and involve multiple sessions.

The quality of the process may be of more significance than the process itself. Poorly conducted mediation could be more dangerous than when unrepresented parties appearing before a well-trained and sensitive judge. In reality, there is not always a clear choice between mediation and the adversarial process. For example, a well-structured, cooperative two-attorney negotiation is more like mediation than a contested trial. Consequently, each abuse survivor must individually evaluate her actual options.

D.   LEGISLATIVE AND JUDICIAL RESPONSES TO DOMESTIC VIOLENCE AND MEDIATION

Courts and legislatures have responded to the consensus that domestic violence cases should be given special treatment in mediation by enacting a variety of rules and statutes to achieve that goal. As of 2004, 42 states have enacted statewide statutes or court rules authorizing mandatory, discretionary, or voluntary court-sponsored mediation programs of selected family law disputes. Of the 42 statutes or rules, 29 create some kind of exception to the court's authority to order mediation when domestic violence and/or child abuse are present or prohibit mediation entirely under these circumstances. Under many of these rules or statutes, mediation is prohibited when domestic violence is present. *See, e.g.,* Colo. Rev. Stat. Ann. § 13-22-311(1) (2000) (court cannot refer cases to mediation when one party claims to be a victim of physical or psychological abuse by the other party); La. Rev. Stat. Ann. § 9:363 (2000) ("no spouse or parent who satisfies the court that he or she, or any of the children, has been the victim of family violence perpetrated by the other spouse or parent shall be court ordered to participate in mediation"); Mont. Code Ann. § 40-4-301(2) (2000) (mediation not permitted if court has reason to suspect one party physically, sexually, or emotionally abused the other party or child). The level of proof necessary to establish the presence of domestic violence varies substantially among jurisdictions. In Florida, there must be significant evidence of abuse in order for a case to be excused from the mediation process. Fla. Stat. Ann. § 44.102(2) (b) (2000) (a "history of domestic violence that would compromise the mediation process" is necessary for a court to be prevented from referring a case to mediation); *see also* Ohio Rev. Code Ann. § 3109.052(A) (2001) (court cannot order mediation if one party was convicted or pled guilty to a crime of domestic violence involving the other party or their children); Minn. Stat. Ann. § 518.619, subd. (2)(2000) (no mediation allowed if there is probable cause that one party has sexually or physically abused the other party or child).

A few statutes make mediation mandatory, even in the presence of domestic violence. *See* Cal. Fam. Code § 3181(a) (2001) (mediator shall meet with parties separately and at separate times, if history of domestic abuse or party alleges under penalty of perjury that domestic violence occurred and party alleging the abuse so requests); Utah Code Ann. § 30-3-38(4)(c) (2001) (mandatory mediation of visitation disputes under pilot program may continue notwithstanding an allegation of physical or sexual abuse of a parent or a child, unless otherwise ordered by a court.) A handful of statutes require the court or mediator to screen for domestic violence. *See, e.g.,* Haw. Rev. Stat. § 580-41.5 (1998) ("a mediator who receives a referral or order from a court to conduct mediation shall screen for the occurrence of family violence"); W. VA. Code § 48-9-202 (requiring the highest court of the state to develop rules for "premediation screening procedures to determine whether domestic violence.would adversely affect the safety of a party."). The remaining statutes give little or no guidance as to how the court should identify domestic violence or provide for exceptions under broad, vague concepts like "undue hardship" or "good cause."

A number of major professional organizations have also weighed in on the need to provide special treatment for family violence cases in mediation. The Model Standards of Practice for Family and Divorce Mediation, attached as Appendix C and endorsed by the American Bar Association and the Association of Family and Conciliation Courts, among others, includes provisions defining domestic violence, requiring domestic violence training for mediators, screening, and setting forth steps to ensure safety during mediation. The Model Standards also recognize that some cases should not be mediated "because of safety, control or intimidation issues. A mediator should make a reasonable effort to screen for the existence of domestic abuse prior to entering into an agreement to mediate. The mediator should continue to assess for domestic abuse throughout the mediation process." Another group of distinguished academics, judges and practicing lawyers, the American Law Institute (ALI), has also addressed the issue of mediating family disputes where domestic violence is present. In its Principles of the Law of Family Dissolution, the ALI takes the position that the risks of coercion and intimidation in mediation for victims of domestic violence require that all mediation programs be voluntary. In order to protect victims in parent education and the development of parenting plans, the ALI would require courts to develop a screening process to identify cases in which there is "credible" evidence that domestic violence has occurred and to conduct evidentiary hearings to evaluate such evidence. The ALI, then, takes the position that the best way to address the risks of domestic violence and mediation is to make certain such cases are identified in the courts and to use mediation only when both parties agree to it.

For a broader discussion of family mediation statutes and rules, see Chapter 6 *supra*.

E. SCREENING FOR DOMESTIC VIOLENCE

Despite the consensus that domestic violence cases require special treatment in mediation, few statutes or rules provide guidance to courts about their obligation to identify domestic violence cases before an order to mediate is issued. As a result, both attorneys of clients in mediation and family mediators have an important role to play in screening cases for domestic violence. The following excerpt provides some guidance as to the role of both these players in mediation.

DOMESTIC VIOLENCE AND MEDIATION: RESPONDING TO THE CHALLENGES OF CRAFTING EFFECTIVE SCREENS[3]

39 Fam. L.Q. 53, 65–67, 69–70 (2005)

By Jane C. Murphy & Robert Rubinson

Best Practices in Screening for Domestic Violence

Screening for domestic violence is not a one-step process. Indeed, many individuals — both lawyers when parties are represented and a wide range of court personnel-can help to narrow the gap between theory and practice in protecting domestic violence victims in the mediation process.

A. *The Role of Attorneys*

An initial problem in approaching the role of lawyers in protecting victims of domestic violence is that the vast majority of such victims cannot obtain counsel. As addressed below, this common situation vastly enhances the responsibilities of the judicial system — both administrators and judges — to protect victims through appropriate screening protocols.

A second problem is when the abuser — sometimes the party with greater economic resources — is represented and the victim is not. Such an instance intensifies an inherent power imbalance, and such an imbalance would, in virtually all circumstances, render the case inappropriate for mediation. In other instances, however, all parties are represented by counsel or the victim is represented and the abuser is not. In such cases, lawyers have a crucial and positive role to play.

First, lawyers are exceptionally well positioned to act as screeners themselves. By learning and understanding the specific circumstances surrounding domestic violence and by knowing and understanding how mediation is likely to be conducted in a given jurisdiction, lawyers can counsel clients about whether or not mediation is an appropriate process. Moreover, lawyers' relationships with their clients enable them to conclude that mediation would not be appropriate as events unfold and more information is gathered. As a result, lawyers can act as screeners at all points in their representation, up to and including the mediation session itself.

Second, lawyers can advise their clients about other potential remedies and, if appropriate, pursue them. For example, pursuing mediation does not preclude seeking a protective order or pressing criminal charges against an abuser. The advisability of such actions, in turn, might influence whether or not mediation is an appropriate alternative.

Third, when possible, lawyers can assess the qualifications and competence of potential mediators. As "repeat players" in the mediation process, lawyers are in a far better position than parties to help insure the choice of a sensitive and sophisticated mediator.

Fourth, lawyers can have a crucial role to play in preparing for and attending the mediation sessions themselves. In so doing, lawyers act as power enhancers and equalizers: they can speak on behalf of clients, evaluate proposed solutions in light of applicable legal norms and the specific experiences of the client, and, if necessary, suggest opting out of the mediation itself if it is not serving the interests of clients.

These constructive roles for attorneys presuppose, of course, effective lawyering. In the context of a case involving a client who has experienced domestic violence, this means attorneys who are sophisticated in their understanding of the special needs and experiences of such clients, are rigorous in their fact investigation, and understand the possibilities and shortcomings of mediation in resolving specific issues facing individual clients.

B. The Role of the Courts

Because so many family law litigants are unrepresented, courts must play the primary role in screening cases for mediation. The obligation to screen should be made explicit in the governing statute or court rule. This shifts the burden of raising domestic violence issues from the victim to the court and lays the groundwork for courts to lobby for appropriate resources for effective screening. In addition, courts, by rule or other directive from the chief judge of the highest court, should provide mediation programs with a protocol defining the obligations of each player in the system. Because there are many points of entry into the family justice system, and because domestic violence issues are often difficult to identify, cases should be screened at several different points in the court system. . . .

Mediation

Despite multiple efforts to screen for domestic violence cases prior to mediation, cases involving abusive relationships will still get to mediation. It is, therefore, critical that mediators are properly trained to identify domestic violence and conduct their own screenings. This is required by mediator's ethical standards and is an essential part of an effective screening system. Mediators have developed a number of their own screening tools for this purpose. To insure quality and consistency, courts may want to prescribe the use of a uniform screening tool to be used by all mediators. A variety of professional organizations have developed lists of questions for mediators and others to use to elicit information to evaluate for the presence of domestic violence in premediation meetings with participants See e.g., Katherine Waits, *Battered Women and Their Children: Lessons from One Woman's Story*, 35 HOUSTON L. REV. 30 (1998) (reprinting screening tool from the American Medical Association); The Impact of Domestic Violence on Your Legal Practice: A Lawyer's Handbook 2-1-2-11 (Goelman, et al. eds. 1996). Even if screening occurs at multiple levels, cases involving abusive relationships will still find their way into mediation. Experts have developed checklists for mediators of behaviors that may be observed in mediation that suggest a power imbalance resulting from domestic violence. These behaviors look at tone of voice, facial expressions, willingness to express needs, outbursts and lopsided agreements. See e.g. Lenard Marlow, *Sampson and Delilah in Divorce Mediation*, 38 Fam. and Conciliation Courts Review 224 (2000). Mediators who observe such behaviors can conduct private caucusing and other screening techniques to determine whether to exclude the case from mediation or implement appropriate power balancing or safety measures if the mediation is to continue.

NOTES AND QUESTIONS

1.　Assume you are a legislator in a state in which the family mediation statute simply provides: "In cases involving custody and mediation disputes, the court shall order the parties to attend a minimum of two sessions of mediation before a court certified mediator." In response to requests from domestic violence advocates, you are considering amendments to the statute to give special treatment to victims of domestic violence. What are your options? Do you provide an exception for cases in which domestic violence is present? Why or why not? If you decide to include an exception, how do you define domestic violence? Do you make the decision to order mediation in the presence of domestic violence discretionary with the court or make the exception absolute? If you decide to permit discretion, what factors should guide the court's discretion?

2.　Should the victim have the opportunity to consent to mediation? Should the fact that the victim is represented or not represented by an attorney affect her right to consent? Del. Code Ann. tit. 13 § 711A(2001) (mediation is prohibited if domestic violence has occurred between the parties or if either party is under a protective order, unless the victim is represented by counsel). For an excellent analysis of the range of family mediation statutes see, Student Note, *Mediation Trends: A Survey of the States*, 39 Fam. Ct. Rev. 431 (2001). For a discussion on the pros and cons giving victims of domestic violence the right to consent to mediation, compare ANDREW SCHEPARD, CHILDREN, COURTS AND CUSTODY at 101 (2004) with Linda K. Girdner, Mediation *Triage: Screening for Spouse Abuse in Divorce Mediation*, 7 Mediation Q. 365, 374 (1990) (arguing that mediation is never appropriate, notwithstanding victim consent, under certain conditions including where weapons are involved or there have been threats to kill the partner or children.)

3.　Substance abuse problems affect large numbers of families facing divorce, separation, or other family disputes. While many believe substance abuse and family violence are connected, most experts agree that family violence is not *caused* by the substance abuse. Rather, the cause is the abuser's need for power and control. Nevertheless, substance abuse and family violence often occur in the same families. The National Center on Addiction and Substance Abuse has concluded that "[c]hildren whose parents abuse drugs and alcohol are almost three times . . . likelier to be physically or sexually assaulted and more than four times . . . likelier to be neglected than children of parents who are not substance abusers." No Safe Haven: Children of Substance Abusing Parents ii (1999). Drug and alcohol problems in a couple, however, interfere with that couple's ability to communicate and make meaningful decisions in mediation. As a result, some family mediation statutes and rules provide exceptions to court ordered mediation where there are allegations of substance abuse. *See, e.g.,* N.C. Unif. Rules Cust. and Mediation Program Rule 8 (court may waive mediation where there are allegations of alcoholism or drug abuse); S.C. Rules Fam. Ct. Rule 2 (2004) (a court may defer or dispense with mediation upon a showing of substance abuse); NH Rev. Stat. Ann. § 458-15-a (1999) ("the court may choose not to order mediation if there is . . . (d) a finding of alcoholism, drug abuse.").

The following excerpt suggests that mediation can be appropriate where there has been domestic abuse and offers "tips" for the mediator to ensure safety.

MEDIATION AND DOMESTIC ABUSE[4]

From DIVORCE AND FAMILY MEDIATION 304–331 (Jay Folberg, Ann L. Milne & Peter Salem, Eds.) (2004)

By Ann L. Milne

. . . Most mediation proponents agree with the following guidelines:

- Some cases involving domestic abuse are inappropriate for mediation.
- Screening is necessary to determine which cases are appropriate.
- Mediators must be well trained in the dynamics of domestic abuse.
- Participation in the mediation process must be safe, fair, and voluntary.
- Victims of abuse should not be required to mediate.

Given these guidelines, proponents of making mediation available in cases of domestic abuse generally start with the argument of the "BATMA": What is the couple's "best alternative to a *mediated* agreement" . . . In short, if mediation is not used, then what? It is argued by both social science experts and legal scholars that mediation is more appropriate and effective than the adversarial process, even in cases of domestic abuse. Some have said that the adversarial process exacerbates the dynamics between partners when abuse is a factor by escalating the conflict and reinforcing the power and control differential and the win/lose aspects of the relationship . . . Few judges and lawyers have expertise in the subject of domestic abuse, whereas many mediators have had training in it. . . .

Reframing the Debate

. . . As in any conflict, the framing of the issues is critical in order to adequately address [these concerns]. Rather than framing the question, *Should mediation be used in cases involving domestic abuse?*, a more useful framing of the issue would be: *What process can we develop that will best help individuals who have been involved in an abusive relationship address the issues between them, so that they can move on with their lives without violence and without the need for ongoing court and legal interventions?* . . .

When providing mediation to batterers and victims, the following are excluded from the list of topics to be addressed:

We are not mediating whether or not the abuse occurred . . .

We are not mediating reconciliation . . .

We are not mediating fault and blame . . .

We are not mediating punishment and consequences . . .

We are not mediating dropping of charges, protective orders, or restraining orders.

("Do this, then she will drop the abuse charges").

We are not mediating contingencies or leveraging of issues . . .

---

[4] Copyright ©2004. Reprinted with permission.

We are not mediating court orders.

We are not mediating threshold issues.

With the above procedural ground rules in place, the following areas can be effectively mediated:

Terms of Living Apart

Matters such as establishing a date for moving out, determining who is going to live where, division of household accessories, establishing a parenting schedule, and payment of household expenses are all day-to-day living arrangements that parties may need to address. The judge often does not have the time to take up each of these individual issues, and paying lawyers to negotiate them can be too costly for many. . . .

Property Division

Mediation can be a very helpful process for dividing up personal possessions such as furnishings, household supplies, photographs, books, tools, and all the other sundry things that family members need to manage their daily lives.

Financial Support . . .

Use of Clothing and Toys . . .

Activities With The Children

Mediation can be a very useful forum in which to share information about what activities the children would enjoy as well as to resolve disputes regarding activities of which a parent disapproves. Is it OK to take the children hunting? To a friend's home? To the corner tavern? . . .

School Contact

How will child-care decisions be made? . . . If a parent is called away from home, will the other parent be given the first opportunity to baby-sit? . . .

Judgment is Important

The role of the mediator is typically described as that of a nonjudgmental neutral party . . . However, when mediating in cases of possible or known domestic abuse, . . . [t]he mediator must continually reevaluate whether this case is appropriate for mediation and whether he or she has the skills needed to work effectively with this couple.

Forget the Balancing Act

Terms such as *maintaining balance, power balancing*, and *level playing field* are often used when describing the mediation process. However, when mediating in a case involving issues of domestic abuse, I find that I am "off-balance" much of the time because I am challenged to keep control of the process.

The Process is Less Collaborative and More of a Facilitated Negotiation

. . . The parties focus more on their separate interests and solutions rather than the mutual interests that I tend to focus on when abuse is not a factor.

Short-Term Agreements

One of the incentives to using mediation in cases involving concerns about domestic abuse is the ability to put in place agreements of a short-term nature and revisit and revise them as needs dictate. Predictability and steadfastness are not often present with these couples. Putting together agreements or court orders that apply over the long haul is often counterproductive . . .

Need for Reliable Resources

The need to establish a scaffolding of support can be very important when mediating in domestic abuse cases. The support of the parties' attorneys, victim and batterer advocates, counselors, and a safety plan can all work together to facilitate the success of the mediation process.

Conclusions

The question of whether or not mediation is appropriate in cases of domestic abuse must be reframed to focus on finding an answer to the question of what kind of system we could design that would provide a safe and secure decision-making process for spouses and parents in dispute. Although a traditional mediation process may not offer the protection necessary in domestic abuse cases, dismissing mediation outright may also be a mistake. The development of hybrid mediation models that embody the self-determination principles of the mediation process while also addressing power, control, coercion, and safety issues must be the goal.

F. CHILD ABUSE AND MEDIATION

Family violence may also involve child abuse. Research demonstrates that domestic violence and child abuse often overlap. Children exposed to domestic violence are at an increased risk of being abused or neglected. A variety of studies reveal there are both adult and child victims in 30 to 60 percent of families experiencing domestic violence. Most statutes and rules creating exceptions from court ordered mediation treat domestic violence and child abuse in the same way, permitting the victim or parent to opt out of mediation upon a satisfactory showing of abuse. Despite the lumping together of these two issues, allegations of child abuse in a family experiencing separation or divorce raise additional issues for the mediator. While screening for intimate partner violence is challenging, the mediator may be even less likely to be able to identify child abuse in a family through interviews with parents. The following excerpt provides valuable information about the incidence of child abuse for attorneys and mediators involved in these cases.

CHILDREN, COURTS AND CUSTODY: INTERDISCIPLINARY MODELS FOR DIVORCING FAMILIES 94; 96–97 (2004)[5]

By Andrew Schepard

Parents are the principal perpetrators of child maltreatment. Mothers and fathers tend to commit different types of child abuse and neglect. Mothers are significantly less likely than fathers to physically abuse their children. The role of mothers in physical abuse tends to be limited to tolerating and sometimes facilitating abuse by male partners. Mothers, however, are more likely to neglect children than fathers. Mothers tend to be the children's primary care-takers and thus are the parents primarily held accountable for any omissions and or failures in care-taking. Females are thus more often guilty of neglect than men (87% to 43%). In contrast, men more often than women physically abuse children (67% to 40%) and are far more likely to commit sexual abuse.

Child abuse has devastating consequences for children — acts of abuse are likely to continue after first being committed, victims are likely to be repeatedly abused, and the longer the abusive behavior continues, the more severe the damage to the child.

There are many different kinds of child abuse, and thus the practice has many different negative effects on children, too many to summarize here. Perhaps the most critical fact is that violence begets violence — child abuse, like domestic violence, replicates itself across generations. Children who are abused are much more likely to be abusers themselves when they grow up than children who are not abused. Intervention to treat both the abuser and the abused is critical to break the intergenerational cycle . . .

Child-abuse victimization rates are generally similar for male and female victims (11.2 and 12.8 per 1,000 children, respectively), except for victims of sexual abuse, where the rate of abuse is about double for girls. About 1 or 2 of every 20 boys will be sexually abused during childhood, whereas about 4 out of every 20 girls will be abused. Most sex abusers of children are not strangers but fathers and men in long-term relationships with their mothers, and the risk of abuse, particularly of girls, significantly increases following divorce.

The child custody court faces significant coordination problems when an allegation of family violence is made in a dispute before it, as those same allegations can be the basis of a criminal prosecution or a child protection proceeding. A father who has a sexual relationship with a minor child, for example, commits a serious crime for which he may be prosecuted. Allegations of child abuse and neglect can also trigger an investigation by a state's child protective services (CPS). CPS can initiate a child protection proceeding against the offending parent to terminate that parent's custody rights if it believes the violence allegations are true. To conserve scarce resources, prosecutors and CPS often count on the child custody court to determine the truth and make appropriate orders.

---

[5] Copyright ©2004. Reprinted with the permission of Cambridge University Press.

"True" and "False" Accusations

Accusations of being an abuser or a batterer made in a child custody dispute are extremely serious. As one state Supreme Court has noted, "a parent's reputation, access to the custody of her children and even liberty may be lost over a false accusation." There are documented instances in which children have made allegations of child abuse that later turned out to be false. The focus on false claims that follows must be placed in context. The problem of family violence is very serious, and a focus on false claims should not be taken to minimize it. "We must always temper the incidence of true disclosures with the possibility of false ones."

Child custody disputes create a particularly troublesome setting for accusations of family violence. Divorce is often a time for disclosure of violence that was previously hidden from public view. Parents may leave the marriage to protect the child and themselves from further violence. On the one hand, parents must be encouraged to bring allegations of violence to the attention of authorities who have the power to provide protection to the vulnerable. On the other hand, parents in a custody dispute are often very angry at each other, misinterpret each others' behavior, and have an incentive to disclose previously unreported child abuse to the court, as the court is more likely to award the non-violent parent greater rights. This constellation of factors leads to some false or exaggerated allegations of violence or abuse.

Different definitions of "false" allegations cloud the question of whether false allegations of child abuse are more common in child custody disputes than allegations made against parents who are not involved in custody disputes. False allegations should not be confused with "unsubstantiated" or "unfounded" allegations as determined by a child protection agency. When a child protection agency finds an allegation to be unsubstantiated, it means only that the agency is of the opinion that there is not enough evidence to continue investigation and file an action in court. A child custody court is not bound by that finding, as it is possible that with further investigation and evaluation, some unsubstantiated allegations might eventually be validated. False allegations, furthermore, can encompass a variety of kinds of behavior ranging from deliberate, malicious false reports to misinterpretation of events and intentional or unintentional coaching of children . . .

NOTES AND QUESTIONS

1.   Detecting child abuse or evaluating claims of such abuse by others is beyond the expertise of most family mediators. But given the rate of incidence described in the Shepard article, family mediators mediating child access disputes should have some training in this area. The Schepard excerpt provides a starting point. *See also* Robin Fretwell Wilson, *Children at Risk: The Sexual Exploitation of Female Children After Divorce*, 86 Cornell L. Rev. 251(2001) (noting the substantial social science research demonstrating that girls are at an elevated risk for sexual abuse after divorce by a parent, step-parent or other person.)

2.   As with intimate partner violence, uncovering child abuse is just the first issue a family mediator must deal with. Assuming it is not a case where the child abuse has already been discovered and adjudicated in some way (*see* Chapter 4[C]), mediator suspicions of child abuse, party allegations, or party admissions raise a variety of questions for the mediator. As discussed more fully in the next Chapter

(Chapter 10[B][3]), most ethical rules governing family mediation obligate media-tors to keep matters discussed in mediation confidential. *See, e.g.,* Model Standards for Divorce and Family Mediation Standard VII. This promise of confidentiality, however, does not extend to threats of future violence of adults or children made during mediation. In the case of child abuse, child protection laws may *require* the mediator to report to appropriate state agencies allegations or admissions about both past and ongoing child abuse disclosed in mediation. *See, e.g.,* MD Family Law 5-704. If a mediator has reasonable grounds to suspect child abuse, she is required to report it and will, as a result, most likely withdraw from the mediation. Many cases, however, may raise suspicions or concerns but not reach the "reasonable grounds" to believe abuse or neglect is occurring to warrant a formal report. These cases raise the difficult ethical and professional issues for family mediators.

Assume you are mediating a child access case. The parties get into a heated argument after the husband/father states that the wife/mother "is a lousy mother who can't take care of herself let alone a child," referring to the parties' five-year-old daughter, Clare. You suggest a private caucus with each of the parties to cool things down and give the mother a chance to talk uninterrupted about whether she is, indeed, overwhelmed in her current role as primary caretaker. During the private caucus with the mother, you learn that Clare stays with her 10-year-old cousin when the after school program is unavailable. He lives in the same apartment building as the mother and daughter and stays by himself after school. About once a week, he walks home with his cousin and they stay at his apartment unattended for about three hours until his mother or Clare's mother comes home.

Putting aside specific statutory-or rule-based ethical mandates (until we get to Chapter 10), what do you think your next step should be as a mediator? Do you tell the husband/father? Do you step out of your role as mediator to "advise" the mother? Do you bring in any third parties? Do you continue to mediate the case?

Chapter 10

ETHICAL ISSUES IN FAMILY MEDIATION

A. INTRODUCTION

The study of "ethics" in family mediation falls into two categories: First, there are formal ethics "codes" and statutes that apply to mediation generally and family mediation in particular. These govern the more "doctrinal" dimensions of ethics, including conflicts of interest and confidentiality. The second category explores issues that are less subject to rules yet still implicates basic ethical and moral issues, such as when or if a mediator should influence the terms of an agreement.

This Chapter will address the first of these categories. We have explored the second category in our treatment of the "Power Critique" in Chapter 8.

B. SOURCES OF FAMILY MEDIATION ETHICS

1. General Sources of Standards Governing Mediation

Family mediators, although engaged in a specialized form of mediation, are still subject to statutes and standards governing the general practice of mediation. Whether these sources have the force of law depends on the law of individual states. In addition to qualification rules, which we have already explored in Chapter 6, these standards typically address, among other things, confidentiality, conflicts of interest, and mediator "neutrality" or "impartiality."

The following represents primary sources of standards governing mediators generally:

- *The Uniform Mediation Act*: An attempt to promote uniformity has been made by the National Conference of Commissioners on Uniform State Laws, which, in 2001, promulgated the Uniform Mediation Act. As of this writing, few states have adopted it. As with other Uniform State laws, it is difficult to anticipate how widely states will adopt the Act.

- *The Model Standards of Conduct for Mediators*: First adopted in 1994 and revised in 2005, the Model Standards are promulgated by the American Arbitration Association, the American Bar Association, and the Association for Conflict Resolution. This is the preeminent unified set of standards governing mediation. While influential, these standards standing alone do not have the force of law.

- *State statutes and rules*: As we have seen previously, both mediation and family law mediation are subject to an ever-changing array of state law and rules that vary from jurisdiction to jurisdiction. An influential set of guidelines for states is the *National Standards for Court-Connected Mediation Programs* issued by the Center for Dispute Settlement and the Institute of Judicial Administration.

2.   Model Standards of Practice for Family and Divorce Mediation

The *Model Standards of Practice for Family and Divorce Mediation* attached as Appendix C, is, by its terms, "aspirational in character" and thus does not have the force of law. It is nevertheless the most recent and influential set of ethical standards addressing family mediation. As such, it articulates current norms governing the practice of family mediation.

The following excerpt traces the *Model Standards'* history and goals. After completing this background, you should review the *Model Standards* themselves.

FORWARD TO THE MODEL STANDARDS OF PRACTICE FOR FAMILY AND DIVORCE MEDIATION (2000)
By Andrew Schepard

The *Model Standards of Practice for Family and Divorce Mediation ("Model Standards")* are the family mediation community's definition of the role of mediation in the dispute resolution system in the twenty-first century. They are the latest milestone in a nearly twenty year old effort by the family mediation community to create standards of practice that will increase public confidence in an evolving profession and provide guidance for its practitioners. The *Model Standards* are the product of an effort by prominent mediation-interested organizations and individuals to create a unified set of standards that will replace existing ones. They draw on existing codes of conduct for mediators and take into account issues and problems that have been identified in divorce and family mediation practice.

Between 1982 and 1984 [the Association of Family and Conciliation Courts ("AFCC")] convened three national symposia on divorce mediation standards. Over forty individuals from thirty organizations attended to explore issues of certification, licensure and standards of practice. Drafts were distributed to over one hundred thirty individuals and organizations for comment and review. The result of the efforts was the 1984 *Model Standards of Practice for Family and Divorce Mediation ("1984 Model Standards")* which have served as a resource document for state and national mediation organizations.

In tandem with the process convened by AFCC, the American Bar Association's Family Law Section drafted *Standards of Practice for Lawyer Mediators in Family Law Disputes* (1984) *(1984 ABA Standards")*. . . . [T]he *1984 ABA Standards* were basically compatible with the *1984 Model Standards*.

Following promulgation of the 1984 *Model Standards* and *1984 ABA Standards*, interest in mediation in all fields, and family mediation in particular, burgeoned. Interested organizations promulgated their own standards of practice. The Academy of Family Mediators, for example, promulgated its own standards of conduct based on the *1984 Model Standards*. Several states and courts have also set standards. *See, e.g.*, Florida Rules for Certified and Court-Appointed Mediators (October, 1995); Iowa Supreme Court, Rules Governing Standards of Practice for Lawyer-Mediators in Family Disputes (1986) . . .

In 1996, the Family Law Section of the American Bar Association came to the conclusion that interest in and knowledge about family mediation had expanded dramatically since the *1984 ABA Standards* were promulgated and a fresh look at that effort was required. It created a Task Force on Standards of Practice for Divorce Mediation (later renamed the Committee on Mediation) ("ABA Committee") to review the *1984 ABA Standards* and make recommendations for changes and amendments. . . . After intensive review and study, the ABA Committee concluded that while the *1984 ABA Standards* were a major step forward in the development of divorce and family mediation they were in need of significant revision.

First, the *1984 ABA Standards* did not address many critical issues in mediation practice that have been identified since they were initially promulgated. They did not deal with domestic violence and child abuse. The *1984 ABA Standards* also did not address the mediator's role in helping parents define the best interests of their children in their post-divorce parenting arrangements. They made no mention of the need for special expertise and training in mediation or family violence.

Second, the *1984 ABA Standards* were inconsistent with other guidelines for the conduct of mediation subsequently promulgated. The ABA Committee believed that uniformity of mediation standards among interested groups is highly desirable to provide clear guidance for family mediators and for the public. Uniformity and clarity could not be provided within the framework of the *1984 ABA Standards*. The ABA Committee therefore decided to replace the *1984 ABA Standards* with a new document.

The ABA Committee [and other organizations] created a new draft of standards of practice for family mediation specially applicable to lawyers who sought to involve themselves in that process. The Committee set several goals for the revised standards. First, the ABA Committee sought to insure that its revised standards were state of the art, addressing important developments in family mediation practice since the adoption of the *1984 ABA Standards* and *1984 Model Standards*. Second, the ABA Committee sought to insure that its recommended standards were consistent, as far as is possible, with other standards of practice for divorce and family mediation.

To meet these goals, the ABA Committee examined all available standards of practice, conducted research, and consulted with a number of experts on family and divorce mediation. It particularly focused on consultations with experts in domestic violence and child abuse about the appropriate role for mediation when family situations involved violence or the allegations thereof.

The Council of the ABA's Family Law Section reviewed the ABA Committee's first draft effort in November of 1997. It concluded that other interested mediation organizations should be included in the process of drafting revised standards of practice for family mediation . . .

The *Model Standards* . . . are thus the result of extensive and thoughtful deliberation by the family mediation community with wide input from a variety of voices. Nonetheless, they should not be thought of as a final product but more like a panoramic snapshot of what is important to the family mediation community at the beginning of the new Millennium. The Symposium hopes the *Model Standards* will provide a framework for a continuous dialogue to define and refine our emerging profession. The Symposium organizers hope that the family mediation organizations, the bench and the bar and the public will use the *Model Standards* as a starting point for discussion and debate. That continuing process should result in identification of new areas of concern that additional Standards should address and proposals for revision of existing *Standards*. . . .

QUESTION

As this excerpt notes, the Model Standards are the result of extensive study and consensus among "interested mediation organizations," which would include both lawyers and non-lawyers. Do you believe distinct disciplines — lawyers and mental health professionals, for example — might view family mediation differently? Even if this is true at the macro level, are there issues of ethics that might be viewed differently by different professionals? If so, which ones?

C.   CONFIDENTIALITY AND ITS EXCEPTIONS

1.   Overview

The issue of family mediation and confidentiality is more complex than one might anticipate. Sources governing confidentiality are, in many respects, a patchwork of different sources of law. The following describes some of the primary sources of confidentiality. Note that special issues regarding disclosure obligations in the context of child abuse are explored separately below.

- *Rules of Evidence*. Federal Rule of Evidence 408 and similar evidentiary rules in most states protect the confidentiality of settlement discussions. Mediation would usually qualify as a "settlement discussion" for purposes of Rule 408 and similar state provisions. In addition, some statutes, including the Uniform Mediation Act, may establish a separate "privilege" for communications in mediation akin to other privileges, such as the attorney-client privilege. It is important to note, however, that typically such rules of evidence, including rules of "privilege," limit the admissibility of evidence at trial. Standing alone, such provisions do not address voluntary disclosure of information outside this narrow context.

- *State statutes.* Most states have adopted confidentiality provisions relating to mediation. Maryland Rule 17-109, for example, provides that "a mediator and any person present or otherwise participating in the mediation at the request of the mediator shall maintain the confidentiality of all mediation communications and may not disclose or be compelled to disclose mediation communications in any judicial, administrative, or other proceeding." As with most confidentiality provisions, there are exceptions "provided by law" or to "prevent serious bodily harm of death." In the family mediation context, this is particularly important given laws that mandate reporting child abuse or domestic violence. It is important to note, however, that again using the Maryland Rule as an example, by its terms, it "appl[ies] only to civil actions in Circuit Court." Thus, private family mediations or mediations that are conducted pre-filing are not protected.

- *Contract.* Many private mediators and mediation programs require mediation participants, including parties and the mediator, to sign agreements that prohibit disclosure of communications in mediation. The remedy for breach of such agreements is, as in all contract matters, a lawsuit for breach of contract.

- *Non-binding family mediation and general mediation guidelines.* The primary example is the *Model Standards of Practice for Family and Divorce Mediation* just discussed. The Standard VII of the *Model Standards* provide the following guidelines regarding confidentiality:

> *A family mediator shall maintain the confidentiality of all information acquired in the mediation process, unless the mediator is permitted or required to reveal the information by law or agreement of the parties.*

> A. The mediator should discuss the participants' expectations of confidentiality with them prior to undertaking the mediation. The written agreement to mediate should include provisions concerning confidentiality

> B. Prior to undertaking the mediation the mediator should inform the participants of the limitations of confidentiality such as statutory, judicially or ethically mandated reporting . . .

2.   Confidentiality and Judicial Enforcement of Agreements in Family Mediation

With increasing frequency, issues have arisen that explicitly confront confidentiality issues in mediation. Courts have been asked to examine the terms of an agreement allegedly reached in mediation and/or whether an agreement was reached at all. The following two cases illustrate two approaches courts have taken in such circumstances.

HUDSON v. HUDSON
District Court of Appeal of Florida, Fourth District
600 So. 2d 7 (1992)

PER CURIAM.

The appellant husband has perfected this appeal from a final judgment of dissolution and from an order denying his motion to vacate said judgment.

It appears that, during the progress of the dissolution proceeding below, the trial court set the case for trial commencing April 1, 1991. In the interim, an order scheduling mediation was entered and a mediation hearing was set for March 27, 1991. At said hearing the parties arrived at what appeared to be an oral agreement settling the issues involved, but no written mediation settlement agreement was signed. Shortly thereafter, the husband apparently had second thoughts about the proposed settlement, and the parties never reduced the alleged oral agreement to writing. The trial date of April 1, 1991, came and the wife and her counsel showed up for trial but neither the husband nor his counsel appeared. The trial judge commenced the final hearing and heard the testimony of the wife and a residence witness.

The transcript of that hearing reflects that the wife apprised the court of the mediation proceeding, the negotiations toward settlement, and the proposed oral agreement. She even produced her written, unsigned version of what the parties had agreed to. Apparently to corroborate that, she had the mediator sign the back of her written version as a sort of certification that this was what the parties had agreed to at said hearing. In addition to these revelations of the "mediation agreements," the court took testimony from the wife relative to the marital property and other pertinent evidence generally submitted to arrive at a distribution of the marital estate and support needs of the parties. A final judgment was entered and in due course the husband obtained a copy. A motion to vacate the judgment was filed and a hearing held thereon, at which the trial court indicated that she did not hear a motion to enforce the oral mediation agreement, but that she tried the case on the merits and entered judgment thereon. The motion to vacate was denied.

Section 44.102(3), Florida Statutes (Supp.1990), the statutory court-ordered mediation provision, provides in pertinent part:

> (3) Each party involved in a court-ordered mediation proceeding has a privilege to refuse to disclose, and to prevent any person present at the proceeding from disclosing, communications made during such proceeding . . . [A]ll oral or written communications in a mediation proceeding . . . shall be confidential and inadmissible as evidence in any subsequent legal proceeding, unless all parties agree otherwise.

The transcript of the dissolution trial leaves little doubt that the trial court was fully apprised of the mediation proceeding and exactly what the wife perceived to have been agreed upon between the parties, albeit there was no written executed agreement. It appears to us that the injection of the so-called agreement prepared by the wife and "certified" by the mediator, and the various testimonial representations of what transpired at said hearing vis-a-vis agreements between the parties, into the trial before the court violates the spirit and letter of the mediation statute.

The confidentiality of the negotiations should remain inviolate until a written agreement is executed by the parties.

Therefore, we hold that the well was poisoned by the admission of the foregoing evidence of the "agreement" and so infected the judgment reached that it should be vacated and the matter tried anew.

Accordingly, except for the provision dissolving the marriage of the parties, the final judgment is reversed and the cause is remanded for a new trial on the remaining issues.

MCKINLAY v. MCKINLAY
District Court of Appeal of Florida, First District
648 So. 2d 806 (1995)

WEBSTER, J., concurred in the result only.

MICKLE, Judge.

John R. McKinlay, the former husband (Husband), appeals from an August 1991 final order disposing of real and personal property. He alleges three errors: 1) the trial court's failure to enforce the parties' mediation agreement and to impose sanctions; 2) the refusal to permit the mediator to testify in response to allegations made by Louise R. McKinlay, the former wife (Wife), who had questioned the fairness and propriety of the mediation proceedings but claimed a privilege as to mediation communications; and 3) the trial court's division of property. Finding error as to the second issue, we are constrained to reverse and remand for a full evidentiary hearing. § 90.507, Fla.Stat. (1989) (waiver of privilege by voluntary disclosure).

The original proceedings in this prolonged litigation were initiated in May 1985, when Wife filed a petition to dissolve the parties' 17-year marriage. After a hearing in 1986, the lower tribunal issued a final judgment of dissolution of marriage, which was reversed and remanded in Husband's first appeal.

Upon remand, the trial court issued orders in October 1989 setting the cause for final hearing but also referring the parties to mediation during the interim period. § 44.302(1), Fla.Stat. (1989) (permitting trial court to refer contested civil action to mediation). Husband, Wife, and their attorneys attended the December 8, 1989, mediation conference and, with the mediator, all signed a "Stipulation of the Parties" indicating their settlement as to terms involving the distribution of real property, an investment plan, boats, cemetery lots, personal property, life insurance policies, and attorney's fees and costs. On the "Disposition of Mediation Conference" form, the mediator checked "Agreement signed (total resolution)." The stipulation and the mediator's report were filed immediately in the trial court.

In a letter dated December 8, 1989, Wife informed her then-trial counsel, "I do not believe the stipulation agreement that we signed earlier today was fair to me." She alleged that she had been "under severe emotional distress" and had been pressured into signing the agreement. In a letter dated December 14, 1989, Wife's former trial counsel notified Husband's lawyer as follows: "Please be advised that I have been informed by Ms. McKinlay that she, as a result of numerous factors occurring at the time of the mediation, feels that she no longer wishes to abide by the terms of the mediation agreement as signed."

On February 1, 1990, Husband filed a motion to enforce the mediation agreement and to impose sanctions, noting 1) the lapse of 10 days since the filing of the stipulation and report and 2) the absence of a written objection to the stipulation by the trial court. Husband argued that the agreement had become binding on the parties pursuant to Fla.R.Civ.P. 1.730 and that Wife had failed to comply with procedural requirements for objecting to the result.

In a February 14, 1990, letter to the trial judge, Wife complained of being "trapped in a dilemma," and she alleged first that Husband's counsel had "badgered" and "intimidated" her at every deposition and hearing and had given "inaccurate information" to the mediator. Second, Wife contended that her own former counsel had instructed her to sign the mediation agreement on the ground that "his attorney fees to pursue this would be more than the outcome would be worth." Third, she stated that the mediator had pressured her into signing the agreement. Wife asserted that she had been under severe emotional distress at the time of the mediation conference because of a family health emergency, and she sought to have the agreement cancelled . . .

Subsequently, Wife hired new counsel . . .

[An] evidentiary hearing [was] held on April 4, 1990, in part to address the issue of enforcement of the mediation agreement. In response to Wife's earlier allegations of intimidation or duress in the mediation proceedings, Husband sought to have the mediator testify. Wife's counsel objected on the ground that mediated matters are privileged and inadmissible over objection pursuant to section 44.101(3) and section 44.302(2), Florida Statutes. Husband's attorney countered that Wife had waived her privilege by challenging the conduct and integrity of the mediation proceedings, and by fully presenting her allegations in writing and in testimony at the unreported hearing. Finding that Wife had exercised her procedural right to object to the mediation results and had not waived her right to exclude testimony concerning mediation communications, the trial court refused to allow the mediator either to testify or to proffer testimony. That ruling constitutes reversible error.

The trial court based its decision first on section 44.101(3), Florida Statutes (1989), which provided in pertinent part:

> (3) Notwithstanding the provisions of s. 119.14 [public meeting and record requirements], all oral or written communications in mediation proceedings . . . shall be confidential and inadmissible as evidence in any subsequent legal proceeding, unless both parties agree otherwise.

Second, the court relied on section 44.302(2), Florida Statutes (1989) [subsequently renumbered § 44.102(2)], which stated:

> (2) Each party involved in the mediation proceeding has a privilege to refuse to disclose, and to prevent any person present at the proceeding from disclosing, communications made during such proceeding whether or not the dispute was successfully resolved. This subsection shall not be construed to prevent or inhibit the discovery or admissibility of any information which is otherwise subject to discovery or admission under applicable law or rules of court. There is no privilege as to communications made in furtherance of the commission of a crime or fraud or as part of a

plan to commit a crime or a fraud. Nothing in this subsection shall be construed so as to permit an individual to obtain immunity from prosecution for criminal conduct.

The trial court found that Wife had not waived her statutory privilege.

The parties have called our attention to *Hudson v. Hudson*, 600 So.2d 7 (Fla. 4th DCA 1992) (as modif. on reh'g), in which the reviewing court reversed upon a finding that admission of evidence pertaining to an *oral* mediation agreement had tainted the judgment. *Id.* at 9. Although *Hudson* supports Wife's position that mediation communications generally are confidential and inadmissible in a subsequent legal proceeding unless all parties agree otherwise, we find several key factual distinctions between the cases. First, the instant mediation proceedings resulted in a signed, written agreement . . . Second, we note that, unlike the case sub judice, *Hudson* and its progeny were subject to an amendment to chapter 44 . . . which provided that "[n]otwithstanding the provisions of s. 119.14, all oral or written communications in a mediation proceeding, *other than an executed settlement agreement*, . . . shall be confidential and inadmissible as evidence in any subsequent legal proceeding, unless all parties agree otherwise" . . .

Third, and most significant, is the fact that as the party who objected to the settlement based on allegations of duress and intimidation, Wife availed herself of the opportunities to file a written letter to the trial judge and to testify at the unreported February 15, 1990, hearing. However, with only her side of the story presented, she invoked a statutory privilege to preclude testimony or a proffer from other witnesses such as the mediator. These particular facts lead us to conclude that Wife waived her statutory privilege of confidentiality and that, as a result of the waiver, it was error and a breach of fair play to deny Husband the opportunity to present rebuttal testimony and evidence.

Our conclusion is bolstered by the general body of law holding that certain analogous statutory privileges, *e.g.*, the psychotherapist-patient privilege and the lawyer-client privilege can be waived. *See, e.g., Procacci v. Seitlin*, 497 So.2d 969 (Fla. 3d DCA 1986) (attorney-client privilege waived by client's suit for malpractice). Section § 90.507, Florida Statutes, provides:

> A person who has a privilege against the disclosure of a confidential matter or communication waives the privilege if he, or his predecessor while holder of the privilege, voluntarily discloses or makes the communication when he does not have a reasonable expectation of privacy, or consents to disclosure of, any significant part of the matter or communication. This section is not applicable when the disclosure is itself a privileged communication.

Given that Wife invoked the privilege at the April 1990 hearing while challenging the prior conduct or statements of the attorneys and the mediator, we are drawn inescapably to conclude that she thereby voluntarily disclosed or consented to the disclosure of a significant part of the matter or communications for which the privilege was claimed . . .

Having found reversible error as to the second issue, we need not reach the final issue relating to the property distribution scheme. The order is REVERSED and the cause is REMANDED for further proceedings consistent herewith.

WOLF, J., concurs.

WEBSTER, J., concurs in result only.

NOTES AND QUESTIONS

1. Both the *Hudson* and *McKinlay* cases involve parties to family mediation who had "second thoughts" about an agreement reached in mediation. Particularly in light of the stressors that, almost by definition, participants in family mediation experience, to what extent, if at all, should mediation participants be allowed to pierce mediation confidentiality to seek judicial vacatur or modification of a mediation agreement? A knotty problem in this regard is that disclosure of confidential information from the mediation is almost always needed in order to prove any claim that an agreement reached in mediation should not be enforced. Do you see any way to address this problem?

2. What impact does unilateral disclosure have on the non-disclosing spouse? Consider *McKinlay*. The wife's disclosure in that case "opened the door," thus allowing the husband to respond by marshaling evidence that would otherwise have been confidential. Does this mean that one spouse can, in effect, force the other spouse to waive confidentiality? Does the *Hudson's* court's remand for a new hearing without consideration of what happened in mediation solve this problem or does it raise problems of its own?

3. Recall the series of cases regarding legal enforcement of mediation agreements in Chapter 6. Three of those cases — *Cloutier v. Cloutier, In re Banks*, and *Vitakis-Valchine v. Valchine* — primarily involved financial issues. One case — *Wayno v. Wayno* — involved child access. Setting aside the specific issue of child abuse, do you think that a court and/or applicable law should provide less confidentiality protection when the best interests of a child are at issue? To what extent should a court, when conducting an independent inquiry as to what custody or visitation arrangements are in the best interest of a child, be able to inquire into what happened in mediation?

3.   Duties to Report Child Abuse

The openness that is so vital to successful mediation can also enable a mediator to learn information which leads her to suspect that one or more parties are engaged in child abuse. Virtually all states have mandatory reporting provisions regarding reporting of child abuse. The scope of these provisions and how they relate to other evidentiary privileges vary from state to state and, similarly, the obligation of mediators to adhere to such provisions also varies from state to state. Art Hinshaw, *Mediators as Mandatory Reporters of Child Abuse: Preservation of Mediation's Core Values*, 34 Fla. St. U. L. Rev. 271 (2007).

Many statutes governing mediation confidentiality include permitted disclosures "required by law," the most obvious of which would be reporting of child abuse. The same is true of non-binding sources of mediator ethics. The *Model Standards of Practice for Family and Divorce Mediation* is typical in this regard:

> If the mediator has reasonable grounds to believe that a child of the participants is abused or neglected within the meaning of the jurisdiction's

child abuse and neglect laws, the mediator shall comply with applicable child protection laws.[1]

This, of course, still only takes a mediator so far given that the mediator still must know and adhere to a particular jurisdictions "child protection laws."

Apart from the issue of mandatory reporting is the question of how mediators should handle questions of child abuse in terms of the mediation itself. Most mediators, when faced with plausible allegations of child abuse, would not agree to mediate the matter or, if the mediation had already begun, would immediately terminate the mediation. Perhaps surprisingly, the *Model Standards* are not quite so definitive. In terms of the acceptability of mediating matters involving child abuse at all, Standard IX A states that a "mediator shall not undertake a mediation in which the family situation has been assessed to involve child abuse or neglect without appropriate training." This obviously contemplates that "appropriate training" — which remains undefined — would enable a mediator to mediate such cases. The *Standards* go on to say that "the mediator should consider the appropriateness of suspending or terminating the mediation process in light of the allegations," thus, once again, contemplating situations where continuing the mediation is acceptable in light of possible child abuse. Do you agree with the *Model Standards'* views on this subject? Could you contemplate continuing or initiating mediation when, at the same time, the mediator must report abuse to appropriate authorities? Would this be to the benefit of parties or the victims of the alleged abuse?

A Scenario

Stating the above principles is much easier than putting them into practice. Consider the following scenario:

You are mediating a divorce involving John Davis and Diane Davis. The only issue is child access. The couple has one child, Jeffrey, who is 9 years old. Neither party is represented at the time of the mediation.

You conduct the mediation and the couple is about to reach an agreement regarding child access. John will pick up Jeffrey Friday evening and will drop him off at Diane's house on Saturday evening. The parties have also made agreements about holidays, which are roughly evenly split between them, and the summer, during which John will take Jeffrey for two weeks in addition to his normal time with him. John and Diane also agreed to joint legal custody.

During the mediation, you observe that John is prone to extreme outbursts of anger. These outbursts include pounding on the table and shouting. It appears to you that virtually anything you or Diane say — even if innocuous — could trigger these outbursts. At one point, John also shouts how Diane is too "soft" with Jeffrey and that he, John, believes in "being tough" with Jeffrey in terms of discipline. In your experience, you have never seen someone as volatile and unpredictable as John.

In contrast, Diane seems to you remarkably composed and not intimidated by John's behavior. You check in with her frequently to insure that her participation

---

[1] *Standards of Practice*, Standard IX C.

and any agreement is voluntary. Given John's behavior, you personally would not leave a child of yours with John.

NOTES AND QUESTIONS

1.   Assume that the jurisdiction in which you are mediating mandates reporting when a person has a "reasonable belief" that abuse has occurred. Do you believe, based upon these facts, that what you know would constitute "reasonable belief" that Jeffrey has been abused? Are there further actions as a mediator that you might employ in light of what has transpired in the mediation thus far?

2.   What is the underlying standard of "reasonable belief" in legal terms? Is it akin to a "preponderance of evidence"? Less? More?

3.   Apart from conceptualizing "reasonable belief" in legal terms, in practice fact interpretation can be an agonizing challenge. In contrast to judge or jury who, at least in theory, assesses facts as presented by others, it is the mediator herself who is the fact finder and who must take a significant action — breaching confidentiality — in the event the "reasonable belief" standard has been met. What factors might incline a mediator to view uncertain facts as constituting "reasonable belief"? What factors might incline a mediator to view uncertain facts as not constituting "reasonable belief"?

4.   A distinct and exceptionally knotty ethical problem faced by mediators in this situation is whether, even in an assessment less than "reasonable belief" such as "possible child abuse," a mediator should terminate the mediation and/or in some way subtle or not so subtle influence child access agreements to better protect the child. Put another way, such actions fall short of reporting yet still, in some measure, protect a child. An example would be to promote the possibility of supervised visitation. Such steps of course generate tension between the mediator's role as empowering parties and interest in protecting a child. How would you balance these factors?

5.   Assume you have made a decision to report child abuse. Do you have an obligation to tell the parties this? Assuming there is no obligation, would it be more appropriate to do so or not to do so? Why?

4.   Potential Death or Substantial Bodily Harm

Many sources of mediator confidentiality permit a mediator to disclose information learned through mediation about potential death or bodily harm to an individual as well as, in the words of the Uniform Mediation Act, communications in mediation that are "intentionally used to plan a crime, attempt to commit or commit a crime, or to conceal an ongoing crime or ongoing criminal activity." The *Standards of Practice for Family and Divorce Mediation* frames this exception in terms of disclosure of "a participant's threat of suicide or violence against any person to the threatened person and the appropriate authorities if the mediator believes such threat is likely to be acted upon as permitted by law."[2]

An interesting side note to these provisions relates to mediator expertise. Presumably an attorney-mediator might be better able to assess whether a crime

---

[2] *Standard of Practice*, Standard VII.

has been or will be committed while a mental health professional might be better situated to assess the legitimacy of threats of suicide — a complicated matter that requires knowledge of psychology. These circumstances recall the difficult question of appropriate mediator qualifications — an issue we have explored in Chapter 6.

5.   Speaking to Parties About Confidentiality

In Chapter 3 we explored the Mediator's Introduction or"Opening Statement" and, among a set of topics most mediators address, we included "a discussion of confidentiality." Given the relative complexity of confidentiality and its exceptions, this can be a delicate and important task. Options are virtually infinite. Whatever formulation one chooses, however, it is often the *manner* of the mediator — how the mediator exudes discretion and professionalism — that might have a greater impact on the willingness of participants to feel willing and comfortable to openly participate in mediation.

NOTES AND QUESTIONS

1.   If you have prepared or delivered an Opening Introduction in your course or as a mediator, consider how you expressed the issue of confidentiality. Upon reflection, how would you assess how you handled this topic?

2.   Consider the following options a family mediator might use in speaking to parties about confidentiality:

- "I cannot disclose anything you say to me in mediation."
- "I have a statutory obligation to disclose child abuse and I have discretion to disclose potential death or substantial bodily" [this assumes, of course, that the jurisdiction in which the mediation is taking place provides for this]

These options represent two ends of a continuum. Craft a new statement or statements in writing and then deliver it orally. As you do so, would you characterize your statement as an accurate statement of the law? Might it be off-putting to participants? If so, could there be a way of formulating your statements to make it less so?

D.   CONFLICTS OF INTEREST IN FAMILY MEDIATION

In contrast to conflicts of interest in legal ethics, which are intricate and often difficult to apply, ethical norms governing mediation and conflicts of interest are straightforward. Standard IV of the *Model Standards of Practice for Family and Divorce Mediation* succinctly expresses the contours of mediator obligations relating to conflicts of interest to which virtually all mediators would ascribe:

> A family mediator shall disclose all actual and potential grounds of bias and conflicts of interest reasonably known to the mediator. The participants shall be free to retain the mediator by an informed, written waiver of the conflict of interest. However, if a bias or conflict of interest clearly impairs a mediator's impartiality, the mediator shall withdraw regardless of the express agreement of the participants.[3]

---

[3] *Standard of Practice*, Standard IV.

Standard IV imposes on the mediator an obligation to "disclose all actual or potential grounds of bias and conflicts of interest reasonably known to the mediator." In practice, many mediators approach this obligation in two distinct ways. First, a mediator should advise parties of any potential conflict *of which the mediator is aware.* An obvious example would include if a mediator knows one or more of the participants in the case, including attorneys, either professionally or personally. Second, some mediators will, as part of their introductory remarks, inquire of mediation participants whether the mediator (or co-mediators) are known to them or if they have any reason to believe that the mediator could not be fair and impartial. This might reveal conflicts of interest of which the mediator is not aware. Apart from insuring that participants have an opportunity to raise connections that the mediator might have forgotten, such a question further enhances the goal of expressing to the parties their control over the mediation process.

In addition, a careful reading of the *Standards* language reveals that some mediator conflicts might so "impair a mediator's impartiality" that participant consent would still not cure the conflict. This means, in effect, that some conflicts reach a level of severity that even informed consent by all participants would still not allow a mediator to continue the mediation. This is a relatively uncommon circumstance. One example might be a mediator's friendship — not acquaintance-ship — with a participant, although in such an instance it is hard to conceive why the other, non-friend party would consent. Another perhaps less obvious example might be a mediator's aversion to one participant. This could be for any reason or even for no articulable reason. Perhaps a participant looks like the mediator's ex-spouse — a potentially substantial issue if the mediator experienced an acrimonious divorce and the mediation involves the same. There are, of course, a virtually unlimited number of associations or "feelings" generated by mediation participants or even circumstances raised by a mediation that might limit a mediator's ability to fairly conduct the mediation.

Under these circumstances, at least formally, it is the obligation of the mediator to inform the parties that it would not be appropriate for the mediator to continue to act as mediator. There would ordinarily be no obligation to detail the reasons why, although it often might be prudent for the mediator to stress that this has nothing to do with the parties individually or (if appropriate) whether the matter should be mediated. It would then be prudent for the mediator to use her best efforts to secure another mediator for the matter.

While all of this sounds fine in theory, mediators might view such "soft" feelings as not a legitimate basis for recusal or that these feelings are more subject to "control" or not likely to inhibit the ability of a mediator to keep an "open mind." Do you agree? Is there any meaningful way to distinguish "feelings" that reach a threshold which warrants recusal? Since these are assessments based upon a mediator's examination of a mediator's own feelings, is this even possible? Should there be some presumption on the mediator's part one way or another?

E. SPECIAL ETHICAL CONSIDERATIONS FOR LAWYER-MEDIATORS

1.   Introduction

A puzzling, intricate, and, in many ways, as yet unresolved issue for lawyers who mediate relates to the interaction of professional ethics governing lawyers and ethics governing mediators. This is truly a new area, albeit one that is of increasing importance as more and more lawyers mediate. For rare treatments of the interaction between lawyer and mediation ethics in the context of family mediation, see Richard E. Crouch, *Divorce Mediation and Legal Ethics*, Fam. L. Q. 219 (1982); Robert Rubinson, *The New Maryland Rules of Professional Conduct and Mediation: Perplexing Questions Answered and Perplexing Questions that Remain*, 36 U. Balt. L. Forum 1 (2005).

A range of issues might face lawyer-mediators. For example, assume a lawyer is acting as mediator and observes a lawyer representing a party who is committing a substantial breach of professional ethics. How is the lawyer's reporting obligation as a lawyer affected by ethical or statutory obligations of confidentiality in mediation? A perhaps even more timely issue confronts attorneys who wish to incorporate mediation into their practice by formally associating with non-lawyers. This has arisen particularly in the area of family law practitioners. This scenario potentially conflicts with prohibitions against fee splitting between lawyers and non-lawyers. For an ethics opinion addressing — and ultimately sidestepping — "ethical implications of system to provide family law mediation," see MSBA Comm. on Ethics, Op. 97-7.

2.   Clarifying Confusion About the Role of Lawyer-Mediators

One important recent development in the area of the role of lawyer-mediator is the adoption in 2002 by the American Bar Association of Rule 2.4 of *The ABA Model Rules of Professional Responsibility*. This Rule, for the first time in lawyer's ethics, explicitly addresses ethical considerations when lawyers act as "third party neutrals." It is primarily concerned with confusion on the part of pro se parties about what role a lawyer-mediator has undertaken in mediation. Given the "pro se" crisis in family mediation that we discussed in Chapter 8, Rule 2.4 has particular importance for family mediators, especially those mediating in court-annexed programs.

Rule 2.4 sets forth two principles. First, the Rule mandates that a "lawyer serving as a third-party neutral shall inform unrepresented parties that the lawyer is not representing them." By its terms this Rule seems to be saying that whenever a lawyer is mediating, the lawyer must both disclose that she is also a lawyer and that the lawyer is not representing anyone in the mediation. Second, where parties to mediation are unclear as to whether the lawyer-mediator is acting as a lawyer or as a mediator, "the lawyer shall explain the difference between the lawyer's role as a third-party neutral and a lawyer's role as one who represents a client."

Model Rule Rule 2.4 is only binding in jurisdictions which have adopted it. Nevertheless, it is worth considering whether it states good mediation practice whenever lawyers are acting as mediators even in jurisdictions which have not adopted Rule 2.4.3

3.   Conflicts of Interest

Conflicts of interest is one issue where there is some formal guidance for lawyers-mediators.

First, ethical rules governing lawyers strictly limit the degree to which mediators can represent a party before or after mediation. Rule 1.12 of the ABA Model Rules of Professional Conduct, which has recently been substantially revised, expressly provides as follows: (1) "a lawyer shall not represent anyone in connection with a matter" in which the lawyer had acted as a mediator "unless all parties to the proceeding give informed consent, confirmed in writing"; (2) a lawyer-mediator shall not negotiate "for employment with any person involved as a party or lawyer" in the mediation.

Second, the norms of mediator ethics as well as legal ethics would prohibit a lawyer representing a party from later mediating a dispute relating to the representation. Such a situation would constitute one of the "non-consentable" conflicts described by Standard IV of the *Model Standards* (see Appendix C) given that the lawyer-mediator's role as advocate would certainly "impair a mediator's impartiality."

Chapter 11

REPRESENTING CLIENTS IN FAMILY MEDIATION

A. INTRODUCTION

Representing clients in family mediation is a subject distinct from how to mediate family disputes. At the heart of the problem is how the norms of family mediation — a collaborative process which often hopes to preserve relationships — squares with the norms of lawyering. Of course, problems multiply because the norms of lawyering themselves are shifting: for example, notions of lawyers as "problem solvers" as opposed to "advocates" are becoming more commonplace. Given the unique qualities of family disputes, this "problem solving" orientation has blossomed into a full-fledged movement in which lawyers who practice family law are engaged in what they explicitly call "collaborative lawyering" — a subject we will explore in later in this Chapter.

As the following material makes obvious, this is an area very much in flux and shot through with uncertainty. It is nevertheless of extraordinary importance as the legal profession absorbs mediation as crucial in the world of the conflict resolution. As explored in Chapter 10, the legal profession has already taken tentative steps into ethical rules governing lawyers as mediators. More will undoubtedly come and new lawyers will become central to the trends and decisions to be made on this issue.

B. CONCEPTUALIZING AN ATTORNEY'S ROLE IN FAMILY DISPUTES

Popular culture and some practitioners persist in viewing lawyers through a "hired gun" lens, with lawyers' dedication to clients' interests generating over the top advocacy. This is far from a new view. English Barrister Lord Brougham expressed it in 1820:

> [A]n advocate, in the discharge of this duty, knows but one person in all the world, and that person is his client. To save that client by all means and expedients, and at all hazards and costs to other persons . . . is his first and only duty; and in performing this duty he must not regard the alarm, the torments, the destruction which he may bring upon others.[1]

This is, however, far from a universal view, particularly in the extreme form articulated by Brougham. Indeed, current norms of advocacy are various and subject to professional choices made by individual lawyers. Some lawyers do view Brougham-like advocacy as crucial to effective representation while others reject conventional advocacy as an appropriate model for lawyers. Most lawyers are somewhere in the middle. The Model Rules of Professional Conduct capture some of this in-between ground:

> A lawyer should . . . take whatever lawful means and ethical measures are required to vindicate a client's cause or endeavor. A lawyer must also act with commitment and dedication to the interests of the client and with zeal in advocacy upon the client's behalf. A lawyer is not bound, however, to press for every advantage that might be realized for a client.[2]

There is consensus, however, that advocacy in family law matters raises distinct issues. The American Academy of Matrimonial Lawyers has issued a set of principles entitled "Bounds of Advocacy." While, for sure, the principles set forth in this document are aspirational and not all practitioners adhere to them in theory or in practice, Bounds of Advocacy does represent a national consensus that Brougham's "torments" and "destruction" do not have a place in family practice. Indeed, there is an explicit call for family lawyers not to act in this manner even when clients demand otherwise:

> Some clients expect and want the matrimonial lawyer to reflect the highly emotional, vengeful personal relationship between spouses. The attorney should counsel the client that discourteous and retaliatory conduct is inappropriate and counterproductive, that the measures of respect are consistent with competent and ethical representation of the client, and that it is unprofessional for the attorney to act otherwise . . . The matrimonial lawyer should make every effort to lower the emotional level of the interaction among parties and counsel. Some dissension and bad feelings can be avoided by a frank discussion with the client at the outset of how the attorney handles cases, including what the attorney will and will not do regarding vindictive conduct or actions likely to adversely affect the children's interests. If the client is unwilling to accept the attorney's

---

[1] MONROE H. FREEDMAN, UNDERSTANDING LAWYERS ETHICS 71 (3d ed. 2004).

[2] ABA Model Rules of Professional Conduct 1.3 Comment [1].

limitation on objectives or means, the attorney should decline the representation.[3]

There are also, at times, explicit limitations on particular strategies that clients may suggest or demand, such as using custody claims merely as a "bargaining chip." If a client wants to persist in this strategy even after the lawyer counsels otherwise, the attorney should withdraw.[4]

C.   LAWYERS' ROLES PRIOR TO AND DURING FAMILY MEDIATION

Setting aside broader conceptions of advocacy, a more pointed question relates to what role or roles lawyers perform in relation to the mediation process itself. As with everything else in mediation, there are numerous variables that go into answering this question: the nature of and complexity of the issues in dispute, the nature of the planned mediation (including whether it is "court annexed" or not), whether or not a client has had experience with mediation before, and so forth.

1.   Counseling Clients About the Mediation Option

Before assessing lawyers' role *in* mediation, what of lawyers' roles in counseling clients about the mediation possibility *prior to* mediation?

If mediation is not mandated or court-ordered, clients have a choice about whether to pursue mediation or not. Increasingly ethical rules governing lawyer's conduct have begun to address lawyer's obligations to discuss the mediation option when a client seeks the lawyer's assistance in a dispute. The ABA Model Rules of Professional Conduct were recently amended to state that "when a matter is likely to involve litigation, it may be necessary . . . to inform the client of forms of dispute resolution that might constitute reasonable alternatives to litigation."[5] This amendment generated and continues to generate a lively debate about whether it should *mandate* counseling about the availability of ADR[6]: its "may be necessary" language is a remarkable melding of the mandatory with the discretionary. Nevertheless, this new Rule demonstrates a movement toward recognizing that engaging in non-adversarial processes is a subject about which lawyers should counsel clients.

If counseling clients about the mediation is ethically mandated or appropriate, consider options in how an attorney might approach the task:

- Should a lawyer "advocate" for mediation itself?
- Should a lawyer present mediation as one of several options without trying to "convince" a client that she should choose mediation?
- If a client decides that litigation is what she wants to pursue, should a lawyer seek to "convince" her otherwise?

---

[3] American Academy of Matrimonial Lawyers, BOUNDS OF ADVOCACY Rule 1.3 Comment (2000).

[4] *Id.* at Rule 5.2, Comment.

[5] ABA Model Rules of Professional Conduct Rule 2.1 Comment [5].

[6] Andrew Schepard, *Kramer vs. Kramer Revisited: A Comment on the Miller Commission Report and the Obligation of Divorce Lawyers for Parents to Discuss Alternative Dispute Resolution with Their Clients*, 27 PACE L. REV. 677 (2007).

Moreover, in terms of counseling, what factors might go into assessing whether mediation is appropriate? Consider the following possibilities:

- Are there power differentials?
- Is there actual or suspected abuse or domestic violence?
- Would either or both parties be open to a collaborative process?
- Will the resources of a client facilitate meaningful time to mediate or, if the possible mediation will be court-annexed, does the structure or resources allocated to the program offer the possibility of a successful mediation?
- What are the legal issues involved and how might they be resolved in adjudication?

Can you think of other factors that might be explored?

As with issues relating to confidentiality discussed in Chapter 10, central decisions also need to be made about word choice in describing the mediation alternative to clients. *See* Robert Rubinson, *Client Counseling, Mediation, and Alternative Narratives of Dispute Resolution*, 10 Clinical L. Rev. 833 (2004). In thinking about this challenging issue, consider how clients, like lawyers, have likely internalized the norms of adjudication advocacy. This is especially true in family law, with movies, television shows, and high profile divorces virtually always involving high drama and intense and confrontational advocacy. Consider this question: has there been a portrayal in popular culture about family mediation?

Given this reality, consider the following word choices as lawyers counsel and explain mediation to clients:

- Characterizing choices as "managing controversy."
- Consciously avoiding the language of advocacy, such as "claims," "defends," "argues," "positions," and "rights." The adjudication process is also embodied in such terms as "testify," "evidence," "relevance," "ruling," and "judgment." Consider alternatives: "interests," "goals," "resolutions," "facilitation," "cooperation," "collaboration," and "perspectives,"

2.   Preparing Clients for Family Mediation

Assuming that a client chooses mediation and the other party agrees, or assuming that the mediation is mandated or court-ordered, the next issue to arise is how a lawyer should "prepare" a client prior to family mediation. Put somewhat differently, the issue can be approached in the sense of assessing how preparing a client for mediation might differ from preparing a client for adjudication. Consider the following possible categories: establishing goals, developing facts, and preparing for the distinctive dynamics of mediation.

a.   Establishing Goals in Mediation

It would usually be important for a lawyer to explore a client's goals for mediation. The openness of mediation should not mask how a lawyer still must work intensively with the client to establish and assess a range of possible outcomes, as well as identifying the interests and probable goals of the other party. In the mediation context, the parties' interests may appear compatible, or they may appear mutually exclusive. Analysis of goals is not complete unless it includes a thorough canvass of alternative routes to satisfying the client's — and the other party's — interests. In the mediation process, increasing the range of settlement alternatives facilitates reaching a mutually satisfactory agreement. When a client is aware of this feature of mediation, she may see the generation and development of alternatives not as a retreat from achieving a particular outcome, but as the means of potentially achieving a satisfactory resolution of the dispute. As a result, she is more likely to engage thoughtfully — both in the planning process and in the mediation session — in generating alternative resolutions.

b.   "Facts"

As we have seen in Chapter 3, "facts" in the context of mediation is much broader than in adjudication. This crucial dimension of mediation should inform how lawyers approach fact investigation prior to mediation. Given that mediation promotes dialogue between parties themselves, a lawyer should seek to understand who the parties are and how they typically interact. Is the parents' relationship such that one party will unfairly dominate in a more open process? Is it a goal of one or more parties to continue the relationship in some form? What sorts of non-either/or ideas might be available regarding financial issues or child access?

c.   Mediation Dynamics and Strategy

The dynamics of mediation suggest that a lawyer plan and perform a particularly difficult balancing act. In litigation and arbitration, the lawyer's formal communications are directed primarily to the decision-maker. In parallel fashion, in negotiation the lawyer is primarily concerned with managing the dynamics of the interaction with the lawyer for the opposing party. But in mediation the lawyer must at once attend to the opposing party, his or her lawyer (assuming the other party is represented), the mediator, and, of course, his or her own client. In other words, in mediation the lawyer must consider, with the direct participation of the client, multiple audiences. Prior to mediation, a lawyer should consider these audiences and, if appropriate, explore this with a client.

Yet another challenge is for a lawyer to move away from the "admit and deny" pattern of other forms of dispute resolution. Rather, a lawyer might consider that a crucial aspect of the attorney role prior to and during mediation is to collaborate with a client to insure that the client's "frame" or narrative is what is meaningful to the client even if it is not, strictly speaking, a "response" to another party's position.

3.   Assessing How a Lawyer Should Approach Her Role in Mediation

An issue that should be explored prior to mediation is how the attorney should act during mediation. This is a large issue and one that warrants more extended consideration.

It is first important to recognize that there remains dispute among and within jurisdictions about the degree to which attorneys should even attend family mediation sessions. There is some support for the idea that attorneys need not be present when the mediation involves child access issues, while they should be present for disputes involving marital property. As with all else, a potentially infinite range of circumstances can inform making these decisions, including attorneys' fees a party might incur in having an attorney present at mediation.

In considering who should do what at mediation, lawyers should consider the characteristics of the client and any barriers that are likely to prevent a case from being resolved. Not all clients are the same. Some are shy; some are articulate; some are highly knowledgeable of legal forums and processes, and others are not. Some make great impressions and some do not; some are even-tempered, and some are quick to anger. It is important to take the client's personality and presentation into account in exploring with the client what role the client and lawyer should play at mediation. In this regard, the question is not only how the client's participation enhances the likelihood of a productive mediation, but also whether the client's interests are such that she would benefit from playing an active role.

In addition, it is also important to consider your own tendencies and impulses as an attorney. Some attorneys have more experience and facility at collaborative forms of bargaining, including mediation. For lawyers accustomed to the highly adversarial litigation process, adjusting to the interest-based, collaborative nature of mediation can be a new, challenging, and disconcerting experience. This might be especially true for newer lawyers. For lawyers whose usual goal in litigation or negotiation is to wrest and maintain as much control over the flow of information and outcome as possible, relinquishing control to the parties and the mediator may seem counterintuitive. Nevertheless, such lawyers — as all lawyers in mediation — should strive to facilitate settlement by framing and complementing the client's voice rather than by acting as the client's "mouthpiece."

In light of these variables, consider the three "models" presented in the following excerpt.

MODELS OF CLIENT INTERACTION WITH ATTORNEYS IN MEDIATION (2002)[7]
By Jonathan Hyman

Here are three models of how a lawyer can interact with a client during mediation.

The (substantive) counselor. The client negotiates in the mediation. The lawyer only provides advice to the client about the risks and benefits of adjudication . . . and reviews the terms of agreement to avoid any hidden traps or unforeseen gaps. Under this model the lawyer need not even attend.

The (positional) negotiator. The lawyer does most of the negotiating at the mediation, and mostly in the positional mode. That is, the lawyer uses the mediation primarily as an opportunity to manage the concealment/disclosure game, trying to extract information from the other side that helps assess the value of the case and the other side's willingness to settle, and trying to conceal harmful information from the other side, and also to convey information that will cause the other side to see their own case in a less favorable light . . . The client decides on the goals, and the lawyer decides on the means. The lawyer's attempt to control the negotiation without continual dialogue with the client is similar to writing motions and briefs and conducting a trial.

---

[7] Copyright ©2002. Reprinted with permission.

The (negotiation) counselor. This approach is more complex. The lawyer and client both participate in the mediation, with the lawyer continually assessing the information exchange, the proposals, and the dynamics of the negotiation. It requires ongoing dialogue with the client about how the negotiation is going, and how to increase the chances of a good outcome with the client. But it also entails some independent action by the lawyer, that can't be subject to dialogue with the client. For instance, the lawyer might see how the various cognitive and affective obstacles to agreement are affecting the client, something the client, almost by definition, can't see. A lawyer might be able to see, in a way the client can't, why the other side isn't effectively communicating [with] the client (and vice versa). The lawyer then has some obligation to try to overcome those obstacles, without the luxury of extended dialogue with . . . the client . . . At the same time, the lawyer should know when the client may have a better chance of getting a good result, either because the client knows the other side better than the lawyer . . . or because it's important for the other side to relate to the client, not the lawyer . . .

NOTES AND QUESTIONS

1.   Do you see additional "models" that Hyman does not describe? What would such a model or models look like?

2.   Do you believe one or more "models" is particularly appropriate to certain issues in family mediation? Would the answer to this question turn on whether the mediation is addressing child access issue or financial issues?

3.   Do you believe attorneys should have different rules if the mediator's orientation is evaluative, facilitative, or transformative?

4.   What variables do you think might come into play into deciding what model you, as an attorney, might choose to adhere to?

5.   As is often the case with mediation, there is often little "purity" in how mediators and attorneys behave in actual mediation sessions. Can you conceive of being prepared to undertake different roles at different points in a mediation session? What might trigger a change in "model" in the midst of a mediation session?

Now consider a different, more extended consideration of the many issues touched upon thus far in this Chapter.

LAWYER'S REPRESENTATION OF CLIENTS IN MEDIATION: USING ECONOMIC AND PSYCHOLOGY TO STRUCTURE ADVOCACY IN A NONADVERSARIAL SETTING[8]
14 OHIO ST. J. ON DISP. RESOL. 269 (1999)
By Jean R. Sternlight

. . . Although lawyers are participating in mediation in record numbers, little has been written regarding what role such lawyers are or should be playing in the mediation process. Two fundamental and interrelated normative questions must be

---

[8] Copyright © 1999. Reprinted with permission.

addressed. First, should an attorney representing a client in mediation serve as an advocate for that client, or should the attorney play a different, less adversarial role when representing a client in mediation? Second, how active should the attorney be in the mediation process, and how should she relate to her client in the mediation? For example, should the lawyer play the role that many play in court, by doing most of the talking for her client and also serving as a buffer between her client and other mediation participants? Or, should a lawyer take what some have called the "potted plant approach" and basically sit quietly in the room and allow the client to be the primary participant in the mediation? Are there other options? Although mediators may often attempt to control the attorney-client relationship by asking the client to play a direct role in the process, attorneys often have a critical impact in determining how they and their clients should behave in mediation . . .

The extent to which mediation can prove useful in bridging economic, psychological, and strategic gaps between attorneys and their own clients is crucially dependent on the roles played by the attorney and client in the mediation. No single lawyer's role is always best in mediation. Rather, the attorney's appropriate role in mediation should vary depending on which barriers seem to be impeding the appropriate settlement of a particular dispute. That is, while the attorney should remain an advocate for her client at all times, she should adjust the manner in which she attempts to further her client's interest depending upon which barriers are preventing the fair settlement of the dispute. For example, given many of the barriers, the attorney should frequently stop herself from dominating the mediation, instead allowing the client to play an active role in the process. In other situations, however, the attorney must be active and assertive to ensure that her client is not coerced by the opposing party or client. The attorney should not herself determine these relative roles, but rather should in most circumstances consult with the client regarding this issue.

While no single lawyer's role in mediation is always proper, lawyers need to be particularly vigilant in guarding against their own tendencies to behave in mediation exactly as they would in litigation. Instead, to serve their clients' interests, and in light of the conflicts of interest and perception between lawyers and their own clients, attorneys should often encourage their clients to play an active role in the mediation, allow the discussion to focus on emotional as well as legal concerns, and work toward mutually beneficial rather than win-or-lose solutions. Those lawyers who, seeking to advocate strongly on behalf of their clients, take steps to dominate the mediation, focus exclusively on legal issues, and minimize their clients' direct participation, will often ill serve their clients' true needs and interests. Such overly zealous advocates are frequently poor advocates . . .

Some clients undoubtedly prefer to have their attorneys take a dominant role during the mediation. For example, for a variety of reasons clients may wish to have their attorneys speak for them. Such clients may be shy; they may believe that their attorneys could express their positions more articulately and cogently than they could; they may fear that a stronger or better educated opponent may take advantage of them if they represent themselves in the mediation; they may worry that they would make an inappropriate admission; they may fear that they would cry or get angry if they had to speak; or they may believe that their speech would anger or upset the opposing party and thereby bring about physical or emotional harm or derail the negotiations. From a strategic standpoint, a party that wishes to settle the dispute but does not want to admit fault may also find it desirable to be represented in the negotiation.

As well, some clients prefer to have their lawyers serve as buffers, limiting the clients' direct confrontations with either the opposing parties, the opposing parties' attorneys, or even the mediators. For example, some clients have been emotionally or even physically abused or harassed by the opposing parties and would find future confrontations emotionally distressing and perhaps physically threatening. Certain clients may also recognize that they would be subject to coercion or be outmatched if they had to go head-to-head with the opposing party or attorney. Mediation may not be an appropriate dispute resolution device for many parties who have such concerns. Or, if the dispute is to be mediated, such clients may prefer to stay home (if this is allowed by the jurisdiction rules) and allow their attorneys to represent them in mediation. At times, a client who has these concerns may choose to attend the mediation but request that the attorney do all or most of the talking and also ensure that neither the opposing side nor the mediator engages in conduct that would be painful or detrimental to the client.

In other cases the client may desire to play an active role in the mediation, but the attorney may believe that such active participation would not serve the client's best interests. For example, the client may desire to speak out but the lawyer may fear that the client would not be a good advocate of her own position, that she would make damaging admissions, or that she would either get mad or make the other side mad, thereby disrupting the negotiation process. Similarly, the client may express a desire to participate actively in the mediation, and perhaps to have the attorney stay home, but the attorney may fear that the client would be bullied or tricked by the opposing party or simply settle the case for less than the attorney might have obtained. Or, the attorney may fear that the client is not up to the emotional stress that will occur if the attorney does not participate actively in the mediation.

All of these concerns of both client and attorney are potentially legitimate. While some, and particularly some mediators, may believe that all attorney participation in mediation intrudes inappropriately into what should be a client-oriented process, situations do exist in which attorneys need to serve as their clients' protectors and spokespersons. It is crucial to consider these important interests in devising guidelines for attorneys' roles in mediation . . .

The worst mistake one can make in determining the appropriate roles of lawyer and client in a mediation is to refuse to see the issue and simply operate out of habit. Too many lawyers and clients have never thought seriously about how the lawyer-client relationship should work in the context of a mediation. Many lawyers, particularly those with extensive deposition or trial experience, have simply transferred their assumptions and behavior from those areas to the mediation forum without thinking through the differences between a trial or a deposition and a mediation. Such lawyers often instinctively try to do all the talking for the client, tell the client not to volunteer anything, try to stifle emotional outbursts, and focus primarily on establishing the superiority of their clients' legal positions rather than on a problem-solving approach. While this dominating approach may be appropriate in certain mediations, adopting it as a general rule will prevent the use of mediation to overcome the various barriers to negotiation.

Equally inappropriately, some lawyers, like some mediators, assume that mediation is exclusively the clients' process and either fail to attend altogether or do attend but act as the much discussed "potted plant." Such a lawyer may figure that because comments made in mediation are protected by confidentiality, and because no settlement can be reached without her client's agreement, the lawyer need not worry much, if at all, about protecting her client's interests. Again, while this approach may sometimes be appropriate, adopting it unthinkingly in every case is a mistake which may subject certain clients to coercion and abuse and ultimately cause them to accept a settlement which is unfair.

Instead of exclusively taking one approach or the other, lawyers and their clients should divide their responsibilities on a case-by-case basis after taking into account such factors as the nature of the clients and their attorneys, the respective goals of these participants, and the nature of the dispute . . .

This Article advocates that attorneys should consult extensively with their clients not only as to what position should be taken in a negotiation and as to whether the case should be mediated, but also as to the respective roles to be taken by lawyer and client in the mediation. It argues that, at a minimum, such consultation is desirable as a matter of good practice for several reasons. First, the determination of roles may well implicate important substantive concerns. For example, a client may wish to give her own opening in the mediation because one of her substantive goals is to be able to explain how she feels directly to the opposing party, even if this strategy might possibly lower the likely dollar value of the case. Or, a client may wish to have her attorney handle all of the questions because the client feels it would be emotionally damaging to attempt to confront the opposing party or her attorney directly, again regardless of the effect on the bottom line. The attorney should not simply assume that the client's only goal is maximizing, or minimizing, a dollar result.

Second, the client likely has more information regarding the client's aptitudes and abilities than does the attorney. If the attorney does not discuss participation issues with her client, she may make false assumptions regarding the client's interest or ability in participating actively in the mediation. A client who appears articulate may for emotional reasons nonetheless be ineffective in certain mediation contexts. Alternatively, a client who appears very shy or inarticulate may be capable of making a very moving and personal opening statement.

Third . . . a number of conflicts of both economic interest and also psychology may exist between attorney and client. Where the attorney makes choices about the respective roles of client and attorney in mediation, she is likely, at least unwittingly, to make a decision that is biased in favor of her own economic and psychological interests. In cases where such conflicts are possible, it is particularly important that an attorney should consult with her client.

Fourth, it would not be costly for attorneys to consult with their clients on these points. Presumably the attorney will, in any event, meet with her client to explain the nature of mediation and discuss the client's case and settlement position. It is merely suggested that attorneys add an agenda item to this preparatory meeting.

Of course, when the attorney consults with the client, the client will sometimes throw the question of roles back to the attorney and ask the attorney to make the decision. It would be preferable to have the attorney outline the pros and cons of various options to the client and let the client make the call. However, if having heard all the options the client still requests that the attorney decide who should make the opening or how it should be structured, the attorney should go ahead and make these decisions . . .

As well, the attorney should ask herself whether the client would benefit by having the attorney protect her from the opposing party. Although, ideally, mediation should be an opportunity for clients to communicate directly with one another, sometimes such direct communication by clients or their attorneys may be undesirable . . . [I]f the client has been subjected to domestic abuse by the opposing party, it may be not only emotionally distressing but also coercive and even unsafe for the victim to converse directly with her abuser . . .

[In the following discussion, "AL" is an attorney for Client A, and "BL" is AL's opposing attorney for Client B.]

Where BL has an exaggerated idea as to the strength of B's case, again it is important to determine the source of the misperception. Where it is legal — i.e., a misunderstanding of relevant precedents — AL should actively attempt to convince BL to rethink the law. Where BL mistakenly thinks her own client will be a terrific witness, AL may be able to show BL that she is wrong . . .

It may well be that BL, rather than B, is the person who is engaging in competitive negotiation behavior. Again, A and AL must attempt to convince BL to take a more problem-solving approach. Probably AL would be more able to talk directly to BL and to have some impact than would A. As noted above, however, where these efforts fail it may be appropriate for AL to discourage A from sharing too much information with the opposing party or her attorney . . .

Perhaps BL is opposing a settlement because of her needs and incentives that are not necessarily consistent with those of her client. As discussed earlier, BL's financial interests might lead her to oppose settlement. Or, BL might oppose settlement for nomonetary reasons such as her own quest for justice or to hone her trial skills. Certainly it will be awkward for either A or AL to deal with such conflicts overtly. Rather than directly confront BL on these issues, A and AL may seek to convince B that the settlement is wonderful, regardless of BL's lack of enthusiasm. A may be able to do this by speaking directly to B, perhaps even outside the presence of the attorneys. Alternatively, AL might attempt to have a conversation with BL in which she subtly sought to convince BL not to let her own needs stand in the way of her client . . . in overly competitive negotiation behavior, she would often be well advised to allow her client to take an active role in the mediation. Clients will typically be more prone to engage in problem-solving than will attorneys, as discussed above. Also, clients will often be better able than attorneys to recognize opportunities for win-win solutions . . .

Anyone who says they have a simple answer to the question of how lawyers and clients should divide their responsibilities in a mediation must be wrong. Either their answer is not simple or their answer is not right. The answer is complicated because the division of responsibilities should vary substantially depending upon who the client is, who the lawyer is, and what factors appear to be blocking a reasonable and fair settlement of the dispute . . . In determining her role in a mediation, a lawyer should do the following: (1) serve as her client's advocate, (2) consult with her client regarding the division of responsibilities, (3) consider who her client is, and (4) take into account whether she or her client is best situated to help to overcome the extant economic, psychological, and principal-agent barriers to a fair negotiated agreement . . .

NOTES AND QUESTIONS

1.   Is Sternlight's approach *too* contextual, that is, should an attorney operate from an initial assumption of minimal participation as opposed to fashioning her role through the analysis Sternlight suggests?

2.   Sternlight alludes to a fact that the preceding discussion has only touched upon: actions of opposing counsel. Note that in conventional adjudication, attorneys interact with each other. Mediation, of course, is different. How does that affect your conception of what lawyers should do in mediation? Is this less of an issue because of the less adversarial norms set forth in the "Bounds of Advocacy" excerpted above?

3.   Sternlight's discussion is not focused on family mediation. To what extent is family mediation different? In thinking about this question, consider the following article, which does focus on family mediation.

RECLAIMING PROFESSIONALISM: THE LAWYER'S ROLE IN DIVORCE MEDIATION[9]
28 Fam. L.Q. 177 (1994)
By Penelope Eileen Bryan

Gayle's Story

When I first met Warren, he was an elected county official and I had just begun working as an administrator in the county tax office. Warren seemed like a dream come true. He was well-known in our community, charming, and good looking. He wined and dined me and within five months of our first date he asked me to marry him. Hardly believing my luck, I accepted.

Six months after I started my job, Warren's parents were killed in an automobile accident near their home in New Jersey. After the funeral Warren spent the next month in New Jersey settling estate matters. When Warren returned home, he surprised me by announcing his intention to run for the state legislature. He urged me to quit my job, explaining that he would need my help in the campaign and that a working-wife would seem too unconventional to conservative Midwestern voters. I resisted, arguing that I recently had received a promotion and that we needed the money I made. Warren then confided that he and his sister each had inherited over $1 million and that we had no need for my income. I had no idea Warren's parents were wealthy. Stunned, I agreed to resign.

Warren ran a successful campaign and began his long tenure as a state legislator. Then came the children. First Stephanie, then Josh, and finally Julie. Years passed. At first I enjoyed being the wife of a popular public official. We entertained frequently, especially before elections. I became a sophisticated cook and hostess.

Over the years, though, some troublesome patterns emerged. Soon after I quit my job Warren took almost exclusive control of family finances. Toward the end of our marriage, my weekly allowance was $200. From this amount Warren deducted any amount I spent on my own needs, such as shoes, clothing, cosmetics, haircuts, or lunches with friends. Warren also gave me a credit card, but he deducted any charge related to my personal needs from my weekly allowance.

In addition to my allowance, Warren deposited $400 a week into my checking account for family expenses. This money was to be spent exclusively on groceries and on the children. Each week Warren required me to justify each expenditure I made from my checking account.

Although I sometimes was resentful, I told no one about our private life. I accepted Warren's control and worried about preserving his reputation in the community. I grew concerned, however, about Warren's relationship with the children. Troubling incidents occurred with increasing frequency. For instance, dinner time became a nightmare. Warren insisted that the children eat efficiently — nothing put on their plates was to be wasted. Warren also maintained that Josh was too self-indulgent and that he needed more discipline. To correct Josh's failings, Warren required me each day to cook one dish Josh disliked. At dinner Warren, with a broad smile, would serve Josh a large portion of this dish. When he was young Josh simply hung his head and quietly ate what his father put before him. As he grew older and bigger, however, Josh's anger frequently flared.

During one angry exchange, Warren lifted Josh's plate that was piled high with lima beans and smashed it on the table. The beans went everywhere. He then towered over Josh and made him eat the beans without using utensils, one at a time, from the table and the floor. Warren yelled at and berated Josh until he had finished. Stephanie, Julie, and I were not permitted to leave the table until Josh was through eating. These incidents made me and the other children sick to our stomachs. They made Josh boil in suppressed anger. Warren created similar disciplinary schemes for Stephanie and Julie.

Control and derision were not the only problems in Warren's interactions with the children. His violent anger frequently led to his use of excessive physical force. During one angry outburst, Warren threw eight-year-old Julie against the wall, almost causing her to faint. This incident led fourteen-year-old Stephanie to complain to our pastor about her father's behavior. She explained that her father drank and that he physically abused her and her siblings when he disapproved of their behavior. In response to Stephanie's complaint, our pastor called me. I was shocked that Stephanie had reported her father to an outsider. The pastor recommended a local psychologist named Paul and suggested that the family undergo counseling. Paul met with Stephanie and then with me and Warren. In the end, Paul assured Stephanie her father never again would abuse her or her siblings — he would not risk his reputation.

Warren did cease physically abusing the children, but his verbal attacks and his financial control increased. Warren would not allow me to purchase $30 lamps to replace the two lamps in the living room which he had broken in a rage. He claimed we could not afford to have routine maintenance performed on the house. All household help was dismissed except the lawn and pool men. I began doing all the housework in spite of an earlier injury to my neck. We stopped entertaining and only infrequently went out together in public. During this time Warren paid cash for a $175,000 motorhome.

After a year of housework, my injured neck rebelled. I had surgery to replace two discs. Afterwards I was told that I could not do the housework and that I would have trouble doing many types of jobs. Warren still insisted we could not afford household help. I continued doing what I could.

Six months after my surgery a pivotal incident occurred. Tension had been mounting in the house and Warren was drinking heavily. The children and I were in the kitchen. I was putting the finishing touches on a Saturday morning breakfast. Warren entered just as Josh reached into the ceramic cookie jar. Warren yelled that Josh would ruin his appetite. Josh glared, extracted a cookie, and took a bite. Warren tried to hit the cookie out of Josh's hand while he grabbed the ceramic jar. Josh retreated to the other side of the room near his sisters. While staring at his father, Josh took another bite from the forbidden cookie. Warren lost it. He hurled the ceramic jar at Josh's head. Fortunately the bloody-marys he had consumed that morning impaired his accuracy. But the ceramic jar caught Stephanie, leaving a two inch split in her cheek. Trembling, I quickly ushered the children out of the house and into the car. As I looked at my sobbing children and Stephanie's bleeding face, for the first time I seriously contemplated leaving Warren. When I returned home that evening with the children, I told Warren he had to quit drinking or I would leave him. He quit, but the problems continued. I entered counseling with Paul.

Warren grew increasingly aware of my dissatisfaction with the marriage. At Christmas he told me that I could hire a maid and a laundress and that he would buy me a new van — if I promised to stay with him. I could not promise. Two months later I announced that I wanted a divorce and I asked Warren to leave the marital home. He refused. Since I wanted the divorce and he did not, he insisted that I and the children should be the ones to leave.

Not knowing where we should go or what we should do, I called Melinda to represent me. I chose Melinda because I knew several other politicians' wives who had used Melinda for their divorces. I explained that the children and I had nowhere to go. Melinda agreed to see me immediately. With the children sitting in the waiting room, Melinda and I had our first conference. Knowing Warren's political and financial status, Melinda told me to rent an apartment for the family until she could work things out with Warren's lawyer.

I left Melinda's office and began a futile search for housing. Landlords would not accept my credit card for rent and I had no cash or money in my checking account. I called Warren. He refused to give me money for housing. He told me to get a job. I felt frightened. Growing desperate, I turned to my friend Marty and asked if we could stay with her for a day or two. Although Marty had three children of her own, she agreed. The "day-or-two" extended to ten.

I again called Warren, explaining that living in another person's house was becoming extremely stressful. After a day and a half of negotiation, Warren agreed that we could live in his motorhome if he could park it in Marty's driveway. With no other alternative available, the children and I moved to Marty's driveway.

I was embarrassed and distressed over living in Marty's driveway. I also was surprised that Warren, upon whom we had depended for many years, showed no concern for where his children were sleeping. Warren's unanticipated behavior made me feel acutely vulnerable. There seemed nothing I could count on.

Approximately four weeks passed with the children and me living in the motorhome. I found the situation intolerable. Although the motorhome was luxuriously furnished, the over-stuffed furniture significantly reduced available space. The width of the motorhome could be traversed with one step, the length with twelve steps. There was only one bed in which Stephanie and Julie slept. I slept on the couch. Josh, tall for his age, had nowhere to sleep but on the foot-wide floor.

The stove did not work, forcing us to take all of our meals with Marty's family. There was no acceptable place to drain the holding tank which collected water from the shower and sinks. At night the children and I sneaked out into Marty's yard to drain the tank. We could not do this during the day because we were afraid the neighbors would think we were draining sewage and would complain, forcing us to leave the only housing we had.

The motorhome's heating and cooling units could not be used. Whenever they were turned on, all the circuits in Marty's house blew. Ventilation and temperature control became oppressive problems, especially with our unstable fall weather . . .

I began calling Melinda almost daily, asking whether something could be done. Finally my psychologist Paul called her and insisted that my living situation had to change. Melinda told him that Warren had been more difficult about paying temporary support than she had expected and that she intended to request a temporary support hearing. She explained that first, however, the law required me to mediate with Warren. Paul expressed his concern about my ability to negotiate with Warren. Melinda assured him that mediation was just a hoop that had to be jumped through to get to court. Melinda and Warren's attorney scheduled a mediation session.

I met with Melinda once before the mediation. I explained that I knew nothing about mediation and that, whatever it was, I did not want to do it with Warren. She insisted that the law required mediation before a temporary support hearing. I should not worry — nothing would happen and she would be there with me. After the mediation we could get our hearing before a judge. We spent the rest of the conference discussing finances.

I could not tell Melinda much about finances. I did tell her, however, that Warren owned stock, a condo in Aspen, a pension plan, a motorhome, and some rental property. I also informed her that, except for the marital home, Warren kept all the property in his name. We then filled out my financial affidavit by approximating and guessing at my household expenses, using Melinda's household expenses as a yardstick.

Melinda asked me about the value of the marital home. I told her that a house about the same size down the street from us sold for approximately $400,000 four years ago. A depression then hit the real estate market. The lot upon which our house sat, however, was five acres larger than the lot of the house that sold. She then suggested that our house probably was worth around $500,000-$600,000. I replied that I thought that figure was too high. She persisted, however, and a $500,000 value was put down on the financial affidavit. On my way out of Melinda's office, I reminded her that the children and I desperately needed to find adequate housing and that we needed money upon which to live. She assured me we would have our court hearing soon.

The entire week before the mediation I was a wreck. I slept little and cried frequently. I chain smoked. My hands constantly shook. I met with my psychologist several times. He helped calm my nerves — but only temporarily. When I left his office my anxiety resurfaced. Worse — I was embarrassed and angry with myself. I could remember a time in my life when I had felt strong and competent. I had trouble believing that I had become this nervous wreck and that my life and my children's lives seemed so vulnerable to Warren's whims.

I knew that my whole life was at stake in the divorce as well as the lives of my children. I was fifty-three, I had no college education and I had not worked in over twenty years. My doctors had told me I would have difficulty holding down any full-time job. Josh and Julie had significant learning disabilities and required a lot of my time, making full-time employment even more difficult. I knew I needed continued psychotherapy to address my anxiety and depression. Medical insurance was a necessity. My financial vulnerability frightened me, but in therapy I had come to realize that divorce was the only choice for me and the children.

The day of the mediation I went to Melinda's office. Soon afterwards Warren and his attorney arrived. To my chagrin, I was shaking and close to tears. I told my attorney's receptionist I had arrived. She nodded briefly and told me to have a seat. Melinda would be out in a moment. I sat as far away from Warren as I could and tried not to look at him or his attorney. The receptionist asked whether Warren would like coffee. She referred to him as "senator." He thanked her for her attentiveness. His old seductive charm was in full-swing. No one asked whether I wanted coffee. Other attorneys in the firm wandered through the waiting room. They each spoke deferentially to Warren, ignoring me completely — even though several of them knew me socially. I began to feel apologetic — uncomfortable with the awkwardness my presence seemed to cause. I went to the bathroom, looked in the mirror and tried to convince myself that I was being overly sensitive. Yet I was becoming apprehensive and I worried whether I could control my tears.

Finally Melinda appeared. She engaged in a casual chat with Warren. Both of them acted as though nothing unusual were happening. I wondered whether I was the only person there who understood the significance of the divorce and the desperateness I felt. I felt extremely anxious and unable to concentrate. Melinda ended her conversation with Warren and called me into her office, explaining there was no need for me to sit in the waiting room with Warren.

Settling into her chair, Melinda told me that the mediator was an attorney named Frank and that they had decided I should not confront Warren directly during the mediation. But first we all had to meet with Frank in Melinda's conference room. I was relieved that I did not have to deal with Warren.

We all sat down at Melinda's conference table. Warren's attorney handed Warren's financial statement to Melinda. Melinda also had the financial disclosure forms that Warren had to submit to the state each year. She noticed that on each form Warren had valued the marital home at approximately $200,000, much lower than the $500,000 we had put on my financial affidavit. She leaned over to me and quietly explained that Warren must have undervalued the home for tax purposes and to make himself look less wealthy to his constituents. The mediator Frank also noticed the discrepancy. He asked Warren about it, and Warren explained that he had put down the assessed value of the home.

Frank then explained the mediation process to all of us, but I could not listen. In Warren's presence, I was too emotionally agitated to listen. Besides Melinda had assured me she would protect me. I was there so that I could get to a judge and get the children and me out of the motorhome. At the end of Frank's talk, Melinda and I left the conference room and returned to her office.

On the way to the office, Melinda's receptionist stopped me and asked that I return the key to the bathroom. Frowning, she told me that my taking the bathroom key into the conference room had caused considerable difficulty for others in the office. I felt ashamed — like a bad child. I started to cry.

After Melinda and I were back in her office and I had calmed down, Frank entered. I told him of the family's need to get out of the motorhome and find suitable housing. I explained what living in the motorhome had been like. He seemed genuinely concerned and he promised that I would get out of the motorhome. I cried again — this time with relief. Regaining my composure, I relaxed some and allowed myself to imagine having easy access to a bathroom. My positive feelings proved premature.

Melinda and Frank left to talk with Warren and his attorney. My first few minutes alone were fine, but as time passed I became anxious — wondering what was taking so long. My imagination conjured up negative images — Warren's refusing to pay support, Warren's deciding that he wanted custody of the children, Warren's convincing everyone that I was malingering. The comfort I experienced earlier gave way to feelings of insecurity and dread. I began pacing.

By the time Frank and Melinda returned I had convinced myself that I was in trouble. I was right. Melinda seemed excited and she told me progress had been made. Warren was willing to leave the marital home and allow me and the children to return. I again cried with relief. Melinda also explained that Warren had offered me ownership of the marital home. She could not believe my good fortune. She had not anticipated ANY reasonable offer — certainly not one as generous as this. No court, she assured me, would award me $500,000.

My relief immediately gave way to panic. I felt numb. I had many jumbled thoughts. I paced the room, trying to calm myself so that I could explain. I did not want the marital home. In order to get any money out of it, I would have to sell it. The real estate market was depressed. I had heard of people who had walked away from their homes because there were no buyers. The house was not worth $500,000. The house needed work before it could be sold. I knew of two leaks in the roof. I could not afford repairs. I did not have any money! Had she forgotten that?

Melinda left the room to confer with Warren and his attorney. She returned and stated that "the senator" said the roof did not leak. That seemed to close the topic.

I asked about financial support. Melinda said that Warren would not pay spousal maintenance — it was "absolutely out of the question." I sank into confused anxiety. I needed spousal maintenance. I could not afford to live in the house without it. Melinda, who knew this, blankly stared at me during my attempt to explain. I could not comprehend what was happening. When I first hired Melinda, she indicated that I was entitled to maintenance. I again explained, as thoroughly as I could, the expenses of maintaining the house and the children, my lack of recent work experience, and my limited ability to work. At a brave moment, looking straight at Melinda, I told her I HAD to have spousal support. Melinda flinched. Frank frowned and explained that courts disapprove of spousal maintenance, making it difficult to get. I felt light-headed. I sensed I was losing control.

I protested. I thought nothing was going to happen today. Mediation was just a hoop. I could not do this. I was not ready. Frank asked Melinda how long it would take to get a temporary support hearing. Melinda replied it would take five or six weeks. I was shocked. If I did not agree, the children and I would spend another six weeks in the motorhome! It would be winter! I had to breathe deeply to keep from getting dizzy. I began to cry.

The pressure increased. Melinda said I could invest $150,000 in another house and then I could live nicely off the interest on $350,000. If I invested the money at 10 percent, she explained, I would have a $35,000 a year income. I did not think to challenge her, even though I knew interest rates had fallen. I did, however, express my belief that the house was not worth $500,000 — so her calculations were inaccurate. We had not even had an appraisal done! I felt ambushed.

Frank then pulled up a chair right in front of me, put his elbows on his knees, and cupped his chin in his hands. Sitting there knee to knee with me, he asked me to tell him about the house. I told him what I already had told Melinda. He asked if the acreage we owned could be subdivided. I said no-the community restrictions would not allow it. After listening to me, he talked about how valuable ten acre home sites were, how people valued space and privacy, and how people were moving to our state because our economy was on the up-swing. Surely the house would sell for $500,000 — perhaps much more. I would be a wealthy woman. He told a story of how his friend's home had sold quickly. Surely mine also would sell quickly.

Frank then stated that, in his experience as a lawyer, Warren's offer was generous. He and Melinda suggested that I should be grateful. I wondered if we lived on the same planet. Melinda repeated that no court would give me $500,000. I was wearing out — but I tried again. I did not want the house. I did not know its worth. I was not sure I could sell it. I could not afford to repair it. "I" knew the roof leaked — even though Warren denied it. I could not afford the expenses and upkeep without spousal maintenance. Someone said that I might refinance to get funds for repairs. I wondered how I could qualify for refinancing with no income. Why did no one understand these things?

Melinda responded that I was being unreasonable — I obviously did not understand the offer — I should stop whining about petty details. If I would just agree I would be a half-millionaire. Her tone became cold and authoritative. I again felt like a "bad child."

Frank suggested that Warren might agree to co-sign for a $50,000 mortgage so that repairs could be made. He left to consult with Warren.

Lunch arrived. Frank returned. The two of them ate. I pushed the food around my plate. I felt confused, exhausted, and defeated. The people I trusted to help me seemed deaf to my concerns. I began doubting my judgment; after all, they were the experts. Maybe I was wrong about the house and my financial vulnerability. One of them told me a judge would review the settlement and make sure it was fair.

Toward the end of lunch I asked how I could afford to stay in the house while I was waiting for it to sell. They looked at each other — pleased that I seemed to be coming around. We discussed whether child support would cover the maintenance and expenses. It would not. They left to talk with Warren. I put my hands over my face and cried.

When they returned my insides were shaking. I did not want to talk to them anymore. I wanted to go back to the motorhome and be alone. But of course I could not — I had to get through this. I could not get a temporary support hearing without mediating. I wondered whether a judge would consider support if we reached agreement on how to split the property. I was too exhausted to ask, and quite frankly, the last people I wanted to ask were my lawyer and that mediator.

Frank explained that Warren now was offering to pay me $1,000 a month, as a property distribution, for eighteen months. Then I could afford to stay in the house. Frank and Melinda assured me that the house would sell within eighteen months. I was getting a great deal. I just nodded, no longer able to argue but wondering what made them clairvoyant. I looked at Melinda and expressed my confusion. Feeling like a child and with tears rolling down my cheeks, I asked her what I should do. She replied that I should accept Warren's offer. I asked her if she was sure. She was.

Soon we all went into the conference room to sign a typed agreement. Melinda explained that she would draft another agreement in the morning, but it would be wise to get something signed now. She handed me the agreement, asking me to read through it. I flipped the pages without much comprehension. I did notice, however, that the agreement said nothing about Warren's signing for a $50,000 mortgage. I asked Melinda why it was missing. She stated that Warren had refused. I could no longer concentrate. I asked whether she was sure I should sign. She was sure. I signed.

I have no memory of my drive "home" to the motorhome. Soon after my arrival I told Marty what had happened. She was surprised I had accepted the marital home because I earlier had told her that I did not want the house. I explained that everyone told me it was a good deal. She then reminded me that her home had been for sale for three years without an offer and that she had lowered the price considerably. She doubted that my house could be sold quickly and that it was worth half a million dollars.

After calling two other friends who shared Marty's opinion, I began to panic. I realized I had to make some changes in the final agreement that Melinda was preparing. I never thought the paper I signed in Melinda's office immediately after the mediation was a "final" agreement. I thought a second agreement was coming — that changes could be made.

The next morning I called Melinda. I told her I wanted Warren to guarantee that the roof did not leak. I also wanted him to guarantee that I would realize at least half a million dollars from the sale of the house. Melinda told me Warren would not sign the agreement if she made the changes. I said that was okay, because I did not intend to sign it unless those provisions were included. Melinda was furious with me. She told me I was a "nit-picking cry-baby" — hat I was going to screw up the whole deal. I was shocked by the way she spoke to me and I retreated, insisting only that she insert a clause about the roof. She then told me she could not insert such a clause — that the agreement I had signed the day before was a binding contract. I could not change its provisions. I had to sign the final copy. I told her I would wait and see what the judge had to say. She told me there would be no temporary support hearing — no judge — the contract I had signed took care of everything. I was stunned. I hung up on Melinda and began to weep. It seemed I had sold myself down the river.

Later that day, when I had regained some control, Marty called a real estate agent who ran comps on the house. The real estate agent said I would be lucky to get $260,000 for the house — especially in the current market. So much for having a half a million dollars! Two days later an inspection revealed a roof in need of replacement for a cost of $35,000.

The next few days I felt numb. No spousal maintenance. No medical insurance. No portion of a pension plan. Just a house worth half of what I had been told it was worth. I could not overcome the feeling that I was responsible for this — that somehow I deserved this situation because of my stupidity and weakness. My sense of personal accountability and defeat made it impossible for me to consider challenging the agreement. Marty, however, argued that I, and especially the children, deserved a better fate. She finally convinced me to talk to another lawyer.

More than a year has passed since the mediation. My new lawyer and I are in the middle of a legal fight with Warren who, understandably, wants the agreement to stand and shows no willingness to compromise. My attorney has no idea what his final fee will be or whether we will win. We struggle with several problems. Because mediation is relatively new, little helpful precedent exists regarding the enforceability of mediation agreements. He also tells me that judges favor mediation and that our judge likely will be reluctant to find the agreement unenforceable. Moreover two of our primary legal arguments, unconscionability and coercion, are difficult because Melinda allegedly represented me during the mediation. In essence, we must suggest that her representation was inadequate.

Despite the problems, however, I am glad I decided to fight. When I look back on the mediation I feel very angry. I cannot believe that I was forced into that experience, that my lawyer abandoned me, and that I almost gave up what I think I deserve after over twenty years of service to my husband and family — a chance for a decent life.

I. Introduction

The initial wave of unabashed enthusiasm for divorce mediation and alternative dispute resolution (ADR) in general has given way to sober reassessment. As stories like Gayle's keep emerging, lawyers and potential mediation participants pause. Yet, enthusiasm for mediation persists among legislators, judges, and judicial administrators who hope for an easy solution to overcrowded dockets and a way to rid judges of unsavory divorce cases. Moreover, ADR proponents tell divorce lawyers that mediation offers a "better way" of resolving divorce disputes. In contrast with traditional lawyer representation, the informality of mediation, they explain, honors client autonomy and family privacy, preserves post-divorce family relationships, fosters greater compliance with final decrees, and permits idiosyncratic agreements unconstrained by the insensitive dictates of formal law. Good lawyers offer their clients mediation and watch from the sidelines while informality works its magic; only bad lawyers talk "rights," obstruct mediation, and sometimes insist upon trial. With advocacy declared illegitimate, many divorce lawyers accept the marketing rhetoric and compromise, as did Melinda, their professional role.

Yet divorce mediation, as the foregoing narrative illustrates, poses hazards that require lawyer intervention and advocacy. This article describes how lawyers can reclaim their professionalism while representing the High-Risk Client

II. The Lawyer's Role in Mediation

A. Introduction

The lawyer's first task is to assess the risk mediation poses for her client by balancing the client's strengths and weaknesses against those of the other spouse. Once a lawyer determines that a client, like Gayle, presents a high-risk profile, the lawyer generally should try to avoid mediation. Avoidance seems especially important when the client has experienced physical or emotional abuse in the marriage.

Some high-risk clients, however, eventually can recover sufficient strength to negotiate effectively with their spouses. For instance, a husband's depression caused by his anticipated loss of a close relationship with his children can subside, and a housewife's low self-esteem and status may increase when she obtains a prestigious new job. Yet recovery usually occurs slowly. Because mediation generally is recommended early in the divorce process, most clients do not have sufficient time to mend.

Increased cost may also suggest the inappropriateness of mediation. To protect a high-risk client's interests, the lawyer must attend and/or spend extensive time preparing the client for and reviewing the mediation sessions. These safeguards can significantly increase the cost of divorce. Moreover, if the lawyer must conduct a largely independent negotiation during mediation, the additional expense of mediation seems unnecessary; traditional lawyer negotiation would suffice.

More often than not, however, a lawyer cannot control whether her client mediates. Mediation rarely is voluntary. Courts commonly require divorcing couples to attempt mediation before allowing them to proceed in the formal legal system. When mediation is mandated for a high-risk client, however, many statutes permit her lawyer to seek an exception. . . .

When a high-risk client is required to mediate, her lawyer should, if permitted to do so, accompany the client to all mediation sessions. Perhaps Melinda chose to attend Gayle's mediation because she recognized Gayle's vulnerability. Rather than protect her high-risk client, however, Melinda abandoned her traditional advocacy role and herself fell victim to the mediation process.

B. Lawyer Participation

When the attorney attends mediation sessions, any resulting agreement will be more difficult to challenge than when a client has mediated alone. For instance, a court might declare that Melinda's presence reduced or eliminated any risk of coercion during Gayle's mediation and presumptively assured that the agreement reflected Gayle's interests. To successfully contest the mediation agreement, Gayle probably must at least suggest that Melinda malpracticed; that her lawyer failed to protect her interests and helped to create the duress that Gayle experienced. This burden is difficult to sustain when the client's story inevitably is contrasted with the stories told by a prestigious lawyer and a mediator who both have their professional reputations at stake. Because of the significance that courts attach to the presence of counsel in mediation and the difficulty of undercutting that significance, a participating lawyer vigilantly must protect her client's interests during mediation.

1. AVOIDING THE PITFALLS

Several circumstances encourage lawyers to compromise their professionalism during mediation: their belief in a "better way," efficiency rhetoric, lawyer self-interest, relationship rhetoric, and diminished professional accountability. Lawyers must anticipate and avoid these pitfalls.

a. Belief in a "Better Way"

Many lawyers want to believe the fashionable rhetoric about a "better way" of resolving divorce disputes. They have been told that the informality of mediation permits parties to avoid the constraints of substantive law and maintain their autonomy. Moreover, mediating spouses can preserve their familial relationships, whereas lawyers and judges generate unnecessary hostility between divorcing parties. A lawyer who uncritically accepts this rhetoric may hesitate to compromise mediation's integrity by insisting on formal discovery and the vindication of legal rights.

Gayle's mediation suggests, however, the problems that can occur when a lawyer compromises her role as the client's advocate. Basic financial information must be obtained and reviewed before mediation. Melinda's failure to obtain an appraisal of the marital home and an evaluation of Warren's pension plan and other property caused her to recommend an inadequate settlement. Moreover, basic legal rights need protection in mediation just as they do in lawyer-to-lawyer negotiation. Melinda's failure to challenge Warren's refusal to pay spousal maintenance and the lopsidedness of the proposed settlement significantly jeopardized her client's financial future. Perhaps Melinda's uncritical belief in mediation's superiority encouraged her to abandon her professional role and to neglect her client's interests.

b. Efficiency Rhetoric and Lawyer Self-Interest

Efficiency rhetoric and lawyer self-interest provide additional disincentives for lawyer advocacy in mediation. Mediation is marketed to the public as a faster and cheaper way of resolving divorce disputes. To fulfill the promise of greater efficiency, mediators will pressure both lawyers and parties to reach agreements quickly. Reaching agreement frequently is easier and faster when the lawyer forgoes formal discovery and abandons legal rights. Had Melinda, for instance, insisted upon earlier responses to discovery requests or upon spousal maintenance for Gayle, agreement might have taken much longer or never have been reached.

Moreover, the lawyer herself may have incentives for reaching agreement quickly. A lawyer with a burdensome case load may be tempted to compromise her role as the client's advocate if an agreement can be produced quickly. Other concerns also may make quick resolution attractive to the lawyer. The mediator's settlement agenda can reinforce the lawyer's self-interest to the detriment of the client.

c. The Preservation of Relationships

Mediators frequently will pressure lawyers and clients to preserve an informal, accommodating atmosphere in order to reduce hostility and to preserve constructive relationships between the divorcing spouses. Melinda's insistence in mediation that Warren honor Gayle's legal right to spousal maintenance undoubtedly would have precipitated his anger and compromised his future relationship with Gayle. The rhetoric of peace is especially likely to affect lawyers who have become uncomfortable with advocacy in divorce proceedings.

The academic and practical literature urges divorce lawyers to recognize the importance of preserving the post-divorce family. The popular press blames lawyers for creating and throwing the grenades of divorce warfare. Films like War of the Roses and television programs like L.A. Law depict the horrors of a hostile divorce. Mediation rhetoric feeds on a collective sense of professional guilt, reminding lawyers of what they have heard elsewhere: bad lawyers talk rights, protect legal interests to the detriment of relationship interests, and unnecessarily cause hostility between divorcing parties.

Yet, in the long run, mediation proves no more effective at containing hostilities than any other form of divorce dispute resolution. Two years after divorce, the hostility between spouses who resolved their dispute through mediation does not differ from the anger between spouses who resolved their divorce through lawyer-brokered settlement or judicial decision.

An exaggerated concern with preservation of the relationship between divorcing spouses usually disadvantages the weaker spouse. Generally, the weaker spouse needs something from the more powerful spouse. If the weaker spouse persists in a request that the powerful spouse rejects, the powerful spouse's anger may threaten preservation of the relationship. Moreover, if continuing cordial relations becomes the paramount value in mediation, mediators will encourage the weaker spouse to retreat. This dynamic existed in Gayle's mediation. Gayle, the weaker spouse, requested spousal maintenance and insisted she did not want the marital home. Warren, the more powerful spouse, refused her request for maintenance and offered her the marital home. The mediator looked to Gayle to abandon her reasonable request, rather than to Warren to fulfill his legal obligation. Gayle's lawyer followed suit.

The rhetoric of relationship preservation also ignores the possibility that provoking Warren's anger might be necessary to preserve Gayle's rights. Forcing Warren to acknowledge Gayle's contributions to their marriage and to provide appropriate maintenance might foster greater respect and less hostility in the long run. Finally, concern with preserving friendly relations during mediation neglects the likelihood of Gayle's hostility, once she recognizes the unfairness of the resulting settlement.

d. Professional Accountability

A different form of self-interest can encourage the lawyer to abandon legal rights talk in favor of the rhetoric of relationship and efficiency. When a lawyer negotiates an agreement that inadequately reflects her client's legal entitlements, the lawyer is open to a professional malpractice claim. In mediation, however, primary responsibility for the agreement's terms rests with the mediating spouses, making a malpractice claim more difficult. A lawyer, then, may not take her responsibility to protect her client's legal rights quite as seriously during mediation as she does when she negotiates for the client herself. When, however, a mediated agreement is grossly unfair, a client may pursue a legal malpractice claim, despite its difficulty. Gayle, for instance, may sue Melinda if the court refuses to set aside the mediation agreement. Regardless of whether Gayle would be successful in her malpractice suit against her attorney, Melinda's life would not be pleasant and her professional reputation likely would be tarnished.

Similarly, when the lawyer negotiates a settlement or conducts a hearing that fails to effectuate her client's legal rights, her professional reputation may suffer. When the client mediates, however, the lawyer has less responsibility, and her reputation may suffer less damage if the outcome seems unjust.

Moreover, proponents claim that mediation generates greater user satisfaction than lawyer-brokered settlements and judicial decision. The promise of a more satisfied client provides an additional reason for the lawyer to remain passive. Again, however, the lawyer might misapprehend her vulnerability to a dissatisfied and angered client. Gayle lives in a small town, has a high-profile divorce case, and frequently discusses her dissatisfaction with Melinda's representation. Melinda's professional reputation has suffered because of her failure to protect Gayle's interests adequately during mediation.

A lawyer must monitor her own responses throughout mediation to be certain that she is not seduced by these disincentives into abdicating her professional responsibility. More specifically, a lawyer always should complete formal discovery before mediation, and should insist that the agreement reflect the substantive legal rights of her client. In so doing, she must expect and be prepared to ignore mediator disapproval and hostility.

2. PREPARING THE CLIENT FOR MEDIATION

The lawyer and client must decide upon their respective roles in mediation. If the client is high-risk, extensive lawyer participation may be necessary. If the client seems sufficiently powerful, however, the lawyer can encourage her participation, interrupting the proceedings only when necessary. However responsibilities are divided, the lawyer must prepare the client for mediation and remain alert throughout the sessions.

a. Educating the Client

A client's self-understanding and knowledge of the mediation process can help her to avoid mediation's pitfalls. If a spouse feels guilty about an extramarital affair, the lawyer can explain that during mediation the client must anticipate, detect, and resist attempts by the mediator, the other spouse, and the other lawyer to manipulate her guilt. If the client's weakness is adherence to a traditional sex role ideology that makes her primarily responsible for preserving family relationships, the lawyer should explain the disadvantage this belief can create and should urge the client to resist exploitation. In addition to alerting the client to potential difficulties resulting from the client's attributes, the lawyer must explain the pressures the client will encounter in mediation. Specifically, the client, like the lawyer, must resist the emphasis on shortsighted efficiency concerns, the seduction of informality, the focus on relationship to the exclusion of rights, the intense pressure to compromise and settle, and the biases characteristic of mediators. Education alone, of course, is insufficient to protect all clients.

3. MONITORING AND OBSTRUCTING THE DISCOURSE

Throughout mediation, a lawyer should monitor the discourse for signs of client weakness and undue influence of mediation rhetoric. For instance, if the client has low self-esteem, the lawyer must obstruct communications by the other party, the other lawyer, and the mediator that suggest the client's unworthiness. Knowing Gayle's low self-esteem, her lawyer should have recognized her duty to support Gayle, rather than join in the mediator's suggestion that Gayle's concerns were irrational and childish. More specifically, Melinda should have identified the mediator's pressure tactics, investigated the value of the marital home, and supported Gayle's request for spousal maintenance.

Similarly, a lawyer must detect when a client seems tempted by the pressure to succumb to preserving of the peace by unwisely compromising a legal entitlement. When a lawyer detects her client's wavering, she should interrupt the discourse, reinforce the client's rights, and/ or request a recess to reorient the client.

In their study of mediation discourse, Cobb and Rifkin found that one disputant's narrative and moral characterization of the dispute tended to dominate and receive the mediator's reinforcement. Most frequently, stories that were presented first controlled the characterization of the dispute by confining the other party to a defensive response during which the contrasting story was never told. Consequently, a lawyer should encourage her client to tell her story first. If this cannot be done, the client should be instructed initially to avoid defensive responses and to tell her contrasting story. Moreover, the lawyer should remain alert to the mediator's tendency to reinforce the first story through the use of sympathetic language and through summaries of the dispute that emphasize the first narrative. If this occurs, the lawyer can interrupt and expose the mediator's biased language and the mediator's unwarranted dismissal of her client's contrasting story.

4. BOTTOM LINES AND NEGOTIATION TACTICS

The lawyer and client should have a firm sense of what result they must obtain through mediation: a benchmark against which to compare an emerging settlement. With this clear understanding, they will be less vulnerable to manipulation. The lawyer and client carefully should develop and set firm bottom lines on each anticipated issue prior to mediation. Of course, these bottom lines may require alteration during mediation. A more favorable result than the lawyer and client anticipated on one issue may warrant their acceptance of a less favorable result on another. However, the lawyer and client privately should clarify and agree to the modification before accepting. Moreover, because compromise is promoted and expected in mediation, initial demands should be set high enough to allow adjustment. None of this, of course, can be accomplished without adequate information, which often can be obtained only through formal discovery.

One can only imagine how different Gayle's mediation might have been if she and Melinda had known the value of all marital assets, and if they had agreed that any settlement must provide Gayle spousal maintenance and should not award Gayle the marital home. Instead, their lack of mutual understanding and commitment made it easier for the pressures of mediation to dictate the outcome.

The client and lawyer jointly must develop negotiation tactics and strategies to avoid undermining their individual effectiveness. Agreement must be reached on the content and timing of demands and information disclosure, potential tradeoffs and negotiation strategy. Personal and legal weaknesses and strengths of both sides require assessment. While a thorough discussion of negotiation tactics and strategies is beyond the scope of this article, it is important to recognize that, prior to mediation, lawyers and clients must discuss and develop negotiation strategies . . .

Conclusion

I recognize that the role I advocate for lawyers compromises the informality of mediation. However, as history reveals, in a society of unequals, formalization frequently proves necessary to protect weaker parties. Moreover, mediation, which encourages lawyers to abandon their traditional role, creates an unacknowledged threat to the legal profession and to the place of law in divorce disputes. The glorification of informality delegitimizes lawyers and law. Mediation "cools out" the legal profession by its reinforcement of lawyer guilt, its appeal to lawyer self-interest, and its insistence upon the inappropriateness of a "rights" focus in divorce disputes. Yet, experience continually reminds us that a client's legal rights and her lawyer's professionalism may be all that stands between her and poverty or the loss of her children. Divorce lawyers must reclaim their professionalism and avoid the seductive call of informality.

NOTES AND QUESTIONS

1.   Do you believe Gayle's story is typical or atypical? Is it appropriate as a basis to reach the conclusion Bryan draws?

2.   Make a list of Melinda's actions that you believe are inappropriate. What would you have done differently? Has she committed malpractice? Has she violated rules of ethics?

3.   While the focus of the article is on the lawyer's role, consider how the mediator performed. If you were mediating this dispute, what would you have done differently? Might Melinda have approached her role differently if you were the mediator? If so, how?

4.   Chapter 8 addresses issues of power differentials and the impact they might have on family mediation. Make a list of the different power differentials you can identify in Gayle's story. In light of them, do you believe Gayle's divorce would ever be appropriate for mediation? Why or why not?

5. In concluding her article Bryan claims that "in a society of unequals formalization proves necessary to protect the weaker parties." Do you agree? Would Gayle have fared better in litigation? What variable might you need to know in order to answer this question?

D.   COLLABORATIVE LAW

In recent years, a fascinating new trend has emerged in the practice of family law in which lawyers act as "collaborate" when representing clients, thus, proponents claim, simultaneously gaining the advantages of legal representation and mediation. As the following excerpt demonstrates, the practice of collaborate law is not without its critics. As you read this excerpt, consider arguments that collaborative law is superior to family mediation.

COLLABORATIVE LAWYERING: A CLOSER LOOK AT AN EMERGING PRACTICE[10]
4 Pepp. Disp.Resol. L.J. 351 (2004)
By William H. Schwab

An Introduction to Collaborative Law

CL originated among family lawyers, particularly in the context of divorce. While there is interest in and efforts toward applying the collaborative model to other types of disputes, the vast majority of collaborative cases continue to be divorce . . .

A Brief History

Stuart Webb was (and still is) a family lawyer in Minneapolis who, in 1988, found himself in a state of "family law burnout" after many years of practice. Besieged by the constant negativity of his practice, Webb was ready to quit the law. It was while considering an alternative career in psychology that the idea of a new way to practice law occurred to him. By 1990, Webb had stopped going to court, resolved to represent his clients only in negotiations in which the clients themselves participated, aimed exclusively at settlement. In those cases where the process broke down, he would withdraw and require the client to seek new counsel to litigate. The process now known as collaborative law was born.

. . . Webb and a few like-minded colleagues founded the Collaborative Law Institute, a non-profit organization whose purpose it is "to create and practice collaborative non-adversarial strategies to help clients in family law matters achieve agreement in a dignified and respectful manner." By 1993 CL had reached California, and CL practice groups have since sprung up in at least twenty-four other states and Canada, and very recently the idea was introduced in the United Kingdom . . .

The essential characteristics of CL are found in the agreements governing the process. While the usual retainer agreement, albeit with some unusual terms, captures the ways in which the collaborative process differs from traditional

----

representation, many collaborative lawyers also present a statement of the principles governing CL, the most central of which are:

- A commitment to good-faith negotiations focused on settlement, without court intervention or even the threat of litigation, in which the parties assume the highest fiduciary duties to one another;

- full, honest and open disclosure of all potentially relevant information, whether the other side requests it or not; and

- if either party decides to litigate, both lawyers are automatically terminated from the case, requiring the parties to seek new litigation counsel.

The last principle, referred to herein as the "disqualification provision," is the primary way in which collaborative lawyers limit the scope of their representation, and is widely seen as the sine qua non of the process. Collaborative lawyers also reserve the right to withdraw or terminate the process if they believe their client is not meeting the "good faith commitments" made up front.

Practitioners can construe the disqualification provision in different ways. Most often, among practitioners, the disqualification provision establishes "a commitment to settlement from the very start" that enables both the lawyers and their clients to focus on a negotiated resolution without the distraction of preparing or threatening to litigate. More theoretically, it is a process-oriented commitment engineered to diminish the value of both parties' BATNA [Best Alternative to a Negotiated Agreement] in an effort to keep them at the table. Divorcing spouses negotiate "in the shadow of the law," and while the existence of other alternative dispute resolution processes may mean that litigation is not always the next preferable choice if CL fails, it is the default to measure alternative processes. By requiring the disqualification of collaborative counsel in the event of impasse or abuse of the process, parties must incur increased costs should they desire to take their dispute to court, making that alternative less attractive. The extent to which this disincentive pressures parties to remain at the table has been a source of concern . . .

CL also requires that the parties jointly retain neutral experts to assist in the divorce (an accountant or home appraiser, for example). The impact of this practice is twofold. First, retaining a single, "neutral" expert to advise both parties eliminates from negotiations the adversarial dynamic of dueling experts with conflicting opinions on the fair market value of the home, or the optimal custody arrangement for the children. Second, retaining one expert costs less than two; to the extent experts are required in a given case, this is one of the ways in which CL can claim to be a cheaper process. Collaborative lawyers also include experts under the disqualification provision, putting them and their work product off-limits for purposes of litigation, thereby further increasing the stakes of failure to reach a settlement.

Within these contractual boundaries, the "four-way" becomes the primary mode of negotiation in which both lawyers and spouses sit down together to negotiate, with the latter actively participating. Pauline Tesler, an early convert to collaborative practice who has since trained hundreds of lawyers in the model and authored the first book-length treatment of the process, describes the four-way meetings as a six-way communication in which each spouse interacts directly with one another, their respective lawyers, and their spouse's lawyer. The counseling that parties receive during these sessions, proponents say, represents an improvement over mediation in that clients receive the benefits of legal advice and advocacy in the moment, while the agreement is being formed. Contrast this with divorce mediation sessions in which lawyers typically do not directly participate. In CL, its proponents see a process offering the settlement orientation of mediation combined with built-in legal advisors and negotiators. Even vis-a-vis mediation in which the parties' lawyers directly participate, Tesler maintains that CL is preferable in that collaborative lawyers are focused solely on settlement, where adversarial counsel are not. For her, and many of her collaborative colleagues, there is no doubt that CL is the "next generation" in dispute resolution . . .

A. The Andersons

Boston couple Tom and Ann Anderson largely resemble other couples who are opting to collaborate in divorce. They are both white, in their mid-fifties, and have one fourteen-year old son. Tom has a master's degree, and Ann had completed two years of college. Their marriage of fifteen years was Ann's first and Tom's second. The couple had worked together to operate a small business out of the family home, yielding a combined income between $40,000 and $50,000 per year.

The Anderson's were in marital counseling when it became clear to them both that their marriage could not be salvaged. At the time, mediation seemed an obvious choice for them. "We didn't want to spend a lot of money, and we really wanted to work out a co-parenting plan," Ann explained. Dan had settled his first divorce via mediation, so the alternative was for him a familiar one. This time, however, the mediation became stalled. For Ann, it was their inability to get past "a couple of tough issues," including deciding who would move out of the family home, that led her to call off the mediation after their fourth session.

While Tom and Ann could not agree on settlement terms, or even about why the mediation had failed, they were both filled with dread at the prospect of going to court. That was when the mediator told them about a new option called collaborative law.

B. Their Lawyers

Ann did not have to go far to get more information about CL. As it turned out, the lawyer she had consulted briefly during the mediation was Doris Tennant, a collaborative family lawyer and member of the Massachusetts Collaborative Law Council (CLC), the state-wide practice group. The case would be Tennant's first collaborative representation, and it came after a time in which she had been "struggling" with litigation. "I didn't want to continue doing it — the whole process was too tense, to stressful, too dishonest, too inefficient." She had heard of lawyers who had stopped going to court, and it sounded to her like a good idea. In April 2000 she joined with local colleagues for Boston's first CL training led by Pauline Tesler, and co-founded the CLC shortly thereafter. For the past two years Tennant has not been to court, and she has no plans to return. Ninety-five percent of her practice is domestic relations work, 40% of which is consists of her own mediation practice. The balance is filled by negotiating settlements, both inside and outside of CL.

Tennant gave Ann a folder of materials produced by the CLC describing the process, including its basic principles as described above in Part I.C. Also included were copies of press articles on the process, some written by collaborative lawyers. Recalling her first conversation about CL, Ann said that Tennant told her to expect "a more compassionate, more human process than litigation." Ann also remembers hearing that the process was ideal for working out co-parenting arrangements, and would cost a mere fraction of the $30,000 she could expect to spend litigating a "normal" case. It did not take long for Ann to decide to try CL. "It was very important to me to feel in control of the process and its outcome. I had these horrible visions of some court-appointed guardian making decisions about our son."

When Ann shared the materials with Tom, he was receptive to the idea. "When the mediation failed, I thought we were headed for court. I was pleased when Ann found an alternative." He read over the articles and contacted one of the authors, family lawyer Rita Pollak, also among the first CL-trained Bostonians and a founding member of the CLC. "I'm over the top about Collaborative Law," says Pollak, who three years ago swore off litigation. She pitches the process to all her clients, though only after telling them about mediation. Like Tennant, she is a divorce mediator with this area comprising about one-third of her practice. Another third is dedicated to collaborative cases, and the remainder is guardian ad litem work. When Pollak explained the disqualification provision and its possible consequences, Tom recalls thinking, "It was fair, given what we were hoping to accomplish — a low cost means to a rational settlement, with the least amount of contention."

The lawyers knew each other, but had never worked together on a collaborative case. "Collegiality in the divorce bar has dissipated," says Pollak. For her, much of CL's value comes from being able to tell her clients that they can trust the other side. "Candor among colleagues works to the benefit of clients." The two lawyers met over lunch to discuss the agenda of the first four-way meeting.

C. Their Process

The Anderson's collaborative dissolution required three four-way meetings over three months in the summer of 2001. Before each they prepared with their respective lawyers. This preparation covered not only what the clients wanted, but also what might happen if they were to go to court. "As much as 40% of my analysis is driven by what a court might do with a situation," says Tennant. "These forecasts made Ann more realistic about what she could hope to accomplish." When they did come together in the four-ways, Tom described the meetings as "pro-forma." "Most of the work was done beforehand in separate meetings." The pre-meetings he refers to are first between client and lawyer, then between lawyers. These communications took place either in person, over the phone, or using e-mail. The lawyers prepared with Tom and Ann, and with each other, before each four-way. Describing the preparation process generally, Pollak works with her clients to "identify explicitly the 'hotspots' that are going to come up. We'll talk about numbers, too." For Ann, the separate contact with her lawyer throughout the process was crucial. "Doris helped me to work through the stress and anger. She was very patient, very attending." At the same time, Tennant was able to guide Ann and keep her focused on the negotiation.

The tough issues that had kept the Anderson's from reaching agreement in mediation, however, persisted at the collaborative table. Among their differences, both felt strongly that the other should be the one to move from the family home; their positions had not changed since the mediation had broken down. Ultimately, it was their shared interest in their son that would keep them talking to one another. "We were both very committed to his welfare," says Tom. But a shared commitment to raising their son did not help decide who would get the house. Indeed, it is not difficult to imagine that divorcing spouses, being equally committed to meeting their child's best interests, could both believe sincerely that they should remain in the home. What finally broke the impasse was the one factor that had changed between the processes: Time.

"I finally backed down on the house and left," says Ann. "Time had passed and emotionally I was more ready to move than I had been during the mediation." In retrospect, Ann also believes that she was more committed to obtaining the divorce than was Tom. In the end, it was a friend's suggestion — not counsel from her lawyer — that led Ann to consider the compromise. Conversations with all four participants clearly indicate that the substantive break-through had not come easily, nor was it the only difficult point of contention. For example, Ann felt strongly that her retirement account should be off limits, while Tom wanted it considered as marital property. He described Ann's approach, at certain times, as, "(w)hat's hers is hers, and what's mine is up for negotiation."

The most difficult process-related moment occurred not between the clients, but between Ann and her husband's lawyer. Ann describes a four-way meeting in which Pollak "surprised (her) with some comments that didn't seem collaborative, but instead more provocative." She left the meeting upset with both lawyers; with Pollak for taking what Ann perceived as an aggressive stance, and with her own lawyer for not defending her at the table. Tennant remembers the moment well. "Ann told me that she felt as though she had just been through the meeting from hell." Tennant had not realized the impact of the moment on her client until afterwards, when she asked Ann's permission to address the matter directly with her colleague. The result was a call from Pollak to Ann, in which she apologized. Tennant suggests that Ann may have been more wary in subsequent meetings, but not to a degree that affected the case. Ann agrees. "It made me feel like the process is human, not seamless, but human." Looking back, she sees the exchange as "just a blip in the process."

D. Postlude: Looking Back at the Settlement

When the Andersons took their agreement to court in November 2001, the judge had never heard of CL. After listening to their description of the process, he congratulated the Andersons for being "pioneers." When interviewed, one and a half years after finalizing their divorce, the ex-couple still agrees that their settlement is working. Asked how well the agreement met their needs, Tom says, "I didn't want to be a weekend father, and I'm not." They share physical and legal custody of their son, fifty-fifty, and say he has adjusted well to the new situation. "The co-parenting is working well, and that was our primary goal," Ann reports. Indicating how important post-divorce concerns were to the outcome of their case, she describes the settlement agreement as their "co-parenting plan." But just how well it is working might be surprising to some . . .

The Anderson's successful co-parenting relationship notwithstanding, both still have different ideas about the compromises made to reach settlement. "I gave more on the intractable points, in the best interests of our son," says Tom. According to Ann, "I negotiated hard, and got what I felt I could . . . in the end I wanted the divorce sooner, and paid for it in terms of the cash settlement." Today the ex-couple is dealing with harsh realities shared by most divorced couples, regardless of the process they chose. "It's tough financially. When I was married there was a cushion. Now there is none," Ann says. She now works as a credit analyst, while Tom continues to run the business. With detectable ambivalence, she reports having no regrets, and at the same time is bothered by a sense that Tom enjoys "a better lifestyle."

Both, it turns out, were quite satisfied with their collaborative experience and would recommend the process to others. But they do say that CL would not be appropriate in all cases. Tom sees divorce "as much a psychological process as it is a legal process," and suggests that collaboration will not work in cases where "people have scores to settle." Ann actually has recommended CL to others since the divorce, including her brother. "It didn't work for them, though. They weren't able to come together."

The Anderson's story calls to mind what has probably been the harshest critique of CL to date. Professor Penelope Bryan, who wrote her critique in response to an introductory article by Tesler, may well look at Ann as the paradigm of what is wrong with CL. For Bryan, "reforms like collaborative divorce that focus on emotions and relationship preservation, almost to the exclusion of substantive concerns are likely to do little to alleviate the post-divorce suffering of women and dependent children." Revisiting the outcome from Ann's perspective, Bryan might say that she traded certain tangible interests in exchange for preserving a working relationship with Tom for co-parenting purposes, the kind of self-defeating trade that women are socially conditioned to make.

As serious as the indictment may be, two responses temper its impact. First, Ann's stated trade was meeting her interest in a quick resolution in exchange for some portion of the cash settlement that she may have won had she kept negotiating. Her interest in expediency may have resulted in a poorer financial outcome, and CL may well have facilitated the trade, but there would appear to be no obvious reason to associate the desire for a quick divorce with sex. Second, in her reply to Bryan's critique, Tesler points out that Bryan's concern is not that CL leads to worse outcomes for women, but that it fails to correct long-standing problems with litigation and mediation that have had a disparate impact on women. CL has never claimed to do as much . . .

NOTES AND QUESTIONS

1.   What arguments exist which support the idea that collaborative lawyering is superior to family mediation? Could you argue the opposite? Which argument or arguments do you find most convincing?

2.   Are you concerned about the ethical concerns raised about collaborative law? There is always the possibility that to the extent collaborative law conflicts with the Model Rules of Professional Conduct, those rules may be amended to explicitly permit collaborative practice. Do you believe such amendments should be adopted? For a consideration of how lawyer ethics should adapt to the "facilitative" goals of

family law, see Steven H. Hobbs, *Facilitative Ethics in Divorce Mediation: A Law and Process Approach*, 22 U. Rich. L. Rev. 325 (1987–1988). A recent ethics opinion by the American Bar Association examines these issues in some detail and concludes that collaborative can be undertaken in accordance with the Model Rules of Professional Conduct. Formal Opinion 07-447.

3. This Article suggests that more affluent parties are far more likely to utilize collaborative law. Do you see a role for collaborative law among low-income parties? In considering this question, recall the discussion of the "pro se crisis" in Chapter 8.

Chapter 12

COMPARATIVE, CROSS CULTURAL AND INTERNATIONAL PERSPECTIVES IN FAMILY MEDIATION

A. INTRODUCTION

Much of the discussion of mediation in this text concerns family mediation in the United States. Developing an understanding of the way mediation is experienced in and by different cultures is critical to representing clients in mediation and being an effective mediation practitioner. This Chapter introduces the multicultural dimension of mediation by looking at the way in which mediation has developed in other cultures and the way in which culture affects participant and mediator behavior in mediation. Finally, this Chapter provides a brief overview to a number of developments in family law over the last decade that have created opportunities for mediation of family disputes where international law may govern the dispute

B. COMPARATIVE PERSPECTIVES IN MEDIATION

1. Roots of Modern Family Mediation

Family mediation as practiced in the 21st century United States has its roots in a variety of formal and informal dispute resolution systems in both this country and others. Modern western mediation has adopted elements of dispute resolution practices from both ancient Chinese and Native American cultures. The following excerpt describes the peacemaking model of mediation as practiced by the Navajo Nation.

PEACEMAKING AS CEREMONY: THE MEDIATION MODEL OF THE NAVAJO NATION[1]

11 INT'L. J. OF CONFLICT MGMT. 267–68, 274–79, 284 (2000)

By Jeanmarie Pinto

. . . Before 1868 the Navajos settled disputes by mediation. Navajos have always understood these concepts. We could have taught the Anglos these things one hundred and fifty years ago.

The Navajo philosophy and system of justice focuses on healing both the wrongdoer and all the people that may have been affected — directly and indirectly. Navajo justice does not try to punish anyone. The focus of Navajo conflict resolution is on *healing* everyone that has been touched by the conflict. Navajo justice listens to everyone who may have been affected and seeks a solution that helps not only those who have been wronged but also the wrongdoer. The philosophy of Navajo *beehaz' aanii* teaches that everyone and everything is connected, so that the actions on one individual affect many others. Punishment of the individual not only does not help him or her — it also does nothing to help the community. . . .

There is a strong sense of interconnectedness in all aspects of life that can be observed among the Navajo people. That sense of relationship of one thing to another is evident in the process of the Peacemaker Ceremony because it promotes the balance of one person to another, one person to the group, and the group to the larger community. It also aids in restoring the balance of body, mind, and spirit within the individual.

Furthermore, the Peacemaker Ceremony illustrates the Navajo perception of connection between spiritual beliefs and the law. The law then becomes more than maxims applied in certain situations — it is a way of conducting oneself in day-to-day activities. The success of the Peacemaker Division is dependent on a shared conception of this sense of interconnectedness in all things. In this way, the application of the Navajo common law using the Peacemaker process transcends the notion of a method of resolving disputes and becomes a powerful tool for healing the inner processes of the individual and the group that contribute to the production of conflict.

Presently, the Navajo Nation Courts are operated in a similar fashion to those in mainstream Anglo-American society. The Peacemaker Division, however, is founded and operates solely in traditional Navajo philosophy. The concepts and foundations are taken from the Navajo Creation and Journey Narratives, which give order and meaning to the Peacemaker system.

The Navajo have found a creative way to use their traditional system of justice and integrate some of the methods of the Anglo-American court system to create a new way to resolve conflicts. The Peacemaker Division stands as an example of the usefulness of learning from other cultures while keeping one's own cultural perspective . . .

The Peacemaker Process

In addition to the philosophical differences between the Navajo ODR and the mainstream ADR, there are practices and steps in the peacemaking process that are not found in mainstream mediation. If we are going to learn from the Navajos, we must look at the process of the Peacemaker session.

ODR revolves around the idea of "talking things out". This Navajo concept of "talking things out" is not as simplistic as it sounds. It involves the interconnectedness of the participants, thereby creating equality by allowing everyone a voice, and addressing all three levels of human beings: body, mind, and spirit. When there is balance within the individual, then balance can be attained in relationships with others.

At first glance, the Peacemaker process appears to be similar to Western mainstream mediation or arbitration — but the similarity ends with appearances. Although the *naat' aanii* (Peacemaker) may appear to be acting as a Western styled mediator, in actuality this person has a much more interactive role with the participants. Neutrality is thought to be an unattainable and undesirable goal and therefore does not have a place in Navajo Peacemaking. Furthermore, the *naat' aanii* is usually known to the disputing parties, either on a personal level or by reputation . . .

The *naat' aanii* does not have to be a religious figure; most of the chapter-appointed *naat' aanii* are not religious figures. If the parties have a relative that they feel is wise and in whom they place their trust, that person may be appointed to be the peacemaker in their session. Peacemaking works with the principles of *k'e* — relationship, responsibility, and respect — and *k'ei* — clan membership — to bring the parties of the dispute closer to healing both themselves and the problem at hand. Through restoration of *k'e*, all parties of the dispute are aided in the restoration of their "being" to achieve harmony on both a personal level as well as on the group level. The ultimate aim of peacemaking is *hozho nahasdlii*, which generally translated into English as "now that we have done these things we are again in good relations."

In the following case, the principles of k'e were brought to the forefront to help facilitate a practical solution. This case also clearly illustrates why it is important in some cases to include interested parties, as well as the primary parties to the dispute.

The Case of the Families Who Weren't Fooled

A young Navajo woman sued a man for paternity. When they got into court, the woman said", "He's the father." The man said, "No. I'm not." The judge sent the case to Navajo Peacemaker Court.

The peacemaker sent notice to the man's and woman's families, and they went to the peacemaking. During the peacemaking, they stopped the "He is/I'm not" talk. The families knew what had been going on all the time and said, "We're going to talk about what to do about *our* child."

The young man didn't have a job, and couldn't afford to pay child support. The woman, who lived in a rural area, relied on firewood for heat and cooking fuel. The families agreed that the young man should supply firewood to the woman until he could pay child support.

By involving the child's family, the discussion turned from paternity to a practical discussion of how to solve a problem. There was no question about paternity — and no need for blood tests — because Navajo families know what their children are doing. They also know what is best for their grandchildren.

A Peacemaking session is meant to be a ceremony of healing, known as *hozhooji naat' aanii*. In a manner quite unlike Western mediation, *hozhooji naat' aanii* calls on "assistance from the Holy People and humans" to restore both the parties and other participants to harmony. Participants are led from *anahoti* (disharmony), to *hozho* (harmony and good relations) using the power of spirit, the wisdom and guidance of the *naat' aanii*, storytelling, and a basic problem solving process.

The Peacemaker process is considered by the Navajos to be a *healing ceremony*, rather than just a way to address conflict. There are two main components of a Navajo healing ceremony: (1) purification of the person in treatment, using symbols and words; and (2) a confirmation of relationship with the community and with the spiritual realm.

Navajo justice and peacemaking are concerned with healing on all levels so that the conflict does not erupt again. Peacemaking travels to where a problem actually starts — inside a person — maybe due to alcoholism or to a recent or past traumatic event. Chief Justice Robert Yazzie describes this attention to the inner cause of conflict in this way: [p]eacemaking gets below the surface of a problem and leads people to the heart of the matter. Speaking of hearts, it uses emotions and the whole person to solve the problem . . .

For Navajos, "monsters" come in many forms — alcoholism, child abuse, ethnic hatred, etc. Part of the storytelling process within peacemaking can involve reminding participants of one of the sacred Navajo Narratives in order to help participants recognize the monsters with which they are dealing.

The healing ceremony is facilitated by the peacemaker, or *naat' aanii*. This person is an active participant in the conflict resolution process. A *naat' aanii* (peacemaker) is a unique figure in the process of peacemaking. He or she may act as a mediator (Navajo style), or as an arbitrator if the parties request that the *naat' aanii* make the final decision.

Navajo style mediation relies on the objectivity — not the neutrality — of the peacemaker. Very often, the parties may choose the *naat' aanii* from their own community, clan, immediate family, or church. The characteristics of wisdom, knowledge, honesty, and leadership are most important for a *naat' aanii*.

A peacemaker is a person who thinks well, speaks well, shows a strong reverence for the basic teachings of life, and has respect for himself or herself and others in personal conduct.

A *naat' aanii* functions as a guide, and views everyone — rich or poor, high or low, educated or not — as an equal. A *naat' aanii* is chosen for knowledge, and knowledge is the power which creates the ability to persuade others.

Through the telling of Sacred Navajo Narratives, and in relating wisdom grained though personal experience, the peacemaker teaches basic Navajo principles and guides the participants from a negative frame of mind to one that is positive enough to promote problem solving.

The *naat' aanii* aids the healing process through *persuasion*, no coercion. Navajo morality and Navajo common law do not allow for the use of coercive force. Freedom and equality are fundamental to Navajo thought, and the phrase "it's up to him" (or her) is illustrative of the belief that no one makes decisions for another. Therefore, the *naat' aanii* may use many techniques to show peacemaking participants where their thinking has gone astray or suggest actions to bring about a resolution — but may not use coercion or authoritarianism. The participants make the final decisions, based on their sense of respect, responsibility, and relationships in *k'e* . . .

The Peacemaking Journey: Steps of the Process

The steps of the peacemaker process are similar to those followed by Western mediators. However, the Navajo peacemaker session begins and ends with a prayer, and the focus is on finding solutions that are grounded in Navajo philosophy. Additionally, the unique relationships that are a result of the clan system and the emphasis on *k'e* and *k'ei* provide a different emphasis than that of Western mediation. Finally, where some Western mediators utilize storytelling as a part of the process, Navajo peacemakers draw their stories from Navajo Narratives, which most participants grew up hearing.

*   *   *

It may seem to some that the biggest value in this merging of traditional conflict resolution beliefs and practices with those of the dominant society is most relevant to non-Western cultures, the theory could be applied to any close-knit community. Every neighborhood has its own climate; unwritten rules about what is acceptable and what is not. The climate may or may not be cultural, in the sense that everyone shares the same country or culture of origin. However, it may be possible to go into a neighborhood, apartment building, or area and assist in identifying what the values, more, and practices of that group are, in order to design a peacemaking method based on that particular "culture." . . .

While it may be true that in much of American mainstream society there is little sense of community, spirituality, or even relationship, there is nothing to say that a peacemaking system — based on the Navajo model — could not work. In Navajo terms, we must summon our courage and utilize all that we have within our grasp to slay the "Mutations and Monsters" that threaten our daily lives.

> One of the most important [pieces of] information of many Navajo sources that establishes the protocol for dispute and problem resolution is the Creation and Journey Narrative, describing Monster Slayer and Born for Water. They were created to enter a Journey to Rid the Earth Surface of the mutations and monsters who came into existence because of irresponsibility, indiscretion, the lack of respect and the improper relations among all the Beings. What live monsters and mutations do we have in our current lives? Consider alcoholism, domestic violence, extra marital affairs, com-

placency, elderly abuse, economic abuse, psychological abuse, dominance and control, and the list goes on and on.

The Navajo Peacemaker process provides a model that recognizes the fears that we all have and offers a pragmatic and spiritual method for dealing with those fears. This model is flexible enough to be adapted for use by any group of people who have the courage to strive to find a more effective way of gaining control over the "Mutations and Monsters" that plague human life.

NOTES AND QUESTIONS

1. Prof. Harold Abramson has summarized some of the dominant features of the mediation model practiced in the United States:

> U.S. practices reflect a culturally shaped view of mediation, a view that is vividly conveyed in the highly regarded original Model Standards of Conduct for Mediators. Its definition of mediation, found in the Preface, reveals much about the problem solving role envisioned in the United States. Mediation is a process in which an impartial third party — a mediator — facilitates the resolution of a dispute by promoting voluntary agreement (or "self determination") by the parties to the dispute. A Mediator facilitates communications, promotes understanding, focuses the parties on their interests, and seeks creative problem solving to enable the parties to reach their own agreement. These standards give meaning to this definition of mediation. This definition, however, has been modified in the recent changes to the Model Standards to reflect a momentous broadening of the term mediation to encompass different "styles." The revised definition provides that: "Mediation is a process in which an impartial third party facilitates communication and negotiation and promotes voluntary decision making by the parties to the dispute" According to the Reporter's Notes "It [the new definition of mediation] is not designed to exclude any mediation style or approach consistent with Standard I's commitment to support and respect the parties' decision-making roles in the process." Therefore, this ostensibly broader definition has a firm limit. It only welcomes those styles of mediation that comport with the Westernized fundamental principle of party self-determination.

Harold Abramson, *Selecting Mediators and Representing Clients in Cross-Cultural Disputes*, 7 Cardozo J. Conflict Resol. 253, 262(2006). In what ways does the Navajo Peacemaking Model of Mediation differ from the U.S. model summarized above?

2. The Chinese, another ancient culture which practiced mediation as a dominant form of dispute resolution, emphasizes the Confucian values harmony and the community over the individual. Like the Navahos, the Chinese also contemplate a different role for the mediator, one that includes the roles of counselor, educator and problem solver. J.A. Wall, Jr., *Community Mediation in China and Korea: Some Similarities and Differences*, 9 Negot. J. 141, 141–42 (1993). This conception of the role of the mediator is common in a number non-Western nations. *See, e.g.,* Amr Abdalla, *Principles of Islamic Interpersonal Conflict Intervention: A Search Within Islam and Western Literature*, 15 J.L. & Relations 151, 161–62, 165, 176 (2000–2001). How does this differ from the role of mediator described in U.S. family

mediation? What are the advantages and disadvantages of the different approaches?

3.   Some scholars have advocated for the use of the Navaho Peacemaking model of dispute resolution in conflicts involving domestic violence. *See, e.g.*, Donna Coker, *Enhancing Autonomy for Battered Women: Lessons from Navajo Peacemaking*, 47 UCLA L. Rev. 1 (1999). Based on your reading of domestic violence and mediation, what, if any, benefits do you see for this model of dispute resolution in claims involving domestic violence? Are there any potential dangers?

2.   Modern Family Mediation Outside The United States

The United States approach to mediation has also adopted elements of mediation from a variety of European and other western nations who have longer histories of using alternative dispute resolution to resolve family conflicts. The excerpt below describes mediation in today's Family Courts in Australia, long regarded as a leader in innovation in family conflict resolution.

AUSTRALIAN FAMILY LAW AND THE FAMILY COURT — A PERSPECTIVE FROM THE BENCH[2]
40 Fam. Ct. Rev. 279, 280–81, 285–87, 291–95 (2002)
By Alastair Nicholson

The Family Court of Australia came into being on January 6, 1976, the commencement date of the Family Law Act that established it. . . .

Today, the Family Court has fifty-three judges, approximately two hundred registrars and mediators, and approximately six hundred other administrative and support staff. It serves 250,000 new clients each year through twenty-two major locations and a large number of rural and provincial circuit locations. It is a self-managed court that receives appropriated revenues of around $110 million per year.

The challenges are linked to the nature and volume of the workload and are magnified by the geographical and cultural diversity of the Australian landscape. By way of example, Australian Bureau of Statistics figures indicate that 48 percent of all Australians were either born overseas or have one overseas-born parent, and of those, 26 percent are people from non-English-speaking backgrounds. Australia is second in the world to Israel in its cultural and linguistic diversity. Thirteen percent of recently divorcing couples were born in the same overseas country, and 29 percent of divorcing couples involved one partner who was born in a different country. The impact of these statistics on the provision of services by the court is that cultural diversity is a mainstream issue.

The Family Court operates across the vast continent of Australia, except for Western Australia. Its jurisdiction brings it into contact with a large cross section of men and women at a time when they are experiencing possibly the most distressing periods of their lives. Many have already been damaged by physical violence, as have their children, and by economic deprivation. Some will come to perceive the family law system as the cause of their problems; others will have unrealistic expectations of what it can deliver.

---

[2] Copyright ©2002. Reprinted with permission.

At a wider level, the court's work intersects with ongoing debates about the recognition of the roles of men and women in marriage and as parents, the protection of the human rights of both adults and children, and the extent to which the financial and psychological consequences of marriage breakdown are private or public responsibilities. In the past decade (and in addition to its day-to-day activities), the court has been required to consider the competing interests of biological and social parents of a child born as a result of surrogacy, the validity of the marriage of a postoperative female to male transsexual, the issue of who can consent to the sterilization of a female child with severe intellectual difficulties, abduction of children to and from Hague Convention countries, and how it can best manage the needs of its large client base of self-represented litigants . . .

PRIMARY DISPUTE RESOLUTION SERVICES

A distinctive feature of the Family Court is its provision of free, in-house conciliation services by staff who have either legal or social science qualifications and experience. The Family Law Act requires the court to provide a range of both voluntary and mandatory non-therapeutic services to help separating couples and their children resolve their disputes without recourse to litigation. Despite their continuing importance in the court's armory, the nature and extent of these services have changed in recent years, as has the terminology used to describe them. For example, recent budget cuts have caused a reduction in the provision of voluntary (pre-filing) counseling, and the 1995 amendments to the act adopted (but did not define) the umbrella term primary dispute resolution (PDR) to cover the processes of relationship and reconciliation counseling, mediation, conciliation counseling, conciliation, and arbitration. The court has recently adopted the generic term mediation to describe its in-house dispute resolution services, and its conciliation staff have received mediation training.

Currently, the act requires the court to offer the following PDR services:

- conciliation conferences in financial matters conducted by a legally qualified registrar,
- conciliation counseling in children's matters conducted by a counselor qualified in either psychology or social work,
- joint conciliation conferences conducted by a registrar and a counselor in enmeshed matters, and
- pre-filing mediation (or post-filing by consent of the parties) in financial and children's matters conducted by a registrar and/or a counselor.

Neither reconciliation nor relationship counseling is offered, but clients seeking such assistance are referred out to appropriate community agencies. An application or request may be made to the court at any time for assistance from the counseling service. No court order is required, frequently no proceedings have been instituted, and matters discussed at such counseling are privileged. Where proceedings are under way, the court may also, of its own motion or upon request, order the parties to attend the counseling service to discuss the welfare of the child and endeavor to resolve any differences relating to the child.

In a contested children's matter, the court may direct a court counselor to provide it with information and expert advice in a report on matters relevant to the proceedings, and the court counselor may include any additional matters that relate to the welfare of the child. These family reports frequently involve a number of interviews with the child and with people relevant to his or her best interests, such as family members and teachers. The judge may direct that a particular aspect (such as the child's wishes or relationship with a stepparent) be explored in the report. The report is released to the parties before the hearing, and its contents frequently provide a sound basis for the settlement of the dispute. The counselor who prepares it may be cross-examined on its contents, but the roles of confidential counseling and report preparation/writing are kept separate, and he or she will not have been involved in any previous privileged counseling involving the parties whose children are the subject of the report.

Children are not permitted to be witnesses in court; nor may they swear an affidavit unless the court orders otherwise. However, a child may apply for a parenting order under a provision that is, not surprisingly, very rarely used. A judicial officer may interview children, but this is most unusual and, as mentioned earlier, children may be separately represented. The Full Court has provided a set of guidelines in which such representation would normally be considered appropriate, including cases involving allegations of child abuse, where there are real issues of cultural or religious difference affecting the child or where neither parent seems a suitable caregiver. After some initial confusion in the early years of the act's operation, it is now generally accepted that the role of the separate representative is to investigate matters that he or she considers are relevant to the best interests of the child, to convey to the court (but not necessarily to endorse) any wishes expressed by a child, and to liaison with and collate the evidence of court counselors and experts such as psychiatrists and pediatricians.

In this way, the child's representative provides the court with a perspective that may otherwise not otherwise be available to it or that may be distorted by a parent who is seeking a particular outcome that may not coincide with the child's best interests. Where a third party, such as a grandparent, applies for a parenting order, the court must first order the parties to attend a conference with a family and child counselor to discuss the proposed order and consider the report prepared by the counselor or officer. The court may further order that compliance with a parenting order be supervised, as far as practicable, by a court counselor or welfare officer. This may involve supervision of compliance with orders relating to a child and/or the giving of such assistance as is reasonably requested by any party in relation to compliance with, and carrying out of, the order.

An order is rarely made for supervision without assistance. In practice, the counselor's role is to remain in regular contact with clients to assist them with ongoing problems related to the welfare of the child, to respond to their requests for help, and to provide support to the child personally. This does not involve the physical supervision of the contact or the handing over of the child for contact. The act requires court counselors or other members of the court staff who have reasonable grounds for suspecting that a child has been abused, or is at risk of being abused, to notify the state child welfare authority of their suspicions and the basis for them. Where a member of staff suspects that the child has been ill treated or exposed to behavior that psychologically harms the child, or that the child is in threat of either ill treatment or psychological harm, he or she may notify that authority of his or her suspicions and the basis for the suspicion.

Mediation was introduced as a separate primary dispute resolution stream in 1991, and until 1999, a co-mediation model involving a staff lawyer (registrar) and a counselor was employed. Subsequently, two changes were made. First, due to shrinking resources, the mediation was limited to a single mediator (except in enmeshed children's and property matters); and second, mediation was integrated with the range of services offered by the court when all these services were put under the single banner of mediation.

In financial matters, a final order cannot be made in proceedings with respect to the property of the parties to a marriage (otherwise than by consent) unless the parties have attended a conference with a staff lawyer (registrar). Parties are required to produce all relevant financial material at such conferences and must make a bona fide endeavor to reach agreement on the matters in dispute. Conciliation conference particulars and negotiations are not admissible in evidence if the matter proceeds to trial. The efforts of the court's counselors and registrars pioneered alternative dispute resolution in Australia, and the models they used have served as a blueprint for other courts in a number of countries since. The fact that counselors were working alongside lawyers and judges in a court was unheard of at the time, and this multidisciplinary problem-solving approach is still quite rare. The court continues to provide the largest primary dispute-resolution service in Australia, despite recent cutbacks and outsourcing of much of its *287 pre-filing work to community agencies. Lawyers have been major supporters of the services and major referrers of clients to them, and mediation is an integral part of the court's case-management system.

The original architects of the act recognized that the adversarial system was an inappropriate vehicle for the resolution of family disputes in the vast majority of cases, particularly where the continued parenting of children was an issue. Although literature on the subject was sparse at the time, it is now widely recognized that mediated outcomes are more likely to be suited to the parties' needs, owned by them, and therefore complied with, than are imposed outcomes. Settlement rates at pre-filing conciliation reached as high as 75 percent of matters dealt with several years ago, when the service had a full complement of staff.

One area of the court's awareness that has increased over the years is that of family violence. The unsuitability of mediation in circumstances of power imbalance is well recognized, and the court has a family violence policy and guidelines for staff (currently being reviewed) that acknowledge the importance of comprehensive intake procedures for identifying the appropriateness of intervention. The use of separate rooms, and telephone and/or video conferencing where necessary, is also catered for. In addition, indigenous family consultants (refer to the Ralph article) provide an important liaison between counselor and client where one or both parties are Aboriginal or Torres Strait Islanders . . .

RECENT DEVELOPMENTS AND INITIATIVES

Over the past few years, the court has developed a range of processes to enable it to meet the evolving or changing needs of families in dispute (including the increase in self-represented litigants) and better understand and manage its workloads.New, pretrial management procedures have been introduced that aim to maximize the use of judge time and encourage an earlier resolution of cases that settle before they reach the court door. These involve changes to the system of evaluating children's disputes, and they also encourage greater compliance with court orders for preparation of trials.

We have also embarked on the conduct of a new, rotating judicial education program that will involve every judge and judicial registrar attending a one-week seminar every three years. The recently completed program contained sessions on judgment writing, violence, child contact, and other subjects of judicial interest. Judicial education has been conducted previously but on a more ad hoc and therefore unsatisfactory basis. Registrars, counselors and other court staff also receive professional in house training.We simplified many of our procedures in early 1996, and the rather verbose and technical Court Rules are now being completely revised and will be rewritten in plain English. A number of unnecessary forms will also be eliminated. . . .

We are also working toward a comprehensive overhaul of our services to culturally diverse clients. The court already produces a wide range of written and audio materials in a large number of languages, conducts training programs on family law issues to community workers specializing in working with ethnic communities, and provides funded interpreter services for all court events. These initiatives are however not always uniformly adopted across all locations, and a national committee is now overseeing this area to ensure that there is a consistent approach to meeting the needs of culturally diverse clients.

*   *   *

THE FUTURE

. . . Western societies have struggled for many decades with the reality, the rhetoric, and the politics of marriage and, latterly, relationship breakdown. We all know that family law is far more than marriage and divorce law. The lives of many mothers and children are blighted, even endangered by the violence they experience directly or witness in the home. Relationships between unmarried heterosexual and homosexual couples continue to increase in proportion to traditional marriages, and medical technology provides us with ways of creating life that were unheard of even ten years ago.

Definitions of family become ever more complex as a consequence of these factors. Policies, programs, and laws have attempted to cope with all of these challenges, with mixed results. Perhaps a good example of this is the 1996 children's reforms Family Law Reform Act of 1995, which was an attempt to take family law forward in this country, particularly in the area of children's matters. Experience to date suggests that it is one thing to legislate but quite another thing to change attitudes and that sometimes legislation has untoward unintended effects.

Of course, disputes involving family members not only generate deep emotional responses but also, on a wider plane, frequently lay bare issues of power, gender, public and private responsibility, and concepts of ownership.

Marriage and relationship breakdown is an issue of great public concern because of its perceived destabilization of society and its effects on children. Issues of family autonomy and state intervention intersect with each other as what was originally a private relationship becomes the subject of public scrutiny. Moral beliefs are challenged as issues such as the recognition of same-sex relationships, surrogacy, and in vitro fertilization have become significant . . .

Limitations on the types of matters about which the Commonwealth can make laws naturally restrict the areas over which the Family Court can adjudicate. The fact that these limitations in no way reflect the circumstances of peoples' lives, and probably never did, is an Australian historical legacy that is not easily rectified; however, I believe that it is time that we, the community, this court, and other courts exercising family law jurisdiction look much harder at the possibility of finding mechanisms to overcome these constitutional limitations or even, dare I say it, amend the Constitution to overcome them. Looking more specifically at the court and the future, I believe that we have proved over our twenty-five year history that we have an extremely significant role to play in the Australian community.

As all aspects of our lives have become less insular and more global in outlook, and as mobility increases, family law generally and the Family Court of Australia specifically have become integral parts of a wider family law system. This is partly due to the ratification of international instruments such as The Hague International Abduction Convention and the Convention on the Rights of the Child. It is also the result of the less formal but significant links that are forged at conferences, both within and outside Australia.

From an international point of view, this court is regarded as a model that has been used to provide assistance to other countries considering changes to their family law systems.

I am confident about the future of this court and heartened by the quality of its judges, its management, and its staff. To work in this jurisdiction requires a high degree of dedication, and that has been demonstrated in full measure over the years. As in the past, family law and the Family Court will continue to be the subject of controversy. But the court will continue to be at the forefront of innovation in the area of family law and in the wider arena of courts generally with respect to case management, court governance, and information technology. Because we build and learn from the past, the court is well placed to meet the challenges that lie ahead.

NOTES AND QUESTIONS

In addition to the basic mediation program outlined in Judge Nicholson's article, Australia has also experimented with a number of specialty family mediation programs. *See, e.g.*, Thea Brown, *Magellan's Discoveries: An Evaluation of a Program for Managing Family Court Parenting Disputes Involving Child Abuse Allegations*, 40 Fam. Ct. Rev. 320 (2002) (describing an interagency, multidisciplinary pilot program for managing parenting disputes that involved allegations of child abuse in the Australian Family Court.) The Australian Family Court's mediation programs provide models for the United States to emulate in its effort to reform family conflict resolution. What characteristics of the United States in terms of both its demographics and legal system would promote or hinder making the kind of widespread, uniform changes in dispute resolution places like Australia, England and New Zealand have experienced in the U.S.? *See* Radoslaw Pawlowski, *Alternative Dispute Resolution for Hague Convention Child Custody Disputes*, 45 Fam. Ct. Rev. 302, fn. 52 (2007).

C. CROSS CULTURAL MEDIATION

Family mediators, like family lawyers and judges, will regularly encounter families of diverse racial, religious, and ethnic composition. Many families will have members who have emigrated from other countries or who share different religious beliefs. They come to mediation with different ethnic, religious and legal traditions. Accommodating diverse family traditions is challenging in courts hearing divorce and other family law cases. Developing a multicultural approach to family law is constrained by constitutional legal norms such as equality and due process. While such values should not be ignored in alternative dispute resolution settings, the informality and ability to allow parties to ignore some legal norms gives mediation the potential to address cultural differences in ways litigation may not.

Drawing on both her own experience and others' research, Allison Taylor has developed the following list of factors that a family mediator may want to explore to identify potential barriers to understanding between parties or between party and mediator in mediations involving multicultural parties.

ASSESSMENT OF CULTURAL FACTORS
From THE HANDBOOK OF FAMILY DISPUTE RESOLUTION:
MEDIATION THEORY AND PRACTICE 234–236 (2002)[3]
By Alison Taylor

In perhaps the most thorough exploration of this topic in the family mediation literature base, Irving and Benjamin (1995) summarize the recent tidal wave of information to find the features within each particular sociocultural, ethnic, or racial group that most relate to this issue of family identity and patterns that can be cross-compared. They list six such factors that should be taken into consideration when analyzing, understanding, or working with a family's identity. Together, these factors form a pattern of interaction that can be observed and handled across families of different cultural backgrounds.

- Modal social class, based on education and income level. This affects the family's resources and opportunities for basic needs and aspirational wants.

- Definition of the family, based on the cultural expectations of who is in and who is out of the socially constructed family expectations.

- Life cycle, based on the stage of development that the family as a whole is experiencing, such as "newly formed couple," or the phase of development of the individuals, such as "young adult." This designation influences and sets the expectations for the behavior of each participant in the different stages.

- Marital relations, based on the cultural expectations of how husband and wife can and should relate, and the acceptable range of variation, regarding their power and decision-making dimensions, the relationship of the marriage to the parent-child responsibilities, and the requirement for commitment to each other under circumstances such as problems and other affiliations.

- Parent-child relations, based on the level of autonomy and deference required between parents and their children, the basic system as democratic or despotic, and the gender differentiation of authority, obedience, and duty.

- Perspective on treatment, based on how culturally consistent it is to have the mediator function as expert, decision maker, helper, or analyst and how open the family should and can be regarding the full dimensions of the problem or its solution.

Missing from this schema are other important cultural factors that a family mediator may want to ask about or understand for the family they are working with — for example,

- The relationship to time orientation, where certain cultures have different understandings of the meaning of timeliness and duration of a problem. Does their lateness for an appointment mean a lack of interest, or is it an expression of their culture, where things happen as they do and being late is acceptable?

- The urge for social or economic mobility, which can lead to stronger bargaining, hardened positions, or a refusal to consider options. Are the participants bargaining from hopes to gain or not to fall back in economic class?

- Hierarchy within the family, both between the generations and interpersonally within the generations. Is the paternal grandmother the real head of the family, or is it the father or the mother who must be listened to and obeyed?

- Common emotional and psychological states, which are not personal pathology but culturally acceptable and predictable behavior and feelings. For example, in Mexican families, those who believe they have been touched by a folk illness such as the evil eye may exhibit symptoms that could appear to be a diagnosable mental health condition to those from a Western medical model of mental health.

- Language capacity — that is, their ability to understand the social and interpersonal discussion and context of mediation efforts with nuances of meaning that convey more than the basics. This is one of the issues in having an interpreter.

- Culturally consistent responses to stress — that is, what people are allowed or expected to do in their culture when experiencing distress. Some cultures have elaborate grief patterns that mimic mental breakdown.

- Communication patterns or requirements, such as directness, the use of intermediaries, the lack of voice, speaking for the entire family unit, or taboo topics within the culture. Asian cultures often have very different communication issues from Western cultures.

- Migration and acculturation issues, or the level at which this process has affected each member of the family. Do they all want to acculturate?

- Dimensions of face, such as typical insults to face, face-saving behaviors, and face-maintenance strategies. This factor is usually associated with high-context cultures.

- Understandings of pain and suffering and mental and emotional illness. In some cultures, stress and problems are more less manifested as somatic complaints and symptoms; in others, a person who is "crazy" has heightened or lowered status and expectations for his behavior.

- The relationship to problems and self-efficacy, such as beliefs that make certain conditions intolerable or unchangeable by people because they believe it was willed by Go and therefore unchangeable.

The reading below gives concrete example of the way in which some of the factors identified in the preceding excerpt may affect party decision making in family mediation. It also some practical suggestions for mediators seeking to become more culturally responsive and navigate the ethical issues.

CROSSING BORDERS INTO NEW ETHICAL TERRITORY: ETHICAL CHALLENGES WHEN MEDIATING CROSS-CULTURALLY[4]
49 S. TEX. L. REV. 921, 922–37, 942 (2008)
By Harold Abramson

. . . II. The Challenge for the Mediator: A Cross-Cultural Dispute

This dispute is a distressing one with an acute cultural overlay. And, despite the obvious unfairness to one party, at least from a Westernized point-of-view, it was not an easy dilemma to resolve. Here is the dispute and the challenge for the mediator: A Muslim woman asked her Imam at her Mosque for advice on obtaining a divorce from her husband. As part of the process of counseling, the Imam met with both spouses and advised them about the principles of Islamic law that they should follow in dissolving their marriage contract or nikkah. Both spouses want to resolve their conflicts Islamically and in accordance with Quranic principles.

Their Imam advised them that a husband can ask for and obtain a divorce for any reason (talaq). However, he is obliged to support his children until they reach the age of majority and provide for the wife's needs for a "waiting period" of seclusion, if the wife remains in the husband's home to observe the waiting period (the iddath, which lasts three menstrual cycles to check that the wife is not pregnant). In addition he is obliged to pay his wife the amount stipulated in the marriage contract (the mahr) that she must receive if the marriage ends. The marriage contract provided for $ 40,000.

A wife cannot receive a divorce without her husband's consent. If she initiates the divorce, she forfeits her right to the mahr although the obligation of the husband to support his children continues until each child reaches eighteen years old.

The Wife is pressing for divorce and the Husband is resisting giving consent. The Wife, who has little means to support herself, is deeply unhappy in the

---

[4] Copyright ©2008. Reprinted with permission.

relationship, especially since her Husband took a second wife, which he is entitled to do Islamically. The Imam advised them that the husband cannot force his wife to continue with him and should not unreasonably withhold his consent — but that giving consent would release him from any obligation to pay his wife the mahr.

The Wife, who is distraught and humiliated, says that she wants permission for an Islamic divorce from her Husband in order to move on with her life. The Husband says that he will not grant her request unless she forfeits her mahr and any other financial support for herself and agrees to give up custody of each child at puberty. The Husband insists that he wants custody of their six-year-old son when he turns seven years old. He wants custody of their thirteen-year-old daughter when she turns fifteen years old. When reaching the stated age, the Husband told the Wife that the child would be taken into the care of the Husband's female relatives.

At the mediation, the Wife capitulates and says she will waive all rights to financial support and agree to his requests regarding the transfer of custody at the given ages so long as the Husband grants her request for a divorce. Having extracted these concessions, the Husband seems pacified. The Wife and Husband are heading toward this agreement. Such an agreement would be broadly supportable under Islamic law principles and within the norms of the Iranian community in which the parties live. What should a western mediator do?

For the mediator, this is a cross-cultural conflict with a twist. Instead of the cultural conflict arising between the parties, the conflict arises between the mediator and the parties. It is in this peculiar context that this hypothetical presents one overarching and challenging feature: The parties agree to a Rule that when applied by these parties results in a mediated agreement that is unfair based on the Mediator's westernized values and may even violate western domestic law.

Consider the way the Husband's power over granting a divorce was being used to extort a one-sided agreement, at least from a westernized point-of-view. A western Mediator would likely view such an agreement as grossly unfair where the unemployed Mother waives needed financial support and relinquishes rights to her children in return for the Husband consenting to the divorce. Under westernized common law and statutory laws, such a one-sided agreement also is likely to be invalid and unenforceable due to the unclean hands of the withholding Husband and the duress suffered by the Mother who wants the divorce.

This culturally shaped family mediation starkly raises an old issue in new packaging: Should a mediator withdraw when the mediator encounters a rule, practice, or emerging agreement that the mediator thinks is unfair? In this dispute, the new packaging entails an objectionable foreign cultural rule and its impact on the resulting mediated agreement. Without this cultural overlay shaping the parties' behavior and resulting agreement, I suspect that many western mediators would withdraw from the mediation, as will be explored later. With the cultural overlay, however, it is less clear what a mediator might do. In analyzing what a mediator might do, I will suggest a four step approach for proceeding ethically and for avoiding the charge of cultural imperialism.

III. Bridging Cultural Conflicts Between Mediator and Parties: A Methodology

Cross-cultural mediators live under the constant threat of cultural imperialism charges. Mediators do not want to be guilty of parochial ignorance and arrogance when objecting to what might be a cultural practice. Mediators want to avoid claiming that they are right and the parties wrong. In order to reduce this risk, cross-cultural mediators should approach mediations with a healthy respect for cultural pluralism and a clear understanding of the other cultural practice. This sequence of four initiatives is designed to guide mediators along this pathway . . .

A. Understand Own Culture

A mediator inescapably views a dispute through his or her culturally shaped lens, whether conscious of it or not. And, a mediator must be self-aware of this perspective in order to distinguish universal behavior and other cultural behavior from the mediator's own cultural views when reading a dispute. Developing self-awareness requires doing some research. I have found it helpful to read articles and books that describe cultural categories like forms of communicating in different cultures and describe American culture for foreigners (and it is especially fascinating to read how others view your own culture). When it comes to mediator ethics in the United States, the Model Standards of Conduct for Mediators provide the primary cultural lens through which mediators see their disputes. So, I began this journey by re-acquainting myself with the Model Standards and especially the values that they reflect.

These ethical standards emerged from a long standing and heated debate over whether a mediator ought to be responsible for the resulting agreement. . . .

This fundamental debate was resolved formally when the Model Standards of Conduct for Mediators in the United States vested mediators with the responsibility of ensuring a fair process, not a fair result, under the assumption that a fair process will result in a fair result from the point-of-view of the parties. The Model Standards implements this vision by establishing as the primary obligation of mediators to tenaciously preserve party self-determination as to process and outcome. The Model Standards define self-determination as "the act of coming to a voluntary, uncoerced decision in which each party makes free and informed choices as to process and outcome." In support of this obligation, the Standards further oblige mediators to conduct an impartial and quality process that includes promoting procedural fairness and party competency. In short, as long as mediators follow these ethical standards, the parties can arrive at whatever result that they choose to adopt.

These principles reflect the values of the mediation culture in the United States. These principles give mediators a rationale for avoiding becoming entangled in judging the fairness of the result. However, these principles of party self-determination, impartiality, and quality process still offer much for mediators to ponder and evaluate, as this hypothetical illustrates.

In view of these principles and without the cultural overlay, the mediator might withdraw from the mediation. The one-sided agreement is unlikely to be viewed as an agreement that the wife entered into voluntarily, consistent with the principle of party self-determination. The agreement is so problematic that it would likely be held invalid and unenforceable because of the unequal bargaining relationship. This westernized view of the emerging agreement may also poison the mediator's view of the Husband, and as a result, compromise the mediator's ability to maintain his or her impartiality. Further, the combination of these two possibilities may make it difficult for the mediator to meet his or her obligation to conduct a quality process. In the face of these types of problems, the Model Standards instruct the mediator to "take appropriate steps including, if necessary, postponing, withdrawing from or terminating the mediation." Frequently, non-mediators object to the Model Rule's focus on process. They are concerned about the mediation process giving its imprimatur to an unfair outcome. Are there any circumstances, I am often asked, when a mediator might worry about substantive fairness of an outcome? It turns out that for family cases like this one a different approach is encouraged. The Model Standards of Practice for Family and Divorce Mediation adopted by the ABA require a mediator to "consider suspending or terminating the mediation" when the mediator "reasonably believes" the agreement to be "unconscionable" or when parties are using the mediation to "further illegal conduct" or to "gain an unfair advantage."

Therefore, both of these model ethical codes provide ample justifications for a mediator to withdraw. But, in a dispute laden with non-westernized practices and behavior, the mediator should take additional steps before deciding whether to withdraw. The mediator needs to research the other culture and try to bridge any cultural gaps, if the mediator wants to avoid the charge of cultural imperialism.

B. Research Other Culture

A mediator cannot help bridge a cultural gap without learning and understanding the cultural practices of the parties. Researching culture is not easy to do, as anyone who has tried knows only too well. In the face of sometimes difficult to find materials that may reveal amorphous, as well as conflicting information, the mediator needs to become acquainted with the terms of a practice as well as its rationale. Learning about someone else's culture can be a treacherous inquiry because the mediator is trying to understand a practice that not only might be contrary to his or her own, but also abhorrent — based on the mediator's cultural upbringing. This inquiry is vital if the mediator wants to avoid the charges of ethnocentrism and cultural imperialism. The inquiry can be an uncomfortable, if not repulsive, one however, because the mediator must be open to the possibility that what appears, in abstract, to be an offensive practice, may turn out to be tolerable when understood in context.

For example, it may feel offensive to be open to investigating a practice of arranged marriages involving payment, a practice apparently condemned in the United Nations Report of the Committee on the Elimination of Discrimination Against Women, but you might find it helpful to learn a justification for the payment practice as explained by one commentator: "The payment of mahr (dower), which involves payment or preferment, is a central feature of the marriage contract in Islam and, as a measure intended to safeguard [a woman's] economic position after marriage, [the mahr is offered to the bride]."

It also may feel repugnant to be open to investigating a practice that gives men a right to a greater share of property, a practice also apparently condemned in the

Convention on the Elimination of All Forms of Discrimination Against Women. But you might find it helpful to learn how it is justified, as the same commentator explained that in Islam, men have financial obligations to others that are not shared with women so men need a disproportionate amount of assets to meet those other obligations.

Of course, neither of these explanations provides the final word. These explanations offer leads that can give the mediator a line of challenging research to pursue.

C. Bridge Any Cultural Gap

With some understanding of the cultural context of the practice, the mediator should next proceed with a sophisticated party self-determination inquiry. As a threshold matter, I assume that the parties have legal counsel. I also assume that the parties were encouraged to seek counsel from a trusted family member or friend so that each party has the benefit of a support system that each party trusts.

The mediator might give the Wife and Husband an opportunity to express their reactions to the Rule and to consider its rationale, benefits, and drawbacks. Then, the mediator might follow-up with clarifying and reality-testing questions. This is not a simple inquiry, giving rise to the old adage that it can be easier to describe what to do than to actually do it. But, it is an essential inquiry if mediators want to seriously pursue party-self-determination. One of two basic scenarios might emerge for the mediator to pursue: the Wife accepts the Rule or the Wife objects to it.

Under the first scenario, if the Wife understands and accepts the Rule despite the disadvantageous trade-offs that it can produce when dissolving the marriage, at least she is making an informed choice to follow the Rule and live with its consequences. Formal consent under these circumstances, however, should not end the inquiry as succinctly emphasized by one insightful commentator on culture and international human rights. She explained that the most difficult situation is when those who do it and those who endure it offer no objection. But this surely does not mean that nothing may be done. First, there is an abiding suspicion that things are not what they seem in such examples. Are they really just as happy? Does the fact that they have no other way of life open to them make a difference? In short, a good deal more information is needed about the conditions those persons face and the sources of our knowledge about those conditions. Second, intervention comes in degrees, not wholesale. [Look for ways to] increase their range of choice. It is one thing to embrace a way of life when none other is available, an entirely different one to cling to it when alternatives present themselves.

The mediator can test consent by tempting the Wife with options. It turns out that the Wife has an alternative if the mediation is taking place in New York State. There is a state law designed to diminish the ability of a husband to extort an unduly favorable settlement under a religious rule that gives the power to divorce to the husband. The mediator might inquire whether the parties or attorneys are aware of the applicable law. (How a mediator might delicately initiate this inquiry is beyond the scope of this article.) Through their attorneys, the parties would learn that New York law authorizes a court to consider whether the Husband exploited a barrier to remarriage when the court determines the distribution of marital property and appropriate maintenance. Therefore, the Wife would have an option for ameliorating the influence of the Rule and a choice to make. She could agree to the onerous terms, or to turn to or threaten to turn to the secular courts to reduce her unequal bargaining power. This may not seem like a real choice for someone who wants to preserve her standing in her own religious community. But it gives the Wife an opportunity to choose which value is more important to her — preserving her standing in her community or improving the terms of divorce . . .

I was unexpectedly aided in my journey by a visit to my office by a bright, articulate, reflective, and extremely distraught female law student. She wanted to talk about her separation and divorce. Her arranged marriage was a disaster; after less than a year, she had moved out the day before. As a practicing Muslim woman born in the U.S. who is determined to live within the customs and practices of her religion, she was deeply upset. To proceed with the divorce would make it difficult to remarry within her Muslim community and to continue with the marriage would make her life painfully miserable — a reality that even her parents recognized. As she told me her choice, I was starkly reminded about our limited role as mediators who persevere to honor the principle of party self-determination. All mediators can do is conduct a process where the parties can make an informed choice, regardless of how personally painful the choice may be to one of the parties and how unfair the result may seem to the mediator.

Under the second scenario, if the Wife, a dedicated member of her religious community, objects to the Rule and its consequences, then the conflicting values between the mediator and one of the parties disappear. The mediator can no longer be accused of imposing his or her values on the parties when those values are being asserted by one of the parties. The cultural values now coincide between the mediator and the Wife, giving the mediator a shield from the charge of cultural imperialism, 32 although not from the charge of partiality. The mediator no longer needs to bridge a cultural conflict between the mediator and the parties. The mediator can now return to the familiar territory of trying to bridge a gap between the parties.

D. Assess Whether to Withdraw

Even in the face of the parties consent or apparent consent, the mediator may still find the practice so personally abhorrent that the mediator may want to withdraw. But, how can a mediator withdraw and avoid the charge of cultural imperialism?

1. Assess Whether Cultural Practice Violates Internationally Recognized Norms

I next pursued the grand inquiry in cultural studies — the search for universal norms, against which the mediator could judge the practice. How to identify these norms is the subject of numerous articles, books, and much debate. Rather than exploring the challenges and highly contested nuances of agreeing on universal norms, I attempted a shortcut, although one with its own hazards, by researching ratified international treaties as a source of norms. Recalling that ratification means approval in accordance with a country's domestic political process, a ratified treaty arguably reflects the values of the ratifying country, shared values of the ratifying countries, or universal values if widely adopted. Then, if the practice, in this case the Rule, violates an international treaty ratified by the parties' country or countries with similar cultures, the mediator could defend against the charge of imperialism by withdrawing, not on the basis of a violation of his or her own cultural norms, but based on the violation of an independently recognized norm.

With this promising approach in mind, I started researching international treaties, reading articles on international human rights, and consulting with human rights professors. I quickly learned about two international treaties with surprisingly relevant and specific provisions.

First, I read the Universal Declaration of Human Rights that was adopted by the United Nations General Assembly and learned that even Iran among other Muslim countries voted for it. And it gets even better because Article 16 (1) is right on point. It provides that, "they [men and women] are entitled to equal rights as to marriage, during marriage and at its dissolution." But, then this pathway turned bumpy. The Universal Declaration turns out not to be a treaty ratified by member nations. It is more of an enabling legislation. Fortunately, it led to an impressive treaty on point.

In the Convention on the Elimination of All Forms of Discrimination Against Women, Article 16 provides that the "States Parties shall take all appropriate measures to eliminate discrimination against women in all matters relating to marriage and family relations and in particular shall ensure, on a basis of equality of men and women: . . . (c) The same rights and responsibilities during marriage and at its dissolution." This treaty was ratified by one hundred and eighty-five countries. Now, that is an impressive level of agreement — except, unfortunately, Iran did not ratify the treaty nor did the United States! Not ready to give up, I next checked to see if any countries in Iran's neighborhood had ratified the treaty and discovered that many did, including Egypt, Iraq, Jordon, Lebanon, Saudi Arabia, and Syria. New hope! But then I noticed these small footnotes called reservations and quickly secured copies of each footnote. Each of these countries either generally or specifically opted out of Article 16(c). The reservations opted out, for example, when the terms violated "norms of Islamic Law" (Saudi Arabia) or were "incompatible with the provisions of the Islamic Shariah" (Syria).

This promising pathway failed. It did not reveal universal norms, but instead, revealed unambiguously the lack of universal agreement for the principle of equality in the dissolution of marriage. This inquiry failed to discover a principled source of internationally recognized standards that could be the basis for withdrawing from the mediation.

2. Assess Whether Still Impartial or Conducting a Quality Process

At last, I reached the final step in this journey. If the Rule does not violate a universal standard, is there any other principled basis for withdrawing? A mediator might withdraw under Standard II of the United States Model Code if the mediator could no longer be impartial because the mediation is being conducted under a Rule that violates the mediator's personal values. Threats to impartiality arise anytime the mediator becomes conscious of something unfair in the mediation that is impacting on one of the parties. This is familiar territory for mediators, and mediators know to withdraw when the mediator thinks he or she can no longer be evenhanded. The mediator also might withdraw under Standard VI if the mediator feels that this unfair Rule compromises the quality of the mediation process. Of course, if the mediator's decision to withdraw is based on his or her own cultural value, the decision would expose the mediator to the ultimate charge of cultural imperialism — the charge that the mediator is claiming that "my cultural value is better than your cultural value." However, the mediator would reach this result as a last resort after respectfully and diligently researching the other cultural practice and confronting fully his or her own value to determine whether the implicated value is so fundamental that the mediator could not mediate a case in which it is violated.

Despite these concerns, I suspect that many westernized mediators would not withdraw. Instead, they would likely rely on the common refrain that "it is the parties'process" — as I and others have often declared — "so we should defer to their choice." Nevertheless, in this particular case, I would likely withdraw, so I thought.

Withdrawal was the direction I was going until my research assistant innocently asked what would happen next. "Would what would happen after withdrawal be better than the mediator continuing," she inquired. Yes. She queried what their BATNA would be if the negotiation in the mediation was prematurely halted.

To work through her inquiry, I ventured down two different pathways. I first wondered whether the BATNA would provide a fair (or at least a fairer) process. If it would, a decision to withdraw would seem easy to make. The parties would be relegated to a better process, and the Wife would have the opportunity to possibly improve her situation.

The second pathway entailed the opposite inquiry — whether the BATNA would not likely lead to a better process. If it would not, a decision to withdraw would negatively impact on the disadvantaged party. If the mediator withdraws, the wife would lose access to help by a third party with expertise in dispute resolution, a third party who might be culturally sensitive to this unequal power dynamic, and who might be able to help the parents negotiate further details within the parameters of the agreement. A mediator who continues with the mediation might be able to help the parties negotiate valuable details that might benefit the children including addressing such issues as visitation by the non-custodial parent and education plans for the children.

This was the most difficult decision moment for me. After trying to research the wife's BATNA and much cogitating, I thought I still would withdraw if faced with this dilemma. I would not want the mediation process (or me) to be associated with such an unfair mediated result. I would want to avoid conferring the imprimatur of mediation on a process and result that violated such a core value of fairness — even when my definition of fairness was shaped by distinctively westernized values. This is what I had concluded in two presentations of the paper and in what I thought was my final draft. Thanks to challenges by colleagues and friends, however, I discovered that I was so determined to withdraw that I had become blinded to the significant benefits of continuing for the parties. I am now inclined to continue to mediate. If both parties want to continue with me and the mediation, I think I should try to mediate the best agreement which the parties are willing to enter into so long as the agreement is not illegal.

Conclusion

When crossing borders, mediators are crossing into new ethical territory. Ethical issues can arise due to differences in culture between the mediator and the parties. In order to navigate this new territory, mediators need to be aware of their own culturally shaped behavior and perspective and be open-minded and nonjudgmental when proactively learning about other ways of behaving. And, mediators should diligently search for ways to bridge any gaps between the mediator and the parties before confronting the difficult possibility of withdrawing. By conscientiously following the four steps outlined in this article, mediators should be able to avoid the charge of cultural imperialism, except when the mediator decides to be imperialistic.

NOTES AND QUESTIONS

1.   Differences in racial, religious, or ethnic backgrounds are the primary way we think of multiculturalism. Reviewing the list of behaviors that might be culturally shaped in the Taylor excerpt, can you identify differences that might be grounded in factors unrelated to race, ethnicity, or religion? What other life circumstances create "cultural" differences?

2.   Professor Abramson identifies four steps to become a more culturally sensitive and ethical mediator: (a) understand your own cultural identity; (b) research the culture of the mediation participants; (c) attempt to bridge cultural gaps by promoting an informed and voluntary decision making; and (d) consider withdrawing as mediator if cultural barriers or agreement compromise the mediator impartiality or the mediation process.

While the first step may appear the easiest to accomplish, understanding one's own culturally shaped behavior is often challenging. Practice this skill by identifying yourself culturally (or by home region or other identifiable group). Behaviors or values that may be shaped by culture include: appropriate spatial distance between people talking with one another; traditional vs. egalitarian gender roles including those related to child rearing and "breadwinning"; meaning of nonverbal behavior (including the appropriateness of eye contact); relationship of individual to family (value of individualism vs., communitarian); deference to authority in private or public context (culture one in which decisions reached by leaders or consensus). Using these examples and others in the list in the Taylor excerpt, identify some of the cultural characteristics of the group with which you identify. Which are grounded in stereotypes and which are rooted in your own behavior or preferences?

For an analysis of cultural characteristics of particular ethnic or racial groups, see Cynthia R. Mabry, *African Americans "Are Not Carbon Copies"of White Americans — The Role of African American Culture in Mediation of Family Disputes*, 13 Ohio St. J. on Disp. Resol. 405 (1998); Jessica R. Dominguez, *The Role of Latino Culture in Mediation of Family Disputes*, 1 J. Legal Advoc. & Prac. 154 (1999).

3.   Consider your role as a family mediator in the following case. A third party child custody complaint has been filed by Bob and Mary Rose seeking custody of 7-year-old Prosper. Prosper's mother was killed in his home country, Rwanda, and his father, Gaheej has struggled since coming to the United States. Bob Rose is a Boy Scout leader who has helped Prosper and for the last three months he and his

wife have taken in him when Gaheej had to move to a shelter. Gaheej has bouts of depression when he remembers how his wife and other children were killed during his country's civil war. He has trouble keeping jobs because he is unskilled, does not speak English, and misses work because of his untreated depression. At a hearing shortly after the custody case was filed, the Roses were given temporary custody, Gaheej was referred for psychiatric counseling and given a specific visitation schedule at the Rose's home, and the case was set for two sessions of court sponsored mediation. If mediation fails, the court has set the date for trial in three months.

At the mediation, the Roses are the first to accept your invitation to make an opening statement. They explain that they took Prosper in at the request of Gaheej, that Gaheej has not moved from the shelter, and that he cannot hold a job. He visits Prosper irregularly and when he does, he seems more distant and polite with Prosper rather than affectionate and loving. The court records also reveal that Gaheej has not attended any of the sessions with the court psychiatrist. When it is Gaheej's turn he seems reserved and formal and simply says, "Sometime from now I will be well. I will take care of my son."

(a) What, if any, conclusions do you draw about the desires of each side to provide primary care for Prosper?

(b) What, if any, conclusions do you reach about what custody arrangement would be in the best interest of the child? Is this relevant to your role as mediator?

(c) Assume the Roses, responding to intense pressure from Prosper, have decided to agree to allow Prosper to move back with Gaheej and limit their contact to monthly visits. In addition to the above facts, you have learned during the mediation that Gaheej believes seeking public assistance will bring shame to him and his son. He plans to move out of the shelter as soon as he can but has no plans to find employment or seek public assistance. You fear allowing the parties to reach an agreement giving Gaheej primary custody will be harmful to Prosper. Use the approach outlined in the Abramson excerpt to determine how to proceed.

For a variation of this approach focused on steps mediators can take when facing cultural conflicts between the disputing parties (rather than between mediator and parties), see HAROLD I. ABRAMSON, MEDIATION REPRESENTATION: ADVOCATING IN A PROBLEM-SOLVING PROCESS 173–81 (2004) (Five Steps: Develop Cultural Framework, Understand Own Culture, Learn Other Culture, Be Open Minded, and Bridge Gap).

D. MEDIATING INTERNATIONAL FAMILY DISPUTES

One of the byproducts of our increasingly global society is the increase in family disputes involving multinational parties. It is important, therefore, to have some understanding of the limits foreign law may place on parties' freedom to enter into agreements on issues that may be addressed by statutory law or agreements entered into in other countries. In many cases, these limits depend on the specific, complex facts of each case. In some cases, an analysis of the facts will produce no clear answers. A thorough examination of the ability of parties to enter into private agreements on issues or parties subject to foreign law is beyond the scope of this Chapter. But the following should help mediators in identifying circumstances when agreements may be wholly or partly unenforceable by U.S. or foreign courts.

1.   Prenuptial Agreements

Mediators often see parties planning to marry and seeking to mediate an agreement about financial or other issues in contemplation of divorce, commonly called a prenuptial agreement. Where the one or both of the parties may return to a foreign country, mediators should inform parties that the enforceability of these agreements varies considerably from country to country. While there was some regional variation in U.S. jurisdictions, most states will now enforce such agreements as long as certain criteria in formation are met. Some non-U.S. jurisdictions — Hong Kong, for example — still view such agreements as against public policy and unenforceable.

2.   Divorce

Mediating agreements which are predicated on the validity of a foreign divorce also raises a number of potential legal issues. Foreign divorces are regularly enforced on principles of comity, even where the divorce is granted by a religious authority. The primary requirement for recognition in this country is that the foreign divorce proceeding embody basic U.S. norms of due process. It is usually sufficient that one of the parties is domiciled in the country granting the divorce and that the defendant has notice and an opportunity to be heard. This norm is also embodied in the Hague Convention on the Recognition of Divorces and Legal Separations (in effect in 17 countries).

Jeremy Morely, a noted international family law attorney, highlights some common issues with foreign divorce:

- Religious divorces, such as (a) Islamic "talaq," which in traditional Islamic law is simply the husbands' triple declaration of divorce; (b) Jewish rabbinic divorce ("get"), which has recognized civil law authority in Israel, and varying degrees of recognition elsewhere in the world; and (c) divorces in Cyprus, which, under Cypriot law, for members of the Greek Orthodox Church can usually only be issued by a church tribunal.
- Registry office divorces, such as in Japan and Taiwan (and, with certain variations, in China and Korea), whereby both spouses merely file a paper in a local registry office and are promptly divorced.
- "Quickie" divorces, such as in the Dominican Republic, whereby one party typically travels there for a couple of days with a consent paper signed by the other spouse, and a court issues a divorce decree quickly thereafter.

Jeremy D. Morely, *International Family Law*, N.Y.L.J, November 24, 2004.

3.   Child access

Given the need for recognition of custody and visitation agreements by third parties such as schools and health care providers, parties domiciled in the U.S. will want to have mediated agreements on child access issues reduced to a US court order. It is critical, therefore, for mediators to alert parties to issues surrounding international custody conflicts.

In families where one or both parents are non-U.S. citizens, parties seeking mediation of child access disputes may be subject to the jurisdiction of a foreign court or subject to a foreign custody order. International custody disputes are also subject to the Hague Convention on the Civil Aspects of International Child Abduction, which has been signed by 74 countries since its promulgation in 1980. Under the Child Abduction Convention, the state from which return is requested is not permitted to "decide on the merits of rights of custody" unless it has already determined that the child is not to be returned.

Another source of foreign law for child access disputes is religious courts. The Hague Child Abduction Convention is generally not in force in those parts of the world in which religious courts exercise jurisdiction over child custody matters. For this reason, courts in the United States determine custody disputes involving Islamic countries by applying interstate custody jurisdiction statutes and the doctrine of comity. Under these doctrines, most American courts have been willing to assume jurisdiction even where there's a religious court order on the basis of the child's best interest.

NOTES AND QUESTIONS

1.   As discussed throughout this text, there is a range of opinion on the extent to which mediators should address the law governing disputes before them. Cases involving international parties and/or law present special challenges in this regard. Based upon the brief overview in this section, what fact gathering or advice would you provide a couple who comes to you with the following facts?

> Mr. and Mrs. Sagumi are both Japanese citizens. They have been in the United States for the last 4 years due to Mrs. Sagumi's academic appointment in a New York college. Mr. Sagumi has been unable to find satisfying work here and has returned to Japan where the parties recently obtained a divorce. They are having conflicts over visitation and Mrs. Sagumi just filed a custody action in local New York court. The court has referred them to you for mediation. Are there any potential limits in the parties' ability to have any agreement they reach reduced to a cour order? *See, e.g.*, *Amin v. Bakhaty*, 798 So. 2d 75 (La. 2001). *See also* Ann Laquer Estin, *Embracing Tradition: Pluralism in American Family Law*, 63 Md L.Rev. 540, 597 (2004).

2.   Treaties like the Hague Convention on Child Abduction make no special provision for mediation of disputes of child access within the treaty's purview. What are the pros and cons of court ordered mediation of these disputes? See Radoslaw Pawlowski, *Alternative Dispute Resolution for Hague Convention Child Custody Disputes*, 45 Fam. Ct. Rev. 302 (2007).

APPENDIX A

SELECTED FAMILY MEDIATION STATUTES AND RULES

CALIFORNIA FAMILY CODE

§ 3164. Qualifications of mediators.

(a) The mediator may be a member of the professional staff of a family conciliation court, probation department, or mental health services agency, or may be any other person or agency designated by the court.

(b) The mediator shall meet the minimum qualifications required of a counselor of conciliation as provided in Section 1815.

§ 3162. Uniform standards of practice; contents; adoption by judicial council

(a) Mediation of cases involving custody and visitation concerning children shall be governed by uniform standards of practice adopted by the Judicial Council.

(b) The standards of practice shall include, but not be limited to, all of the following:

(1) Provision for the best interest of the child and the safeguarding of the rights of the child to frequent and continuing contact with both parents, consistent with Sections 3011 and 3020.

(2) Facilitation of the transition of the family by detailing factors to be considered in decisions concerning the child's future.

(3) The conducting of negotiations in such a way as to equalize power relationships between the parties.

(c) In adopting the standards of practice, the Judicial Council shall consider standards developed by recognized associations of mediators and attorneys and other relevant standards governing mediation of proceedings for the dissolution of marriage.

(d) The Judicial Council shall offer training with respect to the standards to mediators.

MISSOURI RULES OF CIVIL PROCEDURE, SUPREME COURT RULES

88.03. Mediation of Child Custody and Visitation — Mediation Defined

Mediation under this Rule 88 is the process by which a neutral mediator appointed by the court assists the parties in reaching a mutually acceptable agreement as to issues of child custody and visitation. The role of the mediator is to assist the parties in identifying the issues, reducing misunderstanding, clarifying priorities, exploring areas of compromise, and finding points of agreement. An agreement reached by the parties is to be based on the decisions of the parties and not the decisions of the mediator. The agreement reached can resolve all or only some of the disputed issues.

88.04.   Mediation — When Ordered — Appointment of Mediators

(a)   The court may order mediation of any contested issue of child custody or visitation, at any times, upon the motion of a party or the court's own motion.

(b)   No investigation and report will be ordered by the court during the pendency of the mediation.

(c)   If the court orders mediation under Rule 88.04(a), then the mediator shall meet the minimum qualifications required under Rule 88.05.

(d)   The court may appoint a mediator agreed upon by the parties. If the parties cannot agree or if the court dos not approve the agreed-upon mediator, the court may select the mediator.

88.05.   Mediation — Qualifications of the Mediator

(a)   A mediator who performs mediation in a contested child custody matter pursuant to this Rule 88 shall be a person who has stated by affidavit that he or she:

(1)   Is an attorney or a person who possesses a graduate degree in a field that includes the study of psychiatry, psychology, social work, counseling or other behavioral science substantially related to marriage and family interpersonal relationships; and

(2)   Has received a minimum of twenty hours of child custody mediation training in a program approved by the court.

(b)   The court may maintain a list of mediators meeting the requirement of Rule 88.05(a) or rely on such list maintained by a bar organization.

(c)   In appointing a mediator, the court shall consider:

(1)   The nature and extent of any relationship the mediator may have with the parties and any personal, financial, or other interests the mediator may have that could result in bias or conflict of interest; and

(2)   The mediator's knowledge of: (A) the Missouri judicial system and the procedures used in domestic relations cases, (B) other resources in the community to which parties can be referred for assistance, (C) child development, (D) clinical issues relating to children, (E) the effects of the dissolution of marriage on children, (F) family systems theory, and (G) mediation and conflict resolution.

MARYLAND RULES RELATING TO FAMILY MEDIATION

RULE 17-103.   GENERAL PROCEDURES AND REQUIREMENTS

(a)   **In General.** A court may not require a party or the party's attorney to participate in an alternative dispute resolution proceeding except in accordance with this Rule.

(b)   **Minimum Qualifications Required For Court Designees.** A court may not require a party or the party's attorney to participate in an alternative dispute resolution proceeding conducted by a person designated by the court unless (1) that person possesses the minimum qualifications prescribed in the applicable rules in this Chapter, or (2) the parties agree to participate in the process conducted by that person.

RULE 9-205. MEDIATION OF CHILD CUSTODY AND VISITATION DISPUTES

(a) **Scope of Rule.** This Rule applies to any case under this Chapter in which the custody of or visitation with a minor child is an issue, including an initial action to determine custody or visitation, an action to modify an existing order or judgment as to custody or visitation, and a petition for contempt by reason of non-compliance with an order or judgment governing custody or visitation.

(b) **Duty of Court.**

(1) Promptly after an action subject to this Rule is at issue, the court shall determine whether:

(A) mediation of the dispute as to custody or visitation is appropriate and would likely be beneficial to the parties or the child; and

(B) a properly qualified mediator is available to mediate the dispute.

(2) If a party or a child represents to the court in good faith that there is a genuine issue of physical or sexual abuse of the party or child, and that, as a result, mediation would be inappropriate, the court shall not order mediation.

(3) If the court concludes that mediation is appropriate and feasible, it shall enter an order requiring the parties to mediate the custody or visitation dispute. The order may stay some or all further proceedings in the action pending the mediation on terms and conditions set forth in the order.

(c) **Scope of Mediation.**

(1) The court's initial order may not require the parties to attend more than two mediation sessions. For good cause shown and upon the recommendation of the mediator, the court may order up to two additional mediation sessions. The parties may agree to further mediation.

(2) Mediation under this Rule shall be limited to the issues of custody and visitation unless the parties agree otherwise in writing.

(d) **If Agreement.** If the parties agree on some or all of the disputed issues, the mediator may assist the parties in making a record of the points of agreement. The mediator shall provide copies of any memorandum of points of agreement to the parties and their attorneys for review and signature. If the memorandum is signed by the parties as submitted or as modified by the parties, a copy of the signed memorandum shall be sent to the mediator, who shall submit it to the court.

(e) **If No Agreement.** If no agreement is reached or the mediator determines that mediation is inappropriate, the mediator shall so advise the court but shall not state the reasons. If the court does not order mediation or the case is returned to the court after mediation without an agreement as to all issues in the case, the court promptly shall schedule the case for hearing on any pendente lite or other appropriate relief not covered by a mediation agreement.

(f) **Confidentiality.** Confidentiality of mediation communications under this Rule is governed by Rule 17-109.

(g) **Costs.** Payment of the compensation, fees, and costs of a mediator may be compelled by order of court and assessed among the parties as the court may direct. In the order for mediation, the court may waive payment of the compensation, fees, and costs.

RULE 17-104. QUALIFICATIONS AND SELECTION OF MEDIATORS

(a) **Qualifications in General.** To be designated by the court as a mediator, other than by agreement of the parties, a person must:

(1) unless waived by the court, be at least 21 years old and have at least a bachelor's degree from an accredited college or university;

(2) have completed at least 40 hours of mediation training in a program meeting the requirements of Rule 17-106;

(3) complete in every two-year period eight hours of continuing mediation-related education in one or more of the topics set forth in Rule 17-106;

(4) abide by any standards adopted by the Court of Appeals;

(5) submit to periodic monitoring of court-ordered mediations by a qualified mediator designated by the county administrative judge; and

(6) comply with procedures and requirements prescribed in the court's case management plan filed under Rule 16-202 b. relating to diligence, quality assurance, and a willingness to accept a reasonable number of referrals on a reduced-fee or pro bono basis upon request by the court.

(b) **Additional Qualifications — Child Access Disputes.** To be designated by the court as a mediator with respect to issues concerning child access, the person must:

(1) have the qualifications prescribed in section (a) of this Rule;

(2) have completed at least 20 hours of training in a family mediation training program meeting the requirements of Rule 17-106; and

(3) have observed or co-mediated at least eight hours of child access mediation sessions conducted by persons approved by the county administrative judge, in addition to any observations during the training program.

*   *   *

(d) **Additional Qualifications — Marital Property Issues.** To be designated by the court as a mediator in divorce cases with marital property issues, the person must:

(1) have the qualifications prescribed in section (a) of this Rule;

(2) have completed at least 20 hours of skill-based training in mediation of marital property issues; and

(3) have observed or co-mediated at least eight hours of divorce mediation sessions involving marital property issues conducted by persons approved by the county administrative judge, in addition to any observations during the training program.

*   *   *

APPENDIX B

SAMPLE PARENTING PLANS

I. AGREEMENT USED AT THE ERICKSON MEDIATION INSTITUTE[1]

The following Parenting Plan language has been developed from our experiences with clients as well as our work with mediators throughout the United States. This Parenting Plan includes the best of what we have learned from, and shared with, parents and mediators. The Parenting Plan is presented first with an explanation of some of the topics, followed by optional language (in *italics*) to be used by our fictional parents, John and Mary Doe.

Agreements Regarding Parental Responsibilities
Custody Options

In developing a Parenting Plan, parents have many choices about the legal definitions of their arrangement. They may choose to use custody labels that are consistent with the laws of their state, or they may choose not to use any such labels. When they are deciding whether or not to use the labels, their most important consideration is the legal consequence of the labels. In those states that designate two gradations of custody, *legal custody* relates to the legal incidents of parenthood, such as access to school records, signing for medical emergencies, and other legal rights; *Physical custody* generally relates to parental control of the children, which parent is presumed to be in charge, who will receive child support, and what kind of a visitation schedule will be imposed upon the parent losing custody.

Legal Custody

The label of *legal custody* relates to the legal rights and responsibilities of parents. Generally, most states encourage both parents to continue to have joint legal custody of their children after a divorce. This gives them the same legal rights and responsibilities that they had while married. In those cases where a parent does not have legal custody, that parent relinquishes the right to share in the major decision making concerning the children's education, medical care, and religious upbringing. When creating a Parenting Plan, almost all parents consider these important decisions as their joint responsibility. Legal custody language in a Parenting Plan varies from state to state but generally follows language that, in this case, incorporates much of the Minnesota statute with a presumption in favor of joint legal custody.

---

[1] Copyright ©2004. Reprinted with permission.

Joint Legal Custody

John and Mary have agreed that they will share joint legal custody of their children. Joint legal custody means that John and Mary both have equal rights and responsibilities regarding their children's upbringing, including education, health care, and religious training. Neither of their rights is superior to those of the other parent. Neither John nor Mary will do anything that would lead to estrangement between their children and the other parent, nor will either parent perform any act that would interfere with the natural development of love and affection between the children and either of them. Both John and Mary recognize that children have emotional and psychological needs to establish a healthy and satisfying relationship with both parents.

__Major decision making.__ On important matters relating to the health, welfare, and/or education of the minor children, John and Mary will discuss and work toward a mutually acceptable determination of the issues, including, for example, but not limited to, the following:

- *In the event of illness or injury to the children, the parent first learning of the illness or injury will notify the other parent immediately.*
- *The parents will consult with each other regarding the schooling of the children.*
- *Each parent will promptly inform or consult with the other in the event of any serious medical problem of the children.*
- *Each parent will have equal access to the information relating to the children, including but not limited to, access to school, governmental, law enforcement, and medical records, and access to all teachers, governmental officials and officers, doctors, and other professionals having contact with the children.*
- *Both parents may participate, individually or jointly, with the children in special activities including, but not limited to, Scouts, music, sports, school conferences and other activities, etc. Such information and contacts will be available to each parent without notice or any further consent of the other parent.*
- *Each parent is authorized to consent to emergency medical care for the children at the time when the other parent is not easily accessible to give such consent.*
- *Each parent will continue to play a full and active role in providing a sound moral, social, economic, religious, and educational environment for the children. Each parent will inform the other of the children's social and educational activities and appointments, so that both parents might participate, when possible and appropriate, and each parent will further advise the other of the children's emergency situations, illnesses, and problems which may occur when the children are in his or her care.*
- *Both parents agree to resolve all conflicts in a manner consistent with the best interests of the children and, when necessary, to use the conflict resolution mechanisms described in this Parenting Plan.*

Physical Custody

The *physical custody* label described earlier creates difficulties for parents building a Parenting Plan. Parents generally remove the contest assumption of this label in their Parenting Plan by choosing Joint Physical Custody. This choice nullifies the power of the label and frees parents to make practical, workable decisions about how they will address specific concerns in the future, should they present themselves:

Sole Physical Custody

John and Mary agree that [one of them] will have sole physical custody of their children.

Joint Legal Custody

John and Mary have agreed that they will share joint legal custody of their children.

No Designation of Physical Custody

Parenting Plan laws in Minnesota have provided parents with the opportunity to refrain from designating the physical custody of their children in a divorce. Many parents choose not to designate a custodial parent and use the following language:

No Designation of Physical Custody

John and Mary agree not to designate a Physical custodian of the minor children. For purposes of travel to states or countries that do not recognize Parenting Plans, this arrangement may be considered Joint Legal and Joint Physical Custody.

*   *   *

The following paragraphs are examples of the form and language of a Parenting Plan for parents to consider as they create their own plan. Not all of these topics are included by parents in their Parenting Plans, of course, but we offer them here as language that other parents have used for their situations.

General Understandings

As parents, John and Mary are committed to cooperating with each other to provide future parenting of their children that is in the children's best interests. They recognize that they are each very important to the physical, social, and psychological development of their children and that their children need each of them to be actively involved in their lives in the future. John and Mary agree to respect each other's individual parenting role with the children and to be supportive of each other as parents.

John and Mary further understand that sending messages to the other parent through the children places the children in the middle of their conflict and that it is their responsibility to communicate with each other directly. They also know that disrespecting the other parent is harmful to the children's sense of self, and so they each agree to refrain from these behaviors. Instead, they will encourage the children's relationship with the other parent and give each child clear permission to love, and be proud of, the other parent.

Separate Parenting

John and Mary agree that they no longer have a relationship as marriage partners and that they have only a relationship as separate parents with separate lives and homes. As separate parents, they agree to the following:

- *The children will have a meaningful relationship with each of them.*

- *They will communicate with each other directly-either verbally, in writing, or by e-mail and will refrain from sending any messages to each other through the children.*
- *When the children complain to one of them about the other parent, the parent receiving the complaint will ask the child(ren) to discuss it with the other parent. If the child is uncomfortable doing so, the parent receiving the complaint will help the child(ren) communicate with the other parent. Each parent will try to understand the complaint without making a judgment, interfering, or taking sides.*
- *They each understand that their parenting styles may be different and that the differences will enhance their children's growth. They each agree to accept and respect each other's differences.*
- *They will each be supportive of the other's parenting and positively encourage the children in their relationship with the other parent.*
- *When parenting problems arise, they agree that they will deal with the problems as parents, just between them.*
- *They agree that they will refrain from discussing their personal lives and parenting problems or differences with the children.*
- *When they have parenting problems between them that they are unable to resolve, they will seek the services of a professional family mediator, or a professional neutral expert in family and/or child therapy, to assist them in resolving the matter.*
- *They agree to respect each other's boundaries. They agree that their separate lives and private lives are no longer joined. They each agree not to enter the other parent's home or private space without being invited.*
- *Finally, they agree that if either or them enters a new significant relationship that may affect the children, each will inform the other parent of this new relationship. They further agree that they will each assist the children in understanding and adjusting to the new relationship.*

Residential Arrangements

The first question parents ask when divorcing is "Where will the children live?" This issue is at the core of the Parenting Plan. The answer is that the children will live with each parent at separate times. The best way to determine these times is for parents to develop a schedule of times the children will spend at each of their homes and when the children will move from one home to the other.

The earliest type of schedule that was commonly used by courts in the United States before the introduction of joint physical custody statutes was a very unequal schedule that assumed children would remain with their custodial parent in the family home and the other parent would have the privilege of having the children visit every other weekend, from Friday evening to Sunday evening, and every other Wednesday from 5:00 to 7:00 P.M.

States began to legislate the concept of joint custody at the same time divorce mediation was beginning to be offered, and more and more parents began to consider different ways they could both be more involved with their children after divorce. Parents in mediation often chose to create more equivalent time-sharing schedules of when the children would be with each parent. This was especially appealing to parents who chose to continue to reside in close proximity after the divorce. In our practices, parents have designed a variety of schedules that meet the needs of the children, their activities, and the parents' work schedules. We found that most parents wanted to have equal time with the children on weekends, and so they alternated weekends routinely. They would often, however, add Sunday night as an overnight; in this event, children would be exchanged at school or at after-school programs on Fridays and at school or at before-school programs on Mondays. Some parents then added the Monday and Tuesday nights to the schedule, creating a half-time parenting schedule, in which one parent has the children overnight on Mondays and Tuesdays and the other parent has them overnight Wednesdays and Thursdays:

(M, Mom; D, Dad)

	Mon.	Tues.	Wed.	Thurs.	Fri.	Sat.	Sun.
Wk. 1	D/M	M	M/D	D	D/M	M	M
Wk. 2	M	M	M/D	D	D	D	D
Wk. 3	D/M	M	M/D	D	D/M	M	M
Wk. 4	M	M	M/D	D	D	D	D

For infants and toddlers, who need more frequent contact with each parent, parents have used the above schedule and added "touch-base" times when the other parent would spend time with children over a meal to break up the longer periods of time.

Some parents wanted longer periods of time, especially with teenage children. These parents frequently chose I-week periods of time with and without the children, with the exchange time being Fridays after school:

(M, Mom; D, Dad)

	Mon.	Tues.	Wed.	Thurs.	Fri.	Sat.	Sun.
Wk. 1	D	D	D	D	D/M	M	M
Wk. 2	M	M	M	M	M/D	D	D
Wk. 3	D	D	D	D	D/M	M	M
Wk. 4	M	M	M	M	M/D	D	D

Many parents find that they have to help each other out because of their unique work schedules. Pilots, flight attendants, air traffic controllers, physicians, nurses, U.S. armed services personnel, servers, and professional athletes, are examples of parents who find that they have to create unique parenting schedules and plan them out a year in advance. They also need to build flexibility into their agreements, so that either parent can make changes, as necessary, while not misusing the flexibility as a means to manipulate a schedule for other than parenting purposes.

Some parents chose to have special one-on-one time between a child and a parent and scheduled this into their Parenting Plan so that it would occur regularly. This "one-on-one time" may also be scheduled for a period of time, based on a special need of a child.

Parents often begin this approach by trying out a parenting schedule for a few months to see how it works for themselves and the children. They may find it necessary to make adjustments to the schedule so that both parents can make a commitment to maintain it. Parents find that the parenting schedules tend to keep the separate homes organized around the children. When a parenting schedule is part of an entire Parenting Plan, the parents make agreements that enhance the entire parenting experience for them and their children. Children generally like parenting schedules once they have adjusted to residing in two homes with separate parents. Children also like to have the parenting calendar displayed where they have access to it at each home. Once the family has adjusted to a parenting schedule, the arrangements tend to go quite smoothly for everyone.

Residential Arrangements

John and Mary realize that their children's needs playa most important role in how they plan their living arrangements, and also that those needs will change as the children grow older. John and Mary will be sensitive to each child's process of adjusting to their divorce and separate parenting in the future. They recognize that their children will adjust better to the changes if they know what will be happening and the schedule of when they will be with each parent. Therefore, John and Mary will clearly communicate to their children the regular schedule for spending time with each parent and the schedule for their holidays. They will make the schedule available to the children at each of their homes or on the Internet.

John and Mary will try to keep the schedules predictable, specific, and routine, and when either of them needs to make an exception to the normal schedule, he or she will first ask the other parent to care for the children. They will give each other as much advance notice as possible about a need to make a schedule change. If the other parent is unable to care for the children, the scheduled parent will make other arrangements.

From time to time, John and Mary may experiment with different schedules in order to try to find an exchange routine that does not unduly disrupt the children's daily schedule and still allows for significant parenting involvement by each of them. They will follow an initial parenting schedule, as follows:

(M, Mom; D, Dad)

	Mon.	Tues.	Wed.	Thurs.	Fri.	Sat.	Sun.
Wk. 1	M/D/M	M	MID	D	D/M/D	D	D
Wk. 2	DIM	M	MID	D	DIM	M	M
Wk. 3	M/D/M	M	MID	D	D/M/D	D	D
Wk. 4	DIM	M	MID	D	DIM	M	M

* Touch-base time from 5:00 to 7:00 P.M. for dinner.

Summer Parenting and Vacations — Options

- *During the summer, John and Mary may make different parenting arrangements. They will agree on a summer schedule at least a month prior to the end of the school year.*
- *John and Mary will have a preliminary discussion about summer plans, camps, and vacations each year by February with the final plans being decided upon by May.*
- *John and Mary agree that they may each have up to 2 weeks of vacation with the children each year. This time may be in 1-week blocks or a full 2-week block. They agree to discuss their vacation plans with the other parent as soon as each is considering vacation times.*

Holiday Schedule

A few decades ago it would have seemed strange to have to create a schedule of when children would be with their parents on holidays. Now it is commonly known as an area of great conflict for divorced parents. A judge once called our office on

December 24 to ask if he could order parents to meet with us on *that day* to mediate where their children would spend Christmas Eve and Christmas Day. We agreed to see them, and the parents came directly to us from the courtroom to mediate this issue. After some time wrestling with the issue of where the children would be that evening, Christmas Eve, and the next day, Christmas Day, the parents refused to cooperate and continued to find fault with the other's ideas. Finally the mediator said, "Well, I guess you will just have to return to court and have the judge decide." They both became extremely upset, with one of them protesting, "We *can't* go back to court! The judge told us if we did, he would place our children in foster care today!" Needless to say, they reached an agreement. Had they had a schedule in place, if only as a fallback in the event they could not agree upon holiday plans, they would not have been in court or mediation on the day of Christmas Eve. Parents understand that when they make a holiday schedule, they are engaging their best effort to plan how the holidays with the children will be celebrated in the future. It also gives parents time to consider how they might create new traditions with their children after divorce. We make an assumption that all families celebrate holidays, though by no means the same holidays. A holiday schedule must be based upon the family's beliefs and traditions. A typical holiday schedule follows.

Holiday Schedule

John and Mary agree to the following holiday schedule, in which holidays will be treated as an exception to the regular weekly parenting schedule, without the need to have makeup time. The children will spend holidays as follows:

Holiday	Even-numbered years	Odd-numbered years
Spring break		
Passover		
Easter		
Memorial Day		
Fourth of July		
Labor Day		
Rosh Hashanah		
Yom Kippur		
Sukkoth		
Teachers' convention		
Halloween		
Thanksgiving		
Thanksgiving Fri.-Sun.		
Chanukah		
First half-winter break		
Christmas Eve		
Christmas Morning		
Christmas Day		
Second half-winter break		
New Year's Eve		
New Year's Day		
Children's birthdays	According to schedule, and the other parent may have some contact as requested by that parent.	
Parents' birthdays	Time to celebrate with each parent	
Mother's Day	Mom	Mom

Holiday	Even-numbered years	Odd-numbered years
Father's Day	Dad	Dad
Holiday	Even-numbered years	Odd-numbered years
Spring! break	Dad	Mom
Easter	Dad	Mom
Memorial Day	Mom	Dad
Fourth of July	Mom	Dad
Labor Day	Dad	Mom
Teachers' convention	Mom	Dad
Halloween	Dad	Mom
Thanksgiving	Mom	Dad
Thanksgiving Fri.-Sun.	Mom	Dad
First half-winter break	Dad	Dad
Christmas Eve	Dad	Dad
Christmas Morning	Mom	Dad
Christmas Day	Mom	Mom
Second half-winter break	Mom	Mom
New Year's Eve	Dad	Mom
New Year's Day	Mom	Dad
Children's birthdays	According to schedule, and the other parent will have some contact as requested by that parent	
Parents' birthdays	Time to celebrate with each parent	
Mother's Day	Momt	Mom
Father's Day	Dad	Dad

Some parents make some special agreements about Monday holidays, adding the Monday holiday to the on-duty parent's weekend, thereby extending it through Monday. Others acknowledge that the parent normally scheduled for the Monday of the holiday will be responsible for planning the children's activities on that day.

Monday Holidays
When Mondays are a holiday, John and Mary agree that the parent on duty on the Sunday before the holiday may have the children for an extended weekend

Optional Parenting Agreements

Conflict Resolution about Parenting Schedules
If John and Mary disagree about scheduling changes or have disputes about the holiday schedule, they agree to first try to resolve such disagreements on their own but will return to mediation if they have difficulties in resolving these new issues on their own. The future costs of returning to mediation will be shared equally.

On-Duty, Off Duty Parenting
John and Mary recognize that decision making is an important part of their parenting role. They agree that the parent with whom the children are residing on a particular day will be the on-duty parent and, in that capacity, will make decisions about the care and control of the children on that day.

This means that if the children are ill, or either parent had other obligations during their on-duty time with the children, it will be the responsibility of the on-duty parent to make arrangements for the care of the children. John and Mary each expect the on-duty parent to first request assistance from the off duty parent, but they both understand that if the off duty parent is not able to assist the on-duty parent during the scheduled time, it will be the responsibility of the on-duty parent to make alternative arrangements for the children.

Relationships Important to the Children

John and Mary recognize that the children will benefit from maintaining their ties with grandparents, relatives, and people important to them. They will each help the children maintain their relationships with these people and spend time with them periodically. John and Mary further agree that they will ask their friends and relatives to refrain from saying negative or disrespectful things about the children's other parent in the presence of the children or within their range of hearing such remarks.

Education

John and Mary agree that unless the present school boundaries change, the children will continue to attend Washington Elementary School, Jefferson Junior High, and Lincoln High School. Mary and John will each reside within easy access of the schools. They will each attend school conferences and will receive copies of report cards. Each parent will communicate with the children's schools to remain informed about each child's needs, progress, and pertinent special events, including parent-teacher conferences. John and Mary also agree to share with each other any information they receive separately about the children's school progress, behavior, and events.

Higher Education

John and Mary further agree that college or technical training is important for their children, and they will encourage and support each child's efforts for further education. Costs associated with pre-college expenses will be shared. These cost include books, field trips, school supplies, and miscellaneous fees, as well as trips to visit campuses and application fees. Both will jointly share in transportation of the children and are committed to strong support of and involvement in, the children's education.

Removal from School

John and Mary agree to obtain the other parent's advance approval if the wish to remove the children from a day of school. They agree that it is acceptable for the children to miss occasional elementary school days for a special event; however, they also agree that at middle and high school levels, the children may not miss school except for family emergencies or for some very special reason to which they each agree in advance.

Religious Training and Religious Activities

John and Mary agree that the children will continue to be raised in the Presbyterian Church, even though John is Muslim. They will each be supportive of the children's religious upbringing and "agree to agree" regarding all religious activities in advance. All costs associated with religious activities that are agreed to in advance will be shared. While each parent will be respectful of the children's wishes, John and Mary will first agree on travel costs and other matters that require cooperation. Since each parent will have the children for half of the weekends, they agree to communicate frequently about organized religious activi-

ties, so that each parent may be aware of the children's schedule. Mary and John agree that John may introduce the children to his religious faith; however, both agree that John will not indoctrinate the children in his own particular religious beliefs.

Communication

When the children are with one parent, John and Mary agree that the children will have open access to the parent with whom they are not staying. They will each also encourage and help the children communicate frequently with the other parent. They agree to give the other parent the address and phone number where the children can be reached any time they are away from home for more than 24 hours.

Sunday Night Phone Call

John and Mary agree that they will talk to each other every Sunday evening at 9 P.M. to discuss the children. The parent who is on duty with the children will initiate the phone call. They will only discuss issues regarding the children. If either John or Mary becomes uncomfortable with the conversation, that parent has only to say that he or she is uncomfortable with the conversation, that they will need to resume it next Sunday, and then gently hang up the phone. The other parent will respect that response, and they will talk to each other the following Sunday evening at 9 P.M.

Safety

John and Mary each agree not to compromise the safety of the children. They will not leave a child unattended for more than 2 hours, until each child is 12 years old.

Special Safety Concerns

Swimming, jet skiing, and snowmobiling activities require the constant supervision of a parent. John and Mary agree to prohibit the children from riding all ATVs and motorcycles. Both recognize the special danger to children from jet skis and snowmobiles. John and Mary agree that they will each closely monitor and supervise the children's use of jet skis or snowmobiles.

Alcohol or Chemical Abuse

John and Mary agree that neither of them will ever care for the children nor transport them while impaired. If either of them believes that the other parent is about to, or has violated, this agreement, that parent may ask for an immediate chemical dependency test for drugs or alcohol. This test may be requested up to two times per month. Should the test result not show impairment, as defined by the state's DUI laws, the parent requesting the test will pay for the cost of the test. However, should the test show impairment, that parent will enter a 3-day inpatient chemical dependency treatment program and follow the recommendations for aftercare. The parenting schedule will be altered temporarily during the treatment program. The other parent will cooperate with requests by the chemical dependency treatment program for participation of the children in the program. The regular parenting schedule will resume immediately upon the recommendation of the chemical dependency treatment program.

Authorized Caregivers

John and Mary will exchange a list of authorized caregivers for the children, and both agree that they will not allow any babysitters or child-care workers to provide care for the children who are not on the list without the prior consent of each.

Transportation for the Exchanges of the Children

John and Mary each agree that the parent whose home the children are coming to will pick them up. That parent will pick up the children's belongings at the same time he or she picks up the children. In addition, John and Mary will cooperate to help the children remember to take their belongings with them, so each child will have the personal belongings and school supplies they need.

Joint Rules at Each Home

John and Mary recognize that they have different parenting styles and agree that the children will be enhanced by the different experiences at each home. However, they agree there are certain ground rules that should be enforced at both homes. Therefore, they agree to the following:

1. *Bedtimes at both homes will be between 8:30 and 9:30 P.M. on school nights and 10:00 and 11:00 P.M. on weekends.*
2. *Curfew at both homes on weeknights will be 9:30 P.M., and on weekends curfew will be 11:30 P.M., unless there is a special event to which both parents agree in advance.*
3. *Discipline for minor problems will be limited to time-outs and withdrawal of a privilege. Discipline for more serious problems will be limited to greater lack of privilege or grounding; still more serious problems will require consultation between John and Mary. They will cooperate with and support the other in carrying out discipline at each of their homes for serious infractions.*
4. *Mary and John will support each other when a child calls to complain about the other parent. They will help the child discuss the matter, but they will support the other parent and encourage the child to work out the problem with the other parent.*
5. *John and Mary agree that the goal is for the children's entertainment to be beneficial, safe, educational, and expansive. If either is unsure about any entertainment, they agree to consult the other parent in advance. There will be no PG-13 movies allowed for a child until age 13, or any R movies for a child unless one parent is supervising the viewing of the movie.*
6. *John and Mary agree that, in general, the on-duty parent is responsible for the supervision of children's activities and entertainment, and he or she will ensure safety, cleanliness, and appropriate behavior.*
7. *John and Mary will each encourage healthy activities for the children, including attendance at children's museums, reading clubs, Scouts, and church youth groups, and once the specifics are agreed upon, each of them will share in the associated costs. If no agreement can be reached concerning the activity, the initiating parent may enroll the child in the activity and pay for and arrange the transportation. If the activity impacts the other parent's schedule with the children, John and Mary agree to consult and obtain agreement from the other parent before enrolling the child in the activity.*

Location of Parents' Homes

John and Mary agree to reside no more than 10 miles from the other parent's home. As the children reach school age, they will attend the school that serves Mary's residence, and each parent will be responsible for transporting the children to school when they are on duty.

Parent's Move from Current Home

If John or Mary anticipates a move from a current residence that will make it impossible to continue the parenting schedule, John and Mary agree to renegotiate the parenting schedules prior to a move. They will focus on how they can still be significantly involved as parents in a way that would meet the needs of the children.

Travel Out of the Country

John and Mary agree to not take the children out of the country without prior written agreement of the other parent. Each will respond reasonably when the other parent requests to take the children out of the country for vacations or travel. They will keep the children's passports in a safe deposit box, with joint access by Mary and John.

Access to Information about the Children

John and Mary agree that they will each have access to information about the children, either through the use of The Children's Book *[Erickson & McKnight Erickson, 1992], a notebook,* ourfamilywizzard.com, *or another means to record all information necessary to meet the needs of the children (i.e., medical records, doctors' and dentists' names and phone numbers, medical J.D. cards, names and Phone numbers of the children's teachers, coaches, friends, the parenting and holiday schedules, and any other information they may need to effectively and efficiently meet the children's needs at any given time the children are with them). They will exchange the information with the children. They will also write notes to each other about the children. John and Mary further agree that the comments contained in their information or notes may not be admissible in any court proceeding in the future.*

Duration of the Parenting Plan

John and Mary understand that this Parenting Plan will be in effect until they make changes to it, and the court subsequently issues a new court order reflecting the new changes. They agree that all changes to the Parenting Plan will be in writing and dated and signed by both of them. Until their divorce decree is amended to reflect written changes, they realize agreements made in this Parenting Plan will legally govern any dispute.

Future Conflict Resolution

In the future, John and Mary agree to behave flexibly and cooperatively, and to communicate with each other in order to meet the changing needs of their children. When John and Mary cannot agree about the meaning of a part of the Parenting Plan, or if a significant change (such as a move or remarriage) causes conflict, they will make a good faith effort to resolve their differences through mediation, before petitioning the court. Should they be unable to resolve their differences in mediation, they will select and share the cost of a neutral child expert who will meet with the children and with each parent. Then, the neutral expert will present a plan in mediation that will allow the parents to overcome their differences. The costs of the neutral party shall be shared, and the neutral party may not be called as a witness in any court proceeding

[Financial Support of Children Sections Omitted].

II. MODEL PARENTING PLAN USED IN THE CIRCUIT COURT FOR BALTIMORE CITY

_____	
_____	IN THE
PLAINTIFF	**CIRCUIT COURT**
V.	**FOR**
_____	**BALTIMORE CITY**
_____	Case No.: _____
DEFENDANT	

PARENTING PLAN

GENERAL INFORMATION

1.1 This parenting plan is:

  [ ]   A final parenting plan ordered by the court.

  [ ]   A temporary parenting plan.

1.2 This parenting plan applies to the following child(ren):

Name(s)	Birthdate
_____	_____
_____	_____
_____	_____
_____	_____
_____	_____
_____	_____

AFFIRMATION

We, _____ and _____ affirm that we are the parents of the above-named child(ren) regardless of our marital status.

2.1 Voluntary Agreement

  [ ]   We enter into this agreement in order to better meet our responsibilities as parents and to safeguard our child(ren)'s future development and well being regardless of any conflicts that we may have. We recognize that the child(ren)'s welfare can best be served by our mutual cooperation as partners in parenting and by each of us providing a home in which they are loved, and to which they belong — their mother's home and their father's home.

2.2 Good Faith

  [ ]   We agree that we have developed this parenting plan with the assistance of, in good faith and on behalf of the best interest of our child(ren).

2.3 Type of Agreement

[ ]   We acknowledge that this is a temporary agreement which is binding upon us and enforceable by either of us after it is submitted to the Court for approval and entered as an Order and signed by a Judge.

[ ]   We acknowledge that this is our final agreement and that it will be binding upon us and enforceable by either of us after it is submitted to the Court for approval and entered as an Order and signed by a Judge.

Review of Mediation

[ ]   The parties agree and understand that their mediators, _____, and _____, and the University of Baltimore School of Law Family Mediation Clinic, have acted as neutral third parties. The parties agree that each will consult their own attorney to review this Agreement, if they so desire. Upon legal review, any recommendation for substantial change or restructuring of this Agreement shall be referred back to mediation.

I. COMMUNICATION

3.1 Access to Information

[ ]   Does not apply.

[ ]   Both parents will have equal access to all information pertaining to the child(ren)'s:

    [ ]   Health care

    [ ]   Education

    [ ]   School events and extra-curricular activities

    [ ]   Other: _____

[ ]   Each parent will be entitled to duplicate information from either the third party provider or the other parent, if the provider will not provide duplicate information pertaining to the child(ren)'s:

    [ ]   Health care

    [ ]   Education

    [ ]   School events and extra-curricular activities

    [ ]   Other:_____

[ ]   Each parent may initiate contact with:

    [ ]   Heath care providers

    [ ]   Teacher and school personnel

    [ ]   Other: _____

[ ]   Each parent shall provide any information regarding the child(ren) and/or his/her/their activities to the other parent immediately upon receipt of such information.

3.2 Communication between Parents

[ ]   Does not apply.

[ ]   Each parent will keep the other informed of a current residential address, mailing address (if different), home and work telephone numbers (or other numbers at which the parent may be reached during the day or at night).

[ ]   Both parties agree that if either of them has any knowledge of any illness, accident, incident or other circumstances seriously affecting the health and/or welfare of their child(ren), he/she will promptly notify the other of such circumstances.

[ ]   All court related and financial discussions shall occur at a time when the child(ren) is/are not present. These discussions shall not occur at times of

exchange of the child(ren) or during telephone visits with the child(ren).

[ ]   The parents shall communicate with each other as follows:

[ ]   Set schedule as follows: _____

_____

_____

   [ ] Mother may communicate with the father by [ ]Phone [ ]Email [ ]Written

   [ ] Father may communicate with the mother by [ ]Phone [ ]Email [ ]Written

3.3 Communication with the Children

[ ]   Does not apply.

[ ]   The parent with whom the child(ren) is not residing shall have telephone access with the child(ren) as follows:

    [ ]   Set schedule as follows:_____

    [ ]   Parent may call child(ren) at any time.

    [ ]   Child(ren) may call parent at any time.

[ ]   In the event that a parent incurs long distance telephone charges as a result of calls from the child(ren) to the other parent, the costs shall be split as follows:

    [ ]   Does not apply.

    [ ]   Parent receiving call from child(ren) shall be responsible for all charges.

    [ ]   Parents will evenly split costs.

    [ ]   Other:_____

II. RESIDENTIAL SCHEDULE

These provisions set forth where the child(ren) shall reside each day of the year and what contact the child(ren) shall have with each parent.
This parenting plan shall begin on the following date:
4.1 Pre-School Schedule

[ ]   There are no children of preschool age.

[ ]   Prior to enrollment in school, the child(ren) shall reside with the [ ] mother [ ] father, except for the following days and times when the child(ren) will reside with or be with the other parent:_____

_____

_____

4.2 School Schedule

[ ]   Does not apply.

[ ]   Upon enrollment in school, the child(ren) shall reside with the [ ] mother [ ] father, except for the following days and times when the child(ren) will reside with or be with the other parent:_____

_____

_____

4.3 Schedule for Holidays

[ ]   Does not apply.

	With Mother (Specify Whether (Odd/Even/ Every or Other)	With Father (Specify Whether Odd/Even/ Every or Other)
New Year's Eve		
New Year's Day		
Martin Luther King Day		
President's Day		
Easter		
Memorial Day		
Mother's Day		
July 4th		
Father's Day		
Labor Day		
Halloween		
Veteran's Day		
Thanksgiving Day		
Christmas Eve		
Christmas Day		
Religious Holidays (as follows):		
Mother's Birthday		
Father's Birthday		
Child's Birthday		
Child's Birthday		
Child's Birthday		

[ ] For purposes of this parenting plan, a holiday shall begin and end as follows (set forth times):_____

_____

[ ] Holidays which fall on a Friday or a Monday shall include Saturday and Sunday.

4.4 Schedule for Winter Vacation

[ ] Does not apply.

The child(ren) shall reside with the [ ] mother [ ] father during winter vacation, except for the following days and times when the child(ren) will reside with or be with the other parent:_____

_____

_____

_____

4.5 Schedule for Spring Vacation

[ ] Does not apply.

The child(ren) shall reside with the [ ] mother [ ] father during spring vacation, except for the following days and times when the child(ren) will reside with or be with the other parent:_____

_____

4.6 Schedule for Summer

[ ]   Does not apply.

Upon completion of the school year, the child(ren) shall reside with [ ] mother [ ] father, except for the following days and times when the child(ren) will reside with or be with the other parent:_____

4.7 Vacation with Parents

[ ]   Does not apply.

[ ]   The schedule for vacation with the parents is as follows:_____

[ ]   Each parent to notify the other of their respective vacation plans with the child(ren)_____

4.8 Priorities under the Residential Schedule

[ ]   Does not apply.

    [ ]   Neither parent shall schedule activities for the child(ren) during the other parent's scheduled residential time, unless the parents agree in advance to include the activity in the child(ren)'s schedule.

[ ]   For purposes of this parenting plan the following days have priority:

    [ ]   Vacations and holidays shall have priority over the residential schedule.

    [ ]   Other:_____

4.9 Restrictions

[ ]   Does not apply.

[ ]   The following restrictions shall apply when the child(ren) spend(s) time with the

    [ ] mother [ ] father:

    [ ]   _____

4.10 Transportation Arrangements

[ ]   Does not apply.

Transportation arrangements for the child(ren), other than costs, between parents shall be as follows: _____

[ ]   _____

4.11 Changes to Residential Schedule

[ ]   Does not apply.

[ ]   Requests to change the residential schedule shall be submitted by the parent requesting the change to the other parent:

    [ ]   In writing

    [ ]   In person

    [ ]   By telephone

Other:_____

[ ] Requests shall be made at least:

    [ ]   24 hours in advance

    [ ]   One week in advance

    [ ]   Two weeks in advance

    [ ]   Other:_____

[ ] Response to the request shall be made by the parent receiving the request:

    [ ]   In writing

    [ ]   In person

    [ ]   By telephone

    [ ]   Other:_____

[ ] Response shall be made within:

    [ ]   24 hours

    [ ]   One week

    [ ]   Two weeks

    [ ]   Other:_____

4.12 Additional Care

[ ] Does not apply.

[ ] The parent requesting the change shall first contact the other parent who will have the first right of care for the child but is not obligated for such care as a result of the change of schedule.

[ ] The parenting requesting the change shall be responsible for any additional child related expenses (for example, day care) incurred by the other parent as a result of the change of schedule.

[ ] Other:_____

III. DECISION MAKING

5.1 Day-to-Day Decisions

[ ] Does not apply.

Each parent shall make decisions regarding the day-to-day care and control of each child while the child(ren) is/are residing with that parent, except as provided below. Examples of day-to-day decisions include treatment of minor health problems, injuries, diet, TV, house rules and discipline.

[ ] We agree to refrain from doing anything to undermine the other parent's household rules and instead, we agree to support the other parent's rules in their household by explaining to our child(ren) that they are expected to follow rules in each parent's household.

5.2 Major Decisions regarding each child shall be made as follows:

	Mother	Father	Joint
Education Decisions			
Extra-curricular activities			
Child care			
Associations			
Non-emergency health care			
Mental Health treatment			

	Mother	Father	Joint
Religious upbringing			
Other:			

5.3 Emergencies

[ ]   Does not apply.

[ ]   If the child(ren) require(s) emergency care, the parent who is responsible for them at that time will immediately arrange for that care and then notify the other parent immediately thereafter.

IV. FURTHER DISPUTE RESOLUTION

6.1 Dispute Process

[ ]   Does not apply.

[ ]   No dispute resolution process, except court action, shall be ordered because of limiting factors.

[ ]   Disputes between the parties shall be submitted to (list person or agency):

[ ]   Counseling by _____

[ ]   Mediation by _____

[ ]   Other: _____

6.2 Cost of Process

[ ]   Does not apply.

The cost of this process shall be allocated between the parties as follows:

[ ]   _____ % mother _____ % father.

[ ]   based on each party's proportional share of income per the child support guideline worksheets, if available.

[ ]   as determined in the dispute resolution process.

6.3 Initiation of Process

[ ]   Does not apply.

The counseling and/or mediation process shall be commence by notifying the other party by [ ] written request [ ] certified mail [ ] other:_____

6.4 Procedures to be Used

[ ]   Does not apply.

In the dispute resolution process:

[ ]   Preference shall be given to carrying out this Parenting Plan.

[ ]   Unless and emergency exists, the parents shall use the designated process to resolve disputes relating to implementation of the plan, except those related to financial support.

[ ]   A written record shall be prepared of any agreement reached in counseling or mediation and shall be provided to each party.

[ ]   If the court finds that a parent has used or frustrated the dispute resolution process without good reason, the court may award attorney's fees and financial sanctions to the other parent.

[ ]   The parties have the right of review of the dispute resolution process to the Circuit Court.

7.1 Independent Counsel, Parties Fully Informed, Fairness of Terms

[ ]   Does not apply.

[ ]   The parties mutually agree that in entering into this Agreement, each party signs this Agreement freely and voluntarily for the purpose, and with the

intent of determining and permanently / temporarily settling the issues of custody and visitation relating to the child(ren). The parties acknowledge that this Agreement is a fair and reasonable agreement, and that it is not the result of any fraud, duress, or undue influence exercised by either party upon the other, or any person or persons upon either party.

8.1 Further Assurances

[ ]   Does not apply.

[ ]   Each of the parties agree to sign such other and further documents and to perform such acts as may be reasonably required to effectuate the purpose of this Agreement.

I (We) declare that this plan has been submitted in good faith.

_____   _____
Mother   Date

_____   _____
Father   Date

APPENDIX C

MODEL STANDARDS OF PRACTICE FOR FAMILY AND DIVORCE MEDIATION

Overview and Definitions

Family and divorce mediation ("family mediation" or "mediation") is a process in which a mediator, an impartial third party, facilitates the resolution of family disputes by promoting the participants' voluntary agreement. The family mediator assists communication, encourages understanding and focuses the participants on their individual and common interests. The family mediator works with the participants to explore options, make decisions and reach their own agreements.

Family mediation is not a substitute for the need for family members to obtain independent legal advice or counseling or therapy. Nor is it appropriate for all families. However, experience has established that family mediation is a valuable option for many families because it can:

1. increase the self-determination of participants and their ability to communicate;

2. promote the best interests of children; and

3. reduce the economic and emotional costs associated with the resolution of family disputes.

Effective mediation requires that the family mediator be qualified by training, experience and temperament; that the mediator be impartial; that the participants reach their decisions voluntarily; that their decisions be based on sufficient factual data; that the mediator be aware of the impact of culture and diversity; and that the best interests of children be taken into account. Further, the mediator should also be prepared to identify families whose history includes domestic abuse or child abuse.

These *Model Standards of Practice for Family and Divorce Mediation* ("*Model Standards*") aim to perform three major functions:

1. to serve as a guide for the conduct of family mediators;

2. to inform the mediating participants of what they can expect; and

3. to promote public confidence in mediation as a process for resolving family disputes.

The *Model Standards* are aspirational in character. They describe good practices for family mediators. They are not intended to create legal rules or standards of liability.

The *Model Standards* include different levels of guidance:

1.   Use of the term "may" in *a Standard* is the lowest strength of guidance and indicates a practice that the family mediator should consider adopting but which can be deviated from in the exercise of good professional judgment.

2.   Most of the *Standards* employ the term "should" which indicates that the practice described in the *Standard* is highly desirable and should be departed from only with very strong reason.

3.   The rarer use of the term "shall" in *a Standard is* a higher level of guidance to the family mediator, indicating that the mediator should not have discretion to depart from the practice described.

Standard I

A family mediator shall recognize that mediation is based on the principle of self-determination by the participants.

A.   Self-determination is the fundamental principle of family mediation. The mediation process relies upon the ability of participants to make their own voluntary and informed decisions.

B.   The primary role of a family mediator is to assist the participants to gain a better understanding of their own needs and interests and the needs and interests of others and to facilitate agreement among the participants.

C.   A family mediator should inform the participants that they may seek information and advice from a variety of sources during the mediation process.

D.   A family mediator shall inform the participants that they may withdraw from family mediation at any time and are not required to reach an agreement in mediation.

E.   The family mediator's commitment shall be to the participants and the process. Pressure from outside of the mediation process shall never influence the mediator to coerce participants to settle.

Standard II

A family mediator shall be qualified by education and training to undertake the mediation.

A.   To perform the family mediator's role, a mediator should:

1.   have knowledge of family law;

2.   have knowledge of and training in the impact of family conflict on parents, children and other participants, including knowledge of child development, domestic abuse and child abuse and neglect;

3.   have education and training specific to the process of mediation;

4.   be able to recognize the impact of culture and diversity.

B.   Family mediators should provide information to the participants about the mediator's relevant training, education and expertise.

Standard III

A family mediator shall facilitate the participants' understanding of what mediation is and assess their capacity to mediate before the participants reach an agreement to mediate.

A. Before family mediation begins a mediator should provide the participants with an overview of the process and its purposes, including:

1. informing the participants that reaching an agreement in family mediation is consensual in nature, that a mediator is an impartial facilitator, and that a mediator may not impose or force any settlement on the parties;

2. distinguishing family mediation from other processes designed to address family issues and disputes;

3. informing the participants that any agreements reached will be reviewed by the court when court approval is required;

4. informing the participants that they may obtain independent advice from attorneys, counsel, advocates, accountants, therapists or other professionals during the mediation process;

5. advising the participants, in appropriate cases, that they can seek the advice of religious figures, elders or other significant persons in their community whose opinions they value;

6. discussing, if applicable, the issue of separate sessions with the participants, a description of the circumstances in which the mediator may meet alone with any of the participants, or with any third party and the conditions of confidentiality concerning these separate sessions;

7. informing the participants that the presence or absence of other persons at a mediation, including attorneys, counselors or advocates, depends on the agreement of the participants and the mediator, unless a statute or regulation otherwise requires or the mediator believes that the presence of another person is required or may be beneficial because of a history or threat of violence or other serious coercive activity by a participant.

8. describing the obligations of the mediator to maintain the confidentiality of the mediation process and its results as well as any exceptions to confidentiality;

9. advising the participants of the circumstances under which the mediator may suspend or terminate the mediation process and that a participant has a right to suspend or terminate mediation at any time.

B. The participants should sign a written agreement to mediate their dispute and the terms and conditions thereof within a reasonable time after first consulting the family mediator.

C. The family mediator should be alert to the capacity and willingness of the participants to mediate before proceeding with the mediation and throughout the process. A mediator should not agree to conduct the mediation if the mediator reasonably believes one or more of the participants is unwilling or unable to participate.

D. Family mediators should not accept a dispute for mediation if they cannot satisfy the expectations of the participants concerning the timing of the process.

Standard IV

A family mediator shall conduct the mediation process in an impartial manner. A family mediator shall disclose all actual and potential grounds of bias and conflicts of interest reasonably known to the mediator. The participants shall be free to retain the mediator by an informed, written waiver of the conflict of interest. However, if a bias or conflict of interest clearly impairs a mediator's impartiality, the mediator shall withdraw regardless of the express agreement of the participants.

A.   Impartiality means freedom from favoritism or bias in word, action or appearance, and includes a commitment to assist all participants as opposed to any one individual.

B.   Conflict of interest means any relationship between the mediator, any participant or the subject matter of the dispute, that compromises or appears to compromise the mediator's impartiality.

C.   A family mediator should not accept a dispute for mediation if the family mediator cannot be impartial.

D.   A family mediator should identify and disclose potential grounds of bias or conflict of interest upon which a mediator's impartiality might reasonably be questioned. Such disclosure should be made prior to the start of a mediation and in time to allow the participants to select an alternate mediator.

E.   A family mediator should resolve all doubts in favor of disclosure. All disclosures should be made as soon as practical after the mediator becomes aware of the bias or potential conflict of interest. The duty to disclose is a continuing duty.

F.   A family mediator should guard against bias or partiality based on the participants' personal characteristics, background or performance at the mediation.

G.   A family mediator should avoid conflicts of interest in recommending the services of other professionals.

H.   A family mediator shall not use information about participants obtained in a mediation for personal gain or advantage

I.   A family mediator should withdraw pursuant to *Standard IX* if the mediator believes the mediator's impartiality has been compromised or a conflict of interest has been identified and has not been waived by the participants.

Standard V

A family mediator shall fully disclose and explain the basis of any compensation, fees and charges to the participants.

A.   The participants should be provided with sufficient information about fees at the outset of mediation to determine if they wish to retain the services of the mediator.

B.   The participants' written agreement to mediate their dispute should include a description of their fee arrangement with the mediator.

C.   A mediator should not enter into a fee agreement which is contingent upon the results of the mediation or the amount of the settlement.

D.   A mediator should not accept a fee for referral of a matter to another mediator or to any other person.

E.   Upon termination of mediation a mediator should return any unearned fee to the participants.

Standard VI

A family mediator shall structure the mediation process so that the participants make decisions based on sufficient information and knowledge.

A.   The mediator should facilitate full and accurate disclosure and the acquisition and development of information during mediation so that the participants can make informed decisions. This may be accomplished by encouraging participants to consult appropriate experts.

B.   Consistent with standards of impartiality and preserving participant self-determination, a mediator may provide the participants with information that the mediator is qualified by training or experience to provide. The mediator shall not provide therapy or legal advice.

C.   The mediator should recommend that the participants obtain independent legal representation before concluding an agreement.

D.   If the participants so desire, the mediator should allow attorneys, counsel or advocates for the participants to be present at the mediation sessions.

E.   With the agreement of the participants, the mediator may document the participants' resolution of their dispute. The mediator should inform the participants that any agreement should be reviewed by an independent attorney before it is signed.

Standard VII

A family mediator shall maintain the confidentiality of all information acquired in the mediation process, unless the mediator is permitted or required to reveal the information by law or agreement of the participants.

A.   The mediator should discuss the participants' expectations of confidentiality with them prior to undertaking the mediation. The written agreement to mediate should include provisions concerning confidentiality.

B.   Prior to undertaking the mediation the mediator should inform the participants of the limitations of confidentiality such as statutory, judicially or ethically mandated reporting.

C.   The mediator shall disclose a participant's threat of suicide or violence against any person to the threatened person and the appropriate authorities if the mediator believes such threat is likely to be acted upon as permitted by law.

D.   If the mediator holds private sessions with a participant, the obligations of confidentiality concerning those sessions should be discussed and agreed upon prior to the sessions.

E.   If subpoenaed or otherwise noticed to testify or to produce documents the mediator should inform the participants immediately. The mediator should not testify or provide documents in response to a subpoena without an order of the court if the mediator reasonably believes doing so would violate an obligation of confidentiality to the participants.

Standard VIII

A family mediator shall assist participants in determining how to promote the best interests of children.

A.   The mediator should encourage the participants to explore the range of options available for separation or post divorce parenting arrangements and their respective costs and benefits. Referral to a specialist in child development may be appropriate for these purposes. The topics for discussion may include, among others:

1.   information about community resources and programs that can help the participants and their children cope with the consequences of family reorganization and family violence;

2.   problems that continuing conflict creates for children's development and what steps might be taken to ameliorate the effects of conflict on the children;

3.   development of a parenting plan that covers the children's physical residence and decision-making responsibilities for the children, with appropriate levels of detail as agreed to by the participants;

4.   the possible need to revise parenting plans as the developmental needs of the children evolve over time; and

5.   encouragement to the participants to develop appropriate dispute resolution mechanisms to facilitate future revisions of the parenting plan

B.   The mediator should be sensitive to the impact of culture and religion on parenting philosophy and other decisions.

C.   The mediator shall inform any court-appointed representative for the children of the mediation. If a representative for the children participates, the mediator should, at the outset, discuss the effect of that participation on the mediation process and the confidentiality of the mediation with the participants. Whether the representative of the children participates or not, the mediator shall provide the representative with the resulting agreements insofar as they relate to the children.

D.   Except in extraordinary circumstances, the children should not participate in the mediation process without the consent of both parents and the children's court-appointed representative.

E.   Prior to including the children in the mediation process, the mediator should consult with the parents and the children's court-appointed representative about whether the children should participate in the mediation process and the form of that participation.

F.   The mediator should inform all concerned about the available options for the children's participation (which may include personal participation, an interview with a mental health professional, or the mediator reporting to the parents, or a videotape statement) and discuss the costs and benefits of each with the participants.

Standard IX

A family mediator shall recognize a family situation involving child abuse or neglect and take appropriate steps to shape the mediation process accordingly.

A.   As used in these Standards, child abuse or neglect is defined by applicable state law.

B.   A mediator shall not undertake a mediation in which the family situation has been assessed to involve child abuse or neglect without appropriate and adequate training.

C.   If the mediator has reasonable grounds to believe that a child of the participants is abused or neglected within the meaning of the jurisdiction's child abuse and neglect laws, the mediator shall comply with applicable child protection laws.

1.   The mediator should encourage the participants to explore appropriate services for the family.

2.   The mediator should consider the appropriateness of suspending or terminating the mediation process in light of the allegations.

Standard X

A family mediator shall recognize a family situation involving domestic abuse and take appropriate steps to shape the mediation process accordingly.

A.   As used in these Standards, domestic abuse includes domestic violence as defined by applicable state law and issues of control and intimidation.

B.   A mediator shall not undertake a mediation in which the family situation has been assessed to involve domestic abuse without appropriate and adequate training.

C.   Some cases are not suitable for mediation because of safety, control or intimidation issues. A mediator should make a reasonable effort to screen for the existence of domestic abuse prior to entering into an agreement to mediate. The mediator should continue to assess for domestic abuse throughout the mediation process.

D.   If domestic abuse appears to be present the mediator shall consider taking measures to insure the safety of participants and the mediator including, among others:

1.   establishing appropriate security arrangements;

2.   holding separate sessions with the participants even without the agreement of all participants;

3.   allowing a friend, representative, advocate, counsel or attorney to attend the mediation sessions;

4.   encouraging the participants to be represented by an attorney, counsel or an advocate throughout the mediation process;

5.   referring the participants to appropriate community resources;

6.   suspending or terminating the mediation sessions, with appropriate steps to protect the safety of the participants.

E. The mediator should facilitate the participants' formulation of parenting plans that protect the physical safety and psychological well-being of themselves and their children.

Standard XI

A family mediator shall suspend or terminate the mediation process when the mediator reasonably believes that a participant is unable to effectively participate or for other compelling reasons

A. Circumstances under which a mediator should consider suspending or terminating the mediation, may include, among others:

1. the safety of a participant or well-being of a child is threatened;

2. a participant has or is threatening to abduct a child;

3. a participant is unable to participate due to the influence of drugs, alcohol, or physical or mental condition;

4. the participants are about to enter into an agreement that the mediator reasonably believes to be unconscionable;

5. a participant is using the mediation to further illegal conduct;

6. a participant is using the mediation process to gain an unfair advantage;

7. if the mediator believes the mediator's impartiality has been compromised in accordance with *Standard IV.*

B. If the mediator does suspend or terminate the mediation, the mediator should take all reasonable steps to minimize prejudice or inconvenience to the participants which may result.

Standard XII

A family mediator shall be truthful in the advertisement and solicitation for mediation

A. Mediators should refrain from promises and guarantees of results. A mediator should not advertise statistical settlement data or settlement rates.

B. Mediators should accurately represent their qualifications. In an advertisement or other communication, a mediator may make reference to meeting state, national, or private organizational qualifications only if the entity referred to has a procedure for qualifying mediators and the mediator has been duly granted the requisite status.

Standard XIII

A family mediator shall acquire and maintain professional competence in mediation.

A. Mediators should continuously improve their professional skills and abilities by, among other activities, participating in relevant continuing education programs and should regularly engage in self-assessment.

B. Mediators should participate in programs of peer consultation and should help train and mentor the work of less experienced mediators.

C.   Mediators should continuously strive to understand the impact of culture and diversity on the mediator's practice.

Appendix: Special Policy Considerations for State Regulation of Family Mediators and Court Affiliated Programs

The *Model Standards* recognize the *National Standards for Court Connected Dispute Resolution Programs* (1992). There are also state and local regulations governing such programs and family mediators. The following principles of organization and practice, however, are especially important for regulation of mediators and court-connected family mediation programs. They are worthy of separate mention.

A.   Individual states or local courts should set standards and qualifications for family mediators including procedures for evaluations and handling grievances against mediators. In developing these standards and qualifications, regulators should consult with appropriate professional groups, including professional associations of family mediators.

B.   When family mediators are appointed by a court or other institution, the appointing agency should make reasonable efforts to insure that each mediator is qualified for the appointment. If a list of family mediators qualified for court appointment exists, the requirements for being included on the list should be made public and available to all interested persons.

Confidentiality should not be construed to limit or prohibit the effective monitoring, research, evaluation or monitoring of mediation programs by responsible individuals or academic institutions provided that no identifying information about any person involved in the mediation is disclosed without their prior written consent. Under appropriate circumstances, researchers may be permitted to obtain access to statistical data and, with the permission of the participants, to individual case files, observations of live mediations, and interviews with participants.

INDEX

[References are to pages.]

[References are to pages.]

[References are to pages.]